CONTENTS

■ **MAP OF PRINCIPAL SIGHTS**

According to the tourist importance of a place we give:

– the main events of local history
– a description of the Main Sights
– a description of the Additional Sights
– under the heading of Excursions a selection of tours
  starting from the main centres

*The **Michelin Maps**
to use
with this Guide are*

PRINCIPAL SIGHTS

To find a town, a sight or setting, a historical or geographical reference described in this guide, consult the index pp 160-162.

Sights		Conventional signs	
Worth the journey ★★★		● Town described	▲ Miscellaneous sights
Worth the detour ★★		━ Sightseeing route described	◡ Dam
<u>Interesting</u> ★		✝ Religious edifice	🗼 Lighthouse
		⚔ Castle or château	|/ View
		⁘ Ruins	☀ Panorama

A vocabulary on p 8 of the guide gives
the English translation of current tourist phrases.

PRACTICAL INFORMATION

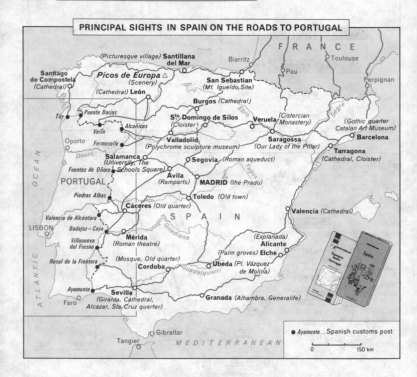

PRINCIPAL SIGHTS IN SPAIN ON THE ROADS TO PORTUGAL

BEFORE LEAVING

The Portuguese National Tourist Office at the Centro de Turismo de Portugal, New Bond Street, London WIYONP, ☎ 01-493 3873 and at the Centro de Turismo de Portugal, 548 Fifth Avenue, New York, N.Y. 10036, ☎ (212) 354-4403 will provide information and literature on application.

In Portugal, the information office of the Direcção-Geral do Turismo in Lisbon (Avenida António Augusto de Aguiar, 86) or the Delegação de Turismo in Oporto (Praça Dom João I, 25) will provide you with information on accommodation and matters of tourist interest on the Portuguese provinces.

Information offices (Posto or Comissão de Turismo) have been established in most tourist resorts. If you write to these in advance they will supply information about the amenities and hotel resources in their immediate area. The sign *Turismo* in a town or resort identifies these tourist offices, where the men and women on duty speak English, often well and always to some degree at least. The addresses of Portugal's main tourist offices are found in the Michelin Red Guide España Portugal.

Customs formalities. – As the entry and customs formalities are liable to alteration we advise tourists to join the AA, Fanum House, Leicester Square, London W.C.2, or the RAC, Pall Mall, London S.W.1, either of which will provide the most recent information and, if necessary, additional papers.

Personal documents. – A valid British Passport or a valid American Passport but no visa is required for a visit of up to 60 days. British Commonwealth citizens with the exception of Australia (up to 90 day's visit) and Canada (up to 60 days) require a visa.

Vaccination certificates are not normally required for entering Portugal or Madeira.

Car documents. – A valid **UK** licence, International Insurance Certificate (Green Card – *see below*) and car registration book are required. If the vehicle does not belong to the driver, the latter should carry a letter signed by the registered owner authorising the use of the vehicle. A GB nationality plate must be displayed. Third party insurance is compulsory.

USA: A valid USA registration card and circulation permit are required, a US nationality plate must be displayed.

An advance warning triangle is compulsory.

Driving. – No person under 18 years of age is allowed to drive in Portugal – either the valid driver's licence or an international driver's licence (available at any AA office) is necessary.

Caravan and boat owners must provide a document giving full details of the vehicle in question, and in the case of caravans an inventory for the customs.

Crossing the Frontier. – The customs' posts indicated on the map above are generally open from 7am to midnight (8am to 8 or 9pm November to March). For information on customs formalities on the Spanish border see Michelin Green Guide to Spain.

Assistance provided by the Motoring Organizations. – The AA and RAC run accident insurance and breakdown service schemes for their members. They also cooperate with the Portuguese Automobile Club (Automóvel Club de Portugal, Rua Rosa Arújo 24, Lisbon, ☎ 56 39 31) in a reciprocal assistance scheme for members. Breakdown service (Lisbon ☎ 77 54 75).

Currency. – There are no Portuguese customs restrictions or special regulations regarding modest amounts of currency which may be taken into or brought out of the country. Special permission through a bank is required for large amounts.

British regulations are subject to alteration and if you do not known them enquire at your bank or travel agency.

In January 1985 the rate of exchange was 195.000 escudos (written $) to £1 and 201.00 escudos (170$) to US $1.00.

HOW TO GET TO PORTUGAL

By Air. – Direct jet services between London and Lisbon, taking about 2 1/2 hours, are operated by BA, TAP (Portuguese Airways), VARIG, etc. There are daily flights throughout the year. Direct jet flights between London and Oporto, taking about 2 hours, are operated by BA and TAP and daily flights, via Lisbon. Direct jet flights by day between London and Faro, taking about 3 1/4 hours, are operated by BA and TAP throughout the year.

For flights to Madeira see p 144.

From the USA, daily flights from New York, Chicago and Boston.

By Sea. – There are no services between Great Britain and Portugal at the moment.

By Rail. – The fastest train is the daily Sud-Express which links Paris with Lisbon in 25 hours.

By Road. – The distance to Lisbon by road when you have landed from the car ferry at one of the Channel Ports is about 1 600 km - 1 000 miles. The most direct route thereafter is by way of Bordeaux, Irun and then either San Sebastian, Valladolid, or Burgos, Salamanca, Vilar Formoso and Coimbra to Lisbon.

For those who prefer not to drive the whole way there is a Motorail service to Lisbon.

A FEW PRICES (early 1985)

Petrol (per litre)	105$
Petrol – super (per litre)	109$
Oil (per litre)	356$
Garage (overnight)	400$
Taxi fare (per km) . . . . 50$ + 26$50 per 138 m	
Letter within Portugal or to Spain	16$50
Airmail letter or postcard to the UK respectively	46$
Airmail letter or postcard to the US respectively	51$
Beer	40$
Black coffee	25$
Portuguese	80$
English or American	150$
English or American newspaper	120-225
Cinema seat (average price)	200$
Theatre ticket (average price)	500$
Dinner followed by a *fado* performance	2 000$
Bullfight (average price)	1 000$
Hairdresser – shampoo and set	500$
Local telephone call in town (3 minutes)	5$50
Bus fare	60$
Underground – single ticket	27$50
Room in a 🏠 or 🏠 hotel in the Michelin Red Guide España Portugal . . 1 450-2 650$ including breakfast	
A la carte meal (average price per person)	1 500$

WHEN IN PORTUGAL

Consulates. – **GB**: Rua de S. Domingos A-Lapa 37 – 1200 Lisbon – ☏ 66 11 22; 60 43 54 or 66 31 81.

USA: Av. Forças Armadas – 1600 Lisbon – ☏ 72 57 17; 72 58 80; 72 01 23 or 72 42 96.

Hotels and restaurants. – *Consult the current Michelin Red Guide España Portugal.*

Pousadas are establishments run under the aegis of the Diracção-Geral do Turismo. The 30 existing *pousadas* have been specially built on selected sites or established in castles of historic interest or former monasteries suitably remodelled to provide every comfort. They are to be found in towns well placed for an overnight stop or as excursion centres. The prices are controlled and the welcome warm and the service attentive. As they are often full it is advisable to book ahead.

Estalagems are similar types of establishments but they are privately owned.

Camping. – The International Camping Carnet is required at certain camping sites. A list of camping sites can be obtained from the tourist centres. Camping outside recognized sites is subject to certain restrictions. Enquire at the tourist centres.

Youth Hostels. – There are about a dozen in all, apply to: Associação Portuguesa das pousadas da Juventude, R. Andrade Corvo, 46 – Lisbon 1 – ☏ 57 10 54.

Tipping. – A service charge of 10% is included in all bills in hotels, restaurants and cafés. It is usual, however, to give an additional tip for personal service; 10% of the fare or ticket price is also the usual amount given to taxi drivers and cinema and theatre usherettes.

Currency exchange. – Hotels, restaurants and shops are not always willing to accept foreign currency and the tourist is, therefore, advised to change cheques and currency at banks, savings banks and exchange offices when these are open. Some or all are to be found in the more important towns or near the larger stations and at frontier posts.

Opening times. – The general opening times are as follows:
– offices: 9.30am to 12.30pm and 2.30 to 6pm
– shops: 9am to 1pm and 3 to 7pm
– banks: 8.30 to 11.45am and 1 to 2.45pm (closed on Saturdays)
– money changers: 9.30am to 6pm (usually closed on Saturday afternoons and Sundays)
– museums and monuments: 10am to 5pm (closed Mondays)
– churches: 7am to 1pm and 4 to about 7pm (do not walk round while services are in progress).

Theatrical performances begin at about 9.30pm; *fados* at approximately 10.30pm

Public holidays. – 1 January, Shrove Tuesday, Good Friday, 25 April (Portugal Day), 1 May, 10 June (death of Camões – national holiday), Corpus Christi, 15 August, 5 October (proclamation of the Republic), 1 November, 1 December (Restoration of Independence), 8 and 25 December. In addition each town or locality celebrates the feast day of its patron saint (St Antony in Lisbon – 13 June).

The time in Portugal is one hour ahead of GMT or the same as BST; there is no alteration at any season of the year.

Electric Current. – The usual voltage is 220.

DRIVING IN PORTUGAL

The speed limits are: motorways 120kph - 74mph; other roads 90kph - 56mph and in towns 60kph - 37mph. It is compulsory for the front passengers to wear seat belts.

Driving is on the right. At crossroads priority should be given to vehicles approaching from the right. The rules for roundabouts are that you go round anticlockwise and allow priority to incoming traffic. To bear left at a crossroads controlled by a policeman, don't go round him, but turn in front of him. When going through towns and villages take great care as children often play at the road's edge and, in the evenings, go slowly, easing your way through the crowds out for an evening stroll. Progress, especially in the north, may also be slowed down by farm carts.

Service stations are chiefly on the main highways or larger roads.

VOCABULARY

For words and expressions used in hotels and restaurants, see p 17; applicable to the history of art, p 21. See also the Michelin Red Guide España Portugal

COMMON WORDS

bank; exchange	**banco; câmbio**	river; stream	**rio; ribeira**
bus; tram	**autocarro; eléctrico**	sir	**senhor**
car	**carro**	square	**largo; praça**
chemist	**farmacêutico**	station; train	**estação; comboio**
customs	**alfândega**	street; avenue	**rue; avenida**
doctor	**mêdico**	thank you	
entrance; exit	**entrada; saída**	(said by a man)	**obrigado**
expensive	**caro**	(said by a woman)	**obrigada**
good afternoon	**boa tarde**	today	**hoje**
good morning	**bom dia**	tomorrow morning	**amanhã de manhã**
goodbye	**adeus**	tomorrow evening	**amanhã à tarde**
halt	**paragem**	to the left	**à esquerda**
I beg your pardon	**desculpe**	to the right	**à direita**
large; small	**grande; pequeno**	town; quarter, district	**cidade; bairro**
letter; postcard	**carta; postal**	where; when?	**onde?; quando?**
letter-box	**caixa de correio**	yes; no	**sim; não**
light	**luz**		
madam (married woman)	**minha senhora**	where is?	**onde é . . .?**
		the road to. . .?	**a estrada para . . .?**
madam (single woman) miss	**menina**	at what time?	**a que horas . . .?**
		how much?	**quanto custa . . .?**
much; little	**muito; pouco**		
petrol; oil	**gasolina; óleo**	road works	**obras**
please	**(se) faz favor**	danger	**perigo**
post office; stamp	**correio; selo**	prohibited	**prohibido**

SIGHTS, PLACES, MONUMENTS

albufeira	reservoir	mercado; feira	market; fair
andar	storey	miradouro	belvedere
barragem	dam	paço, palácio	palace, château
Câmara Municipal	town hall	praia	beach
capela	chapel	quinta	country property
casa	house	Sé	cathedral
castelo	castle, citadel	século	century
chave	key	solar	manor house
citânia	prehistoric city	tapete, tapeçaria	tapestry
convento, mosteiro	convent, monastery	tesouro	treasure, treasury
cruz; cruzeiro	cross; calvary	torre	tower
escada	stairs, steps	torre de menagem	keep
excavações	excavations	túmulo	tomb
fechado, aberto	closed, open	vista	view, panorama
igreja	church	dirigir-se a . . .	apply to . . .
mata	wood	pode-se visitar?	may one visit?

8

PRINCIPAL FOLKLORE AND RELIGIOUS FESTIVALS

Religious processions, folk dancing, bullfights and fireworks are usually integral features in any Portuguese festival, fair – *feira* – or pilgrimage – or *romaria (p 31)*. A detailed calendar of festivals appears in the leaflets produced monthly by the Direcção-Geral do Turismo. We indicate below some of the most picturesque.

DATE AND PLACE *(1)*	TYPE OF FESTIVAL
Days before Shrove Tuesday . ⑬ **Ovar** - ⑯ **Torres Vedras**	Carnival *(4 days)*: cart processions, masked groups.
⑩, ㉒ **Loulé**	Carnival and Almond Gatherers' Fair *(4 days)*: cart processions, battles of flowers, folk groups.
Holy Week . . . . **Braga**	Holy Week ceremonies: processions.
Easter Sunday . . . . ⑩, ㉒ **Loulé**	Pilgrimage of Our Lady of Pity: processions.
3 May . . . . **Barcelos**	Festival of Crosses and pottery fair: folk dancing.
The lst Sunday after 3 May . . . . **Monsanto**	Festival of the Castle *(p 107)*.
3-5 May . . . . **Sesimbra**	Festival of Our Lord Jesus of the wounds (fishermen's festival going back to the 16C). 4 May: procession.
2nd Sunday in May . . ⑪ **Vila Franca do Lima**	Rose Festival: Mordomias procession in which the mistress of the house bears on her head a tray of flowers arranged to represent one of the many provincial coats of arms. The trays are said to weigh nearly 90 lbs.
12-13 May . . . . **Fátima**	First great annual pilgrimage.
Last Sunday in May . . . . **Braga**	First pilgrimage to the Sameiro Sanctuary: procession.
Whitsun . . . . **Matosinhos**	Pilgrimage to Senhor of Matosinhos *(15 days)*: folk dancing.
1st Saturday and Sunday in June . . . . **Amarante**	St Gonsalo Festival *(2 days — p 44)*.
1st fortnight in June . . . . **Santarém**	National Agricultural Fair: International Folklore Festival.
13-20 June . . . . **Vila Real**	St Anthony's Festival: procession, fireworks.
16-24 June . . . . **Vila do Conde**	The lacemakers' procession *(p 138)*.
16-30 June . . . . **Oporto**	Popular Saints' Festival: the night of the 23rd to the 24th is a gala occasion.
23-24 June (St John's Day) . . . . **Braga**	King David's procession, etc *(p 52)*.
28-29 June . . . . **Póvoa de Varzim**	St Peter's Festival: processions, torchlight tattoo *(rusgas)*, barbecue of grilled sardines.
29 June	**Sintra**	St Peter's Craftsmen's Fair.
1st fortnight in July *(odd years)* . . **Tomar**	*Tabuleiros* Festival *(p 133)*.
1st fortnight in July *(even years)* . **Coimbra**	Festival of the Queen Saint *(p 63)*.
1st Saturday and Sunday in July **Vila Franca de Xira**	Festival of the Red Waistcoats *(Colete Encarnado — p 138)*.
25 July to 8 August . . . . **Setúbal**	St James' Fair: bullfights, folk groups.
1st week in August . . . . ⑪ **Meadela**	Folklore Festival *(3 days and nights)*.
1st Sunday in August . . . . . . ⑪ **Guimarães**	St Walter's Festival *(Gualterianas)*: fair, decorated streets, giants' procession, torchlight procession, bullfights, fireworks.
1st fortnight in August . . . . . . ⑪ **Portuzelo**	Folklore Festival *(3 days and nights)*: morodomias procession, international folklore festival.
2nd weekend in August . . . . ⑰ **Alcochete**	Festival of the Green Hat *(Barrete verde)*: blessing of the saltworks, bullfights and bull running in the streets.
2nd Sunday in August . . . **Serra da Estrela**	Festival of Our Lady of the Holy Star *(p 72)*.
10-15 August . . . . **Gerês**	São Bento da Porta Aberta Pilgrimage *(15 km - 9 miles southwest)*.
August (or July) . . . . **Aveiro**	La Ria Festival and decorated prow competition.
3rd week in August . . . . . . **Viana Do Castelo**	Pilgrimage of Our Lady of Sorrow *(3 days — p 136)*.
3rd Sunday in August . . **Miranda de Douro**	Dance of the Pauliteiros *(p 105)*.
Last Sunday in August . . . . **Braga**	Second pilgrimage to the Sameiro Sanctuary.
1st Sunday in September . . . . . . **Palmela**	Grape Harvest Festival: benediction of the grapes, bull running through the streets, folk dancing and music, fireworks.
6-8 September . . . . **Miranda do Douro**	Pilgrimage to Our Lady of Nazo at Póvoa *(11 km - 7 miles north)*: fair and festival.
Beginning 8 September . . . . **Nazaré**	Festival of Our Lady of Nazareth at Sítio: procession, folk groups, bullfights.
9-11 September . . . . **Vila Viçosa**	Capuchin Festival: *romaria*, fair.
Last Sunday in September . **Cape Espichel**	Festival of Our Lady of the Cape: fishermen's festival dating back to the 13C.
1st Sunday in October . . **Vila Franca de Xira**	Fair, bull running through the streets, bullfights *(5 days)*.
2nd Sunday in October . . . . **Santarém**	Great Fair of Our Lady of Sorrow: market, bullfights.
12-13 October . . . . **Fátima**	Second great annual pilgrimage.
19-21 October . . . . **Tomar**	Fair and Festival of St Irene: dried fruit fair *(1st day)*, sale of craft work.
1st fortnight in November . . . . . ⑯ **Golegã**	National Horse Fair and St Martins Day Regional Fair: blessing of horses (dating back to the 17C).
11 November . . . . **Portimão**	Great November Fair.

(1) The fold on Michelin map ⬛⬛ *is given for all places listed above not mentioned in this guide.*

INTRODUCTION TO THE TOUR

APPEARANCE OF THE COUNTRY

Portugal has a great variety of landscape within its relatively small area of 88 994km² - 34 361sq miles and few of the monotonous vistas to be found in the Spanish *meseta*. Generally speaking the altitude decreases from the Spanish border towards the Atlantic and from north to south; the Tagus divides a mountainous region in the north from an area of plateaux and plains in the south.

Topography. – In the Primary Era the northern half of the country was affected by the Hercynian Folding which resulted in the raising of hard granite and shale mountain ranges. These were worn down in the Secondary Era to form a vast plateau out of which still arose some of the heights impregnable to erosion such as the Serra de São Mamede. The Tertiary Era, which saw the raising of the Alps and the Pyrenean Folding, brought a brutal upheaval of the plateau, dislocating it into a series of small massifs, such as the Serras do Marão and da Estrela. The massifs were divided by fissures near which emerged thermal and mineral springs and, in the north especially, metal deposits. The upheavals were accompanied in some cases by eruptions of a volcanic nature which formed ranges such as the Serra de Sintra and the Serra de Monchique. It was at this time that the Tagus and Sado Basins were hollowed out and the coastal plains rose up, folding into the low ranges of the Serra do Aire and the Serra do Caldeirão. The coastline became flatter in the Quaternary Era through erosion of the Estremadura and Alentejo Cliffs and alluvial accumulation, forming shorelines in the Aveiro and Sines areas.

The Interior. – North of the Douro, the foothills which continue the Cantabrian Ranges southwest, appear as massive mountain chains separated by valleys.

Between the Douro and the Tagus, the Castilian Sierras reach into Portugal as a particularly high relief. This is the area of the Serra da Estrela with the Torre itself, the second highest peak in Portugal, standing at an altitude of 1 991m - 6 532ft. Particularly wide valleys – Mondego, Zêzere – surround this giant ridge.

South of the Tagus lies the great plateau which drops down towards the sea. The vast horizons are scarcely interrupted by the minor rises which form the Serras de Monchique and do Caldeirão.

The Coast. – Great ports have been established at the mouths of the principal estuaries: Oporto on the Douro, Lisbon on the Tagus and Setúbal on the Sado.

Fishing ports, such as Portimão, have grown up in the most advantageous bays, or, as with Peniche and Lagos, in the protection of capes. Others, such as Faro and Aveiro, have been built in flat coastal regions protected only very slightly by offshore sandbanks or not at all as in the case of Ericeira, which stands on the beach, facing the Atlantic.

In all, the coast (837km - 520 miles) offers incredible variety. There are interminable strands, beaches of fine sand sheltered by rock cliffs or dunes, creeks confined on either side by promontories; there are long tongues of sand on the islands off the Algarve, and narrow shafts of sand enclosing *rias* or lagoons as at Aveiro; there are impressive promontories like Cape Carvoeiro, Cape Espichel and Cape St. Vincent, the most southwesterly point of continental Europe.

The water is cooled by a current from the Canary Islands which turns and flows down the coast from north to south, dissipating the warmth of the Gulf Stream.

LANDSCAPES AND THE COUNTRYSIDE

The old provinces of history define the large natural regions of the country.

The Minho and the Douro. – The greater part of these two most northern provinces of Portugal is made up of granite hills covered by dense vegetation, only the summits of the Serras do Gerês, Soajo and Marão standing stripped and bare. The fields, enclosed by hedges and climbing vines, sometimes produce two crops a year, while here and there small clumps of eucalyptus, pines and oaks stud the landscape. Olive, apple and orange trees grow on the best exposed hillsides. There are numerous small villages.

The Trás-os-Montes. – This province, lying "beyond the mountains" *(trás os montes)* of the Marão and Gerês Ranges, consists of high plateaux relieved by rocky crests and deeply cut valleys. The plateaux, dominated by bare summits and covered with stunted vegetation, serve as sheep fells. The few villages, with houses built of granite or shale, merge into the landscape. The valleys, more populous and with flourishing fruit trees, vines, maize and vegetables, seem like veritable oases in the bleak countryside. The edges of the plateaux and the slopes down to the Douro and the Tua have been terraced so that olive, fig and almond trees can be cultivated, and particularly the famous vine which produces the grapes for port wine. Fine white houses stand out among the vineyards.

The Beira Litoral. – This low lying region, cut by many water courses, corresponds approximately to the Lower Valleys of the Vouga, the Mondego and the Lis. The country-side in the irrigated areas around Soure and Aveiro consists, for the most part, of ricefields. Pinewoods – Pinhal de Leiria and Pinhal do Urso – anchor the coastal dunes, while at Aveiro the *ria* or lagoon provides an original touch to the scenery. Inland, small fields of wheat and maize are planted also with fruit trees or olives and vines.

The Beira Alta and the Beira Baixa. – This, the most mountainous region of Portugal, is geographically an extension westwards of the central Spanish *cordillera*; the landscape consists of a succession of raised rock masses and eroded basins.

The mountains, of which the principal ranges are the Serras da Estrela and da Lousã, have densely wooded slopes crowned by summits, in some cases bristling with rock outcrops, but more often covered with grass on which sheep graze. Occasional lakes formed artificially behind dams fill the sites of ancient glaciary corries or gorges hollowed out of the quartz. Old villages look down on valley floors terraced into squares of land on which grow maize, rye and olives.

The greater part of the population lives in the Mondego and Zêzere Valleys. The Mondego Valley, a vast eroded corridor and a main means of communication, is blanketed with rich arable land; where the hillsides face the sun, vines may often be seen extending the vineyards of the Dão Region; the Upper Zêzere Valley, known as the Cova da Beira, where oleanders grow, specializes more in rearing livestock. In the south, around Castelo Branco, the vegetation becomes more southern in character.

Most of the granite built villages are still protected by a castle or ramparts, reminders of former wars between Portugal and Spain.

Estremadura. – This was formerly the southern extremity – hence the name – of the lands reconquered from the Moors. Today it is the province surrounding the capital, Lisbon.

Between Nazaré and Setúbal the countryside is gently undulating.

Villages of single storey or low cottages are surrounded by areas of cultivation, small in the north and larger in the south, tended with minute care; fields of wheat and maize, olives, vines and fruit trees grow between clumps of pines and eucalyptus.

Along the coast, where tall cliffs alternate with attractive sand beaches, there are many fishing villages. The Serra de Sintra is a pleasant wooded range only a few miles from Lisbon. The Serra da Arrábida, south of the Tagus, provides shelter for several small seaside resorts.

The Ribatejo. – The "riba do Tejo", or bank of the Tagus, is an alluvial plain formed in the Tertiary and Quaternary Eras. On the hills, along the right bank, the farmers go in for a mixed cultivation based on olives, vines and vegetables. The terraces along the left bank are used by large scale landowners to grow wheat and olives.

The plain, which can be flooded by irrigation, is covered with ricefields, market gardens and above all by vast meadows on which horses and black fighting bulls are raised.

The Alentejo. – The immense province of Alentejo which occupies nearly a third of the total land area of Portugal, is flat and, with the exception of the Serra de São Mamede, practically without relief.

There is almost no natural vegetation in Alentejo. But in spite of the difficulties of irrigation, the land is seldom left fallow.

THE PROVINCES
The towns shown are district capitals

11

Alentejo, the Portuguese granary, is also the region of the cork oak, the evergreen oak and the olive tree; in addition plums are grown around Vendas Novas and Elvas. Flocks of sheep and herds of black pigs eke out an existence on the poorer ground.

The large landowners live in *montes* or large farmhouses built singly upon hillocks and limewashed to deflect the sun. The other local inhabitants live in villages of low houses, equally dazzling in their whiteness and surmounted by huge chimneys.

The coast is generally uninviting and there are few harbours. Windmills can still be seen turning here and there on the heights above the river banks.

The Algarve. – Portugal's southernmost province takes its name from the Arabic *El-Gharb* meaning "west" for this was in fact the most westerly region conquered by the Arabs in the Iberian Peninsula.

This small area, separated from the Alentejo by shale hills, is like a garden; flowers grow alongside crops and beneath fruit trees so that one sees geraniums, camellias and oleanders, cotton, rice and sugar cane and carobs, figs and almonds. Most cottage gardens are surrounded by hedges of agaves. The villages consist of groups of the flat roofed houses cut at many levels by open terraces and decorated with attractive chimneys.

To the west rises a mountain range of granite rock, the Serra de Monchique, covered in lush vegetation.

The coast is very sandy and east of Faro is protected by shoreline sandbanks. To the west the beaches are backed by high cliffs which form the impressive promontory of Cape St. Vincent.

CLIMATE

The summer dryness and heat which can be felt even among the Minho heights have made geographers describe the climate as Mediterranean, though no Mediterranean wave laps Portugal's shores. The Atlantic, however, has considerable influence on the weather, bearing humidity and welcome rains, reducing the length of the summer drought and moderating the temperature.

The Seasons. – The movement of the Azores anticyclone determines the major features of the weather at all times of the year. In **summer,** lying northwest of Portugal, it assures fine weather – the sun reigns undisputed, but not for long. Although the temperature may exceed 40°C - 104°F the coast enjoys an almost permanent, gentle sea breeze – nevertheless, resorts and the more exposed beaches only come alive after 4 or 5pm. In the vast Alentejo Plains no breath of air ruffles the odd pools of water lying in the dried out river beds. The mountains, however, are always cool by comparison, fanned by valley breezes.

Winter passes with not more than a couple of weeks of frost in most parts of the country. Snow is exceptional and only lies in the highest *serras*. The weather is generally bright and warm, though the nights can be cold.

Autumn and **spring** have their sunny days but also days when it rains and the sky is darkened by heavy clouds brought by west winds. April in Portugal does not always live up to its reputation.

Regional Characteristics. – Generally speaking, and in spite of the difference of the relief of the hinterland and the 560km - 348 miles which separate the northernmost from the most southerly point, the Portuguese **coastline** enjoys a uniform climate. The temperature at Viana do Castelo is almost the same as that at Cape St. Vincent and if there is slightly more rain, it is offset by there being more humidity in the south.

Inland, as you leave the coastal belt and approach the Spanish *meseta,* it gets drier and there are greater variations in temperature. In the north, while heavy rain soaks the Serra da Estrela, the more sheltered Trás-os-Montes endures a rugged climate much resembling that of the upper plateaux of the *meseta*. The centre of the country is a transitional area and a perfect example of a temperate climate. The Alentejo, lacking high mountains, is drier and more southern in character. The Algarve, with mild winters, has a subtropical climate.

Average daily temperature (centigrade)

maximum in black 11
minimum in brown 6
13°C or higher
18°C or higher
Centigrade 0   10   20   30
32   50   68   86 Fahrenheit

	J	F	M	A	M	J	J	A	S	O	N	D
Torquay	9 / 3	8 / 3	11 / 4	13 / 6	16 / 8	19 / 11	20 / 13	20 / 13	18 / 12	15 / 9	12 / 6	10 / 4
Bragança	8 / 1	10 / 1	13 / 3	16 / 5	19 / 8	24 / 11	28 / 13	27 / 13	24 / 11	18 / 8	12 / 4	8 / 1
Oporto	14 / 6	15 / 6	17 / 8	18 / 9	20 / 11	22 / 13	23 / 15	23 / 14	23 / 14	21 / 12	17 / 8	14 / 5
Lisbon	14 / 8	15 / 8	18 / 10	20 / 11	22 / 13	25 / 16	28 / 17	28 / 17	26 / 17	23 / 14	18 / 11	15 / 8
Évora	12 / 6	14 / 6	16 / 8	19 / 9	22 / 11	27 / 14	30 / 16	30 / 16	27 / 15	22 / 13	16 / 9	13 / 6
Faro	15 / 9	16 / 9	18 / 11	20 / 12	23 / 14	26 / 17	29 / 19	29 / 19	26 / 19	23 / 16	19 / 12	16 / 9
Funchal (Madeira)	19 / 13	18 / 13	19 / 13	19 / 15	21 / 16	22 / 17	24 / 19	24 / 19	24 / 19	23 / 18	22 / 16	19 / 15

VEGETATION

The number and diversity of plants in Portugal is a visual reminder of the different types of soil and even more of the contrasts in climate to be found within its borders.

The **robur** and **tauzin oak,** together with chestnuts and a few birches and maples, grow on the very wet peaks of 500m - 1 500ft in height (in north Portugal on the Serras de São Mamede and Monchique). Heather, ferns and gorse make up the underbrush. The **Lusitanian oak,** although it thrives best along the right bank of the Tagus, may be seen throughout the country except in the extreme south.

South of the Tagus and in the Upper Douro Valley where the summers are very dry, there are dense woods of **evergreen** and **cork oaks** close by heaths and moorlands sparsely covered by cistus, lavender, rosemary and thyme. The evergreen and cork oak may be seen everywhere in Portugal, the trees would grow 20 to 25m - 60 to 75ft if they were not lopped to facilitate the gathering of acorns from the one and the stripping of cork from the other.

Eucalyptus, with its characteristic scent (the eucalypti were first introduced in Europe in 1856) and **pines** (sea pines, Aleppo pines – in the Serra da Estrela – and umbrella pines, of which the kernels are edible) are widely distributed, often appearing in plantations (Leiria Pinewood). Pines are most often chosen for afforestation since they are resistant to wind, grow rapidly and flourish on otherwise difficult hilly or mountain sites and light soil. The hardwood is used for timberwork and carpentry. The pines also produce pit props and beams, many of which are exported to the United Kingdom, as well as resin, pitch and turpentine.

Finally certain types of fruit trees have become so acclimatized and have flourished to such a degree that they could now be considered indigenous. Among these are the **carob,** associated with the almond and fig trees of the Algarve – almonds are also common on the Upper Douro – **olives** *(see map p 15)* and orange trees (Algarve, Ribatejo).

TREES AND FORESTS
MAIN SPECIES

Deciduous oaks Eucalyptus
Evergreen oaks
Pine trees Caroubs

Minho
Lima
Braga
Bragança
Tâmega
Sabor
Oporto
DOURO
Douro
Viseu
Aveiro
Mondego
Coimbra
Zêzere
Côa
Castelo Branco
Leiria
Tagus
TAGUS
Portalegre
S P A I N
LISBON
Setúbal
Évora
Beja
GUADIANA
Sado
Mira
Monchique
Faro
0   100 km

Tropical Flora

Most tropical species acclimatize satisfactorily in Portugal. The Buçaco Plantations of the 17-19C and the 19C Pena Park at Sintra have produced outstanding results. The botanical gardens in Coimbra and Lisbon, the Cold Greenhouse in Lisbon, the Monserrate Park in Sintra are all highly decorative.

Madeira particularly, in its public gardens, *quintas* and in the mountains, displays within its small area, specimens of the most beautiful flowers of every continent on earth.

The Carob *(Alfarrobeira)*

The short and deeply furrowed trunk measures some 15 to 20m - 45 to 60ft. It is an evergreen; the edible fruits or seeds, carobs, are embedded in a soft pulp in a long hard pod.

The Cork Oak *(Sobreiro)*

The cork oak flourishes in Portugal. Its evergreen leaves are deep green and glossy on their upper sides and greyish green underneath.

Eucalyptus *(Eucalipto)*

The eucalyptus sometimes grows to a height of 80m - 250ft. Specimens often stand close to sea pines and rise to twice the latter's height.

THE ECONOMY

The area of Portugal in Europe is 88 994km^2 - 34 361sq miles or more than one sixth of the Iberian Peninsula. The frontier with Spain is 1 215km - 755 miles long.

The 1981 census gave the population as 9 833 014 (including Madeira and the Azores). More than a third of all Portuguese live in two of the eighteen areas of which the country is made up – namely Lisbon and Oporto. The density of the population averages 286 per sq mile. The north is more populous than the south.

Portugal has undertaken a vigourous policy of economic development in an effort to catch up on the standards of the major European Powers. The apparent abundance within an attractive landscape and general topography disguises the poverty of the soil, the scarcity of mineral deposits and the difficulties of their development between the mountains of the north and the aridity of the south.

Nevertheless, the Portuguese have succeeded in building factories, in improving the soil by cultivation and irrigation (Alentejo), in building suburban areas in their towns, in constructing giant bridges across the Douro and the Tagus and in building motorways which will further speed the country's development, as well as developing the tourist industry on the western (Figueira da Foz Troia Peninsula) and southern (Alvor, Vitamoura) coasts.

The figures cited below concern Portugal only (not Madeira and the Azores).

AGRICULTURE

Portugal, despite its poor natural resources, has remained basically an agricultural country. Over 30% of the population works on the land and the 5 600 000ha - 14 000 000 acres under cultivation represent approximately two thirds of the country's total area.

In the north the land is divided into innumerable small parcels with a few trees and a small patch of grazing completing the economy of each smallholding. It is from this overpopulated area that nearly 50% of the Portuguese come, who emigrate to France and Germany. The centre of the country, occupied by the Tagus and Mondego Basins, is the country of the vine, maize and rice; the south with its vast properties, that of wheat, olives, cork oaks and orange orchards.

Cereals. – Cereals cover a quarter of the land under cultivation. **Wheat** is king, especially in the Ribatejo and the Alentejo, where the 1983 production reached 326 839 tonnes; **maize** grows in the damp northwestern area running to 424 357 tonnes a year, and **rice,** which requires both considerable quantities of water and heat grows in the central and southern alluvial plains where annual production averages 109 059 tonnes.

Vines. – Vines grow everywhere in Portugal below a height of 700m - 2 200ft but they flourish especially north of the Tagus. Portugal is among the leading producers of wine in the world with an output of 10 030 972 hectolitres in 1982 (more than 50% for port). England once Portugal's greatest customer for port has given top place to France.

Olives. – Olives are cultivated in all areas but they thrive best in the northeast. Portugal is sixth in the world's producers of olive oil. The average yearly production is 474 819 hectolitres.

Fruit and vegetables. – Production of fruit and vegetables has been increasing steadily. A wide variety of fruit is grown: 438 267 tonnes in 1983 including apples, pears, grapes, oranges, almonds, figs for drying, etc. Olives and tomatoes go to canning centres from which quantities are exported particularly to the United Kingdom.

Trees. – *See p 13*. Trees cover an area of more than 3 000 000ha - 7 413 000 acres or nearly 50% of the land under cultivation. Cork oaks – planted over a fifth of the wooded areas and equal in number to one third of the whole world's cork oaks – provide the material for a whole manufacturing industry of the bottle corks, insulating materials and agglomerates. **Cork** alone makes up 4,5% of the value of Portugal's exports and makes the country the world's greatest producer of cork.

Stockraising. – The Portuguese raise the smaller animals such as sheep and goats and pigs.

INDUSTRY

Industry takes precedence over agriculture in the nation's economy and the development of Lisbon and Oporto where 60% of the country's production takes place are evidence of its continuing growth.

Mining. – Portugal hopes by constructing hydro-electric power stations to compensate for its limited coal deposits (250 000m tons of anthracite per annum from the north) despite the lignite deposits, which it is about to exploit.

The country draws considerable economic benefit from its wolfram, copper and tin mines. It is one of the world's largest producers of **wolfram** (2 010m tons in 1983) or tungsten which is mined chiefly at Panasquiera, northwest of Fundão; 279 960m tons of **cuprous iron pyrite** was extracted during 1983 in the Alentejo. Considerable deposits remain either untouched or awaiting expansion. **Tin** (525m tons of tin bearing ores in 1983) is dug out of many, but small, mines (Montesinho, north of Bragança). Moncorvo has large **iron** deposits. The most important deposits of **uranium** are at Cunha Baixa, southeast of Viseu, and at Nisa, northwest of Portalegre; the uranium reserve amounts to an approximate total of 9 200m tons.

Quarries also afford appreciable wealth: rock salt (429 231m tons in 1983), marble (Alentejo), granite and slate all being cut and exported.

Energy. – The country's main effort is directed to exploiting its immense natural resources in the hydro-electric field. The forty dams and power stations, having produced 8 milliard kWh in 1983, give an idea of the magnitude of the achievement since the middle of the century, in particular in the Douro Basin *(p 68)*. Furthermore more than 6 milliard kWh were produced in 1983 by the thermal power stations.

Manufacturing Industries

- Iron and steel
- Fish canneries
- Timber (cork, paper pulp)
- Cement
- Chemicals
- Textiles
- **Braga** Major industrial town
- Industrial area

Mining Industries

- Minerals
- Other resources

Sources of energy

- Oil refinery
- Hydroelectric station
- Thermal power station

0   50   100 km

The Sea

- Shipyard
- Fishing port
- Commercial port

Agriculture

- Cereals
- Olive trees
- Rice fields
- Vineyards

INDUSTRIES

AGRICULTURE

Until the present, the quest for oil, inland and offshore, has proved fruitless. Portugal is, therefore, developing her facilities for receiving large oil tankers. In addition to improvements already made to the ports of Lisbon and Leixões (the outer port of Oporto), work, on a grand scale, is now in progress at Sines.

Manufacturing Industries. – Among the greatest achievements are the erection of oil refineries at Lisbon, Oporto and Sines, a fertilizer factory at Setúbal, the ironworks (blast furnaces) at Seixal Naia, Viseu and Vial Real, wiremills manufacturing copper and tin wire (cables), production of silica in electric ovens, dockyards for shipbuilding, cork manufacturing plants, cement works (at Coimbra, Figueira da Foz, Loulé and Setúbal), textiles (cotton at Oporto and Braga, and wool at Covilha), hosiery and clothing at Oporto, Braga and Lisbon and ropemaking at Oporto and Aveiro, chemical industry at Aveiro, Povoa de Santa Iria and Sinés, and canneries for fruit and vegetables and especially fish.

THE SEA

Throughout her history Portugal has been orientated towards the sea, in 1983 about 18 820 ships were registered under the Portuguese flag.

Fishing. – 11 177 boats and 40 115 men are engaged in the fishing industry which provides a substantial part of the nation's food supply. It also provides the raw material for the fish canning industry which employs 8 764 workers in 99 factories.

The catch in 1983 amounted to 223 486 metric tons; of this 86 233 metric tonnes were sardines from the coastal waters, 9 680 metric tonnes were cod from the waters of Newfoundland and Greenland and 7 307 metric tonnes were tunny from the sea off Madeira and Azores; sardines above all (70% of all fish conserved) and tunny are canned before being exported. Europe takes 60% of the fish canned. The cod, usually dried, is consumed locally.

The Merchant Fleet. – The 96 ships (in 1982) comprising Portugal's merchant fleet conduct trade with Great Britain, the United States, the main European ports, Brazil, West and South Africa, and assures the transport of crude oil from the Persian Gulf to the Mediterranean. Imports are chiefly cereals, food products and raw materials (ore, oil and its by products). Exports are chiefly wine, canned sardines and tomatoes, cork, marble, resinous products, paperpulp, shoes and textiles.

For a stay in Portugal's hinterland consult the map of quiet and secluded hotels in the Michelin Red Guide España Portugal.

FOOD AND WINE

FOOD

Portuguese meals are copious, wholesome and tasty. The menu consists of several dishes, usually prepared with olive oil and flavoured with aromatic herbs such as rosemary, bay leaf, etc. The best dishes, often composed of local products which are difficult to obtain elsewhere, are little known abroad.

Eggs play an important part in Portuguese cookery: they are used in soups and often accompany fish and meat dishes and they form part of most desserts. Rice, for which the Portuguese acquired a liking following their voyages to the Far East, is the most favoured vegetable but French fried potatoes are found everywhere.

Olive oil which is almost tasteless and with no aroma is the oil most widely used. Its dark colour makes it difficult to distinguish from vinegar.

Soups. – Soup, which is served at most meals, can consist of a mixture of the most diverse materials. Among many are *canja de galinha*, a clear chicken soup with rice, *sopa de peixe*, fish soup, *sopa de mariscos* or seafood soup, *sopa de coelho* or rabbit soup, and *grão* or chick pea soup.

The most famous is the Minho **caldo verde** which is served widely north of the Mondego. This consists of a stock of mashed potatoes to which is added the green coloured Galician cabbage, finely shredded, which gives the dish its name; finally olive oil and slices of black pudding, *tora*, are mixed in to cook with the vegetables.

Breads soups or *açordas* are to be found in all regions, those of the Alentejo having many variations such as the *sopa de coentros* made with coriander leaves, olive oil, garlic, bread and, floating on top, a poached egg.

In the south, **gaspacho,** a soup of tomatoes, onions, cucumbers and pimentos seasoned with garlic and vinegar, is served cold with *croûtons*.

Fish and Crustacea. – Fish is basic to the Portuguese cuisine. **Cod**, *bacalhau*, is the most common fish, particularly in the north. It is said that there are 365 ways of preparing cod but it has become relatively expensive.

Many other fish, however, are to be found in some part or other of the country: grilled sardines can be scented in the streets of every town along the coast; fish of many types are mixed into the **caldeirada** or fish stew to be found everywhere. You will get tunny fillets on the Algarve, river lampreys and salmon beside the Minho, shad beside the Tagus.

Seafood is plentiful and is used frequently as a garnish. Shellfish, which are always cooked, are delicious and very varied, especially in the Algarve. A special copper vessel, a **cataplana,** is used in the Algarve to cook **clams** to which are added aromatic herbs and sausages, producing a most delectable dish.

Crayfish *(lagosta)* **prepared in the Peniche way,** or casseroled, are justly famous.

Meat and Game. – Apart from pork and game, Portuguese meat is often very ordinary. Pork is cooked and served in a variety of ways. The **roast suckling pig**, *leitão assado*, of Mealhada (north of Coimbra) is delicious. Meat from various parts of the pig is also to be found in stews, in smoked pigs' tongue sausages, *linguiça*, in smoked pork fillets, *paio*, and in **smoked ham**, *presunto*, at Chaves and Lamego. Ham and sausages are added to the *cozido à Portuguesa*, a hot pot of beef, vegetables, potatoes and rice and also to the local tripe prepared in the Oporto way, *dobrada*, a dish of pig or beef tripe cooked with haricot beans.

Pork in the Alentejo way – *Carne de porco à alentejana* – is pork marinated in wine, garnished with clams. Other meat is mostly minced and consumed as meat balls, although lamb and kid are sometimes roasted or served on skewers.

Cheeses. – Ewes' milk cheeses should be tried between October and May, notably the *Queijo da Serra*, the *Queijo de Castelo Branco* and the creamy *Queijo d'Azeitão* and such goats' milk cheeses as the *cabreiro*, the *rabaçal* from the Pombal region and the small **white cheeses** *queijinhos* from Tomar, often served as an hors d'œuvre as is the fresh goat's cheese, *Queijo fresco*.

Desserts. – Portuguese pastries are infinite in their variety. Nearly all include eggs in their recipes which come in most instances from old specialities prepared in convents. Each locality has its own pastry and the most delicious have been listed in the guide under the appropriate place name. The dessert most frequently seen on menus, however, is the *pudim de flan*, a sort of custard cream mould, while rice pudding, *arroz doce*, sprinkled with cinnamon forms a traditional part of any festive meal. In the Algarve, the local **figs** and **almonds** result in the most delicious sweetmeats and tit-bits.

Drinks. – Portugal produces excellent mineral waters, such as the Água de Luso and the aerated waters of Castelo, Carvalhelhos, Vidago and Pedras Salgadas. The beer is of the lager type and light. The fruit juices, both still, concentrated and of great variety, and aerated, are excellent and refreshing.

WINE

Portugal has a rich variety of wines, including the world famous **Port** *(p 17)* and **Madeira** *(p 145)*. The wines one buys locally or drinks in a restaurant at reasonable prices are of good quality, suitable for all occasions and deserve to be better known. In most restaurants one can ask for the *vinho da casa*, usually an unbranded local wine.

Vinho Verde. – *Vinho Verde* from the Minho and the Lower Douro Valley *(p 68)*, with its low alcoholic content (8° to 11.5°), is light and sparkling with a distinct bouquet and what might even be described as a very slightly bitter flavour. Its colour can be white (tendency to gold) or deep red.

Dão. – Vines growing on the granite slopes of the Dão Valley produce a sweet red wine with a velvety texture and a heady bouquet which most closely resembles a Burgundy. A fresh white wine is also grown.

Colares. – On the Serra de Sintra the vines grow in a sandy topsoil over a bed of clay, producing a velvety red wine which has been famous since the 13C *(p 132)*.

Bucelas. – Bucelas is a dry, somewhat acid straw coloured white wine produced from vineyards on the banks of the Trancão, a tributary of the Tagus.

Other table wines. – The Ribatejo vineyards produce good everyday wines: full bodied reds from the Cartaxo region and whites from Chamusca, Almeirim and Alpiarça on the far bank of the Tagus. Also worth trying are the wines of Torres Vedras, Alcobaça, Lafões and Agueda, the Pinhel and Mateus rosé and the sparkling wine from the Bairrada Region which goes wonderfully well with roast sucking pig.

Dessert Wines. – **Setúbal muscatel** from the vineyards of the chalky clay slopes of the Serra da Arrábida is a generous fruity wine which acquires a particularly pleasant taste with age. The equally fruity **Carcavelos** is a very popular.

Spirits. – The wide variety of Portuguese brandies includes *ginginha*, cherry brandy from Alcobaça, *medronho*, arbutus berry brandy and *brandimel*, honey brandy from the Algarve. *Bagaço or bagaceira*, a grape marc, served chilled, is the most widely drunk.

PORT

The vines of the Upper Douro, cultivated in a particular way in an area specifically defined by law since 1757 *(map pp 68-69)*, produce a generous wine which is shipped only after it has matured, from the port which has given it its name, Oporto.

Port's inestimable quality is due no less to the exceptional conditions under which the grapes are grown and ripened than to the processing of the fruit when harvested.

The cut grapes go into the press where mechanical crushing is gradually taking the place of the human treading which, with its songs and rhythmic tunes, was so highly picturesque. The must ferments in granite vats until it reaches the correct sweetness when a fortifying brandy is added which stops further fermentation and retains the sweetness. The wine is transferred into casks and transported to the vaults of Vila Nova de Gaia where it matures further in enormous casks *(p 113)*.

Wines from outstanding harvests, on the other hand, are shipped direct to England.

Vintage ports are especially selected from the best wines of a particularly fine year. They mature in bottle for 8 or 10 years or more before being served. On the contrary **blended ports** (Tinto or Red, Tinto-Alourado or Ruby, Alourado or Tawny, Alourado-Claro or Light Tawny) are mixtures of several years, and mature in wood.

The port wine trade with England remains of considerable importance *("The English and Port wine" p 113)*.

Port, which is red or white according to the colour of the grapes from which it was made, has many subtleties – it can be dry, medium or sweet. The white (branco), dry or extra dry, is a good apéritif; the sweet or medium sweet red is served at the end of a meal as an accompaniment to cheese or dessert and good conversation.

FOOD AND WINE	**Muscatel**	Wine regions
0 — 100 km	**● Bucelas**	Principal vineyards

HOTEL AND RESTAURANT VOCABULARY

Hotels and accommodation:

estalagem: inn, private hotel, similar to a *pousada*
pensão: establishment not quite of the standing of a hotel
pensão residencial: board only (no meals available)
pousada: hotel standing alone, under state management
quarto (de casal): bedroom (for two persons)
quarto com banho: room with bathroom attached

At a restaurant

(pequeno) almoço	(breakfast) lunch
azeite	olive oil
conta	the bill
ementa, carta	the menu
jantar, ceia	dinner
lista	menu (à la carte)
óleo	groundnut oil
pimenta; sal	pepper; salt
prato do dia	dish of the day

Drinks:

água; copo	water; a glass
café com leite	white coffee
cerveja	beer
fresco	cold, iced
gelo	ice cream, ice cube
sumo de fruta	fruit juice
vinho tinto	red wine

HISTORICAL FACTS

BC

9-7C The Greeks and the Phoenicians establish trading posts on the coasts of the Iberian Peninsula, inhabited in the west by Lusitanian tribes.

3C-2C The Carthaginians master the country; the Romans intervene (second Punic War). Viriate, Chief of the Lusitanians, organizes resistance and is assassinated in 139. Lusitania comes under Roman administration.

AD

5C The Sueves and the Visigoths occupy the major part of the Iberian Peninsula.

THE MOORISH OCCUPATION AND THE DAWN OF A NATION *(details p 19)*

711 The Moorish invasion from North Africa.

8-9C Pelagius leads the reconquest from the Asturias; his successors endow the wars which follow with the spirit of a Crusade. By the 9C the region of Portucale, north of the Mondego, has been liberated *(p 112)*.

1139 Afonso Henriques proclaims himself king under the name Afonso I *(p 84)*.

1249 With the recapture of Faro, the Moors are finally driven from the Algarve.

THE BURGUNDIAN DYNASTY — THE WARS WITH CASTILE

1279-1325 King Dinis I founds the University of Coimbra *(p 63)* and establishes Portuguese, a dialect of the Oporto region, as the official language.

1369-1385 Fernando I, taking advantage of the trouble in Castile, attempts to enlarge his kingdom; he fails and proposes the marriage of his only daughter, Beatrice, to the King of Castile. On Fernando's death in 1383, Castile claims the succession; but João I, bastard brother of the late king and Grand Master of the Order of Avis is acclaimed ruler.

16 June 1373 First Treaty of Alliance with England (signed in London).

14 Aug. 1385 Victory over the Castilians at Aljubarrota *(p 49)*.

1386 Treaty of Windsor with England.

THE AVIS DYNASTY — THE GREAT DISCOVERIES *(details p 19)*

1415 The capture of Ceuta in Morocco marks the beginning of Portuguese expansion.

1481-1495 João II on the throne; Bartolomeu Dias rounds the Cape of Good Hope (1488). The Treaty of Tordesillas, 1494, divides the world into two spheres of influence, the Portuguese and the Castilian.

1495-1521 Manuel I on the throne; Vasco da Gama discovers the sea route to India in 1498 and Pedro Álvares Cabral lands in Brazil in 1500. Magellan is the first man to circumnavigate the world, 1519-22.

4 Aug. 1578 King Sebastião I is killed in Morocco in the Battle of El-Ksar El-Kebir. The king's death marks the end of Portugal's supremacy.

THE SPANISH DOMINATION

1580 Philip II invades Portugal and has himself proclaimed king under the name Felipe I.

1 Dec. 1640 Uprising against the Spanish. Duke John of Bragança takes the title João IV of Portugal; the family remain as the ruling dynasty until 1910.

1668 Spain recognizes Portugal's independence.

THE BRITISH ALLIANCE AND THE NAPOLEONIC WARS *(details p 20)*

1703 Britain and Portugal sign the Methuen Treaty and a Trade Treaty facilitating the shipping of port to England *(p 112)*.

1 Nov. 1755 An earthquake destroys Lisbon *(p 89)*.

1793 Portugal joins the first coalition against Revolutionary France.

1807 French invasion under Junot. The royal family goes into exile in Brazil.

1808 Landing of first detachments of British troops; Wellington in command.

1810 Wellington victorious at Buçaco *(p 56)*; last major battle on Portuguese soil in the Peninsular Campaign.

THE DOWNFALL OF THE MONARCHY

1822 Independence of Brazil.

1834 The civil war ends in favour of Dom Pedro with the Convention of Evoramonte *(p 79)*.

1890 The British Ultimatum ends direct contact between Angola and Mozambique.

1899 Treaty of Windsor with England.

1 Feb. 1908 Assassination of King Carlos I and the heir to the throne.

5 Oct. 1910 Abdication of Manuel II and Proclamation of the Republic.

THE REPUBLIC

1910-1933 The Republic cannot restore order and economy. Entering into the war against Germany in 1916, and sending troops to France only makes the home situation worse, critical in 1928. Dr. Salazar is appointed Minister of Finance, then in 1932, Prime Minister: he restores economic and political stability but in 1933 promulgates the Constitution of the "New State" instituting a corporative and dictatorial regime.

1961-1974 In 1961 India annexes Goa. Salazar, whose illness prevents him from taking part in affairs of state at the end of 1968, dies in July 1970. His successor, Caetano, continues a ruinous and unpopular anti-guerilla war in Africa.

25 April 1974 The Armed Forces movement seize power *(p 89)*.

1974-1975 Portuguese possessions in Africa attain independence. More than 750 000 refugees flock to the home country.

1976 General Ramalho Eanes is elected President of the Republic.

THE FOUNDING OF THE KINGDOM

At the end of the 11C, Alfonso VI, King of Castile and Léon, undertook the reconquest of New Castile. He called on many French knights, including Henri of Burgundy, descendant of the French king Hugues Capet, and his cousin Raymond of Burgundy. When the Moors had been vanquished Alfonso offered to the princes his daughters in marriage: Urraca, heir to the throne, married Raymond; Teresa brought as her dowry in 1095 to **Henri of Burgundy,** the *portucalense* county *(p 112),* so creating him Count of Portugal. Henri dies in 1114; Queen Teresa becomes regent pending the coming of age of her son Afonso Henriques. But in 1128 the latter forces his mother to relenquish her power *(p 84):* in 1140 he breaks the vassalage bonds imposed on him by Alfonso VIII of Castile and proclaims himself King of Portugal: Castile finally agrees in 1143.

Afonso Henriques also continues the reconquest and after the victory at Ourique (1139) he takes Santarém, then Lisbon (1147).

The capture of Faro in 1249 marked the end of the Moorish occupation.

THE GREAT DISCOVERIES

Grand Designs. – On 25 July 1415 a fleet of more than 200 ships under the command of King João I and his three sons, of whom Prince Henry was one, set sail from Lisbon. The Portuguese seizure of **Ceuta** put an end to the Barbarians' acts of piracy along the coast and assured them control of the Straits of Gibraltar. Further, the Portuguese hoped the expedition would furnish them, at low cost, with gold and slaves from the Sudan and finally they considered that it would keep up their prestige with the Castilians who had just taken possession of the Canary Islands. The spirit of the Crusades was not altogether lacking either from this enterprise in which Christians opposed Mohammedans: the Portuguese aimed to join their kingdom to that of the Christian Prester John who was said to rule a country beyond the Moorish territories.

And finally the idea of discovering a new world, of pushing back the boundaries of the unknown, was constantly in the minds of men of ambition at that time.

The Sagres School. – Ceuta taken, Prince Henry realized that the victory did not, in fact, make the spice route between the Mediterranean and India safe from attack by Barbarian pirates. He retired to the Sagres Promontory together with cosmographers, cartographers and navigators to try and work out a sea route from Europe to India. The idea was born in his mind of rounding Africa by the south. To ensure that his hypotheses should ultimately be proved correct, Prince Henry called on experienced navigators to journey ever further south: **Madeira** ① was discovered in 1419 *(p 144),* the **Azores** ② in 1427 and in 1434 **Gil Eanes** *(p 86)* rounded **Cape Bojador** ③, then the furthest point known to Western man. To ensure the success of these expeditions the Sagres School improved the caravel itself and also instruments of navigation *(p 124).* Each time they discovered new land the mariners erected a cairn and established trading rights. Prince Henry inspired new methods of colonization in the setting up of trading posts, exchanges and banks. These offices, established and run by private individuals, sometimes fostered the development of towns independent of the local powers, such as Goa, or they created companies to control trade in one commodity, of which they often acquired monopoly rights, and also deeds of gift, usually of land, to ships' captains with the charge that an area be developed. Henry died in 1460 but the stage had been set.

The Sea Route to India. – **Diogo Cão** reached the mouth of the **Congo** ④ in 1482 and in 1488 **Bartolomeu Dias** rounded Tempest Cape, which was immediately rechristened by João II, the **Cape of Good Hope** ⑤. A few years earlier **Christopher Columbus,** the Genoese navigator married to a Portuguese, had the idea of sailing to India by a westerly route. His proposals, rebuffed in Lisbon, found favour with the Catholic Monarchs and in 1492 he discovered the New World for his patrons.

In 1494 under the **Treaty of Tordesillas** the Kings of Portugal and Castile divided the newly discovered and as yet undiscovered territories of the world between them: everything west of a meridian which was 370 sea leagues west of the Cape Verde Islands was to belong to Castile; everything east of the meridian to Portugal. The position of the dividing meridian has made some historians speculate as to whether Portugal knew of the existence of **Brazil** ⑥ even before its official discovery by **Pedro Álvares Cabral** in 1500.

The exploration of the African coast by the Portuguese continued. On 8 July 1497 a fleet of four ships commanded by Admiral **Vasco de Gama** sailed from Lisbon with the commission to reach India by way of the sea route round the Cape. By March 1498 Vasco de Gama had arrived at **Mozambique** ⑦ and on 20 May he landed in Calicut (Kozhikode, southern India): the sea route to India had been discovered. This epic voyage was later sung in *The Lusiads* by the poet Camões who had joined the ship's company. In 1501 **Gaspar Corte Real** discovered **Newfoundland**, but King Manuel was interested primarily in Asia. Within a few years the Portuguese had explored the coastlines of Asia; by 1515 they were in control of the Indian Ocean, thanks to fortified outposts such as **Goa** ⑧ which had been established by **Afonso de Albuquerque** in 1510. Commercial relations were established in 1540 with China and later with Siam and the East Indies.

It was, however, on behalf of the King of Spain that the Portuguese, **Fernão de Magalhães** (Magellan), set out in 1519 and landed in India in 1521. Though he himself was assassinated by the natives of the Philippines, one of his vessels continued the journey, so being the first to circumnavigate the world (1522). Finally in 1660, **David Melgueiro**, in a Dutch ship, linked Portugal with Japan, by voyaging north of Iceland.

The Bonus. – The Discoveries, coming in a troubled period at the end of the Middle Ages, were of very great consequence in the development of Western civilization at the dawn of the Renaissance. From the beginning of the 16C, monopoly of the trade with India, which up to that time had always been in the hands of the Turks and the Arabs, passed to the Portuguese; Mediterranean and Baltic trading posts such as Venice, Genoa and Lübeck declined in favour of ports on the western seaboard, particularly Lisbon; merchants from northern Europe came to trade their arms, cereals, silver and copper for African gold and ivory, famous Indian spices – pepper, cinnamon, ginger and cloves – Chinese silks, Persian carpets and the precious metals of Sumatra. New products – the sweet potato, maize, tobacco, cocoa and indigo – were introduced to Europe; the gold of Africa and America flowed in to the mouth of the Tagus.

Portugal and Spain became great powers, establishing vast colonial empires, while the countries of Islam lost their importance; the influence of Europe was felt throughout the world. The discovery of the existence of formerly unknown peoples posed religious problems: were the men of the New World marked by original sin? Doubts presaged the Reformation; the birth of criticism and curiosity, of modern science; the fields of geography and anthropology expanded. The need for cheap manual labour brought slavery; the traffic in "black Ebony" introduced African Negroes to America.

Evanescent Riches. – Portugal, however, had overspent its strength; in thirty-four years (1521-55) thirty-two ships had been lost; the population had dropped from 2 to 1 million, many having gone overseas; riches encouraged idlers and adventurers; land was not tilled and wheat and rye had to be imported; crafts and skills were lost; the cost of living rose steeply. Gold was exchanged for goods from the Netherlands and France until Portugal's riches were dissipated and virtually nothing remained. On 4 August 1578 the young King Sebastião I was killed at El-Ksar El-Kebir; two years later Portugal came under the domination of Spain which divided the greater part of her overseas territories with the Netherlands.

THE NAPOLEONIC WARS

Portugal joined the first continental coalition against Revolutionary France in 1793. In 1796 Spain left the Convention and allied itself to France. When Portugal refused to renounce her alliance with England, Spain invaded in 1801 and the resulting war was known as the **War of the Oranges** *(p 70)*. To ensure a strict application of the blockade on Britain, Napoleon invaded Portugal but his commanders had little success in a country supported by English troops under the command of Wellesley. The future Duke of Wellington, preferred guerilla tactics and finally forced the French from the Peninsula.

Portugal suffered violence and depredations by both armies; material poverty and the political and moral effects were tragic; rival factions, supported at times by both the English and the French, emerged ultimately to fight in civil war (1828-34).

THE ANGLO-PORTUGUESE ALLIANCE

"Our Oldest Ally". – This alliance dates back more than 600 years to a treaty signed in London in 1373. This was ratified in 1386 by the Treaty of Windsor which followed the Battle of Aljubarrota (1385) in which English archers helped João I, the new King and Nuno Alvares, to beat the Castilians. This treaty of perpetual peace and friendship has been reratified and invoked several times since, for military, commercial and dynastic reasons.

Military assistance began at the time of the Crusades when in 1147 the reconquest of Lisbon was achieved by Afonso Henriques with the help of an army of Crusaders on their way to the Holy Land. Troops were sent by Richard II in 1398 to aid the expulsion of Don Dinis, a pretender to the Portuguese throne, and again in 1415 to help the expedition to Ceuta in North Africa. In an unsuccessful attempt to break the Spanish domination of Portugal (started in 1580) Elizabeth I provided one of the pretenders to the throne, António, Prior of Crato, with an army in 1589. Military assistance continued throughout the centuries *(see Napoleonic Wars above)*.

"Our Oldest Ally". It was in these terms that Winston Churchill described Anglo-Portuguese relations in the House of Commons in 1943 when announcing the latest agreement providing facilities for British shipping in the Azores during the Battle of the Atlantic (Portugal remained neutral in the Second World War). The alliance also included trade agreements. As early as the 13C trade flourished in English wool and textiles and Portuguese wax, leather and skins, fruit and olive oil. The Methuen Treaty of 1703 *(p 113)* provided conditions for the shipping of port wine to Britain.

Many marriages further strengthened relations, among the most notable being that of Philippa, daughter of John of Gaunt, Duke of Lancaster in 1386 to João I, King of Portugal and founder of the House of Avis which was to reign until 1580, and that of Catherine of Bragança with King Charles II in 1662.

THE ARTS

A few prehistoric sites and ruins dating from Roman times such as those of the city of Citânia de Briteiros *(p 55)*, the town of Conimbriga *(p 67)* and that of the temple at Évora *(p 75)* will interest the lover of antiquity, but it is from the 11C onwards, shortly before the country gained its independence, that Portuguese art and architecture took on a specifically national character.

THE MIDDLE AGES (11-15C)

Romanesque Art. – The Romanesque influence arrived late, in the 11C, in Portugal and, brought from France by Burgundian knights *(p 19)* and monks from Cluny and Moissac, it retained many French traits. Nevertheless, the influence of Santiago de Compostela produced in north Portugal, where it is best represented, a style more Galician than French and further differentiated from its sources by being exemplified in granite. The rock has given the monuments a massive and rough appearance with capitals reflecting the material's solid resistance to the mason's chisel.

Cathedrals, often built on a height in the centre of a town, were reconstructed at the same time as local fortified castles and, therefore, often resemble them outwardly. Both acted as supports to the Portuguese military, at that time occupied in attacking the Mohammedan forces.

Country churches, whose architecture was influenced later, sometimes possess richly carved main doorways. The interior design, frequently including pointed arches and even groined vaulting, has been transformed in many cases by Manueline or Baroque additions.

(After Secretaria de Estado da Informação e Turismo photo)

Coimbra — The fortified Cathedral.

The late 12C rotunda of the Knights Templar at Tomar, copied from the Temple in Jerusalem, has no equal anywhere else in the country.

Gothic Art. – Gothic art developed most vigorously at the end of the 13C in the areas around Coimbra and Lisbon where the calcareous nature of the rock encouraged the building of several churches and monasteries, particularly at Santarém. All the churches, which are designed with three equal aisles and polygonal apses and apsidal chapels, retain the proportions, the mass and the simplicity of the Romanesque style. The Abbey at Alcobaça served as a model to the architects of the 14C Cistercian cloisters of Coimbra, Lisbon and Évora Cathedrals. Flamboyant Gothic found its most perfect expression in Batalha Monastery even though this was only completed in the Manueline period.

Sculpture. – Gothic sculpture developed in the 14C particularly for the adornment of tombs, but continued to ignore the possibilities of decoration on tympana and doorways. Capitals were ornamented only with geometric or plant motifs with the exception of a few stylized animals or occasional human forms (capitals in Celas Monastery at Coimbra).

Funerary art flowered in three centres, Lisbon, Évora and Coimbra from where, under the direction of **Master Pero,** it spread throughout northern Portugal and in particular to Oporto, Lamego, Oliveira do Hospital and São João de Tarouca. The most beautiful limestone tombs are those of Inês de Castro and Dom Pedro in Alcobaça Abbey.

The effulgence of Coimbra continued into the 15C under **João Afonso** and **Diogo Pires the Elder.** A second centre developed at Batalha inspired by Master Huguet.

Statuary, influenced by the French, particularly at Braga, is characterized by minuteness of detail, realism in the carving of the head and gentleness of expression.

Military Architecture. – The Portuguese, in the wars first against the Moors and then the Spanish, constructed castles which remain today as prominent features of the landscape. The first series mark the successive stages of the Reconquest, the second, dating from the 13 to 17C, guard the most frequented routes of communication. Most of these castles, built in the Middle Ages, have a strong family likeness. Double perimeter walls circle a keep or Tower of Homage *(Torre de Menagem)* which was usually square, massive and crowned with pyramid capped merlons, a last trace of the Moorish influence.

The last castles to be built were those constructed in the 17C to protect such frontier towns as Valença do Minho, Almeida and Elvas, when they where given fortifications based on the principles of the French military architect, Vauban.

Some History of Art terms to be found in this Guide

Coro alto. – From the Latin *chorus*: choir. Architecturally, a gallery over the west end of the nave, facing the east end or sanctuary *(capela mor)*. Like the sanctuary, the *coro alto* frequently contains carved wood choir stalls *(cadeiral)*.

Coro baixo. – "Lower choir" situated beneath the gallery.

Mozarabic. – The term applied to work by Christian craftsmen working for Mohammedan masters and influenced by Moorish art.

Mudejar. – Designation applied in Portugal to works completed between the 13 and 16C in which Moorish influence can be traced.

Plateresque. – A style evolved in Spain in the 16C. The highly ornate decoration recalls the work of silversmiths *(plateros)* from which it derives.

Sé. – From the Latin *sedes*: seat, hence episcopal seat, hence cathedral.

THE MANUELINE PERIOD

The Manueline style marks the transition from Gothic to Renaissance in Portugal. It flowered in the reign of Manuel I and, despite its brief duration from 1490 to 1520, was so original that it is of major importance in all aspects of Portuguese art.

It reflects the passion, which inspired all Portugal at the time, for the sea and the faraway territories which had just been discovered and it manifests the strength developing on the banks of the Tagus and the riches also accumulating there.

Architecture. – Churches remained Gothic in their general plan, in the height of their columns and network vaulting – but novelty, originality and movement appeared in the way columns were twisted to form spirals; triumphal arches were adorned with mouldings in the form of nautical cables; ribs of plain pointed arched vaulting were supplemented by heavy liernes in round or square relief; these, in their turn, were transformed by further ornamentation into four-pointed stars or were supplemented by decorative cables occasionally given additional bulk by being intertwined in mariners' knots. The contour of the vaulting itself evolved, flattening out and resting on arches supported on consoles. The height of the aisles was increased, so giving rise to true hall churches.

Sculpture. – The Manueline style shows its character most fully in sculpture in the field of decoration. Windows, doorways, rose windows, balustrades are covered with branches of laurel leaves, poppy heads, roses, corn cobs, acorns and oak leaves, parasol type

(After Secretaria de Estado da Informação e Turismo photo)
Setúbal — The church of Jesus.

flower heads, artichokes, cardoons, pearls, scales, ropes, anchors, terrestrial globes and the armillary spheres on which the concentric circles enabled navigators to make certain astronomic observations. The Cross of the Order of Christ, repeated everywhere, forms a part of every decorative scheme.

The Artists. – Boytac (d before 1528), was the author of the first Manueline building, the Church of Jesus at Setúbal, and of Guarda Cathedral. He also contributed to the construction of the Hieronymite Monastery in Lisbon. The church of the Monastery of the Holy Cross at Coimbra, and the monastery at Batalha. His artistry lay in magnificent complication: twisted columns, of which he was the master, were covered with overlapping scales and rings; doorways, which were a major element in Manueline art, stand in a rectangular setting bordered by turned columns crowned by spiralled pinnacles; in the centre of the whole or above it stand the Manueline emblems of the shield, the Cross of the Order of Christ and the armillary sphere.

Mateus Fernandes, who brought a Manueline touch to Batalha, was distinctly influenced in his art by the elegance of Flamboyant Gothic. Decoration, which he designed usually as an infinitely repeated plant, geometric or calligraphic motif, takes precedence over the size of the area ornamented – the doorway to the Unfinished Chapels at Batalha is outstanding for the exuberance of its decoration.

Diogo de Arruda was the most original Manueline artist. He designed the famous Tomar window where imagination marvels at the inventiveness. Marine and nautical themes became a positive obsession with this artist.

Francisco de Arruda was the architect

Lisbon — The Belém Tower.

of Lisbon's Belém Tower. He rejected the decorative excesses of his brother, preferring the simplicity of Gothic design which he embellished with Moorish motifs.

The Arruda brothers were recognized equally as the "master architects of the Alentejo", where they displayed their skill in combining the Gothic and Moorish styles with Manueline themes in such a way as to evolve an entirely new style, namely the **Luso-Moorish.** This is characterized by the horseshoe arch adorned with delicate mouldings.

Simultaneously, as Manueline architecture was reaching its greatest peak at the end of the 15C, Portuguese sculpture came under Flemish influence due to Olivier de Gand and Jean d'Ypres – their masterpiece is the carved wood altarpiece in Coimbra's Old Cathedral. **Diogo Pires the Younger** followed, adopting Manueline themes in his work of which the best example is the font in the Leça do Balio Monastery (1515).

At the beginning of the 16C several artists came from Galicia and Biscay to work in north Portugal. There they took part in the construction of the churches of Caminha Braga, Vila do Conde and Viana do Castelo. The obvious influences in their work are Flamboyant Gothic and Plateresque. From 1517 onwards two Biscayan artists, **João** and **Diogo de Castilho,** worked successively in Lisbon, Tomar and Coimbra. Their art, which had much of the Plateresque in it, became integrated in the Manueline style (the Hieronymite Monastery).

Painting

The Portuguese painters, freeing themselves from foreign influence and lagging somewhat in time behind the architects and sculptors, nevertheless, illustrated in their own way their country's prodigious political ascent.

The Primitives (1450-1505). – The early painters were influenced by Flemish art whose penetration into Portugal was favoured by the close commercial ties between Lisbon and the Low Countries.

Only **Nuno Gonçalves,** author of the famous St Vincent polyptych *(p 99)*, remained truly original, not least in the way the picture in its composition evoked a tapestry more than a painting. Unfortunately none of his other works are known except for the cartouches for the Arzila and Tangier tapestries which hang in the Collegiate Church of Pastrana in Spain.

Among the Flemish painters who came to Portugal, Francisco Henriques and Frei Carlos stand out for their tendency to "Lusitanise" or "Portuguese" their art by accentuating the luminosity of the colours.

The Manueline Painters (1505-50). – The Manueline painters created a true Portuguese school of painting which was characterized by delicacy of design, beauty and accuracy of colour, realism in the composition of the backgrounds, a true illustration of the height and size of human figures and an expressive naturalism in the portrayal of people's faces tempered, however, with a certain idealism. The major artists in the school worked either in Viseu or Lisbon.

The **Viseu school** *(p 141)* was under the artist, **Vasco Fernandes,** known as "Grão Vasco". **Gaspar Vaz,** who had begun painting at the Lisbon school, in fact painted his best pictures when he went to Viseu. The works of these two masters, though still influenced by Flemish art, nevertheless revealed their own considerable originality.

The **Lisbon school** established around **Jorge Afonso,** Painter to King Manuel I, saw the development of several talented artists:

(After Secretária de Estado da Informação e Turismo photo)

Portrait of Prince Henry the Navigator.

– **Cristóvão de Figueiredo** evolved a technique which recalls the later Impressionists (the use of spots of colour in place of the longer brushstrokes) and the utilization of black and grey in portraiture. His style was imitated by several artists including the Master of Santa Anna in his altarpiece for the original Church of the Madre de Deus in Lisbon.

– **Garcia Fernandes,** sometimes archaic in style, affected also a certain preciosity in his portraits.

– **Gregório Lopes,** whose line and modelling were harsher, was the painter of life at Court. He excelled in backgrounds which always present in exact detail contemporary Portuguese life, whether in the country, in town or at court (altarpiece in the Church of St John the Baptist at Tomar). His influence may be seen in the work of the Master of Abrantes, even though the latter's style was already Baroque.

The Minor Arts in the Manueline Period. – Manueline taste in the minor arts exhibits an exuberance in decorative motifs, often inspired by the Orient. Ecclesiastical plate, which was particularly sumptuous in the 15 and 16C, owed much to Oriental exoticism. Pottery and china were influenced by Chinese porcelain. Furniture adopted Oriental decorative techniques with the use of lacquers (China) and inlays of marquetry, mother of pearl and ivory (India).

(After Tabacaria Nilo photo)

Coimbra — The pulpit in the Church of the Holy Cross.

THE RENAISSANCE

The Renaissance, which retained its essential Italian and French characteristics in Portugal, spread out from Coimbra, where several French artists had settled *(details p 63)*.

Nicolas Chanterene, whose style remained faithful throughout to the principles of the Italian Renaissance, undertook the decoration of the north door of the Hieronymite Monastery in Lisbon before becoming the master sculptor of the Coimbra school. The pulpit in the Church of the Holy Cross in Coimbra is his masterpiece.

Jean de Rouen excelled in the production of altarpieces and low reliefs (Celas Monastery in Coimbra).

Houdart succeeded Nicolas Chanterene in 1530 at Coimbra as grand master of statuary. His sculptures are easily recognizable for their great realism.

The advance in architecture, which came later than in the other arts, was brought about by native Portuguese: **Miguel de Arruda** introduced a Classical note to Batalha after 1533; **Diogo de Torralva** completed the Convent of Christ at Tomar; **Afonso Álvares** began the transition to Classical design by giving buildings a monumental simplicity.

CLASSICAL AND BAROQUE ART (17-18C)

Classical Art. – 17C. The Classical period saw the triumph of the Jesuit style with **Filippo Terzi,** an Italian architect who arrived in Portugal in 1576 and **Baltasar Álvares** (1550-1624); churches became rectangular in plan and were constructed without transept, ambulatories or apses. Painting came under the influence of Spain and produced only two major artists: **Domingos Vieira** (1600-78), whose portraits are vividly alive, and Josefa de Ayala, known as **Josefa de Óbidos** (1634-84 – p 110). A feeling for Classical composition is also apparent in the work of the silversmiths and goldsmiths of the period (altar in the Cathedral at Oporto). The 17C was also famous for the Indo-Portuguese style of furniture, typified by marquetry secretaires inlaid with rare woods and ivory.

Baroque Art. – Late 17-18C. The Baroque style, which owes its name to the Portuguese word *barroco* – a rough pearl – corresponds, in the artistic sense, to the spirit of the Counter-Reformation.

Architecture. – Baroque architecture abandoning the symmetry of the Classical style, sought movement, volume and a sense of depth through the use of curved lines for which it had a predilection. It also sought to give an impression of grandeur. In Portugal, the beginning of Baroque architecture coincided with the end of Spanish domination and the restoration of the country's independence *(p 18).*

In the 17C, architecture, therefore, took on an austere and simple appearance under the guidance of **João Nunes Tinoco** and **João Turiano.** But from the end of the century onwards façades becames alive with figures of angels, garlands, and the interplay of curving lines, particularly at Braga. The architect **João Antunes** advocated an octagonal plan for religious constructions (the Church of Santa Engrácia, Lisbon). In the 18C King João V invited artists to come to Portugal from abroad. The German **Friedrich Ludwig** and the Hungarian, **Mardel,** both trained in the Italian school brought with them a monumental style, as can be seen in the Monastery at Mafra.

(After Secretaria de Estado da Informação e Turismo photo)

Bom Jesus.

True Baroque architecture developed in the north and can be seen in both ecclesiastical and civil buildings (Bom Jesus do Monte Church near Braga and the Mateus Manor near Vila Real), where the aesthetic appearance of the façades is accentuated by the contrast between the white limewashed walls and the granite pilasters and cornices which frame them.

At Oporto, **Nicolau Nasoni,** who was of Italian origin, adorned façades with floral motifs, palm leaves and swags. In Braga, architecture approached the Rococo in style (the Raio Palace at Braga and the Church of St Mary Magdalene at Falperra).

Decoration. – *Azulejos (p 25)* and **Talha dourada** were popular forms of decoration, the latter being the Portuguese name for the heavily gilded wood used in the adornment of church interiors from 1650 onwards. Wood was also used to make altarpieces but, though described in the same way, was first carved before being gilded.

In the 17C, altarpieces resembled doorways: on either side of the altar and the foot of steps leading to the bishop's throne, rise up twisted columns while the screen itself was covered in such decorative motifs in high relief as vines, bunches of grapes, birds, cherubim, etc. Altarpieces in the 18C were often out of all proportion, invading the ceiling and the chancel walls. Entablatures with broken pediments crown columns against which stand atlantes or statues. Altarpieces were also surmounted by baldachinos.

Statuary. – Numerous statues generally of wood were to be found on the altarpieces which decorated the churches. In the 18C statuary largely followed the styles of foreign schools: at Mafra, the Italian Guisti and his colleagues instructed many Portuguese sculptors, among them **Machado de Castro** *(details p 103)*; in Braga, Coimbra and Oporto, **Laprade** represented the French school; however at Arouca, the Portuguese **Jacinto Vieira** in a personal style made his carvings very alive.

The idea of Baroque cribs or manger scenes, to be seen in many churches, originated in southern Italy. In Portugal they are more naïve (often inspired by traditional pilgrimages) but not without artistic merit. The figures in terracotta often being the work of Machado de Castro, **Manuel Teixeira** or **António Ferreira.**

The talent of the Baroque sculptors is also evident in the many fountains found throughout Portugal especially in the Minho Region. The monumental staircase of Bom Jesus *(see illustration above)* near Braga, is made up of a series of fountains in the Rococo style.

Painting. – Painting is represented by **Vieira Lusitano** (1699-1783) and **Domingos António de Sequeira** (1768-1837), the latter a remarkable portrait painter and draughtsman.

Baroque angel.

FROM THE END OF THE 18C TO THE PRESENT DAY

Architecture. – The second half of the 18C saw a return to the Classical style which may be seen in the work of **Mateus Vicente** (1747-86 – Queluz Palace), **Carlos da Cruz Amarante** (Church of Bom Jesus) and the Lisbon architects, particularly **Eugénio dos Santos** who created the so called Pombal style *(p 89)*.

Currently, architectural imagination and skill are best exemplified in the bridges which have been constructed across the Douro at Oporto, and on a vast scale over the Tagus at Lisbon and in the Monument to the Discoveries, also at Lisbon.

Sculpture. – **Soares dos Reis** (1847-89) tried to portray in sculpture the Portuguese *saudade (p 30)*; his pupil, **Teixeira Lopes** (1866-1918) revealed an elegant technique particularly in the painting of children's heads, while **Francisco Franco** (1885-1955) was the outstanding Portuguese sculptor at the beginning of the 20C.

Painting. – Two painters, **Silva Porto** (1850-93) and **Marquês de Oliveira** (1853-1927), belonged to the Naturalist movement, while **Malhoa** (1855-1933), the painter of popular festivals, and **Henrique Pousão** (1859-84) were closer to Impressionnism; **Sousa Pinto** (1856-1939) excelled as a pastel artist and **Columbano Bordalo Pinheiro** (1857-1929) achieved renown with his portraits and still lifes.

Portuguese painting at the beginning of the 20C stuck to Naturalism; two artists only diverged to follow the general trend: **Amadeo de Souza Cardoso** (1887-1918), the friend of Modigliani, worked in Paris assimilating the lessons of Cézanne and after finding his true expression first in Cubism, emerged into a highly coloured variant of Expressionism. **Maria Helena da Silva** was born in 1908 and went to Paris in 1928. Her whole art derived from the Paris school, but in her space paintings, the influence of pattern juxtaposition and the colours of *azulejos* can occasionally be seen.

AZULEJOS

Origin and Manufacturing Processes. – The art of decorated pottery, already known to Antiquity, was probably introduced to the Iberian Peninsula by the Moors who had learned it from the Persians. The **alicatados** technique, employed in the 14C by potters in Andalusia, consisted of cutting already painted clay with a file and fitting the pieces together as in marquetry. In the **tacelos** technique practised at Toledo and Jaén at the same period, motifs were outlined in the clay before it was fired. In the 14C also the use of glazes with a lead base and metal based iridescent enamels spread fairly rapidly.

The **cuerda seca** process, brought to the country by the Christians, made it possible to separate colours by covering strokes marked on the fresh clay with linseed oil or manganese. In the 16C the first moulds to be made in relief, the **Cuenca** process, pointed the way to ceramic mass production. In 1517 in Sevilla, the Italian Francisco Nicoloso invented the **Majolica** technique, the painting of colours on the still wet clay tiles.

Portuguese Azulejos. – The Portuguese discovered the appeal of *azulejos* when they started to explore Morocco shortly after the capture of Ceuta in 1415. The first Portuguese made *azulejos* date from 1584 – until then only Moorish, as in the Royal Palace at Sintra, or Andalusian tiles were used. These first Portuguese *azulejos* were blue or *azul*, hence the name.

In the 17C the Portuguese completely mastered the craft and began to experiment. Multicoloured *azulejos* appeared with blues, yellows, purples and greens all used to add to the decorative effect of designs which, however, remained for the most part purely geometric. After 1650, the tiles began to take on a new character: public buildings started to be ornamented with *azulejos* pictures or panels illustrating hunting scenes, picnics, landscapes and other scenes of outdoor life; friezes became crowded with blazons, garlands and cherubs. An *azulejos* craze beset the country, but the demand was so great that the tile makers of Rotterdam and Delft, long noted for and highly skilled in the production of blue and white tiles, were able to win a market for themselves and in the course of time destroy the market in multicoloured *azulejos*. All the while the decoration was drawing closer to the contemporary tapestry and fresco styles.

In the 18C **António de Oliveira Bernardes** and his son **Policarpo** set up what was virtually an *azulejos* school to combat the Dutch influence in the craft. The fashion

(After Secretaria de Estado da Informação e Turismo photo)

18C Azulejos.

for Baroque both in architecture and art called for tiles to be made more as frames and settings rather than as pictures themselves. Such themes as were illustrated came, for the most part, from the Old Testament. In about 1740 *azulejos* began to be manufactured industrially: quantity increased at the expense of quality. After the 1755 earthquake the creation of the Rato Royal Pottery Factory revived interest in *azulejos*: polychromy once again found favour and the new *azulejos*, suiting the Rococo style then in fashion, were used to decorate fountains, seats, kitchens, etc. At the end of the 18C the neo-Classical style of architecture called for a return to simplicity in decorative motifs and restraint in colour so that designs were limited to flowers, medallions and birds and tones of yellow, brown and green only.

Jorge Barradas (1894-1971) allied colour and perspective in vast compositions.

MAJOR WRITERS

Open to outside influences which are assimilated quickly and successfully, Portuguese literature is none the less original and capable of imagination. It reflects the lyrical and nostalgic spirit of the people, as in the *fado (p 30)* – and also a critical sense, rapidly inclined towards the satire of injustice or the absurdity in each era. This is why poetry has always held a privileged position with, as a figurehead defying the centuries, the monumental work of Camoens.

Middle Ages. – The earliest known Portuguese literature is at the end of the 12C with the poetry of the troubadours, influenced by Provençal lyricism. To one of these can be attributed the real authorship, in Portuguese, of the well known Spanish courtly romance *Amadis of Gaul.* After King Dinis I, a poet himself, who imposed the official use of Portuguese *(p 18)* the princes of the Avis dynasty (João I, D. Duarte, the infante D. Pedro, Afonso V), in the 15C all personally contributed to the enrichment of the growing literature.

16C. – The Renaissance introduced humanism and a renewal of poetry and dramatic art which can be seen at its best in Sá de Miranda, **Bernardim Ribeiro** (also author of a well known novel *Child and Damsel*), **António Ferreira** (Lusitanian Poems, Castro), but mainly **Gil Vicente** and **Luis de Camões** or Camoens (1524-80) who, in the vast portrayal of *The Lusiads* (1572) which retraces the epic voyage of Vasco de Gama, shows himself to be the poet of the Great Discoveries. He also wrote some beautiful sonnets. The vogue of the courtly romance ends gloriously with the *Palmeirim of England* by Francisco de Morais.

Camões.

Classicism. – In the 17C during the 60 years of Spanish domination, Portuguese literature is restricted to the Academies in Lisbon and the provinces; Baroque affectation prevails, but at the same time there is "Sebastianism" (belief in the "return" of King Sebastião I – *p 20* – that is to say in the restoration of independence and the greatness of the country). The Jesuit António Vieira (1608-97) in his sermons and letters as a missionary in Brazil, reveals the growing personality of the immense colony.

The Age of Enlightenment can also be seen in Portugal, through its scholars, historians and philosophers. Theatre and poetry are affected by French influence. **Manuel M. B. du Bocage** (1765-1805) of French descent, is the great lyric and satirical poet of the 18C.

19C. – Romanticism takes a firm hold due to **Almeida Garret** (1799-1854), who was not only a poet *(Flores Sem Fructo, Fôlhas Caídas)* and master of a whole generation of poets, but also playwright *(The Blacksmith of Santarem)*, and novelist *(Travels in my land)*. Other remarkable poets appear during the century, such as **António F. de Castilho** *(Amor e Melancolia)*, João de Deus *(Fields of Flowers)*, the Azorian, Antero de Quental *(Morning Hymn)*; playwrights such as Leal and D. João da Câmara; novelists, amongst whom **Camilo Castelo Branco** (1826-90), author of the well known *Fatal Love* made into a film, **Eça de Queirós** *(Cousin Bazil, Barbaric Prose)*, **Guerra Junqueiro** *(The Old Age of the Eternal Father)*; historians: **Alexandre Herculano** and **Oliveira Martins**, both authors of a *History of Portugal*.

Contemporary authors. – **Fernando Pessoa** (1888-1935) a complex and precursory genius *(Maritime Odes)* renews Portuguese poetry. Amongst his successors, special mention should be made of **José Régio** *(Poems of God and the Devil)*, João Gaspar Simões, António Boto, António Ramos Rosa, Natalia Correia and Herberto Helder. Amongst the playwrights, José Régio again *(Jacob and the Angel)*, Luis de S. Monteiro, and Miguel Franco *(The Riot)*. Amongst the main novelists: **Fernando Namora** *(The Wheat and the Chaff)*, **Ferreira de Castro** (1893-1974) who drew upon his experiences during a long stay in Brazil *(The Jungle, The Mission)*, Manuel Texeira Gomes *(Letters with No Moral)*, Urbano T. Rodrigues *(Bastards of the Sun)*, Paço de Arcos *(The Cement Forest)*, Augustina Bessa Luis *(The Sibyl)*, Almeida Faria *(Passion)*, and the regionalistic authors such as **Aquilino Ribeiro** and **Miguel Torga**.

The former Portuguese colonies contribute greatly to Lusitanian literature, particularly Brazil with, at the present time, Jorge Amado and Lins do Rêgo, etc.

BOOKS TO READ

A New History of Portugal – H. V. Livermore – *Cambridge University Press.*

Contemporary Portugal – Richard Robinson – *George Allen & Unwin Ltd.*

Camões – The Lusiads, translated by Sir R. Fanshawe – *Centaur Press Ltd*

Machado de Assis – Esau and Jacob – translated by Helen Caldwell – *Owen*

Unknown Portugal – George Pillement – *Johnson*

A Visit to Portugal, 1866 – Hans Christian Andersen – translated by Grace Thornton – *Peter Owen Ltd.*

The towns and sights described in this guide are shown in black on the maps.

TRADITIONAL AND FESTIVE PORTUGAL

Portugal has preserved a distinct civilization of its own. This can be seen very clearly in its domestic architecture, the vitality of its craftsmen and the vivacity of its religious and public festivals. These folklore celebrations permit the tourist to admire the people dancing and wearing their traditional costume so rarely seen now in everyday Portugal.

DOMESTIC ARCHITECTURE

Rural Houses. – Houses in the country are generally low lying; stables, wine and other storerooms and the washhouse occupy the ground floor, and the owner and his family the first floor, which is reached by an outdoor staircase, sometimes horseshoe shaped. Each region has developed its own local style from this general basis.

Minho and the Beiras. – The houses, built of granite, are massive with tiled roofs. The chimneys are very small or even nonexistent, the smoke has to escape through gaps in the roof, the doorway or the large windows.

The outside staircase leads to a stone balcony or veranda large enough to be used as a living room.

A Minho house.

Trás-os-Montes. – The local shale provides the material for the tiles which are hung all over the light structured houses of the region. The stables are separate, built round a yard.

In the Douro Valley, the large vineyard owners build virtual manorhouses *(solar)*. Their elegant, stylish façades are often whitewashed, enabling them to be clearly seen against the terraced vine clad hillsides.

Estremadura, Beira Litoral. – The limestone with which the houses are built considerably enhances their appearance. The façades are often ornamented with cornices and stucco; the staircase has disappeared indoors.

Around Aveiro are several fishermen's villages where the houses, which are built of wood, stand on piles to prevent their being buried by drifting sand.

Alentejo. – The houses, built to shelter the inhabitants from the summer glare and heat, are low lying single storey structures with whitewashed walls and minimal sized doors and windows. Nevertheless the winters are so harsh that huge square or cylindrical chimneys (at Mourão) are also a local feature. Building materials vary according to the region; usually *taipa* or dried clay, or adobe, mud mixed with cut straw and dried in the sun, being used as they were in Moorish times. Bricks, laid in decorative patterns, are used to construct chimneys, crenellations and verandas, while around Estremoz marble is utilized.

Door and window frames are often painted blue, pink or orange.

(After Secretaria de Estado da Informação e Turismo photo)

An Alentejo house.

The Algarve. – The white houses squat low, several cubes juxtaposed making up each dwelling. Sometimes the roof of rounded tiles is replaced in the east, by a terrace to catch rainwater or to dry fish on. The white flat roofed houses to be found in Olhão and Fuseta resemble the villages of North Africa. Very occasionally the terrace is replaced by a four sided, peaked roof, *telhado de tesouro*, which some attribute to the influence of Hindu temple roofs. Peaked roofs are mostly to be seen at Tavira and Santa Luzia.

Doorways are surmounted by arches and covings. Chimneys are slender and elegant, gracefully pierced, painted white or built of brick laid in ornamental patterns and crowned with a ball, a finial, a vase, or an ornament of some kind such as a lance or scythe.

Streets and pavements are often finely **tessellated** with small blocks of basalt, sandstone, granite and limestone.

An Algarve house.

Granaries (Espigueiros). – The granaries, found particularly throughout the Minho (particularly in Lindoso), are small and built of granite or wood on piles. They act as drying floors for maize and form part of the way of life of the rural middle class. The sacredness of maize is symbolized by the cross upon the roof.

Windmills and Watermills. – There are more windmills turning in Portugal today than in any other country in Europe. The 2 000 said to exist stand mostly on the hills near the coast around Viana do Castelo, Nazaré, Lisbon and Sines. Watermills are even more numerous, there being more than 25 000 in different parts of the country scattered beside rivers and streams. The number of mills is explained by the fact that until very recently each peasant ground his own maize.

Today watermills are used mostly for irrigation.

Animal Drawn Wheels. – Animal drawn wheels, in Portuguese *atafonas,* are to be seen in the Alentejo and in Beira Litoral in places where watercourses are scarce and the winds uneven and low.

Water Wheels. – Horizontal water wheels *(sesicas)* are widespread throughout the country, particularly where it is hilly. They use the power from small swift running streams or the force of water dropping from reservoirs as in the Trás-os-Montes. Winter sometimes sees the wheels beside rivers submerged or washed away in the floods.

Tidal water wheels which go back in history to the 13C may still be seen on the Tagus and Sado estuaries and in those to the rivers of the Algarve.

The **vertical water wheel** *(arzenhas),* introduced to Portugal by the Moors, stands beside watercourses where the flow is more even. By changing the buckets the wheel can be used either for irrigation or to mill grain.

Windmills. – The first windmills in Portugal would appear to date from the 11C *(p 60).* Those most common today are the Mediterranean type in which a cylindrical tower built of stone, beaten earth or wood, supports a turning conical roof bearing a mast. The mast carries four triangular sails controlled by ropes. In the Lisbon area the mills are decorated with little clay (or shell) jugs strung along the ropes which whistle stridently as the sails turn.

(After Casa de Portugal photo)

Windmill.

Between the Vouga and the Mondego (central Portugal) a very special type of mill is to be found. The mill itself, which is small and prismatic in shape on a triangular base, is mounted on a pivot, steadied by two wheels. The sails and roof are fixed to the base. To face the wind the whole mill on its base is turned by means of a lever.

Pillories. – Nearly every village in Portugal has its pillory. The column usually stands in the centre of the village square near the old village council hall *(paços do concelho).* It would seem that pillories were invented by the Romans who constructed them in Gaul and that the idea reached Portugal in the 12C. Pillories were then plain columns supporting a revolving cage in which wrongdoers, forgers and robbers were exposed. With time the cage lost its importance, being replaced by iron hooks to which miscreants were chained.

Pillories were usually distinct from gibbets which were erected outside villages, although some were used as gallows.

In the Middle Ages, pillories were also the symbol of triumphant municipal power. Those who had power to dispense justice, whether as a municipal authority anticipating municipal freedom or a private person, could erect a pillory. This is why many stand beside town halls, cathedrals and monasteries which were then generally seats of jurisdiction. They continued to be erected until the 18C.

The Pillory at Rua.

Chief Types of Pillory. – Pillories before the 15C had no particular style. Those erected in the 16C can be recognized by their Manueline decoration *(p 22)* and the armillary sphere with which many are crowned. They are also the most numerous because King Manuel dispensed privileges widely. The columns of 17C pillories are nearly always twisted.

Prismatic (as at Mogadouro), pyramidal (Santiago do Cacém), conical (Tomar), twisted (Chaves) or cylindrical **columns** may be decorated with straight or spiralling ribs (Elvas), roses (Colares), carved discs (Castanheira), scales (Castelo Novo), knots or geometric motifs (Cerveira).

The **superstructure** is ornamental, often deriving in design from the original cage and taking the form of a miniature cage with small columns (Pinhel), a solid sphere (Vila do Conde), a sort of pine cone (Estremoz), a prism (Freixo de Espada-à-Cinta) or quite simply a flat block surmounted by small columns (Murça). The top can also equally well be a smooth or armillary sphere (Leiria) and this, in turn, may be crowned by a weather vane or an arm brandishing the sword of justice (Vila do Conde). In the Bragança Region most of the pillories end in four arms of stone in the form of a cross from which hang iron hooks (Vinhais).

Finally the decoration may take human or animal form or derive from heraldry as with the Cross of the Order of Christ where shields and coats of arms are used.

DAILY LIFE AND HANDICRAFTS

It is the spontaneity of the street scenes that make a trip to Portugal a delight. The visitor will recall women fish and flower sellers in the curve of an alleyway or at the corner of a square; a woman returning from the local pump, a pitcher of water on her head; a group of women washing linen beside a river bank or walking home heavy laden; carved or painted wax candles; vast ox yokes decorated with a Solomon's seal; mule caravans.

Craftsmen offer a wide variety of objects, which are simply and stoutly made and serve as a perennial souvenir.

The weekly markets held in most towns and particularly the fairs, known also for their crowds crowds and their picturesque qualities, usually have stalls which give a good idea of the skill of Portuguese craftsmanship.

Ceramics. – There are many village potters producing domestic and decorative earthenware which varies in shape and colour according to the region of origin. In Barcelos, pots are glazed, colours vivid (yellows and reds) and ornament consists of leaves, stems and flowers; handsome multicoloured cocks are also made locally *(illustration p 49)*; around Coimbra, the colour used is green with yellow and brown overtones and the ornament is more geometric; the potters of Caldas da Rainha use a bright green and produce pots with

Ceramic display at Alcobaça.

surprising shapes: vine leaves, snails, caricature figures, etc; those of Alcobaça and Cruz da Légua work to more classical designs, distinguishing their ware by the variety of blues they use in its decoration.

In the Upper Alentejo (in Redondo, Estremoz – *details p 74* – and Nisa) the clay is encrusted with shining quartz particles or marble chips; in the Algarve amphorae are still made after Greek and Roman forms; finally in the Trás-os-Montes the potters damp down their ovens at the end of the firing to give the ware a black colour.

Lace. – A popular saying goes "Where there are nets, there is lace" and, in truth, lace is made virtually all along, but only along, the coast (Caminha, Póvoa de Varzim, Vila do Conde, Azurara, Peniche, Setúbal, Lagos, Olhão) or near the ports (Valença do Minho, Guimarães, Silves). The only exception is Nisa. The decorative motifs used are pinecones, flowers and trefoils at Viana do Castelo, where the lace looks more like tulle, and seaweed, shells and fish at Vila do Conde.

Filigree Work. – The working by hand of gold or silver wire which reached its height in the reign of King João V (1706-1750) is still held in high regard in Portugal. The chief centre is the small town of Gondomar not far from Oporto. Hearts *(illustration p 112)*, earrings, guitars are all fashioned from the wire, but the craftsman's skill and the gold wire's pliability reach their peak in the intricate caravels, so sturdy and at the same time so delicate. In the Minho, filigree jewelry ornaments and enhances the local costume.

Basketwork. – Osiers, rushes, willows and rye straw are all used to fashion decorative and utilitarian baskets. Pack saddles may be seen in the Trás-os-Montes so constructed as to have twin pairs of deep cylindrical baskets on either side of the mule or donkey.

Hand Weaving, Carpet Making and Tapestries. – Hand weaving still flourishes in some mountain villages. Lengths of heavy frieze are woven on old looms to make capes and tippets. Guimarães specializes in the production of bedspreads and curtains in rough cloth bordered with classical motifs in vivid colours.

The hemp or linen based carpets embroidered in wool at Arraiolos are the best known of their type *(details p 46)*, because of their pleasing interplay of colours and naïvety of design.

Woodwork. – Outstanding among the infinite number of carved wood objects are the **ox yokes** of Barcelos.

Fishing boats are the work of craftsmen and decorators combined. Tall slender prows enable them to face strong seas without danger; while their painted decoration is often inspired by Christian or pagan motifs *(illustration p 47)*.

FESTIVE PORTUGAL

The Portuguese, so often contrasted with the more volatile Castilian and in spite of his reputation as a reserved character with a bent for **saudade** or nostalgia, will always greet you politely and can, on occasion, be most cordial.

He likes to be surrounded by friends and remains attached to tradition, periodically called to mind by innumerable local festivals *(pp 9 and 31)* and *touradas (p 31)* organized all over the country. Music, folk songs and dances help him to escape from the sometimes harsh reality of daily life.

THE FADO

Fados, sad and monotonous chants derived from the troubadour songs of the Middle Ages, are usually about the forces of destiny (the name of *fado* is said to come from the latin *fatum*: destiny) or human passions.

The *fado* first made its appearance at the end of the 18C in the form of sentimental sailor's songs. It became popular in Lisbon in 1830 and by 1840 had taken on its present form. The singer Amalia Rodriguez has helped to make the *fado* well known abroad. The singer, often a woman, *fadista,* is accompanied by one or two players. The Portuguese guitar *(guitarra)* differs from the Spanish (viola) in having twelve as opposed to six strings, and is thus a more subtle instrument. Attempts to modernize the style and evolve a gay *fado* with greater variety in the rhythm have been frowned on by some devotees.

The **Lisbon Fado,** which can be heard in restaurants in old parts of the town such as the Alfama, the Bairro Alto and the Mouraria, more closely resembles the original *fado* form than does the **Coimbra fado** *(p 64)*.

(After Secretaria de Estado da Informação e Turismo photo)

Fado at Coimbra.

REGIONAL LIFE AND FOLK DANCING

The local dances reflect many provincial idiosyncrasies and even the difference of character of the people living in different regions.

Minho and the Douro Coast. – The inhabitants, so rarely seen but most friendly, come together to harvest grapes and for other important tasks, singing to encourage themselves. An equal gaiety is found in their dances which are famous throughout Portugal. **Viras,** a type of round to the accompaniment of traditional songs, have a strong rhythm. The **gota** or **vira galego** is even more energetic. The **malhão** and **perim** folk dances show off the beauty of the local girls who wear attractive costumes for the occasion, sometimes embellished with jewelry and gold bracelets *(illustration p 136)*.

Trás-os-Montes and the Beiras. – In the mountain provinces of Trás-os-Montes and the Beiras, where life is hard, the community life has not totally disappeared. Communal ovens, mills and wine presses still exist. The house traditionally held several generations (often three). It was also a tradition that only the eldest son should marry, the others remaining but staying single. Nowadays the younger brothers have tended to drift away, founding their own families, and often even emigrating. The dances, **chulas** and **Dança dos Pauliteiros,** illustrate the humbleness of a woman before her lord and master.

Beira Litoral, Estremadura, Ribatejo. – Merry-making plays a less important part in life, except between Ovar and Nazaré where the **vira** reappears. As danced by the fisherfolk of the area, the *vira* with its deft figures becomes a joy to watch while in Nazaré a further pleasure is added by the interplay of colours of the petticoats worn by all the girl dancers.

The Atlantic breaks so strongly along this shoreline that it has never been possible to build breakwaters; even the small fishing ports along the coast afford no protection to the boats which sail from them and which, on their return, therefore, have to be hauled up the beach above the high water line.

The wide plains of the Ribatejo are the homeland of the *campinos* or cattlemen who, in their brilliant costumes, raise and guard the fighting bulls.

The Estremenho, or man from the Estremadura, is a fine talker and said to be the braggart of Portugal; the Ribatejan is more reserved, and dances alone in the **fandango** and the **escovinho.** Women dress simply in short skirts, light blouses, broad low heeled shoes and woollen scarfs to cover their heads.

Alentejo. – The woman dresses in clothes well suited to her hard work in the fields. The man, a character of few words, dances while singing slow and mournful measures of **saias** and **balhas.**

Algarve. – The people of the Algarve are dynamic and full of joy. Their dance, the **corridinho**, has a lively rhythm and though the women dress in black they dress smartly.

(After Casa de Portugal photo)

Woman gathering the harvest in the Alentejo.

ROMARIAS

Romarias are religious festivals held in honour of a patron saint. The most important take place in northern Portugal, particularly in the Minho Province where religious observance is strong.

Small *romarias* in mountain chapels only last one day; but the big ones in towns last several days and are followed by lay celebrations. Some social and professional groups hold their own *romarias* as, for instance, the fishermen of Póvoa de Varzim; others form the basis for a major pilgrimage in honour of a saint and draw pilgrims from distant regions and even from Spain.

The Collection. – A few days prior to the festival the organizers make a collection to defray expenses. Gifts, in both kind and cash, are collected in baskets decked with flowers and garlands and are then auctioned. The collections, which thus mark the start of the festivities, are enlivened by players such as the *gaitero* or bagpiper, the *fogueteiro* or man who lights the fireworks and, in Alentejo, even the *tamborileiro* or tambourine player.

The Candle (*Círio*). – The most important part of the religious ceremony often consists in the solemn bearing of a candle, from which comes the name *círio* given to the focal point of the *romaria,* or the parading of a banner, from a sometimes distant place to the sanctuary. The candle is borne on an ox drawn wagon or in a flower decked farm cart; behind, led by the *gaitero,* follows a procession from which emerges the statue of a saint or the Virgin covered in garlands, lace and artificial flowers.

(After Secretaria de Estado da Informação e Turismo photo)

Tomar — The Tabuleiros Festival.

When it reaches the church the procession circles the sanctuary two or three times to the raucous accompaniment of fire-crackers, musical instruments and shouts from the crowd. The candle or banner is then set down near the altar and the faithful advance to kiss the feet of the saint.

The "Saints of Intercession". – To win especial favour from certain saints, believers perform such acts of penance as praying as they go round the sanctuary on their knees or attending the saint's day in silence. The votive offerings, *ex-votos*, on these occasions often take the form of models of the organ or limb for which recovery is being sought – eyes, ears, hands, etc.

Matchmaking saints (St John, St Antony, St Gonsalo) were very popular in olden times; while the festivals of saints said to protect animals (St Mamede, St Mark, St Sylvestre) were attended not only by pilgrims but also by the particular animals concerned.

Popular rejoicings. – As soon as the religious ceremonies are completed and the vows made, the participants organize a gigantic picnic as a prelude to the lay festivities to follow.

The evening rejoicings, which begin after the procession is over, give everyone a chance to enjoy the wonderful regional costumes, the folk dancing and, not least, the beautiful fireworks.

Every *romaria* has its attendant fair where local crafts are sold.

BULLFIGHTING

The Portuguese refuse to see in a fight between a man and a bull a contest of intelligence versus instinct; for them it is a display of skill, of elegance and of courage – the bull is only the instrument.

The Portuguese **tourada** is, therefore, quite different from the Spanish *corrida*. The presentation of the participants is done in 17C style and is more spectacular; they, in turn, salute not only the patrons but also the public.

The *tourada* opens with mounted horsemen *(cavaleiros)* riding against the bull whose horns are covered *(emboladas)* with a leather thong; in the Spanish style fight it is possible for a situation to arise in which the *toureiro* finds himself fighting the bull on foot. The **cavaleiro's** role is first to provoke and later exhaust the bull as he places the *banderillas* or, in Portuguese, *farpas* on the beast. For his part in the spectacle the *cavaleiro,* mounted on a magnificent caparisoned stallion, wears an 18C style costume of gold embroidered coat of silk or velvet, plumed tricorn hat and shining kneeboots with silver spurs.

Bulls have not been killed in the ring in Portugal since the 18C when the Marquis of Pombal forbade it following an accident to the Count of Arcos. When the bull shows signs of exhaustion the *cavaleiro* makes way for the *moços-de-forcado,* men formerly armed with a kind of fork or *forcado*. The eight *moços* have to master the bull, a stage in the contest known as the **pega**: the leader attempts to seize the bull by the horns while his fellows immobilise it; if this feat is too difficult, the leader has to seize the animal's withers *(pega de cernelha)* from the side while the others pull on its tail. The vanquished bull is usually slaughtered next day.

The bullfighting season in Portugal lasts from Easter to October; contests are usually held twice weekly, on Thursdays and Sundays. The best known fights take place in the Praça de Touros in Lisbon, Santarém and Vila Franca de Xira, near the areas in the Ribatejo where the bulls are bred.

TOURING PROGRAMMES

⬭	Overnight stop
⚔	Castle or château
✝	Religious building
⁙	Interesting ruins
▲	Miscellaneous sights
p 159	Route described on p 159

★ Valença do Minho
p 135
Monção
Monte do Faro ★★
Caminha
N 13 69
Ponte de Lima   N 203   Bravães ★
★ VIANA DO CASTELO
N 13 31
N 103
Barcelos
N 205 28
Póvoa de Varzim
Vila do Conde
N 13 34
Matosinhos
★ OPORTO
N 105-2 51
N 105 34
★ Guimarães
Trofa ★
★ AMARANTE
N 15 47
★ Serra do Marão
p 104
Bom Jesus ★★
Rio Cávado
33
N 201
★ Caniçada Reservoir
★ BRAGA
N 101
p 62
Upper Cávado Valley ★
★ Paradela Dam
15
N 103
Alto Rabagão Dam ★
Montalegre
39
43   N 103
CHAVES
N 2
Rio Tâmega
64
Vila Real
Mateus ★
N 15
25   N 2   Sabrosa
N 322
Peso da Régua   N 222   Pinhão
58
Lamego
13
Douro Valley ★
p 68
DOURO
RIO

THE WINE REGION AND UPPER CÁVADO (750 km)

0   20   40 km

★★ Ria de Aveiro
Rio Vouga
Trancoso
N 102 22
VISEU ★
★ Pinoucas
Caramulo
N 16
55 Celorico da Beira
Mangualde   N 16 29
★ AVEIRO
N 230 98
Cabeço da Neve
★★ Caramulinho
N 235 78
Mealhada
N 1
★★★ Buçaco Forest
★★ COIMBRA
N 1
Mondego
40   N 342   Lousã
★ Conimbriga
Serra da Lousã ★
p 102
Castanheira de Pera
N 236-1
Figueiró dos Vinhos   N 350
Cabril Dam ★
167
N 112
★ GUARDA
Manteigas
N 232 20
61 ▲ Hell's Well ★   Centum Cellas ★
★★★ Torre
Belmonte
Covilhã
Serra da Estrela
p 72
N 18
Rio Zêzere
58
N 239 N 239
Monsanto ★
N 238
N 233 49
CASTELO BRANCO

THE BEIRAS (700 km)

0   30 km

---

*The **Michelin** map **37** at a scale of 1: 500 000
(1cm: 5 km) covers the whole of Portugal.
You may pick out at a glance*

> the motorways and major roads for a quick journey
> the secondary or alternative roads for a traffic free run
> the country lanes for a leisurely drive.

This map is a must for your holidays.

TAGUS BASIN-LISBON (850 km)

0   20   40 km

★★ Nazaré
LEIRIA
83   N 1   Batalha ★★★
N 242   Fátima   86
TOMAR ★★
★★ Alcobaça   N 113
Berlenga Island ★★   Mira de Aire Caves ★   35   Castelo do Bode Dam ★
N 8   Caldas da Rainha   Almourol ★★   Abrantès   Castelo do Vide ★
Peniche   N 114   N 118   N 246   Marvão ★★
ÓBIDOS ★★   115   p 127
N 8-2   R. Sorraia   ★ Serra de São Mamede
90   ★ Flor da Rosa   N 119
ERICEIRA   Alter do Chão   PORTALEGRE
Mafra ★
Serra de Sintra ★★   79
★ Sintra   97   Queluz ★   Estremoz
Estoril ★   Evoramonte ★
★ Cascais   106   LISBON ★★★   N 18   N 245
Vila Nogueira   MONTEMOR-O-NOVO   76
de Azeitão   71   N 4   N 114
Serra da Arrábida ★   Setúbal ★   Evora ★★★
p 45
Sesimbra
★ Cape Espichel

ALGARVE AND LOWER ALENTEJO (900 km)

0   20   40 km

Spring Pisões-Moura ▲   Moura
Beja   31   N 586   35
N 260   N 255   SERPA
94   53
N 391   GUADIANA
110   N 595   N 265
N 266   Mértola
Almodovar   N 122
Nave Redonda   71
Monchique   N 2   76   Castro Marim
Serra de Monchique ★   53   N 125
p 106   Silves   Vila Réal de
★ Bravura Dam   Portimão   26   Albufeira ★   Almansil   Santo António
★ Lagos   95   Tavira
Vila do Bispo   78   N 125   Armação   Vilamoura   N 125   Olhão
N 268   de Pera   Olhão
★★ Cape   Sagres   ★★ PRAIA
St. Vincent   DA ROCHA   FARO ★
Sagres Peninsula ★★
p 124

*The **Michelin Red Guide España Portugal**
should be your guide in finding a hotel or restaurant
in Portugal.*

It gives:
    details of hotel accommodation in towns
    a selection of quiet and secluded hotels
    a map of places where the cuisine is outstanding.

PLACES TO STAY

The map below and opposite and the tables on the following pages give information concerning accommodation and leisure facilities offered by a series of towns.

The towns whose names are shown in sepia letters on the maps are not included in the tables, as it is taken for granted that they have all the necessary facilities of a tourist resort.

SERVICES AND ACCOMMODATION

Hotels. – The letter H indicates that a selection of the town or resort's hotel resources are to be found in the annual Michelin Red Guide **España Portugal**. The listings include establishments of all classes ranging from the luxury hotel to other recommended accommodation at moderate prices. The entries also include the recreation facilities offered by each hotel, eg swimming pools, tennis courts, gardens, etc.

Also included are a selection of restaurants worthy of your attention be it for a carefully prepared meal at moderate prices or with a high standard of cooking indicated by stars.

The resorts without an H offer alternative possibilities of accommodation, camping, rental, etc.

Camping. – *See practical information p 7.*

Accommodation for rent. – Addresses available from tourist information centres.

Tourist information centres. – *See practical information p 6.*

Pleasure boat harbours. – All waters sufficiently sheltered to provide moorings for pleasure craft have been listed in this column.

Boat trips. – The availability of organized boat trips by sea or up or down the river is indicated by the symbol ⇌

Cinemas. – The symbol ▥ indicates a cinema with at least one show per week. Films are generally shown with the original sound track and subtitles.

SPORTS AND OUTDOOR ACTIVITIES

Swimming pools. – Swimming pools are numerous throughout the whole country but particularly on the west coast, where the sea tends to be cold and rather rough. Only public pools are indicated.

Angling. – The Portuguese rivers, lakes, rias and coast provide excellent sport. Only places with a club affiliated to a federation are included.

Sailing; water skiing; skin diving. – Only places with a club affiliated to a federation are included.

Tennis. – Courts are indicated where they are available for hire by visiting tourists.

Golf. – Only golf courses within a radius of 5km - 3 miles from a resort are indicated. However the Michelin map ▦ shows all Portugal's golf courses.

Bullfights. – *See p 31.*

Festivals. – The most important local festivals are shown in the table on p 9.

PLANNING YOUR ROUTE

The Michelin map ▦ at a scale of 1: 500 000 (1 cm: 5 km) covers the whole of Portugal. Route planning becomes easy as it differentiates between motorways, major roads (red) and other roads (yellow).

Towns listed in the hotel and restaurant guide are underlined in red and places with a town plan in the same guide are also indicated.

Touristic details cover such themes as: golf courses, racecourses, viewpoints, panoramas, scenic routes and interesting sights.

If you would rather plan your own itinerary
look at the map in this guide of the principal sights (pp 4-5)

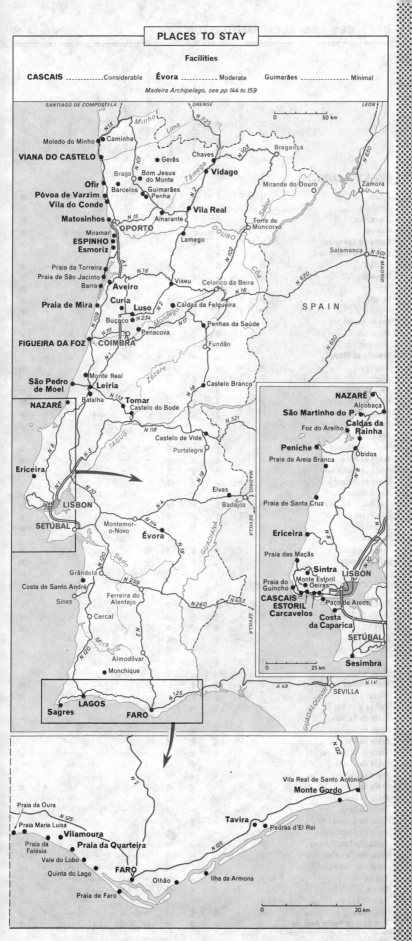

PLACES TO STAY

Facilities

CASCAIS .... Considerable   *Évora* .... Moderate   Guimarães .... Minimal

Madeira Archipelago, see pp 144 to 159

SANTIAGO DE COMPOSTELA   ORENSE   LEÓN

0   50 km

Moledo do Minho   Caminha
VIANA DO CASTELO
Gerês   Chaves   Bragança
Braga   Bom Jesus do Monte   **Vidago**
Ofir   Guimarães   Miranda do Douro   Zamora
Póvoa de Varzim   Barcelos   Penha
Vila do Conde
Matosinhos   Amarante   **Vila Real**
Miramar   **OPORTO**   Torre de Moncorvo
ESPINHO   Lamego   Salamanca
Esmoriz
Praia da Torreira   Viseu   Celorico da Beira
Praia de São Jacinto
Barra   **Aveiro**
Praia de Mira   Curia   **SPAIN**
Luso   Caldas da Felgueira
Buçaco   Penhas da Saúde
FIGUEIRA DA FOZ   **COIMBRA**   Penacova
Fundão
Monte Real
São Pedro de Moel   **Leiria**
Batalha   Castelo Branco
NAZARÉ   **Tomar**
Castelo do Bode
Castelo de Vide
Ericeira   Portalegre
Elvas
LISBON   Badajoz
SETÚBAL   Montemor-o-Novo   **Évora**
Grândola
Costa de Santo André
Sines   Ferreira do Alentejo
Cercal
Almodôvar
Monchique
LAGOS
Sagres   **FARO**

Inset (Lisbon region)

NAZARÉ
Alcobaça
São Martinho do P.
Caldas da Rainha
Foz do Arelho
Peniche   Óbidos
Praia da Areia Branca
Praia de Santa Cruz
Ericeira
Praia das Maçãs
Sintra   **LISBON**
Praia do Guincho   Monte Estoril   Oeiras
CASCAIS
ESTORIL   Paço de Arcos
Carcavelos
Costa da Caparica
SETÚBAL
Sesimbra

0   25 km

Inset (Algarve)

A 49   SEVILLA   GUADALQUIVIR

Vila Real de Santo António
Monte Gordo
Tavira   Pedras d'El Rei
Praia da Oura
Praia Maria Luisa
Vilamoura
Praia da Falésia   **Praia da Quarteira**
Vale do Lobo   **FARO**
Quinta do Lago
Olhão   Ilha da Armona
Praia de Faro

0   20 km

35

	Hotels = H	Tourist information centre = T	Doctor = ⚕	Chemist = ℞	Pleasant site = ◁	Particularly attractive town = ◇	Pleasure boat harbour = ⚓	Fishing port = 🐟	Boat trips = ⛵	Casino = ♠	Cinema = 🎬
WEST COAST											
Aveiro	H	T	⚕	℞	◁	◇	⚓	🐟	⛵	–	🎬
Caminha	H	T	⚕	℞	◁	◇	–	🐟	–	–	🎬
Carcavelos	H	–	⚕	℞	◁	–	–	–	⛵	–	🎬
Cascais	H	–	⚕	℞	◁	–	⚓	–	–	–	🎬
Costa da Caparica	H	–	⚕	℞	◁	–	–	–	–	–	🎬
Costa de Santo André	–	–	–	–	◁	–	–	–	–	–	–
Ericeira	H	T	⚕	℞	◁	◇	–	🐟	–	–	🎬
Esmoriz	–	–	–	–	◁	–	–	–	–	–	🎬
Espinho	H	T	⚕	–	–	–	–	–	–	♠	🎬
Estoril	H	T	⚕	℞	◁	–	–	–	–	♠	🎬
Figueira da Foz	H	T	⚕	℞	◁	–	–	🐟	–	♠	🎬
Foz do Arelho	–	–	⚕	℞	◁	–	–	–	–	–	🎬
Matosinhos	–	T	⚕	℞	–	–	⚓	🐟	–	–	🎬
Miramar	H	–	–	–	–	–	–	–	–	–	–
Moledo do Minho	–	–	⚕	–	◁	–	–	–	–	–	–
Nazaré	H	T	⚕	℞	◁	◇	–	🐟	–	–	🎬
Ofir	H	–	⚕	℞	◁	–	–	–	–	–	–
Paço de Arcos	–	–	⚕	℞	–	–	–	–	–	–	–
Peniche	H	T	⚕	℞	◁	–	–	🐟	⛵	–	🎬
Póvoa de Varzim	H	T	⚕	℞	◁	◇	–	🐟	–	♠	🎬
Praia da Areia Branca	–	T	–	–	◁	–	–	–	–	♠	–
Praia da Barra	–	–	⚕	℞	◁	–	–	–	–	–	–
Praia das Maçãs	–	–	–	–	◁	–	–	–	–	–	🎬
Praia de Mira	H	–	⚕	℞	◁	–	–	–	–	–	–
Praia de Santa Cruz	H	–	⚕	℞	◁	–	–	–	–	–	–
Praia do Guincho	–	–	⚕	℞	◁	–	–	–	–	–	–
São Jacinto	–	–	⚕	℞	–	–	–	🐟	–	–	–
São Martinho do Porto	H	T	⚕	℞	◁	–	⚓	–	–	–	🎬
São Pedro de Moel	H	T	⚕	℞	◁	–	–	–	–	–	🎬
Sesimbra	H	T	⚕	℞	◁	◇	⚓	🐟	–	–	🎬
Torreira	–	T	–	–	◁	–	⚓	🐟	–	–	–
Viana do Castelo	H	T	⚕	℞	◁	◇	–	🐟	–	–	🎬
Vila do Conde	–	T	⚕	℞	–	–	–	🐟	–	–	🎬
SOUTH COAST (ALGARVE)											
Albufeira	H	T	⚕	℞	◁	◇	–	🐟	–	–	–
Armação de Pera	H	T	–	–	–	–	–	–	–	–	🎬
Faro	H	T	⚕	℞	◁	◇	⚓	🐟	–	–	🎬
Ferragudo	–	–	⚕	–	◁	–	–	🐟	⛵	–	–
Ilha da Armona	–	–	–	–	◁	–	–	–	–	–	–
Lagos	H	T	⚕	℞	◁	◇	⚓	–	⛵	–	🎬
Meia Praia	H	–	–	–	◁	–	–	–	⛵	–	–
Monte Gordo	H	–	⚕	℞	◁	–	–	–	–	♠	🎬
Olhão	–	–	⚕	℞	–	◇	⚓	🐟	–	–	🎬
Pedras d'El Rei	–	T	⚕	–	–	–	–	–	–	–	–
Praia da Falésia	–	–	–	–	◁	–	–	–	⛵	–	–
Praia da Luz	–	–	–	–	◁	–	–	–	–	–	–
Praia da Oura	–	–	⚕	℞	◁	–	–	–	–	–	–
Praia da Quarteira	–	T	⚕	℞	◁	–	–	–	–	–	🎬
Praia da Rocha	H	T	–	℞	◁	–	⚓	–	⛵	–	–
Praia da Salema	H	–	–	–	◁	–	–	🐟	–	–	–
Praia de Alvor	–	–	–	℞	◁	–	–	–	–	♠	🎬
Praia de Dona Ana	H	–	–	–	◁	–	–	–	–	–	–
Praia de Faro	H	–	–	–	◁	–	–	–	–	–	–
Praia do Carvoeiro	H	T	–	℞	◁	–	–	–	–	–	–
Praia do Martinhal	H	–	–	–	◁	–	–	–	–	–	–
Praia dos Três Irmãos	H	–	–	–	◁	–	–	–	–	–	–
Praia Maria Luisa	H	–	–	–	◁	–	–	–	⛵	–	–
Quinta do Lago	H	–	⚕	–	◁	–	–	–	–	–	–
Sagres	H	T	⚕	–	◁	–	–	🐟	–	–	–
Tavira	H	T	⚕	℞	◁	–	⚓	🐟	–	–	🎬
Vale do Lobo	H	–	–	–	◁	–	–	–	–	–	–
Vilamoura	H	–	⚕	℞	◁	–	⚓	–	⛵	♠	🎬
Vila Real de Santo António	H	T	⚕	℞	–	◇	⚓	🐟	⛵	–	🎬

Legend: Swimming pool = ⌇ · Sailing school = ⛵ · Boats for hire = L · Water skiing = ⌇ · Skin diving = ⌇ · Fishing = ⌇ · Tennis = ✗ · Horse riding = ● · Golf course = 9 or 18 · Bullfights = ● · Page in guide · Number of fold on Michelin map 37

WEST COAST

Swimming pool	Sailing school	Boats for hire	Water skiing	Skin diving	Fishing	Tennis	Horse riding	Golf course	Bullfights	Page in guide	Michelin fold	Place
●	●	–	–	●	●	●	–	–	–	46	⑬	Aveiro
–	–	L	–	–	–	–	–	–	–	59	⑪	Caminha
–	–	–	–	–	–	–	–	–	–	–	⑰	Carcavelos
●	●	L	●	●	●	●	●	18	●	60	⑰	Cascais
●	–	–	–	–	–	●	●	–	–	68	⑰	Costa da Caparica
–	–	–	–	–	–	–	–	–	–	–	⑱	Costa de Santo André
–	●	–	–	–	●	●	–	–	–	71	⑯	Ericeira
–	–	L	–	–	–	–	–	–	–	–	⑫	Esmoriz
●	–	–	–	–	●	–	●	18	●	–	⑫	Espinho
●	●	L	●	●	●	●	–	18	–	72	⑰	Estoril
●	●	–	–	–	●	●	–	–	–	82	⑭	Figueira da Foz
–	–	L	–	–	–	●	●	–	–	–	⑮	Foz do Arelho
●	●	–	–	–	–	●	●	–	–	116	⑫	Matosinhos
–	–	–	–	–	–	–	–	9	–	–	⑫	Miramar
–	–	–	–	–	–	–	–	–	–	–	⑪	Moledo do Minho
–	–	L	–	–	●	●	–	–	●	108	⑮	Nazaré
●	●	–	●	–	●	●	–	–	–	–	⑪	Ofir
–	●	–	–	–	–	–	–	–	–	–	⑫	Paço de Arcos
–	–	–	–	–	●	●	–	–	–	119	⑯	Peniche
●	●	–	●	–	●	●	–	–	–	122	⑫	Póvoa de Varzim
–	–	–	–	–	–	–	–	–	–	–	⑯	Praia da Areia Branca
–	–	L	–	–	●	●	–	–	–	48	⑬	Praia da Barra
●	–	–	–	–	●	●	●	–	–	132	⑰	Praia das Maçãs
–	–	L	–	–	●	●	–	–	–	–	⑬	Praia de Mira
–	–	–	–	–	–	–	–	–	–	–	⑯	Praia de Santa Cruz
●	●	–	●	●	●	●	–	–	–	60	⑰	Praia do Guincho
–	–	–	–	–	●	–	–	–	–	48	⑬	São Jacinto
–	–	L	–	–	–	–	●	–	–	110	⑮	São Martinho do Porto
–	–	–	–	–	–	●	–	–	–	–	⑮	São Pedro de Moel
–	–	–	–	–	●	●	–	–	–	128	⑰	Sesimbra
–	●	L	–	–	–	●	–	–	–	48	⑬	Torreira
●	●	–	–	–	●	●	–	–	●	136	⑪	Viana do Castelo
–	●	–	–	●	●	●	–	–	–	138	⑫	Vila do Conde

SOUTH COAST (ALGARVE)

Swimming pool	Sailing school	Boats for hire	Water skiing	Skin diving	Fishing	Tennis	Horse riding	Golf course	Bullfights	Page in guide	Michelin fold	Place
–	–	–	–	–	–	–	–	–	–	41	⑳	Albufeira
●	–	–	–	–	–	–	–	–	–	44	⑳	Armação de Pera
–	●	L	–	–	●	●	–	–	–	79	⑳	Faro
–	–	–	–	–	–	–	●	–	–	123	⑳	Ferragudo
–	–	–	–	–	–	–	–	–	–	35	—	Ilha da Armona
●	●	L	–	–	–	–	–	18	●	86	⑳	Lagos
●	●	–	–	–	–	●	●	18	–	–	⑳	Meia Praia
–	–	–	–	–	–	●	–	–	–	140	⑳	Monte Gordo
–	●	–	–	–	●	–	–	–	–	111	⑩	Olhão
–	●	L	–	–	–	●	●	–	–	35	—	Pedras d'El Rei
●	–	L	–	–	–	●	●	–	–	35	—	Praia da Falésia
–	–	–	–	–	–	–	–	–	–	–	⑳	Praia da Luz
–	–	–	–	–	–	–	–	–	–	–	⑳	Praia da Oura
●	–	–	–	–	–	●	–	–	–	–	⑳	Praia da Quarteira
–	●	L	–	–	–	●	–	–	●	123	⑳	Praia da Rocha
–	–	–	–	–	–	–	–	–	–	–	⑳	Praia da Salema
–	–	–	–	–	–	●	–	–	●	–	⑳	Praia de Alvor
–	–	–	–	–	–	–	–	–	–	86	⑳	Praia de Dona Ana
–	–	L	–	–	–	●	–	–	–	80	⑩	Praia de Faro
–	–	L	–	–	–	–	–	–	–	123	⑳	Praia do Carvoeiro
–	–	–	–	–	–	–	–	–	–	–	⑳	Praia do Martinhal
●	–	–	–	–	–	●	–	–	–	–	⑳	Praia dos Três Irmãos
–	–	–	–	–	–	●	–	–	–	–	⑳	Praia Maria Luisa
–	–	L	–	–	–	●	●	18	–	–	⑳	Quinta do Lago
–	–	L	–	–	–	●	–	–	–	125	⑳	Sagres
●	●	–	–	–	–	●	●	–	–	132	⑩	Tavira
–	–	–	–	–	–	●	–	18	–	–	⑳	Vale do Lobo
●	●	L	–	–	–	●	●	18	–	139	⑳	Vilamoura
–	●	L	–	–	–	–	–	–	●	140	⑩	Vila Real de Santo António

INLAND

	Altitude in metres	Hotels = H	Tourist information centre = T	Doctor = ⚕	Chemist = ℞	Pleasant site = ◁	Particularly attractive town = ◇	River, lake or stretch of water = ●	Spa = ⚘	Casino = ♣	Cinema = ▦
Alcobaça	42	H	T	⚕	℞	–	◇	–	–	–	▦
Amarante	100	H	T	⚕	℞	◁	◇	●	–	–	▦
Barcelos	39	H	T	⚕	℞	◁	–	●	–	–	▦
Batalha	71	H	T	⚕	℞	◁	–	–	–	–	▦
Bom Jesus do Monte	400	H	–	–	–	◁	◇	●	–	–	–
Buçaco	400	H	–	–	–	◁	◇	●	–	–	–
Caldas da Felgueira	200	H	T	–	–	◁	–	–	⚘	–	–
Caldas da Rainha	50	H	T	⚕	℞	–	–	–	⚘	–	▦
Castelo Branco	375	H	T	⚕	℞	–	–	–	–	–	▦
Castelo de Vide	575	H	T	⚕	℞	◁	◇	–	–	–	▦
Castelo do Bode	100	–	–	–	–	◁	–	●	–	–	–
Chaves	350	H	T	⚕	℞	◁	◇	●	⚘	–	▦
Curia	40	H	T	⚕	℞	–	–	–	⚘	–	▦
Elvas	300	H	T	⚕	℞	–	◇	–	–	–	▦
Évora	301	H	T	⚕	℞	◁	–	–	–	–	▦
Gerês	400	H	T	⚕	℞	◁	–	●	⚘	–	▦
Guimarães	175	H	T	⚕	℞	◁	◇	–	–	–	▦
Lamego	500	H	T	⚕	℞	◁	◇	–	–	♣	▦
Leiria	50	H	T	⚕	℞	◁	–	●	–	–	▦
Luso	200	H	T	⚕	℞	◁	–	–	⚘	–	▦
Monchique	458	H	–	⚕	℞	◁	–	–	–	–	–
Monte Estoril	50	H	–	⚕	℞	◁	–	–	–	–	–
Monte Real	50	H	T	⚕	℞	–	–	●	⚘	–	▦
Óbidos	75	H	T	⚕	℞	◁	◇	–	–	–	▦
Penacova	240	H	–	–	℞	◁	–	–	–	–	▦
Penha	575	–	T	–	–	–	◁	–	–	–	–
Penhas da Saúde	1475	–	–	–	–	–	◁	●	–	–	–
Penina	20	–	–	–	–	–	–	–	–	–	–
Sintra	200	H	T	⚕	℞	◁	◇	–	–	–	▦
Tomar	75	H	T	⚕	℞	◁	–	–	–	–	▦
Vidago	350	H	T	⚕	℞	◁	–	–	⚘	–	▦
Vila Real	425	H	T	⚕	℞	◁	◇	●	–	–	▦
Viseu	483	H	T	⚕	℞	◁	◇	●	–	–	▦

WHEN TO VISIT PORTUGAL

Portugal has a relatively mild climate *(p 12)*. If a tour of the whole country is planned, spring or autumn is best.

Spring. – Spring is the time when the flowers which adorn so many houses come into full bloom and the countryside is green. April offers as extra attractions the ceremonies of Holy Week and Tourist Day organized in honour of visiting tourists (end of the month).

Summer. – Inland, the summer months are hot and dry, but the coastal climate is tempered by sea breezes. *Romarias,* festivals, and sporting events proliferate *(p 9)*.

Autumn. – In the north especially, the countryside takes on some lovely tints. The Douro Valley comes alive during the grape harvest (mid-September to mid-October).

Winter. – On the Algarve Coast, where one can bathe from March to November, along the Costa do Sol and, above all, in Madeira *(p 145)*, winters are mild and sunny. The Algarve landscape is transformed at the end of January when the almond trees are in blossom. The Serra da Estrela provides a terrain for winter sports enthusiasts.

SHOOTING AND FISHING

Shooting. – Temporary shooting licences are obtained from the Direcção-Geral dos Serviços Florestais e Aquícolas, Avenida João Crisóstomo, 26-28, Lisbon
A permit is needed to import a shotgun and a deposit must be paid to the customs. For anyone continuing on to Spain an authorization is required to carry arms.

Angling. – A permit can be procured from the Direcção-Geral dos Serviços Florestais e Aquícolas *(address as above)* or from the local water departments found in some towns (apply to a tourist information centre for a list of these towns and also for the opening dates for river fishing).

Sea fishing. – Sea fishing is free and no permit is required, as is the case for underwater fishing.

INLAND

Swimming pool	Sailing school	Angling club	Golf course	Tennis	Horse riding	Ski tows	Bullfights	Page in guide	Number of fold on Michelin map	
–	–	–	–	✗	–	–	–	41	⑮	Alcobaça
–	–	●	–	✗	–	–	–	44	②	Amarante
●	–	●	–	✗	–	–	–	49	⑪	Barcelos
–	–	–	–	✗	–	–	–	49	⑮	Batalha
–	–	–	–	✗	–	–	–	54	⑪	Bom Jesus do Monte
–	–	–	–	✗	–	–	–	56	⑭	Buçaco
–	–	–	–	–	–	–	–	–	③	Caldas da Felgueira
●	–	●	–	✗	●	–	●	58	⑯	Caldas da Rainha
●	–	●	–	✗	–	–	–	60	⑤	Castelo Branco
●	–	●	–	✗	●	–	–	61	⑥	Castelo de Vide
–	–	–	–	–	–	–	–	134	⑮	Castelo do Bode
●	–	●	–	✗	–	–	–	63	①	Chaves
●	–	●	–	✗	–	–	–	–	⑭	Curia
●	–	●	–	✗	–	–	–	70	⑦	Elvas
●	–	–	–	✗	●	–	●	75	⑦	Évora
●	–	–	–	✗	●	–	–	118	①	Gerês
–	–	–	–	✗	–	–	–	84	①②⑫	Guimarães
–	–	–	–	–	–	–	–	87	②	Lamego
●	–	●	–	✗	●	–	–	88	⑮	Leiria
–	–	–	–	✗	–	–	–	66	⑭	Luso
–	–	–	–	–	–	–	–	106	⑳	Monchique
–	–	–	18	–	–	–	–	–	⑫	Monte Estoril
–	–	–	–	✗	–	–	–	–	⑮	Monte Real
–	–	–	–	–	–	–	–	110	⑯	Óbidos
–	–	–	–	–	–	–	–	–	⑭	Penacova
–	–	–	–	✗	–	–	–	86	②	Penha
–	–	–	–	–	–	✗	–	72	④	Penhas da Saúde
●	–	–	18	✗	–	–	–	34	—	Penina
–	–	–	–	✗	●	–	–	130	⑰	Sintra
●	–	●	–	✗	●	–	●	133	⑮	Tomar
–	–	–	9	–	–	–	–	–	①	Vidago
●	–	●	–	–	–	–	–	139	②	Vila Real
●	–	●	–	✗	–	–	–	141	③	Viseu

TOURS WITH A SELECTION OF PLACES TO STAY

Listed below is a selection of places to stay which are situated on or at close proximity to the towns described, on pp 41-141.

Braga Region *(p 54)*. – Barcelos, Bom Jesus do Monte, Guimarães.

Buçaco Forest *(p 56)*. – Buçaco, Curia, Luso, Penacova.

Upper **Cávado** Valley *(p 62)*. – Bom Jesus do Monte, Chaves, Gerês, Vidago.

Douro Valley *(p 68)*. – Lamego.

Serra da **Estrela** *(p 72)*. – Penhas da Saúde.

Serra de **São Mamede** *(p 127)*. – Castelo de Vide.

Serra de **Sintra** *(p 131)*. – Praia das Maçãs, Sintra.

Peneda-Gerês National Park *(p 118)*. – Gerês.

Serra da **Arrábida** *(p 45)*. – Costa da Caparica, Sesimbra.

Serra da **Lousã** *(p 102)*. – Penacova.

Serra do **Marão** *(p 104)*. – Amarante, Vila Real.

Serra de **Monchique** *(p 106)*. – Monchique, Penina.

Sagres Peninsula *(p 124)*. – Praia da Salema, Praia do Martinhal, Sagres.

Join us in our never ending task
of keeping up to date.
Send us your comments
and suggestions please.

Michelin Tyre Co Ltd
Tourism Department
81 Fulham Road, LONDON SW3 6RD.

CONVENTIONAL SIGNS

Sights

★★★ **Worth a journey**
★★ **Worth a detour**
★ **Interesting**

Italic type indicates natural sights.

Town plans		Maps				Town plans
	Sightseeing route				Castle - Ruins	
	Walk				Miscellaneous sights	
	Start of sightseeing tour				Cross - Fountain	
	Best parking place when sightseeing				Viewing table	
AZ B	Letter pinpointing a sight on a town plan				Panorama - View	
	Church, chapel				Dam - Factory or power station	

Roads

Town plans		Maps		Miscellaneous		Town plans
AUTO-ESTRADA	Motorway			Reference number common to town plans and Michelin maps		4
	Road					MICHELIN
	Road in uncertain condition			Michelin Branch		
	Footpath			Church, chapel		
	Distance in kilometres	12		Castle - Ruins		
	Portuguese customs			Fort, ramparts - Tower		
	Frontier			Monument, statue, isolated building		
	Spanish customs			Public building with main entrance		
	Pass			Main post office (with poste restante)		
	Through route			Tourist Information Centre		
	Dual carriageway			Covered market - Cemetery		
	Tree lined street			Hospital		
	Road closed, unsuited for traffic or restricted			Stadium		
	Pedestrian street			Public - Private gardens		
	Stepped street			Woods		
	Road under construction			Landing stage: Passenger transport only Passenger and car transport		
	Street passing through arch, tunnel, gateway			Car ferry (Barcaça)		
	Level crossing, railway passing under road, over road			Racecourse - Airport		
	Railway line and station			Cross or calvary - Fountain		
	Tram or trolleybus route			Water tower - Lighthouse		
	Rack railway, funicular			Underground station		
	Ascent - Descent (ascent in the direction of the arrow)	1 in 25 to 1 in 14 / 1 in 14 to 1 in 9 / More than 1 in 9		Coach station		
				Dam - Factory or power station		
P	Public car park			Golf course		
		△ 1174		Altitude in metres		

37 fold 12	Number of Michelin map and fold	G	District Government Office *(Governo Civil)*	T	Theatre *(Teatro)*
Pop 6 578	Population	H	Town Hall *(Cãmara municipal)*	U	University *(Universidade)*
Rtn	Return, round trip	M	Museum *(Museu)*	E	European Road
Áurea (R.)	Shopping street	POL.	Police *(Polícia)*	N	National Road
				Tarouca	Reference point

Plan of Tourist area

Detailed design showing entire street system and reference points

Dark brown

Overall town plan

and surrounding area Sketch plan showing main arteries and general layout only

Light brown

TOWNS, SIGHTS
AND TOURIST REGIONS

ABRANTES

Michelin map **37** folds 5, 6, 15 and 16 – Pop 7 349

Abrantes, a town in central Portugal, occupies an open site★ on a hillside overlooking the right bank of the Tagus. The Tramagal road, on the south side of the river, affords excellent views of this fine town of white stone.

The commanding fortress had fallen into decay more than two hundred years before the Peninsular War when the town was entered first by French troops in 1807 and later by Wellesley who made it his headquarters briefly in 1809.

The town is also known for its delicious confections, "Abrantes straw" or *palha de Abrantes,* so called because the eggs from which it is made appear in it in yellow strawlike streaks.

Old Fortress. – The way up to the fortifications is through a maze of alleyways brilliant with flowers. The ruined keep has been converted into a **belvedere** from which there are views of the middle valley of the Tagus to the point, downstream, where it is joined by the Zêzere, southwards of a countryside carpeted with olive trees on which, here and there, appear groups of white houses in a village. To the north can be seen the upstanding ranges of the Serra do Moradal and the foothills of the Serra da Estrela.

The Church of Santa Maria, which was rebuilt in the 15C, includes a small **museum** *(open 10am to 12.30pm and 2 to 5pm; closed Mondays and holidays)* which contains a 16C carving of the Trinity in polychrome stone and, on the high altar, a beautiful statue of the Virgin and Child dating from the 15C.

AGUIAR DA BEIRA

Michelin map **37** fold 3 or **441** fold 34 – Pop 1 264

The granite houses of the town of Aguiar da Beira, which stands in the austere landscape of the Serra da Lapa, are grouped round a main square which has kept all its medieval character. In the centre is a 12C pillory, and framing the perimeter, a tower crowned with pyramidal merlons, a Romanesque fountain similarly crenellated and a house, typical of the Beira Region, with an outside staircase.

ALBUFEIRA ★

Michelin map **37** told 20 – Pop 14 237 – *Facilities p 36*

A former Arab stronghold, today Albufeira is a fishing town, a large seaside resort and probably the most frequented tourist attraction in the Algarve.

The Site★. – From the residential quarter on the west – at the top of the highest cliff – or from the signal station above the fishing port on the east, are the best views over the golden coloured hills and cliffs where the dazzling white houses of Albufeira cling together. On the vast beach curving below, protected from the swell by the rocky point of Baleeira on the west, there is a strange crook-shaped rock towering up.

A picturesque jigsaw. – From the upper town, with its cobbled **alleys** and vaulted Moorish arches with lanterns, steep roads run down and converge on the main square (Largo E. Duarte Pacheco) where tourists gather. A cliff overhang separates the fishermen's beach from that of the bathers, which can only be reached by a tunnel bored through from the uphill end of the main street (5 de Outubro). Pleasant corniche roads overlook this beach with its rock.

ALCOBAÇA ★★

Michelin map **37** fold 15 – Pop 5 383 – *Facilities p 38*

Alcobaça, built at the confluence of the Alcoa and the Baça, in an agricultural region, cultivated by Cistercian monks from the time of their arrival in the 12C, is now an important fruit market and also the production centre for a full flavoured wine.

For seven hundred years the town was the seat of a powerful religious community which exercised considerable cultural influence throughout Portugal. The vast abbey is famous to this day for its architectural splendour.

Alcobaça is also an active sales centre for the local pottery. Pots, fountains and platters of every shape, but all traditional in pattern *(illustration p 29)* and with blue the predominating colour in their decoration, invade the pavements of the vast square, known formerly as the Rossio, which extends before the monastery façade.

A Posthumous Coronation. – **Inês de Castro,** who had accompanied the Infanta Constanza of Castile to Portugal in 1340, found herself exiled from the Court by King Afonso IV. The monarch sought in this way to separate his son, Dom Pedro, the husband of the Infanta Constanza, from the lady-in-waiting whose beauty he had been unable to resist.

In 1345, on the death of Constanza, the beautiful Inês returned to her lover at Coimbra, installing herself in the St. Clare Convent. The presence of Inês and her children angered Afonso IV who, in his anxiety to keep his kingdom free from all Castilian pretensions, raised no objection to Inês's murder on 7 January 1355.

ALCOBAÇA★★

Dom Pedro took up arms and laid siege but failed to capture the city of Oporto. Two years later he succeeded his father, wreaked justice on the assassins and revealed that he had been married in secret to Inês. In 1361 he had Inês's body exhumed and, legend has it, dressed the cadaver in a purple robe, put a crown upon its head and compelled the nobility of the realm to come and kiss the decomposed hand of the "dead queen". A solemn nocturnal procession then accompanied the remains to the church of the monastery of Alcobaça.

After António Ferreira in his tragedy *Castro*, Camões *(p 26)* made this dramatic event the basis of several episodes in *The Lusiads* and in 1942, the French writer Montherlant again took up the theme in his play *La Reine Morte*.

■ SANTA MARIA MONASTERY★★ *tour: 3/4 hour*
Open 9am to 5pm; closed holidays; 70esc.

King Afonso I, in fulfilment of a vow made to St. Bernard after the capture of Santarém from the Moors in 1147, gave the domain of Alcobaça to the Cistercian Order. The monks began to build the monastery in 1178.

Of the original façade altered by the successive 17 and 18C reconstructions, only the main doorway and the rose window remain. The statues which are 17C represent from below upwards St Benedict and St Bernard and then the four Cardinal Virtues and at the top, in the central niche, Our Lady of Alcobaça.

Church★. – The church has been restored and in the process rediscovered all the nobility and clean lines of its original Cistercian architecture. The nave is very spacious; the crossed ribbed vaulting is supported by beams which, in turn, rest on mighty pillars and engaged columns. By terminating the latter 3m - 10ft above the ground the architect succeeded in considerably increasing the space available to the congregation and in giving the church a unique perspective. The side aisles have striking vertical lines.

The 14C tombs of Inês and Dom Pedro are in the transept. Carved in a soft limestone in Flamboyant Gothic style they were considerably damaged by the French soldiery in 1811.

Inês de Castro's Tomb★★ (*north transept – 1*). – The beautiful reclining figure, supported by six angels, lies upon a tomb on which the four panels are surmounted by a frieze bearing the Portuguese and Castro coats of arms. On the sides are depicted scenes from the Life of Christ: at the head is a Crucifixion in which the Virgin may be seen mourning at the foot of the Cross. The Last Judgment which adorns the panel at the feet of the statue is interesting for its particularly realistic detail; at the bottom on the left, the dead, as the tombstones rise, are standing before God in Judgment, and at the bottom on the right, the damned are being hurled into the jaws of a monster symbolizing Hell.

(After Secretaria de Estado da Informação e Turismo photo)

Inês de Castro's Tomb.

Dom Pedro's Tomb★★ (*south transept – 2*). – Beneath a severe reclining figure, Dom Pedro's tomb depicts, on its sides, the life of St Bartholomew, the King's patron saint. The panel at the head of the tomb is occupied by a beautiful rose representing the wheel of fortune, or, according to some archaeologists, scenes from the life of Inês and Pedro, a theme taken up in the tomb's upper frieze. The panel at the foot depicts Dom Pedro's last moments.

A terracotta of the death of St Bernard in a chapel off the south transept (**3**) was modelled by monks in the 17C. The decoration of two beautiful doors (**4**) which open off the vast ambulatory circling the chancel is Manueline, dating from the 16C.

Cloisters and Abbatical Buildings★. – The Cloister of Silence, which was erected early in the 14C, has an attractive simplicity of line; between buttresses slender twin columns support with great elegance three rounded arches which are surmounted by a rose. The upper storey was added in the 16C by Diogo and João de Castilho.

The chapterhouse, opening off the east gallery, has archivolts resting on graceful small columns and vaulting in which the ribs fan out from central pillars and wall brackets. A staircase (5) leads to the monks' dormitory, a vast Gothic hall.

The kitchens, reconstructed in the 18C, are flanked on the east by the storeroom. The chamber is of monumental proportions, being 18m - 58ft high and with enormous open fireplaces; water is laid on, flowing in as a tributary of the River Alcoa.

The refectory is a large hall with ribbed vaulting. A stairway, built into the thickness of the wall and surmounted by a fine colonnade, leads to the reader's pulpit; opposite the door, a lavabo and 17C fountain jut out into the close.

In the 18C Kings' Hall a frieze of *azulejos* illustrates the foundation of the monastery; the statues carved by monks represent the Portuguese Kings to Joseph I. Note also a beautiful Gothic Virgin and Child.

■ ADDITIONAL SIGHT

Wine Museum (Museu de la Junta Nacional de Vinho). – 1km - 1/2 mile on the N 8 (towards Leiria), on the right. Open 9am to 12.30pm and 2 to 5.30pm.

In the warehouse of a cooperative which makes wine from local production (p 17), hundreds of bottles are gathered together (old Port and Madeira), as well as wine vats, large casks, wine presses, stills, and enormous 19C earthenware fermenting jars.

ALMANSIL

Michelin map 🕮 south of folds 10 and 20 – Pop 5 945

This modest village which borders the road between Portimão and Faro (N 125) is well known to art lovers.

St Lawrence's★. – 2km - 1 mile east of Almansil, to the north of the road, in the hamlet of São Lourenço. Apply at the house to the left of the church. Time: 1/2 hour.

This Romanesque building, which was remodelled in the Baroque period, is faced inside with **azulejos★★** dating from 1730, the work of Bernardo, an artist known as Policarpo de Oliveira Bernardes (p 25). The walls and vaulting are covered with tiles depicting the life and martyrdom of St Lawrence: on either side of the chancel there are scenes depicting the curing the blind and the distribution of moneys gained from the sale of sacred vessels; in the nave, on the south altars there is the meeting between the saint and the pope, the saint in prison, and on the north altars, preparation for the martyr's torture and St Lawrence on the grid being comforted by an angel.

Outside, at the church's flat east end, a vast panel of *azulejos* shows St Lawrence and his gridiron beneath a Baroque scallop shell.

ALMOUROL Castle ★★

Michelin map 🕮 folds 15 and 16 – 18km - 11 miles west of Abrantes

The fortress of Almourol, which stands with towers and crenellations on a small rocky island covered in greenery in the centre of the Tagus, was constructed by Gualdim Pais, Master of the Order of the Templars in 1171 on the site of an earlier Roman castle.

The outstandingly romantic setting has given rise to many legends being woven around the castle. In Francisco de Morais's long prose romance of chivalry, *Palmeirim de Inglaterra (Palmeirim of England)*, duels and fights follow in quick succession at the foot of the ramparts, beneath the eye of the local giant, Almourol.

Almourol Castle.

Tour. – Access from the N 3, north of the Tagus (2km - 1 mile east of Tancos). Leave the car along the river bank opposite the castle. From the landing stage, there is a good view of the castle in its **setting★★**. The castle can either be reached direct by boat (25esc) or circled by boat (100esc per person). The double perimeter wall, flanked by ten round towers, is dominated by a square keep (access to the top by 85 steps and a low door) commanding a panoramic **view★** of the river and its banks.

ALTER DO CHÃO

Michelin map 🕮 fold 6 – Pop 2 794

Alter do Chão stands grouped round its 14C castle. The upright crenellated towers overlook the main square which is paved in a black and white mosaic pattern.

The **view** from the top of the keep looks down from a height of 44m - 71ft onto the city and the olive groves all around.

On the square, north of the castle, a 16C marble fountain is surrounded by elegant slender columns whose Classical capitals support a beautiful entablature.

Michelin map **37** west of fold 2 or **441** fold 23 – *Local map p 68* – Pop 4 757 – *Facilities p 38*

Amarante is a picturesque small town, its 16, 17 and 18C houses, complete with wooden balconies and wrought iron grilles, being built in tiers up a hillside overlooking the Tâmega.

The town, well known for its pastries *(lérias, foguetes, papos de anjo)* and its *vinho verde* or sharp wine, comes alive each year on the first Saturday in June when it celebrates the feast day of its patron saint, Gonsalo.

Gonsalo lived as a hermit in the 13C. He was also the patron saint of marriage.

■ **SIGHTS** *time: 1 hour*

St Gonsalo Bridge. – This granite bridge over the Tâmega was built at the end of the 18C. A marble plaque on one of the obelisks at the entrance to the bridge on the left bank recalls the successful resistance at this spot on 2 May 1809 of General Silveira, the future Count of Amarante, against a detachment of Napoleon's troops.

Church of St Gonsalo Monastery. – The church, which was erected in 1540, possesses a side doorway adorned by three tiers of small columns in the Italian Renaissance style, crowned by a Baroque pediment. A central niche at the level of the first tier contains the statue of St Gonsalo. The four statues on the piers of a loggia to the left of the doorway are of the four kings who reigned while the monastery was still being constructed. A cupola, with an *azulejos* decorated lantern tower, rises above the transept crossing.

The interior, modified in the 18C, has some lovely gilded wood Baroque furnishings: an altarpiece in the chancel, two pulpits facing each other, and above all the **organ case** ★ (early 17C) which is supported by three Tritons. St Gonsalo's tomb (d 1259) lies in the chapel on the left of the chancel; the chapel on the right, called that of the Miracles, contains votive offerings.

At the end of the north arm of the transept, a door opens on to the Renaissance cloister, restrained in style, but where the vaulted cloisters surround a fountain with grotesques.

Town Hall. – The town hall occupies what were formerly the conventual buildings *(in the market square, to the right of the church).*

A small **museum** *(open 10am to 12.30pm and 2 to 5pm; closed holidays)* on the first floor contains archaeological remains, sculptures and modern paintings including works by the Cubist painter, Amadeo de Souza Cardoso, who was born near Amarante *(p 25).*

St Peter's (Igreja São Pedro). – This 18C church has a Baroque façade decorated with statues of St Peter and St Paul.

The unique nave, beneath a stucco-work barrel vault, is decorated with 17C bands of blue and yellow *azulejos*; the chancel beneath a stone vault with sunken sculpted panels, has a gilded wood altar. There is a coffered chestnut wood **ceiling** ★, with elegant carving in the sacristy.

EXCURSION

Travanca. – Pop 2 505. *18km - 11 miles by the N 15 going towards Oporto – about 3/4 hour.*

The 12C **church** forms part of an ancient Benedictine monastery built in the hollow of a small wooded valley. The structure is of granite and presents a wide and robust façade in surprising contrast to the interior which, with its three aisles, is completely harmonious in its proportions.

The historiated **capitals** ★ adorning the doorways, the triumphal arch and the chancel are outstanding. The subjects represented include birds with interlaced necks, dragons, serpents, deer, sirens, etc.

To the left of the church stands a machicolated tower with battlements, its doorway decorated only roughly.

The former monastery is now a charitable home.

Michelin map **37** south of fold 20 – Pop 2 894 – *Facilities p 36*

This fishing village is also a rapidly growing seaside resort, due to its large and very safe beach and its shaded sea front.

Boat trip ★★. – *As far as Cap Carvoeiro, to the west, leaving from Armação (eastern beach). Apply to the fishermen near the "Balneários sanitarios". Time 2 hours. Price: approximately 2 500esc. fot 8 people for hire of a motorboat.*

The trip, on a calm sea, takes you past the sandstone cliffs and the rocks strangely sculpted by erosion, where you can discover 18 **sea caves** ★★ considered the most beautiful on the Algarve coast (Pontal, Mesquita, Ruazes, etc.).

Nossa Senhora da Rocha Chapel. – *3km - 2 miles to the west.* This lovely white chapel with its pointed steeple, well situated on a headland in the cliffs, has a doorway framed by two columns with sculpted capitals; the interior is covered with *azulejos* and has charming votive offerings (ships). *In the nearby creek, boats can be hired to visit the caves.*

*To drive to Portugal use **Michelin** maps:*

no **986** *Great Britain and Ireland*

no **989** *France*

no **990** *Spain and Portugal*

Michelin map **37** northwest of fold 3 or **441** fold 33 – *Local map p 68* – Pop 2 340

The Arouca Monastery and a few houses on its perimeter lie deep in the hollow of a small green valley surrounded by wooded heights. Founded in 716 but rebuilt in the 18C after a fire, the monastery forms a Baroque but unadorned group.

Monastery Church. – The single nave contains numerous gilded Baroque altars and several statues in Ançã stone carved by Jacinto Vieira. The 18C tomb worked in silver, ebony and quartz in the second chapel on the south side of the church, contains the mummy of Queen Mafalda (1203-52), daughter of King Sancho I.

Lower Chancel (Coro baixo). – *Guided tours (time: 3/4 hour) 9.30am to 12.30pm and 2.30 to 3.30pm; closed Mondays and the day after a holiday; 30esc including the museum.*

The chancel is ornamented with an 18C gilded organ loft, stalls with richly carved backs and graceful statues of religious by Jacinto Vieira.

Museum. – This museum on the first floor of the cloister contains Portuguese primitive paintings★ dating from the late 15C to the early 16C of the Viseu school, and works, including an Ascension, by the 17C artist Diogo Teixeira. There is also a statue of St Peter dating from the 15C.

ARRÁBIDA, Serra da ★

Michelin map **37** fold 17

The Serra da Arrábida rises and falls over the southern part of the Setúbal peninsula, covering 35km - 22 miles between Cape Espichel and Palmela. The line of hills is made up from the ends of Secondary Era limestone deposits, pushed back, broken and buried beneath more recent terrain, reappearing on the north side of the Tagus abutting on the Sintra Massif. The two sides of this small range of mountains, which is less than 6km - 4 miles wide, are completely different in character.

The northern side, which has a more rounded relief, was covered by forests until the abrogation, in the 18C, of the decree providing for royal hunt preserves. Today the landscape is one of vineyards, orchards and olive groves and, on poor ground, of brush and pine woods, as it was originally.

The southern side slopes down to the ocean, ending in cliffs 500m - 1 500 ft high. The indented coastline, the white or ochre colours of the limestone strata, the blue of the Atlantic, the heathlike vegetation where pines and cypresses rise out of a thick undergrowth of arbutus, myrtle and lentisks, is more reminiscent of a Mediterranean than an Atlantic landscape.

Round tour from Sesimbra – *74km - 46 miles – about 4 hours*

The road, climbing up from Sesimbra *(p 128)* to Santana, has some beautiful views on the right, of the coastal cliffs and the southern slopes of the Serra da Arrábida.

Cape Espichel★. – *13km - 8 miles from Santana, to the west. Description p 72.*

After Santana, the N 379 taken on the right, winds between hills enlivened by orange trees and windmills.

2.5km - 1 1/2 miles before Vila Nogueira de Azeitão, turn right on to the N 379-1.

After a brief run through olive groves and vineyards, the road begins a winding climb through dense vegetation. The sea appears in the far distance and, at a bend to the left, the meandering coastline.

After the bend take the lower corniche road (N 10-4) for 2.5km - 1 1/2 miles until on the right the road leading to Portinho appears (1km - 1/2 mile of steep descent becoming very narrow towards the end).

Portinho da Arrábida★. – The Bay of Portinho da Arrábida, at the foot of the *serra's* green slopes *(watch out for falling rocks)*, forms an even curve, its transparent waters edged by a beautiful semicircular beach of fine white sand.

Continuing as a **corniche road★★** the main route (N 379-1) affords pretty views of the Mount Formosinho (alt 499m - 1 637ft), the *serra's* highest peak, on the left, the steep and indented coastline, Portinho in its setting and the Sado Estuary on the right.

A drop in the height of the mountain crestline affords several glimpses of the wooded interior, while the Tróia Peninsula and its coastal headland jut out into the ocean. Below, in the foreground, abutting on a cliff overlooking the sea stands a 16C convent *(not open to the public)* guarded on all sides by cypresses. In the final descent and in the vicinity of a cement works and its accompanying housing, Setúbal can be seen encircling the end of the bay of the same name.

Setúbal★. – *Description p 128.*

Leave Setúbal north, by the N 252 and take before the motorway the N 379 to the left. The approach to Palmela, perched on a height gaily bedecked with windmills, is picturesque.

Palmela. – *Description p 117.*

The N 379 runs near to Bacalhoa (on the N 10) which can be reached from Vendas, on the left.

Bacalhoa Domain. – *Description p 48.*

The N 10 goes to Vila Nogueira de Azeitão, through a landscape of orchards and vineyards.

Vila Nogueira de Azeitão. – Pop 1 719. Important regional economic centre. The main street (N 379) is bordered with lovely Baroque fountains as well as the buildings and gardens of the age-old José Maria de Fonseca wine-producing firm, where the famous moscatel of Setúbal is made.

Return to Sesimbra by the N 379 and Santana.

ARRAIOLOS

Michelin map **37** west of fold 7 – Pop 3 567

This charming village, which stands perched on a hill in the great Alentejo Plain, is famous for its vividly coloured wool carpets and also for its sausages – *paios*.

The 14C castle and even its approach commands a good **vista** of the olive groves growing in the plain, of the reservoir, Lake Divor and, in the foreground, of the white houses with door and window frames painted blue.

Arraiolos Carpets. – Communications developed early between the Portuguese and the Orient so that by the 16C there was such was a liking for Indian and Persian carpets that they were being imported in considerable numbers. In the second half of the 17C a small industry was established and grew up in the Arraiolos Region, manufacturing hemp and linen carpets which were then embroidered with wool and used as chest and wall coverings. At first the carpets followed the Indian and Persian designs, but soon the Oriental patterns and colourings were abandoned in favour of more popular themes in which blue and yellow predominate.

Nowadays Arraiolos carpets *(on sale at the Cooperativa de tapetes de Arraiolos or Fabrica Kalifa)* are popular for their simple designs and bright colours.

AVEIRO *

Michelin map **37** fold 13 or **441** fold 32 – Pop 29 646 – *Facilities p 36 – See town plan in the current Michelin Red Guide España Portugal*

Aveiro stands in a totally flat landscape at the bottom of the Ria de Aveiro *(p 47)*: before it lies a 45km - 28 miles long lagoon cut off from the sea by a littoral strand; all around are salt marshes, beaches, lagoons and canals.

Historical notes. – Like the neighbouring villages of Ovar, Ilhavo and Vagos, which now actually lie a couple of miles inland, Aveiro was a seaport. In the Middle Ages it took on the status of a municipal city, developing apace in the 15 and 16C due to Princess Joana's presence *(see below)* and as a result of the deep sea cod fishing off Newfoundland.

In 1575 disaster struck. A violent storm closed the lagoon; the harbour silted up and the city, deprived of its industries – fishing, salt production and trade – fell into decline. Its population dropped. An effort under the Marquis of Pombal to rehabilitate it in the 18C came to nothing as did several plans to cut the strand to the sea.

Finally in 1808 with the aid of breakwaters constructed from stones and boulders taken from the old town walls, a passage was opened once more from the lagoon to the sea; to the north of the town the Rio Novo took over in a direct line the former winding course of the Vouga. Ceramic and chinaware industries developed, bringing prosperity and with prosperity came expansion and renown: Aveiro became a centre of Baroque art with a famous school of carving. The town was soon littered with monuments.

Aveiro today. – The town still lives by its saltpans, grazing, rice and land made fertile with seaweed gathered from the sea bottom. But it remains primarily a fishing town, gaining its living from the sea: lamprey and sea perch are caught in the lagoon, sardines and skate on the coast. Industry is, however, the mainstay of the region: traditional pottery making (Ilhavo, Vista Alegre), fish processing and canning, shipyards, engineering industries (bicycles, tractors, car assemblying) and iron and steel works (Ovar).

Gourmets visiting the town should try the *ovos moles,* a type of egg sweet, usually served in miniature painted wood barrels. A great exhibition fair is held each year during March and April. In July or August, for the La Ria Festival, a competition takes place on the central canal to find the best painted prow from the fleet of *moliceiros (p 47)* gathered together for the occasion.

A distinctive feature. – Canals crisscross the town spanned by several small bridges; the graceful *moliceiros* as well as their mooring posts inevitably bring to mind Venitian gondolas and their *palli*. The immediate proximity of the Ria and its labyrinth of waterways gives Aveiro its originality.

In addition, the town centre has several lovely buildings, a fine museum, a pleasant park, and a main avenue with plenty of shade *(Avenida Dr Lourenço Peixinho)*.

■ MAIN SIGHTS *time: 2 hours*

Canals *. – Some canals of the Ria continue right into the town; they are shored up by embankments on which the water laps over at high tide.

Central Canal. – Part of it is bordered by noble dwellings, their Classical façades reflected in the water, and there is a continuous spectacle of small boats, *moliceiros* or launches moving about on it, or tying up. The best viewpoint is from the wide bridge-tunnel with balusters which divides it half way along, and is the main crossroads of the town *(Praça Humberto Delgado)*.

São Roque Canal. – It borders the built up area to the north, and is spanned (in front of the Rua do Vento) by an elegant stone humpback footbridge. It divides the salt marshes from the salt warehouses which line the embankment amongst the low roofed houses of the fishing quarter. The canal is used for the picturesque operation of **unloading salt**: there is then an unceasing shuttle between the boats at the wharf and the warehouses; young men run, carrying on their heads a heavy basket loaded with salt which they tip out into the warehouse.

Former Convent of Jesus - Museum *. – *Rua Santa Joana. Open 10am to noon and 2 to 5pm; closed Mondays and holidays; 50esc.*

The Convent of Jesus was erected from the 15 to the 17C. Princess Joana, daughter of King Afonso V, retired there in 1472 and remained there the last eighteen years of her life. In the 18C a Baroque façade was superimposed on the older front.

Church *. – It dates from the 15C, but the interior decoration was completed in the early 18C. The interior has some exceptionally sumptuous carved and gilded wood, particularly in the chancel★★, a masterpiece of Baroque exuberance with its colums, altars, coffered and rose ceiling beautifully intermingled and prodigiously wrought; scenes from the life of Saint Joana can be seen on *azulejos* panels. The lower chancel *(coro baixo)*, holds **St Joana's tomb**★ (early 18C). This masterpiece by the architect João Antunes *(p 24)* in polychrome marble mosaic, is supported by sitting angels, also in marble. The gallery *(coro alto)* is decorated with paintings and a 14C Crucifixion in which Christ's expression changes according to the angle from which it is viewed.

Museum★. – The museum itself exhibits various collections, sculptures of the Coimbra school (16C), Portuguese primitive paintings on wood (one of which is a lovely **portrait of Princess Joana**★ late 15C, attributed to Nuno Gonçalves, remarkable for the severe sculptural features of the young girl dressed in court finery), Italian paintings (a Virgin with honeysuckle 15C anonymous); 18C paintings on copperplate; pottery, sacerdotal ornaments, religious objects and 17C lecterns.

In the rooms devoted to Baroque art, there are statues in polychrome wood of the Aveiro Angels *(illustration p 24)*, a strange Holy Family in earthenware from the workshop of Machado de Castro, a lacquered wood writing desk (containing a small 15C Flemish Virgin and Child in wood), another "portrait" of Princess Joana, in 18C style, by Pachini; the room where Saint Joana died in 1490 is now an oratory decorated with altarpieces and gilded wood.

■ ADDITIONAL SIGHTS

Cathedral (Sé). – Originally a simple church, it has been greatly modified since it was first built in the 16C. It has a Baroque façade and inside, a strange mixture of styles; ancient and beautiful *azulejos* have been added to the renovated walls of the nave and a 17C organ has been installed in the north of the transept. To the left of the entry, there is an early Renaissance Entombment with busts of all the personages except Christ.

Church of the Misericord. – It has an imposing 17C doorway, finely worked. Inside, the height of the nave should be noted and the 17C *azulejos*, as well as, opposite the pulpit, the churchwardens' pew with gilded wood back.

Railway Station (Estação). – The *azulejos* panels which decorate the outside and inside façades (by the platforms) are a pleasant and interesting illustration of Aveira's monuments as well as its region, and the traditional crafts and costumes of the Ria.

EXCURSION

Ilhavo; Vista Alegre. – *7.5km - 5 miles by the N 109.*

Ilhavo. – Pop 13 622. This small fishing port has an interesting **museum** on the history of the fishing industry and the sea. There is also a display of Vista Alegre ceramics *(guided tour - time: 1 hour - 9am to 12.30pm and 2 to 5.30pm; Sundays 2 to 6pm; closed Mondays and holidays).*

Vista Alegre, since 1824, has been a manufacturing centre of good chinaware and glass. A **museum** in an actual works recounts the developments since the earliest days *(guided tour - telephone in advance to M. Daird Cristo ☎ 22261 - 8am to 12.30pm and 2 to 5.30pm; closed Saturdays, Sundays and holidays).*

AVEIRO, Ria de ★★

Michelin map **37** fold 13 or **441** fold 32

The Ria de Aveiro appears as a vast lagoon marked by tides, with scattered islands and crisscrossed with channels, bordered with salt marshes or pine forests, behind a sandy offshore bar some 45km - 28 miles long and not more than 2.5km - 1 1/2 miles wide, with a narrow bottleneck (Barra Channel) linking it to the ocean. This remarkable natural site, the result of the blending of sea water with that of small coastal rivers is in the shape of a triangle. The base is the offshore bar and the top the mouth *(ria)* of the Rio Vouga and the outlet of the Rio Antúa further to the northeast. The expanse of water at high tide covers about 6 000ha - 23sq miles, for an average depth of 2m - 6 1/2ft.

Very rich in fish, fertile in the parts above sea level (market gardening) providing a lot of seaweed and iodized salt *(p 46)*, the *ria* is also, due its picturesqueness and its beaches, a place to visit and stay.

Tour. – Several roads have interesting views over the *ria;* the N 327 *(30km - 19 miles of undulating road, speed-limit)* from Ovar to São Jacinto runs along the north offshore bar the whole way between pine trees and the lagoon; the road from Aveiro to Barra *(8km - 5 miles)* is bordered with farm land, shipyards, and above all the salt marshes where you can see the conical heaps of salt (usually protected by a coating of straw and dried mud) and the nearby huts of the salt workers. But to appreciate fully the charm and originality of the *ria*, a boat trip should be taken. *See p 48.*

The moliceiros. – These flat-bottomed boats, with prows curved like swans' necks and painted with naive motifs in vivid colours, are used for collecting seaweed *(moliço)* which is used as a fertilizer. They have a sail or are propelled with a pole. The prongs of the rakes *(ancinhos)* for scraping or gathering up seaweed, are picturesquely hung round the tip of the prow, once the work is over.

A Moliceiro Prow.

AVEIRO, Ria de ★★

■ TOWNS AND SIGHTS

Aveiro ★ . – *Description p 46*.

Praia da Barra. – *Facilities p 36*. Seaside resort in full development, sheltered by an offshore bar of sand dunes behind which there is an immense beach stretching southwards, beyond the Costa Nova.

Barra Lighthouse. – This lighthouse, built in the 19C, guards the access to the channel which is practicable for sea-going boats, where the ocean and the *ria* meet.

Bico. – One reaches this spot by the N 109-5 which crosses the large built up area of **Murtosa** (Pop 3 233). Bico, a small **port** ★ on the lagoon is worth a visit for its crowded mass of *moliceiros* and the busy men unloading fish, crabs, bundles of seaweed, and rushes intended for cattle litter.

Costa Nova do Prado. – A growing family resort, shaded by umbrella pines and conveniently situated on the edge of both the Atlantic beaches and those of the lagoon. The small houses with façades decorated with vertical strips of painted wood give it a very cheerful aspect.

São Jacinto. – Pop 1 035. *Facilities p 36*. Small resort in the pine woods, but also a military camp and port, at the end of the north offshore bar, on the Barra Channel.

Torreira. – Pop 2 059. *Facilities p 36*. Small fishing port on the *ria*.

■ BOAT TRIPS ★★

Regular services link Aveiro to various points on the lagoon, including Forte da Barra and São Jacinto. In addition, in season, two motorboats *(lanchas)* take tourists round the *ria (hiring by the hour: 250esc. per person). Allow a whole day for the complete tour, including 1 hour of relaxation on shore. For additional information and reservations apply to the Aveiro Tourist Centre (Commissâo Municipal de Turismo, praça de Republica).*

The boat glides out of Aveiro by the canals which surround the salt marshes and reaches the *ria*. It then goes round the flat islands, and mingles with the sailing or motorboats and pleasure craft, as well as the boats of saltworkers, fishermen, peasants, and moliceiros collecting seaweed.

AVIS

Michelin **37** southwest of fold 6 – Pop 1 893

The first glimpse of Avis comes as a welcome sight as one crosses the monotonous Alentejo Plateau, which is covered mostly with cork oaks and olives trees. The town which has retained traces of its early fortifications overlooks the confluence of the Seda and Avis Rivers, now drowned below the waters of the reservoir serving the Maranhão power station, 15km - 9 miles downstream.

The N 243 to the south, affords the best **view** ★ of the town. Ramparts, a few medieval towers and the church of the Monastery of St Benedict, rebuilt in the 17C, stand witness today of the city's brilliant past.

It was in this town at the beginning of the 13C that the military order founded in 1147 by Afonso Henriques to fight the Moors, became geographically established. The oldest order of chivalry in Europe bore several names and followed the rules of several other orders before finally becoming the Order of St Benedict of Avis. It prospered in the Tagus area until 1789.

Avis was also the cradle of the dynasty which was to reign over Portugal from 1385 to 1580. On 7 August 1385 João, Grand Master of the Order of Avis, was proclaimed king with the title João I.

BACALHOA Domain

Michelin map **37** fold 17 – 12km - 7 miles west of Setúbal

This seigneurial residence, built at the end of the 15C and remodelled in the early 16C by the son of Afonso de Albuquerque *(p 20)* is a pleasant building combining both Romanesque and Moorish styles.

The gardens. – *Guided tour (time: 1/2 hour) 1 to 5pm (closed Sundays and holidays); 20esc. Ring at the entrance at the end of a short shaded alley.*

The gardens have unity and a pleasing freshness. In the formal gardens, inspired by the style current in 16C France, clipped box trees alternate with fountains in the form of mythological figures. Glance back and you will see an elegant Renaissance gallery. A fruit garden where mandarin orange and walnut trees, bamboo and cinerias grow, ends at a basin lined by a series of arcaded chambers, their walls tiled in fine 16C polychrome **azulejos** ★. Note the panels representing the rivers of Portugal and the one of Susannah and the Elders, which is the oldest dated one in Portugal (1565).

The tour ends in a walk beside a two storey 15C gallery decorated with busts.

To drive to Portugal
  use Michelin maps (1 in: 16 miles):
  no 989 France
  no 990 Spain and Portugal

When in Portugal
  use Michelin map no 37 (1 in: 8 miles)

BARCELOS

Michelin map ▨ fold 11 or ▨ fold 22 – Pop 4 031 – *Facilities p 38*

Barcelos is an attractive small town situated on the right bank of the Cávado in a green and fertile region. The town which was the capital of the first county of Portugal and residence of the first duke of Bragança is now a busy agricultural market and a well known centre for the production and sale of pottery, *santons,* carved wood yokes and especially decorated cocks. There is a lively market on Thursdays. Numerous shops can be found in the Rua D. António Barroso, a pedestrian street.

There is a good view from the terraces of the Largo Guilherme Gomes Fernandes at the southern end of the Gothic bridge, of the ducal palace esplanade which overlooks the river's steep banks, often enlivened by local women doing their laundry.

The Barcelos Cock. – A pilgrim on his way to Santiago de Compostela was accused of theft as he was about to leave Barcelos.

In spite of his honesty he found himself unable to offer a satisfactory defence and he was condemned to die by hanging. He made one last plea. But the judge refused to be swayed in his condemnation of the stranger. The pilgrim therefore sought the protection of St James and noticing the judge's repast of roast cock, declared that in proof of his innocence, the cock would stand up and crow. The miracle occurred. The judge, in recognition of the pilgrim's innocence, set him free, and he, in memory of the miracle, erected a monument; it may now be seen in the municipal archaeological museum in the Former Palace of the Ducal Counts of Barcelos.

The Barcelos Cock.

■ **SIGHTS** *time: 1 hour*

Parish Church. – The 13C church, modified in the 16 and 18C, has a plain façade, flanked on the right by a square belfry with a Romanesque doorway. In the interior★ glittering with gold and bordered by Baroque chapels, the walls are covered with 18C *azulejos*, some of the capitals are historiated.

Pillory. – The pillory, erected in the Gothic period, has a hexagonal column upon which stands a graceful granite lantern.

Solar dos Pinheiros. – Beautiful Gothic manor house built of granite.

Former Palace of the Ducal Counts of Barcelos. – 15C. A small archaeological museum has been installed in the palace ruins. The most interesting of its contents is the 14C monument set up in honour of the cock which saved the life of the pilgrim.

A worthwhile ceramic museum occupies the basement *(open 10am to noon and 2 to 5pm; closed Mondays).*

Our Lady of Terço. – The church was formerly part of a Benedictine monastery which was founded in 1707. The walls of the nave are covered in beautiful 18C *azulejos* depicting events in the life of St Benedict. The vaulting consists of forty wood caissons painted with Biblical scenes. The pulpit of gilded wood is richly ornamented.

BATALHA ★★★

Michelin map ▨ fold 15 – Pop 7 683 – *Facilities p 38*

The monastery of Batalha stands in a green valley, a mass of gables, pinnacles, buttresses, turrets and small columns – the rose gold outpouring of its architecture is one of the masterpieces of Portuguese Gothic and Manueline art.

The Battle of Aljubarrota. – On 14 August 1385 on the Plateau of Aljubarrota, 15km - 9 miles south of Batalha, two pretenders to the throne of Portugal and their respective allies faced each other prepared to do battle: Juan I of Castile, nephew of the dead king, and João I, Grand Master of the Order of Avis *(p 48)*, who had been crowned king only seven days previously. The opposing forces were of very different strengths: against the organized forces and sixteen cannon of the Castilians, the Constable **Nuno Álvares Pereira** could only muster a squad of knights and foot soldiers, João I of Avis, appreciating that defeat meant Portugal passing under Spanish domination, made a vow to raise a superb church in honour of the Virgin if she would grant him victory. The Portuguese troops resisted and victory was won. A few days later Nuno Álvares pursued the enemy back into Spain as far as Castile and Portugal had secured independence for two centuries.

Three years later the Monastery of St Mary Victorious, subsequently known as the Monastery of Batalha, began to rise.

The Building of the Monastery. – Work was begun by the Portuguese architect Afonso Domingues and was continued from 1402 to 1438 by Houget, an Irishman, who designed in Flamboyant Gothic style the founder's chapel where lie João I, his English queen, Philippa of Lancaster, daughter of John of Gaunt, and his sons. Death prevented the completion of the octagonal mausoleum of the King Duarte I.

During the reign of Alfonso V (1438-81), the Portuguese architect Fernão d'Évora built the so-called Alfonso V cloister in a sober style. Mateus Fernandes the Elder, one of the masters of the Manueline style, succeeded as architect, cooperating with the famous Boytac *(p 22)* in the backing of the arcades of the Royal Cloister and continued the erection of the chapels round the octagon. The chapels, however, were never completed, for King João III (1521-57) abandoned Batalha in favour of constructing a new monastery, the Hieronymite in Lisbon.

■ THE MONASTERY★★★ *time: 1 hour*

Church★★. – The church, which in accordance with the Dominican rule, has no belfry, possesses innumerable pinnacles, buttresses and open balustrades above Gothic and Flamboyant windows. The building is in fine textured limestone, which has taken on a lovely ochre colour with time. The complicated structure at the east end demonstrates the architectural problems arising from joining on to an earlier apse an octagonal rotunda, which, by means of pillars, was to bear a vaulted ceiling. In the event the vault was never constructed and the pillars never completed.

The founder's chapel, off the south aisle, is surmounted by an octagonal lantern.

The main façade is divided into three by pilasters and buttresses: the central part, decorated by a network of lancet shaped blind arcades, is pierced high up by a beautiful Flamboyant window; the main doorway is richly carved, bearing statues (new copies) of Christ in Majesty, surrounded by the Evangelists on the tympanum, the twelve Apostles on the sides, and angels, prophets, kings and saints on the arching. The doorway's proportions appeared to better advantage when the church stood, as it did originally, below the level of the terrace outside.

The church's vast interior, is very plain, the outstanding element being the upward sweep of the vaulting.

The chancel is lit by **stained glass windows★** which date from the 16C Manueline period and depict scenes from the life of the Virgin and Jesus Christ.

Founder's Chapel★. – This square chamber, lit by Flamboyant windows, is covered by an octagonal lantern topped by a star shaped cupola. The massive piles supporting the lantern are linked by festooned tierpoint arches. In the centre is the tomb of King João I and his wife Philippa of Lancaster, the two figures reclining beneath delicately carved canopies. Bays on the south and west sides contain tombs of the founder's children, including that of Prince Henry the Navigator which is covered by a canopy.

Royal Cloister★★★. – The Gothic and Manueline styles mix most successfully in the Royal Cloister, the simplicity of the original Gothic design not being obscured by Manueline detail. The fleur-de-lys balustrade and the flowered pinnacles provide a motif which harmonizes well with the Manueline tracery backing the carved marble arcades. The slender columns supporting the back are adorned with coils, pearls and shells.

Chapterhouse★★. – The chapterhouse contains the tomb of the Unknown Soldier where, in fact, lie the bodies of two Portuguese soldiers who died in the First World War, one in France, the other in Africa. The **vaulting★★★** is an oustandingly bold feat, after two unsuccessful attempts the architect succeeded in launching a square vault of some 20m - 60 ft without intermediary supports. It was so dangerous that it is said to have been accomplished by convicts condemned to death. The chamber is lit by a window containing beautiful early 16C **stained glass★** representing scenes from the Passion.

(After Secretaria de Estado da Informação e Turismo photo)

The Royal Cloister.

Lavabo★. – The lavabo in the northwest corner of the cloister consists of a basin with a festooned curbstone surmounted by two smaller basins. The light, filtering through the stone tracery between the arches, gives a golden glow to the stone and the water.

There is a beautiful view of the church dominated by the north transept bell turret, from this corner of the cloister.

The old refectory, which has a fine Gothic ceiling, contains the **Unknown Soldier's Museum.**

Alfonso V Cloister★. – The coat of arms on the keystones to the vaulting in this fine Gothic cloister are those of King Duarte I and King Alfonso V.

Go round the outside of the chapterhouse and through the porch to the Unfinished Chapels.

Unfinished Chapels★★ **(Capelas Imperfeitas).** – One enters the chapels beneath a vast transitional Gothic Renaissance porch. This **doorway**★★, which was initially Gothic in style, was ornamented in the 16C with Manueline decorations of a rare exuberance; it opens towards the church with a curved arch beneath a powerful multilobed arch. The cut away ornament of the festoons and the detailed decoration on the arching and the columns are well worth looking at.

Seven chapels radiate from the octagonal rotunda, divided from each other by the famous incomplete pillars. These pillars are deeply carved all over, their ornament contrasting sharply with the plain lines of a Renaissance balcony added above by King João III in 1533.

EXCURSION

Cruz de Légua; Cumeira. – *12km - 7 1/2 miles to the southwest.*

Passing through these villages (on the N 8) there are picturesque displays of glazed pottery★ all along the road.

BEJA

Michelin map 🗺 southwest of fold 8 – Pop 19 968

The town of Beja covers a height on the wide Alentejo Plateau, at the watershed between the Sado Basin to the west and the Guadiana Basin to the east.

The town which had been a brilliant Roman colony *(Pax Julia)*, was under Mohammedan domination for four centuries.

Today Beja, a town of white houses and straight streets, lives principally on the trade in local wheat and oil, and has all the appearance of a flourishing agricultural market town.

The Portuguese Letters. – In the world of literary correspondents Beja has been known for three centuries as the town of the Portuguese Religious. In 1669 there was published in France the translation of the *Portuguese Letters* written to Count Chamilly by Mariana Alcoforado, a religious in the Poor Clares Convent of the Conception in Beja. The five love letters, in which passion, memory, despair, entreaty and reproaches of indifference all mingle, caught the public imagination and became famous overnight.

The letters' authenticity and origin, however, was soon in question; critics, struck by the quality of the "translation", suggested that the work had been composed in French by the writer Guilleragues, secretary to Louis XIV.

Others, however, given the nobility of the sentiments and the quality of their expression, believed the letters proved the existence of a former romance of Count Chamilly who had left in 1661 to fight in Alentejo against the Spaniards and had only returned in 1668 at the end of the War of Devolution.

■ **SIGHTS** *time: 1 1/2 hours*

Former Convent of the Conception. – 15C. The church and cloister, crowned with a pierced Gothic balustrade, now house the **regional museum.** *Guided tour (time: 1/2 hour) 9.45am to 1pm and 2.30 to 5pm; closed Sundays and holidays; 25esc, free Saturdays.*

Enter through a chapel whose Baroque interior is lined with gilded and carved woodwork. The cloister on the right contains interesting Christmas crib figures and Visigothic sculptures. Beyond the chapterhouse, where the walls are decorated with beautiful 16C Moorish *azulejos* and the vaulting adorned in the 18C with geometrical designs, hang several pictures, including *St Jerome* by Ribera (17C) and a 15C *Ecce Homo.*

The first floor contains a display of Alentejo costumes and a reconstruction of the cell window through which Sister Mariana Alcoforado is said to have talked with Count Chamilly.

Castle. – *Guided tour 10am to 1pm and 2 to 6pm; (time: 20 minutes) in summer; 9am to noon and 1 to 4pm in winter; closed holidays; 20esc, free Sundays.*

The 13C castle's crenellated perimeter wall, flanked by square towers, is overlooked at one corner by a high keep *(military museum)* topped by pyramid shaped merlons. The first floor, which is reached by a spiral staircase, has fine star vaulting resting, on Moorish styled veined corner squinches. A gallery runs the full length of the wall just below the top of the keep, providing a remarkable lookout over the Alentejo Plain now under wheat.

Not far from the castle stands the small Santa Amaro Church, a building with Visigothic origins dating back to the 6C.

BELMONTE

Michelin map 🗺 fold 4 or 🗺 fold 34 – Pop 2 475

Perched at an altitude of 600m - 2 000ft on the spine of a hillock near the Serra da Estrela, Belmonte can be seen from afar by the square keep of its ancient castle.

The great navigator Pedro Álvares Cabral who discovered Brazil in 1500 was born here. His statue stands on the main street.

Castle. – *Open 8am to noon and 1 to 5pm.*

Built in the 13-14C by King Dinis I, only the keep ringed with battlements remains and the enclosure partly demolished, restored in 1940. The corner tower on the right of the keep has 17C balconies with console brackets, and the section of the wall adjoining it on the left has a double Manueline window.

If you walk round the perimeter wall there is a fine **view**★ of the countryside below, the Baira heights and the rooftops of Belmonte.

BELMONTE

Church (Igreja de São Tiago). – *Open 8am to noon and 1 to 5pm.*

Next to the castle and of an earlier period but modified in the 16C, it still has some interesting elements inside dating from the Romanesque period; capitals, remains of 12C frescoes, baptismal fonts, a fine pulpit with a sounding-board and a 13C polychrome *Pietà* carved from a single block of stone. There are also the granite tombs of Cabral and his mother.

Roman Tower of Centum Cellas★. – *4km - 2 1/2 miles to the north. Take the N 18 towards Guarda then, on the right, the road to Comeal da Torre where there is a dirt track road leading to the foot of the tower.*

This impressive ruin is probably that of a Luso-Roman inn. Its square mass, made of pink granite-blocks laid with dry joints, still stands, with rectangular openings, on three levels.

BERLENGA Island ★★

Michelin map **37** fold 16 – *Facilities p 36*

Berlenga Island which rises, a reddish coloured mass, 12km - 7 miles out to sea from Cape Carvoeiro is the main island in an archipelago consisting of a number of rocky islets, the Estelas, the Forcadas and the Farilhões.

Berlenga, 1 500m - 4 921ft long and 800m - 2 625ft at its widest point, reaches a height of 85m - 279ft above the sea swell. The major attractions of this block of bare granite lie in its numerous indentations and points and in its marine caves.

Berlenga is famous for its underwater, line and harpoon fishing.

Access. – *There is a regular boat service to the island from Peniche between June and September, fare per person: 300esc Rtn; time for crossing: 1 hour; apply for information to the Viamar Company which has an office on the Peniche harbour.*

The boat sails parallel to the south shore of the Peniche Peninsula, then passes close to Cape Carvoeiro and the curious "Crows' Ship" (Nau dos Corvos), a rock resembling a ship's prow circled by screaming gulls.

It moors at the foot of an ancient fortress (1676) now an inn.

Boat trip★★★. – *Apply at the inn or hire a fishing boat (charges not available).*

The trip is especially interesting because of the variety of small islands, reefs, arches and marine caves hollowed out of the red brown cliffs.

Among the most striking sights on the trip are, south of the inn, the Furado Grande, a marine tunnel 70m - 230ft long which ends in a small creek (Cova do Sonho) walled by towering cliffs of red granite; beneath the fortress itself is a cave known locally as the "blue grotto", where light refracts on the sea within, producing an unusual and most attractive emerald green pool.

Walk★★. – *Time: 1 1/2 hours.* Take the stairway from the inn to the lighthouse. Halfway turn to look at the fortress in its **setting**★; on reaching the plateau take a path on the left which goes to the west coast or Wild Coast. There is a good **view**★ from the top of the rocks of the sea breaking below and, in the distance, the other islets of the archipelago.

Return to the lighthouse and descend by a cobbled walk leading to a small bay bordered by a beach and a few fishermen's cottages. Halfway down, and to the left, one sees a creek where the sea roars and smashes in bad weather.

Places, historical characters,
natural phenomena, monuments
described or illustrated in this guide
may be found rapidly through the index
on pp 160-162.

BRAGA ★

Michelin map **37** east of fold 11 or **441** fold 22 – *Local map p 62* – Pop 64 113

Today the capital of the Minho is an animated city living by such industries as leather, textiles, brick manufacture, soap making, engineering and smelting. Like all the towns in the region, a considerable number of craftsmen are still at work, their artifacts being sold each Tuesday on the fairground *(largo da feira)* at the yoke fair.

HISTORICAL NOTES

Bracara Augusta, an important Roman town, was made into their capital by the Suebi when they advanced upon the area in the 5C. The town was captured subsequently first by the Visigoths and then the Moors and only regained prosperity after the Reconquest when it became the seat of an archiepiscopal see.

From this time onwards the influence of the Church became paramount, a feature now particularly apparent in the richness of the architecture; in the 16C the archbishop patron Dom Diogo de Sousa presented the town with a palace, churches and Calvaries in the Renaissance style; in the 18C the two prelates, Dom Rodrigo of Moura Teles and Dom Gaspar of Bragança, made Braga the centre of Portuguese Baroque art.

Braga, once the seat of the Primate of All Spain, is still strongly ecclesiastical in character. Holy Week is observed with marked devotion and is the occasion for holding most unusual processions. The Feast of St John the Baptist on 23 and 24 June attracts local people in great crowds, and even many from Galicia, to attend the processions, the folk dancing and firework displays in the brilliantly decorated and illuminated town.

■ THE CATHEDRAL★ (Sé) *time: 1 1/2 hours*

There subsists today, of the original Romanesque structure, only the south door and the arching over the main doorway, ornamented with scenes from the medieval Romance of Renart, the Fox. The portico with festooned Gothic arches is the work of Biscayan artists brought to Braga in the 16C by Diogo de Sousa. The moulded window frames date from the 17C.

This same archbishop is responsible for the construction of the cathedral's east end bristling with pinnacles and balusters. The graceful **statue★** of Our Lady Suckling the Holy Child (Nossa Senhora do Leite) beneath a Flamboyant canopy which adorns the east end exterior is said to be by the sculptor, Nicolas Chanterene *(p 23)*.

Interior★. – It was transformed in the Baroque period. The contrast between the richness of the woodwork and the simplicity of the nave is striking. The font is Manueline: to the right, in a chapel closed by a 16C grille, lies the bronze tomb (15C) of the Infante Dom Afonso.

The Chapel of the Holy Sacrament contains a fine 17C polychrome wood altar representing the Church Triumphant after a picture by Rubens.

The chancel *(no access)*, which is covered by intricate ribbed **vaulting★** in the Flamboyant style, contains a Flamboyant **altar★** of Ançã stone carved on the front with scenes of the Ascension and of the Apostles. Above the altar is a 14C statue of St Mary of Braga. To the left of the chancel is a chapel decorated with 18C *azulejos* by António de Oliveira Bernardes depicting the life of St Pedro de Rates, first bishop of Braga.

A harmoniously Baroque group is formed by the two 18C **cases★** on either side of the balustraded organ loft.

Treasury★. – *Guided tour 8.30am to 12.30pm and 1.30 to 6pm; 25esc includes the visit to the treasury and chapels.*

On the second floor are 16-18C sacerdotal vestments including those belonging to Dom Gaspar of Bragança. Among the ecclesiastical plate are a Manueline chalice, a Byzantine influenced 11C **cross**, a 17C silver-gilt reliquary cross, a 10C Mozarabic chest made of ivory, a 16C chalice and Dom Gaspar of Bragança's 18C silver-gilt monstrance adorned with diamonds.

The first floor contains fine **azulejos★** dating from the 16C, statues, including a 13C Christ, and also the church gallery *(coro alto)* and its 18C gilded wood stalls. In a neighbouring gallery is an amusing statue of St Crispin, patron saint of shoemakers, facing his Portuguese counterpart, São Crespiniano (St Crispinian).

St Catherine's Chapel (Capela da Santa Catharina). – Decorated with wax votive offerings (arms, heads), the chapel contains a Baroque altarpiece with carved cherubs and bunches of grapes.

Kings' Chapel (Capela dos Reis). – *Same times and charges as the Treasury; also valid for the chapels listed below.*

This chapel, with Gothic vaulting resting on beautiful brackets sculpted with human heads, contains the 16C tombs of Henri of Burgundy and his wife Teresa, parents of the first king of Portugal, and the mummy of Dom Lourenço Vicente (14C), archbishop of Braga, who fought at Aljubarrota *(p 49)*.

St Gerald's Chapel (Capela de São Geraldo). – The walls of this fine Gothic chapel are entirely covered with 18C *azulejos* representing the life of St Gerald who was the first archbishop of Braga.

Chapel of Glory★ (Capela da Glória). – This Gothic building is decorated with 14C mural paintings in the Mudejar style. The sides of the Gothic **tomb★** of the founder, Dom Gonçalo Pereira, in the centre of the chapel, bear reliefs of the Crucifixion and the figures of the Apostles, the Virgin and Child and clerics at prayer.

■ ADDITIONAL SIGHTS

Former Episcopal Palace (Antigo Paço Episcopal) (U). – The palace is made up of three edifices dating from the 14, 17 and 18C. The library, where the reading room has a beautiful gilt coffered ceiling, includes 9C documents. The medieval north wing looks out over the pleasant Santa Bárbara Gardens (the 17C fountain of St Barbara).

Coimbras Chapel (Capela dos Coimbras) (B). – The 16C chapel, next to an 18C church, has a crenellated and statue ornamented tower built in the Manueline style. The interior is faced with *azulejos* of Adam and Eve.

There are, in addition, two Renaissance **works★** of the Coimbra school of sculpture: the Entombment of Christ, and on the altarpiece, the Virgin and Child between St Anne and St Joachim.

Biscainhos Museum (M). – *Guided tour 10am to 12.15pm and 2 to 5pm; closed Mondays and holidays; 10 esc.*

This archaeological and ethnographic museum is in an ancient 17C nobleman's palace, where the patio embellished with a fountain opens on to a garden with an ornamental pond and statues in the style of the 18C.

The collection includes ancient relics (Roman helmet), Portuguese and Dutch pottery (Delft) of the 17 to 19C, traditional artistic creations (18C wooden crib) and upstairs, Indo-Portuguese and French furniture, earthenware, glassware and 18C *objets d'art*.

Pelican Fountain (C). – In front of the town hall there is a lovely Baroque fountain where the water spouts from a pelican and bronze cupids.

House of Screens (Casa das Gelosias) (E). – An unusual 17C house with grilles and screens of Arabic design.

Church of the Holy Cross (Igreja Santa Cruz) (F). – 17C Baroque edifice.

Raio Palace (Casa do Raio) (K). – The front of this 18C Rococo residence, sometimes known as the House of the Mexican (Casa do Mexicano), is faced with *azulejos*.

Chapel of Our Lady da Penha de França (L). – The chapel is embellished with fine *azulejos* painted by Polycarpe de Oliveria Bernardes and a lovely 17C Baroque pulpit of gilded wood.

EXCURSIONS

Round tour★ to the east of Braga. – *44km - 27 miles – about 3 hours. Leave Braga by ② on the map.*

Bom Jesus do Monte★★. – *Facilities p 38.* This neo-Classical church was erected between 1784 and 1811 by Carlos Amarante, at the top of a monumental Baroque staircase.

From the foot of the stairway, the visitor has a choice of several methods of ascent:

– the funicular *(up: 20esc)* which climbs the 116m - 381ft to the sanctuary in a few minutes;

– the road winding in hairpin bends through the greenery;

– the staircase itself, Holy Way, the path usually taken by pilgrims: it affords the best views from which to appreciate the magnificence of the Baroque architecture *(illustration p 24)* and the natural beauty of the setting.

If you choose the staircase leave the car near the entrance porch to the Holy Way. The path designed as a Way of the Cross, is bordered with chapels. At each chapel a scene from the Passion is evoked by life size terracotta figures of astonishing reality. A fountain, ornamented with mythological motifs, also plays near each chapel.

The **Stairway of the Five Senses** is a double staircase with crossed balustrades; the base consists of two columns entwined by a serpent; water pours from the serpent's jaws, flowing back over the length of the body. Above the Fountain of the Five Wounds (water falls from the five bezants of the Portuguese coat of arms), each level is embellished by a fountain designed allegorically as one of the five senses and each balustrade is ornamented with obelisks and statues of Old Testament personages. The **Stairway of the Three Virtues** which follows is adorned with chapels and fountains evoking Faith, Hope and Charity.

Turn, on reaching the church parvis, to enjoy the fine **vista** ★ of the Baroque staircase and the nearby hills wooded with oaks, eucalyptus, mimosas and camelias.

The **church**, in a chapel on the right, contains a multitude of reliquary busts of St Clement in tiered rows above the saint's shrine. The sacristy is adorned with a large ivory Christ and photographs of the church's benefactors.

Nearby, hidden amidst the dense foliage, is a small lake *(boats for hire; 80esc for 1 hour)*.

Return to the car by funicular.

Monte Sameiro ★. – Mount Sameiro is crowned by a late 19 early 20C sanctuary to the Virgin and is a very popular pilgrimage. A staircase *(265 steps; 5esc)* climbs to the cupola's lantern tower (alt 613m - 2 011ft) from which there is a vast **panorama** ★★ over the Minho; in clear weather Mount Santa Luzia overlooking the Viana do Castelo can be seen in the northwest, the Serra do Gerês in the northeast and the Serra do Marão in the southeast. Below, in the foreground, are traces of the prehistoric city of Briteiros and, facing it, the sprawling mass of Braga.

Citânia de Briteiros. – The ruins of Citânia de Briteiros stand on a hillock 337m - 1 102ft high. The city existed from the Iron Age – 8 to 4C BC – and measured 250 x 150m - 820 x 492ft. Three perimeter walls protected its 150 huts. Two huts have been reconstructed by the archaeologist Martins Sarmento. The objects unearthed in the course of excavations are to be seen in the Martins Sarmento Museum at Guimarães *(p 84)*.

Serra da Falperra. – On a wooded slope of this small *serra* stands the **Church of St Mary Magdalene**. Supposedly built by the architect of the Raio Palace in Braga, it has an unusual 18C Rococo style façade in which there is not a single straight line.

Return to Braga by the N 309.

São Frutuoso de Montélios Chapel. – *3.5km - 2 miles. Leave Braga by ⑥, going towards Ponte de Lima; bear right at Real for São Frutuoso.*
The 18C Church of St Francis incorporates this Chapel of St Fructuosus, which was originally constructed in the 7C and is said to have been destroyed by the Moors and rebuilt in the 11C *(to visit apply to the priest or the sacristan)*. It is in the form of a Greek cross and, although very badly damaged, remains an interesting specimen of Byzantine art in Portugal. The Church of St Francis (São Francisco) contains 16C Renaissance stalls from Braga Cathedral.

On your way to Portugal
*visit Spain with the help of the **Michelin Green Guide Spain**.*

BRAGANÇA ★
Michelin map 🔢 fold 13 (inset) or 🔢 fold 26 – Pop 14 662

Bragança, lying within the boundaries of the austere province of Trás-os-Montes, occupies a high combe at an altitude of 660m - 2 165 ft in the Serra da Nogueira.

On the height which overlooks the modern city, there still stands within the shade of its tall ramparts the medieval city which was raised to the status of a duchy in 1442, and became also fief to the House of Bragança.

This family, which had renounced all claim to the throne while the country was occupied by Philip II of Spain, reigned over Portugal from 1640 *(p 140)* until the Revolution of 1910 and over Brazil from 1822 to 1889. During this period the title of Duke of Bragança was given to the heir to the throne.

(After Secretaria de Estado da Informação e Turismo photo)

Bragança and its Fortifications.

BRAGANÇA ★

■ **SIGHTS** *time: 3/4 hour*

A Baroque calvary stands before the cathedral in the lower town.

Make for the citadel (castelo) by way of the picturesque St Vincent Square. Leave the car outside the ramparts.

Old Town ★. – The old town crowns a hilltop, enclosed within a long and fortified wall.

Castle. – The castle, which was built in 1187, comprises a tall square keep, flanked by battlemented turrets, and several towers; two halls are lit by paired Gothic windows. From the keep platform, the panorama extends over the old town, the lower town and the surrounding hills.

Pillory. – The Gothic style pillory, which rests on a wild boar hewn out of the granite, is said to date from the Iron Age.

St Mary's Church. – 16C. The church door is framed by two twisted columns decorated with vine plants; inside, a fine ceiling has been painted in *trompe-l'œil*, with a representation of the Assumption.

Domus Municipalis. – *Apply at no 40, Rua Dom Fernão o Bravo da Cidadela Bragança.*

This pentagonal-shaped building, erected in the 12C, is the oldest town hall in Portugal. It is pierced on every side by small rounded arches; a frieze of carved modillions runs beneath the steep roof. The interior is one vast chamber while, below, the basement is occupied by an ancient cistern.

BRAVÃES ★

Michelin map **37** north of fold 11 or **441** fold 22 – 13km - 8 miles east of Ponte de Lima – Pop 653

The church at Bravães is one of the finest Romanesque buildings in Portugal.

São Salvador ★. – *When closed apply in the nearby café.*

A remarkable **doorway ★** opens the façade of this small Romanesque church (12C), its arching covered in an intricate decoration amidst which can be discerned doves, monkeys, human figures and geometrical motifs; richly historiated capitals crown naïvely carved statue columns. The tympanum, resting on the stylized heads of a pair of bulls, is ornamented with two angels in adoration of Christ in Majesty.

A low relief of the Holy Lamb is carved into the tympanum (of the south doorway) which is supported by two griffins.

Inside, the triumphal arch is embellished by a frieze influenced by Arabic design.

BUÇACO Forest ★★★

Michelin map **37** northeast of fold 14 or **441** fold 32 – *Facilities p 38*

Buçaco National Park, where a wide variety of trees grow, crowns the northernmost peak of the Serra do Buçaco, a range bristling with peaks. In a clearing in the centre of the park stands a former royal hunting lodge – now a hotel. Its appearance is unusual, the design being a pastiche of the Manueline style. A Baroque Way of the Cross leads from here up the hillside to the Cruz Alta, which is built on top of one of the peaks of the massif. Fountains of limpid water scattered among the age old trees bring freshness to the walk.

HISTORICAL NOTES

A Well Guarded Forest. – As early as the 6C Benedictine monks from Lorvão built a hermitage at Buçaco among the oaks and pines of the primitive forest; from the 11C to the start of the 17C the forest was jealously maintained by the priests of Coimbra Cathedral who had inherited it; in 1622 Pope Gregory XV forbade women to enter the forest on pain of excommunication.

In 1628 the Barefoot Carmelites built a monastery, on the site of the present hotel, and surrounded the domain by an unbroken wall. They continued to preserve the forest and, further, planted many new varieties including maples, laurels, Austrian oaks and Mexican cedars. In 1643 a new papal bull threatened anyone damaging the trees of Buçaco with excommunication.

The Battle of Buçaco. – September 1810 found Wellington once more facing the French, this time from the "damned long hill" at Buçaco. (By this time the French had already made two unsuccessful attempts to invade and conquer Portugal; and Wellington, although he had won victories as far east as Talavera in Spain, had been forced to retreat to Portugal to safeguard his lines of communication and reorganize his and the Portuguese armies.)

Masséna made a frontal attack through the mist at dawn; attack followed attack until the rolling volleys of the Anglo-Portuguese forced the French troops back down the hill. Charge and counter charge, regroupings and finally bayonets won the day and what was considered by all a great victory was won against the general whom Wellington considered "the ablest after Napoleon".

Sylvan Buçaco. – A decree dated 28 May 1834 abolished all religious orders throughout Portugal and the Carmelite friars were therefore expelled from Buçaco. The forest was given into the care of the Waters and Forests Department which extended the new plantings so that today the 105ha - 250 acres of woodland at Buçaco includes 400 native varieties of tree (eucalyptus, lentisks, etc) and about 300 exotic varieties (ginkgos, monkey-puzzles, cedars, Himalayan pines, thuyas, Oriental spruces, palms, arbutus, sequoias, Japanese camphor trees, etc).

Besides the trees there are also tree ferns, hydrangeas, mimosas, camellias, magnolias, philarias and even lilies of the valley.

TOUR

The three walks suggested start from the car park in front of the hotel.

The remains of the 17C Carmelite monastery comprise a chapel, the cloisters and, of particular interest, several monks' cells lined with cork to keep out the cold.

The hotel was constructed between 1888 and 1907 by the Italian architect, Luigi Manini. A sort of keep flanked by a small tower surmounted by an armillary sphere dominates the whole. The outstanding feature is the gallery of double arches, an imitation of the cloisters in the Hieronymite Monastery at Lisbon; *azulejos* by Jorge Colaço beneath the arcades illustrate Camões' *The Lusiads*. The great hall is decorated with *azulejos* representing the Battle of Buçaco.

① THE PARK'S FLORA AND FOUNTAINS

Round tour of 1 1/2 hours on foot – local map below

Hermitage of Our Lady of the Assumption (**Ermida de Nossa Senhora da Assunção**). – The hermitage is one of ten hermitages standing alone in the forest to which the monks used to retire.

Cold Fountain (**Fonte Fria**). – The waters rise in a cave and spill out to form a cascade down a stone staircase of 144 steps; at the bottom, hydrangeas and magnolias surround the pool into which the waters flow and which also mirrors some nearby majestic conifers. A path, lined with magnificent tree ferns, rhododendrons and hydrangeas, follows a small stream to a very lovely lake beside which grow several thuya trees.

Fern Alley (**Rua dos Fetos**). – This beautiful alley embellished with pine and very tall cypresses leads to the Grottoes Gate (Porta das Lapas).

BUÇACO Forest ★★★

The Coimbra Gate (Portas de Coimbra). – 17 and 19C. The gate on which can still clearly be seen on the exterior façade the text of the two papal bulls *(p 56)*, opens on to an attractive terrace arranged as a belvedere.

Return by way of the Cedar Alley (Avenida dos Cedros), an avenue of superb cedars.

② The CRUZ ALTA by the forest paths

Round tour of 2 1/2 hours on foot – local map p 57

Take the **Way of the Cross** (Via Sacra) constructed at the end of the 17C in the Baroque style. Terracotta figures enact the scenes in the chapels along the way.

Cruz Alta. – Alt 545m - 1 788ft. The **panorama** ★★ from the Cross is immense: to the right is the Serra do Caramulo; ahead a large number of white villages scattered over the coastal plain; below the hotel emerging through forest greenery; far away to the left, the built up mass of Coimbra and on the horizon on the far left, beyond the Mondego Valley, the heights of the Serra de Lousã and the Serra da Estrela.

Return by the woodland paths marked on the map or combine this walk with the next in such a way as to return by the road.

③ The CRUZ ALTA by road

6km - 4 miles – local map p 57

A few hundred yards from the hotel square glance at the waterfall *(cascata)*, which cascades into the St Sylvestre Fountain (Fonte de São Silvestro) set amidst ferns and hydrangeas.

Military Museum. – *Open 9am to 5.30pm; closed Mondays and holidays; 15 esc.*
The museum, which is outside the wall, features the Battle of Buçaco and the campaigns of 1810.

Obelisk. – The obelisk, which is topped by a glass star, commemorates the battle of 27 September 1810.
There is a wonderful **view** ★ of the Serra da Estrela and the Serra do Caramulo from the monument.
The road subsequently climbs through pine trees to the gate which leads to the Cruz Alta *(see above)*.

> **Remember: Monuments and museums close on Mondays**
> **Churches are open every day but usually close 1 to 4pm.**

CALDAS DA RAINHA

Michelin map 🔢 north of fold 16 – Pop 19 128 – *Facilities p 38*

Caldas da Rainha, a spa with a long established reputation, is a large agricultural centre with a crowded market. The town is also famous for its ceramics which vary considerably in design: vine leaves, snails, caricature figurines, etc.

The Queen's Baths (Caldas da Rainha). – In 1484 **Queen Leonor**, wife of King João II, when travelling to Batalha to take part in memorial rites on the anniversary of the death of her father-in-law Alfonso V, caught sight of some peasants bathing in evil smelling steaming pools at the roadside. Intrigued, she asked for information and was told that the water cured rheumatism. She thereupon decided to bathe before continuing on her way to Batalha. The queen then resumed her journey but had proceeded less than 6km - 4 miles when she began to feel the good effects of the sulphuric waters. This decided her immediately to postpone her religious observances in order to continue the cure. The village where the queen turned has been known ever since as Tornada (which means "return from a trip").

In 1485 Leonor's generosity impelled her to sell jewels and lace to raise sufficient funds to found a hospital in the town which she decided to administer personally. Later the queen commanded that a large park be laid out and a church built near by.

■ SIGHTS *time:1hour*

Spa Park ★. – The delight and green freshness of the park lies in its weeping willows, palms, flowers, lawns, statues and stretches of water.

Malhoa Museum. – *Open 10am to 12.30pm and 2 to 5pm; closed Mondays and holidays; 50esc, free Sundays.*
The museum, which is in the park, contains 19 and 20C paintings sculpture and pottery. Worth noting are the works of José Malho *(p 25)*, painter of popular scenes whose best known canvases include *Promises (as Promessas)* and the *Last Interrogation of the Marquis of Pombal*. Malhoa's style is characterized by his use of intense light and colours and realistic themes.
Another painter, Columbano (1857-1929) known also as the Master of Half Light, has left some fine portraits, notably *Boy's Head (Cabeça de Rapaz)*.

Nossa Senhora do Pópulo Church. – *Times and charges not available at the time of going to press.*
The church, which was built at the end of the 15C at the command of Queen Leonor, is crowned by an elegant belfry with paired Gothic windows bearing Manueline decoration. Inside, the walls are entirely covered with 17C *azulejos* and the altar frontals with fine 16C Moorish *azulejos* in relief. Above the Manueline style triumphal arch is a beautiful **triptych** ★ of the Crucifixion attributed to the early 16C Cristóvão de Figueiredo.

Michelin map ██ fold 11 (inset) or ███ fold 22 – Pop 1 878 – *Facilities p 36*

The fortified town of Caminha was formerly part of Portugal's northern frontier defence against Galician aspirations. It occupied a key position at the confluence of the Coura and the Minho and also controlled the Minho estuary, overlooked on the Spanish side by the Santa Tecla. Caminha is now a fishing village and craft centre for coppersmiths.

Praça do Conselheiro Silva Torres. – The square is still largely medieval in character with ancient buildings grouped round a 16C granite fountain. The 15C **Pitas Palace** is Gothic, its emblazoned façade elegant with curved windows. The **town hall** (Paços do Concelho) has a lovely coffered ceiling in the council chamber. The **clock tower** (Torre do Relógio) was once part of the 14C fortifications. *Go through this gate to Rua Ricardo Jão de Sousa which leads to the parish church.*

Parish Church (Igreja Matriz). – The building was built in the 15-16C as a granite church fortress. Apart from a few Gothic elements such as the pinnacles, the style is basically Renaissance as is particularly evident in the façade doorways. The south door is framed by carved pilasters supporting a gallery on which are statues of Saints Peter, Paul, Mark and Luke. The pediment contains a Virgin supported by two angels. The east end of the church is Plateresque in style rather than Manueline.

Inside is a magnificent *artesonado* **ceiling★** of maplewood carved by a Spaniard in the Mudejar style. Each octagonal panel, framed in stylized cabling, bears a rose at its centre. On the right, stands a statue of St Christopher, patron saint of mariners.

The Chapel of the Holy Sacrament, to the right of the chancel, contains a 17C gilded wood tabernacle illustrated with scenes from the Passion by Francisco Fernandes.

Michelin map ██ fold 14 or ███ fold 32 – Pop 7 498

Cantanhede is a large agricultural town and a commercial centre for wine, cereals and wood. The famous white limestone known as Ançã stone is quarried from the countryside between Cantanhede and **Ançã** (*10km - 6 miles to the southeast*). It is as easy to carve as wood and has always been much liked by local sculptors and architects, particularly those of the Coimbra school (*p 63*). Time turns the white stone a lovely golden colour, but it has a tendency to crumble and wear away.

Parish Church. – The church contains several 16C works attributed to Jean de Rouen, in particular, in the second chapel on the right, the altarpiece with a Virgin of Intercession and, in the Chapel of the Holy Sacrament to the right of the chancel, two tombs surmounted by statues of the prophets.

EXCURSION

Varziela. – *4km - 2 miles. Take the Mira road and bear left after 2km - 1.2 miles (signpost).* The chapel contains an **altarpiece★** of Ançã stone attributed to Jean de Rouen. There is considerable detail in the carving which shows a Virgin of Intercession surrounded by two angels and the kneeling figures of dignitaries of the Church and Court.

Michelin map ██ southwest of fold 3 or ███ fold 33

Caramulo is a spa at an altitude of 750m - 2 461 ft on a wooded hillside in the Serra do Caramulo. Parks and gardens enhance this town on the schist and granite massif which is wooded with pines, oaks and chestnuts and also has such crops as maize, vines and olives. The western slope, which descends gently towards the Aveiro coastal plain, is completely different from the eastern where the sharper relief is cut away by tributaries of the Mondego.

Museums. – *Guided tour 10am to 6pm.*

Car Museum. – *80esc.* An interesting collection of fifty cars.

Art Museum. – *150esc.* The collections include statues from the 15C Portuguese school among which is a Virgin and Child, a series of tapestries from Tournai representing the arrival of the Portuguese in India and a large number of paintings by contemporary artists: Picasso (still life), Fernand Léger, Dufy, Dali, Braque, etc. It also has thirty-six cars including an 1898 Peugeot and a 1902 Darraco.

EXCURSIONS

Pinoucas★. – *3km - 2 miles. Leave Caramulo to the north by the N 230; after 2km - 1 1/2 miles bear left on a dirt track road which, 1km - 1/2 mile further on, ends at the watchtower.* From the top (alt 1 062m - 3 481ft) there is an impressive **panorama★** over the Serra do Caramulo.

Caramulinho★★; Cabeço da Neve. – *7.5km - 4 1/2 miles. Leave Caramulo to the west by Avenue Abel de la Cerda which becomes the N 230-3 and where 3km - 2 miles further on you pass on your left the branch road leading to Cabeço da Neve.*

Caramulinho★★. – *1/2 hour on foot Rtn, by a rocky path which has 130 steps cut into its face.* The tip of the Serra do Caramulo (alt 1 075m - 3 527ft) makes an excellent **viewpoint★★** over the Lapa Range in the northeast, the Estrela Range in the southeast, the Lousã and Buçaco Ranges to the south, over the coastal plain to the west, and over the Serras da Gralheira and do Montemura to the north.

Return to the Cabeço da Neve branch road, which you then take to the viewpoint.

Cabeço da Neve. – Alt 995m - 3 264ft. This balcony summit has a plunging view to the south and towards the east, with views over the lower wooded mountain, dotted with villages, the Mondego Basin and the Estrela Range. Viseu can be seen to the northeast.

Michelin map **37** folds 12 (inset) and 17 – Pop 29 882 – *Facilities p 36*
See town plan in the current Michelin Red Guide España Portugal

Cascais is both a fishing port of age old tradition and a bustling holiday resort. The town has everything in its favour: a mild climate in which sea air combines with cool air from the Sintra Massif and a fine sand beach lining a beautiful bay on the radiant Costa do Sol.

Men have appreciated this particular site since the earliest times. Prehistoric man from the Palaeolithic era was followed in turn by Romans, Visigoths and Moors. Cascais gained its independence at the same time as Lisbon and by the middle of the 14C had acquired the status of *Vila*, but at the end of the 16C, in 1580 and again in 1597, it was sacked first by soldiers of the Duke of Alba and later by those of Mary Tudor. The earthquake of 1755 destroyed the town again, just as it was really recovering. The *azulejos* which decorate the **Church of the Assumption** (Assunção) date from this period.

The bent to tourism came in 1870 when the Court moved to Cascais for the first time for the summer. With the Court came a tradition of elegance and train of architects. The royal palace or former citadel on the promontory which protects the bay to the southwest is now a residence of the Head of State.

Museum-library of the Counts of Castro Guimarães. – *Guided tour 10am to 5pm; closed Mondays; the library is closed Saturday afternoons.*

On the coast road, this 19C noble residence, with a central patio, has a collection of 17C Portuguese and Indo-Portuguese furniture and *azulejos,* 18 and 19C Portuguese gold and silversmith work and pottery, 18C bronzes, carpets, and Chinese vases, valuable books (one of which is a 16C Chronicles of D. Alfonso Henriques) and a strange organ chest dating from 1753.

In the park there is a large fountain with *azulejos.*

EXCURSIONS

Boca do Inferno★ (Jaws of Hell); Praia do Guincho★. – *8km - 5 miles to the west by the coast road.* Pass the former royal palace on the left and then the municipal park on the right.

Boca do Inferno★. – When the road turns to the right, a house and a café with a few pines standing on the left, mark the site of this **abyss★** formed by marine erosion. The sea, entering under a rock arch, booms and crashes particularly vociferously in bad weather.

The road continues as a *corniche* above the sea, giving some fine views of the wild coast. Beyond Cabo Raso (small fort), where the road turns off towards the Serra de Sintra, stretches of sand being pounded by rough seas can be glimpsed between the rocky points. Farther on the immense beach, **Praia do Guincho★** *(facilities p 36)*, is backed by windswept dunes, and the imposing headland, Cabo da Roca (p 132) can be seen on the horizon.

Ibne-Mucane Monument. – *5km - 3 miles by the N 9 going towards Alcabideche.*

A stele, erected in honour of the Arabic writer Ibne-Mucane, who was born at Alcabideche in the 10C and is believed to be the first poet to sing praises in Europe of windmills, bears the following inscription on the stone: "If you are really a man you need a mill which turns with the clouds and is not dependent on water courses."

Michelin map **37** fold 5 – Pop 24 287 – *Facilities p 38*

Castelo Branco lies near the frontier and has, therefore, suffered a number of attacks and even occupations – events which have left few historic monuments. The maraudings of the Napoleonic troops in 1807 were among the most devastating.

The capital of Beira is today a peaceful flower bedecked city living by its trade in cork, cheese, honey and olive oil; it is particularly known for the fine bedspreads *(colchas)* embroidered in variegated colours by young girls who perpetuate a tradition going back to the 17C, as each prepares her trousseau.

CASTELO BRANCO

■ **SIGHTS** *time: 1 1/2 hours*

Follow the itinerary indicated on the town plan.

Tavares Proença Regional Museum (M). – *Open 9am (10am Saturdays and Sundays) to 12.30pm and 2 to 5.30pm (6pm Mondays and Tuesdays); closed holidays; 30esc, free Sundays.*

Established in the old episcopal palace, it has an interesting collection: on the ground floor, archaeological and stone relics, coins, earthenware and ancient weapons, pieces of broken flasks and Roman pottery; in the staircase, 16C Flemish tapestries *(Story of Lot);* upstairs, other 16C Flemish tapestries, paintings of the 16C Portuguese school (a *Santo António* attributed to Francisco Henriques), documents and antique Portuguese furniture (a beautiful 17C carved cupboard), and embroidered bedcovers from Castelo Branco. On the same floor, there is a room with a weaving loom and rustic tools, and another room devoted to modern art.

Gardens of the former Episcopal Palace★ (Jardim do Antigo Paço Episcopal). – *Closed 1 January and 25 December. 10esc.*

The 17C gardens form an unusual ensemble of clipped box trees and hedges, banks of flowers, ornamental pools and Baroque statues. (Signs of the Zodiac, Doctors of the Church, the Seasons, the Virtues, etc.)

An alley which runs beside the Crown Lake and ends in two flights of steps, is lined by balustrades peopled with statues: the Apostles and the Evangelists on the right face the Kings of Portugal on the left – note the irony by which the sculptor has depicted the kings who suffered Spanish domination by considerably reducing their size.

Pass beneath the arcaded staircase which bestraddles the Rua de Frei Bartolomeu da Costa.

Cross of St John (A). – The Manueline style (16C) twisted column is surmounted by a carved cross placed over a crown of seaweed.

Leave the car in front of the Church of St Mary of the Castle and take, to the left of the ruins of the Templars' Castle, the stairway to the Miradouro de São Gens.

Miradouro de São Gens (B). – This shady esplanade bright with flowers affords an extensive view of the town and the surrounding landscape speckled with olive trees.

CASTELO DE VIDE ★

Michelin map **37** north of fold 6 – *Local map p 127* – Pop 2 558 – *Facilities p 38*

Castelo de Vide is a small spa, bunched together at the foot of its castle which stands perched on an elongated foothill of the Serra de São Mamede. It owes its attraction to old whitewashed houses stepped high up the hillside along winding alleys brilliant with flowers.

General view★. – *5 km - 3 miles.* A narrow surfaced road branches off the N 246–1 to the right, 2km -1.2 miles south of Castelo de Vide, to climb round rocks and pines to the **Chapel Nossa Senhora da Penha** (700m - 2 296ft). From the front of the chapel there is a good view of Castelo de Vide.

■ **SIGHTS** *time: 1 hour*

Praça Dom Pedro V. – On this square the Church of Santa Maria stands opposite two 17C buildings, namely the Baroque Torre Palace and the Santo Amaro Hospital. Also overlooking the square are a fine 18C mansion and the late 17C town hall.

Take an alleyway to the left of the church going to the castle (signposted), leaving the Jewish Quarter on your right. Some of the doors and windows are decorated in the Manueline style.

Castle (Castelo). – *Go through the outer walls.* A stairway at the foot of a 12C round tower leads to the keep. From a room with a Gothic cupola and a cistern, there is a picturesque **view★** of the town. At the top of the staircase note, on the right, a 12C Arabic system of ventilation using tracery brickwork high up beneath the roof.

Jewish Quarter★ (Judiaria). – A picturesque quarter where houses in the small streets are all white and many have Gothic doors.

Fonte da Vila. – Below the Jewish Quarter in the centre of a pretty little square, a Baroque granite fountain can be seen.

CASTRO MARIM

Michelin map **37** fold 10 – Pop 4 549

Castro Marim abuts on a height overlooking the ochre coloured and marshy Lower Guadiana Plain near its outflow into the Gulf of Cádiz. Facing the commanding Portuguese town across the estuary – and the border – is the Spanish town of Ayamonte.

Castro Marim, which was already in existence in Roman times, became, in 1321, on the dissolution of the Order of Templars in Portugal, the seat of the Knights of Christ until this was transferred to Tomar in 1334 *(p 133).*

The ruins of Castro Marim's fortified castle which was built of red sandstone and demolished by the earthquake of 1755, stand to the north of the village, while the remains crowning a hill to the south are of the 17C Fort of St Sebastian.

Castle. – *Open 9am to 6pm (8pm June to September); closed Sunday.*

Within the castle are the ruins of an even older castle dating back to the 12C. The parapet walk affords a good circular view over the small city with the 17C Fort of St Sebastian in the foreground, the saltmarshes, the Guadiana and the Spanish town of Ayamonte to the east and Vila Real de Santo António and the coast to the south.

The course of the Cávado River above Braga is steeply enclosed between the Serra do Gerês and the Serras da Cabreira and do Barroso. In this rocky upper valley, as in its tributary, the Rabagão, a series of dams control reservoir lakes of a deep blue colour which are surrounded by wooded mountain slopes crested by bare peaks – altogether a highly picturesque landscape.

Development. – The Cávado, which is 118km - 73 miles long rises at an altitude of 1 500m - 4 859ft in the Serra do Larouco not far from the Spanish frontier; after crossing the 15km - 11 miles of the Montalegre Plateau, the river course drops sharply, losing 400m in 5km - 1 300ft in 3 miles as it follows a series of rock faults running northeast-southwest. The hydro-electric development of this upper valley, facilitated by the impermeable quality of the granite rocks through which the river had cut its course, began in 1946. Dams exist at Alto Cávado, Paradela, Salamonde and Caniçada on the Cávado, at Alto Rabagão and Venda Nova on the Rabagão and at Vilarinho des Funas on the Homen. These installations generated 1 414 million kWh in 1983, or 17 per cent of the total hydro-electric power produced in Portugal.

From Braga to Chaves — *171km - 106 miles – about 4 hours – Local map below*

Leave Braga (p 52) by ② and take the N 103 on the left going towards Chaves.

Immediately on leaving Braga, the Cávado Valley on the left becomes deep and wild; the road climbs along the south slopes which are covered in pine trees and eucalyptus. 8km - 5 miles along on the left side of the road, a belvedere affords a view of the last green stretch of the valley. Further on and to the right, a hillock crowned with rocks looks like a medieval fortress, and 3km - 2 miles further still, the castle of Póvoa de Lanhoso with its keep rising up behind Pinheiro can be seen. After this village, the Cávado Valley is hidden, while on the right the parallel valley of the Rio Ave appears, sparkling and scattered with hamlets. Then the road climbs up through a landscape of bare and rocky crests often topped with rocks resembling ruins; on the slopes there are beautiful spherical rocks; also *espigueiros (p 27)* and a few cattle.

A little before Cerdeirinhas, the N 103 turns downwards and overlooks the Cávado River which it follows, running along the edge of the Peneda-Gerês National Park *(p 118)*.

Gerês. – *14km - 9 miles from the N 103. Description p 118.*

The road then begins to wind and turn, affording precipitous **views**★ of the 15km - 9 mile long **Caniçada Reservoir**★ and of the Salamonde Reservoir. Both lie below pine scattered slopes, dominated by the bare summits of the Serra do Gerês.

Bear left off the N 103 on the Paradela road over the Venda Nova Dam's crest: at the next crossroads bear right.

As the *corniche* style road rises rapidly the **views**★★ of the Serra do Gerês become even more beautiful. A little before Paradela, on the left there is a village built on a rocky projection at the foot of a shale hillock, which has been strangely slashed and hollowed out at the back of a gigantic quarry.

The road crosses Paradela, and now unsurfaced arrives at the dam of the same name.

Paradela Dam★. – The reservoir lake at an altitude of 112m - 367ft above the River Cavado has a lovely mountain **setting**★.

Return to the N 103. The road runs alongside the **Venda Nova Reservoir.**

Vila da Ponte. – Pop 390. A village perched upon a rock spur.

After Pisões, a path to the right leads to Alto Rabagão Dam.

Alto Rabagão Dam★. – The dam stands as a massive concrete wall. Go to the end of the road to the crest of the dam from which there is a good **view**★ over the lake.

Return to the N 103. The road skirts the north edge of the lake before turning left to Montalegre.

Montalegre. – Pop 1 739. Montalegre was built at 966m - 3 170ft in a beautiful **setting**★. Old red roofed houses encircle the walls of the 14C castle (in ruins) whose keep commands the wild and mountainous plateau. Looking out one can see to the north-east the Serra do Larouco where the Cávado, which crosses the plain below, rises.

Return by way of the N 308 to the N 103. The road crosses arid rock strewn moors covered with heather and cut by streams. The plateau suddenly disappears as the **view**★★ extends dramatically to take in a vast green and cultivated basin at the far end of which can be seen the low lying old villages of **Sapiãos** and **Boticas**. The road climbs through magnificent pine forests before joining the lovely agricultural Tâmega Valley to reach Chaves *(p 63)*.

Trás-os-Montes is an arid province, but Chaves is well favoured since it was built on the banks of the Tâmega, in the centre of a sunken basin which is particularly fertile.

The small town of Aquae Flaviae, known to the Romans for its thermal springs, was transformed into an important stopping point on the Astorga–Braga road when Trajan built a bridge over the Tâmega, within its bounds. In 1160, after being recaptured from the Moors, Chaves was fortified to ensure its command of the valley in face of the Spanish fortress of Verin. In the 17C ramparts after the style of the French military architect Vauban were added. Even now the old castle huddled close by picturesque white houses with corbelled balconies give the town considerable style.

The quiet spa town, where the alkaline springs rise at a temperature of 73°C - 160°F, provides treatment for rheumatism and digestive disorders to this day.

It is also equally known for its excellent smoked ham *(presunto)*.

■ SIGHTS *time: 1 1/2 hours*

Bridge. – One can get a general view of the bridge from the gardens which run down to the river. With the years it has lost its stone parapets and even some arches, but it, nevertheless, adds considerably to the charm of the setting. The milestones at the southern end still bear legible Roman inscriptions.

Municipal Museum (Museu de Regiào Flaviense). – *Open 9.30am to 12.30pm and 2 to 5pm; closed Saturday and Sunday mornings, Mondays and holidays; 20esc.*

Archaeological and ethnographical, it includes on the ground floor a room of prehistoric stone relics – the main piece in the collection is a megalithic **figure in human form** (about 2 000 years BC) – and Roman remains. Upstairs there are ancient coins and a banknote plate, a magic lantern, and radio receivers dating from early "wireless" days.

Keep. – This is all that remains of the castle; a massive square tower with battlements at the corners, still surrounded by its quadrangular outer wall. Built by King Dinis, it was the residence of the first Duke of Bragança, illegitimate son of John I.

Military Museum. – *Tour combined with that of the municipal museum (see above).*

It covers four floors of the keep, the first two have ancient weapons and armour, the third evokes the First World War (machine guns, uniforms), the fourth, colonial wars (Portuguese and native weapons). From the platform summit *(121 steps)* there is a panoramic view over the town, the ramparts and the cultivated valley of Chaves.

Church of the Misericord★. – A small Baroque structure, the façade is pleasantly embellished with balconies and twisted columns. The inside walls are covered with *azulejos* showing scenes from the life of Christ, and the Bible. It has a larged gilded wooden altarpiece; the ceiling is decorated with 18C paintings, one of which, in the centre, is a Visitation.

Pillory. – A pillory in the Manueline style stands on the nearby square in front of the parish church.

COIMBRA ★★

Michelin map **37** fold 14 or **441** fold 32 – Pop 79 799

Coimbra, on a hillside at whose foot flows the Mondego, is overlooked by the tall tower of its old University. Many poets, inspired by the romantic setting, have immortalized the charm of this town, the first capital of Portugal, and have helped to make it a city of fine arts and letters. Today Coimbra, with many important buildings preserved from its past, is a quiet commercial and industrial town (textiles, tanneries, potteries and cameras), roused occasionally by some ancient university tradition.

In even years, in July, a torchlight procession is held on the feast day of Queen Saint Isabel, the town's patron saint, during which her statue is borne from the New Convent of St Clare to the Holy Cross Monastery.

The site★. – You can get a good general view of the town in its setting from the **Vale do Inferno** belvedere *(miradouro). 4km - 2 miles. To get there leave by ③ and take a narrow road on the right towards the Vale do Inferno (steep climb); at a fork bear right.*

The most attractive view, however, is from the southern end of the Santa Clara Bridge where lines of women doing their washing add a picturesque touch to the scene.

From Mount Helicon to the banks of the Mondego. – "The first king (King Dinis) honoured the noble art of Minerva at Coimbra, calling on the Muses to leave Mount Helicon to come and play in the smiling meadows of the Mondego" – thus Camões describes the founding of Coimbra University in *The Lusiads (p 26)*. In fact, it was in Lisbon that King Dinis founded the University in 1290. It was transferred to Coimbra in 1308, and it was only permanently established in Coimbra by King João III in 1537 when he installed it in his own palace. Teachers from the Universities of Oxford, Paris, Salamanca and Italy were drawn to the new University, making the town one of the most important humanist centres of the period.

The Coimbra School of Sculpture. – Early in the 16C there came to work in Coimbra several French sculptors from a group of artists under the protection of the Cardinal patron Georges d'Amboise, the promoter in Normandy of what was known as the "methods and style of Italy". Nicolas Chanterene, Jean de Rouen, Jacques Buxe and Philippe Houdart joined with the Portuguese João and Diogo de Castilho, in about 1530, to create a school of sculpture in the town. Their art was learned and sophisticated, inspired by Italian decorative forms: doorways, pulpits, altarpieces and the low reliefs surrounding altars were delicately carved out of the fine Ança stone *(p 59)*. The new style of decoration spread first to the region round Coimbra (Cantanhede, Montemor-o-Velho, Penela, etc.), then, on evolving into a complete architectural style, throughout Portugal.

COIMBRA

The students' life. – The city, peaceful throughout summer, reawakens with a start at the beginning of the academic year. The 13 000 students retain traditions, which, in some cases, go back 400 years and have been codified in dog Latin. The students still adorn their briefcases with different coloured ribbons *(fitas)* to denote their faculty. Romantics all, they play guitars and sing *fados* distinguishable from those of their rivals at Lisbon by the intellectual or sentimental nature of the themes *(p 30)*. The students band themselves into groups of "republics" of twelve or thirteen, usually from the same region and live communally, renting lodgings, managing the group budget in turn and hiring a servant to cook for them.

■ **MAIN SIGHTS** *time: 3 hours*

The sights lie in the old town on the Alcáçova Hill, reached by a tangle of narrow and picturesque alleys sometimes cut by significantly named steps – Escadas de Quebra-Costas: Broken Ribs Steps.

Leave the car in the Avenida Emidio Navarro and follow the route marked on the plan.

Almedina Gate (Z A). – This 12C gate surmounted by a tower is one of the last survivals of the medieval town wall.

Sub-Ripas Palace (YZ B). – The palace is a private residence which was built at the beginning of the 16C in the Manueline style; opposite stands the **Casa do Arco** (Y C).

Old Cathedral (Sé Velha) (Z E). – The cathedral, erected between 1140 and 1175 by two French master craftsmen, Bernard and Robert, has all the appearance of a fortress complete with pyramidal merlons *(illustration p 21)*. The main façade is plain in contrast to the doorway added to the north face in about 1530. This door, which is attributed to Jean de Rouen and is, unfortunately, badly damaged, was one of the earliest items to show Renaissance influence in Portugal. On the east side, the tower, disfigured by the addition of a Baroque lantern turret, is well integrated with a beautiful arcaded gallery where the design of the capitals shows Oriental influence.

Inside, the nave is lined by a wide gallery with Byzantine capitals on the supporting columns. The Flamboyant Gothic **altarpiece**★ in gilded wood at the high altar is by the Flemish masters Olivier de Gand (Ghent) and Jean d'Ypres. At the base, the four

Evangelists support the Nativity and the Resurrection; above, surrounded by four saints, an attractive group celebrates the Assumption of the Virgin, who has been carved with a most graceful face. The top of the altarpiece is crowned with a calvary beneath a fine canopy.

In the **Chapel★** of the Holy Sacrament, to the right of the chancel, there is a good Renaissance composition by Tomé Velho, a disciple of Jean de Rouen.

To the left of the chancel lies the Chapel to St Peter ornamented with *azulejos* in the Mudejar style and a Renaissance altarpiece *(in poor condition)* by Jean de Rouen, representing the life of St Peter.

Cloisters. – *Access through the first door in the south aisle.* The cloisters, built at the end of the 13C, are an example of transitional Gothic architecture; they were restored in the 18C. Blind arcades are surmounted by round bays filled with a variety of tracery; in the first chapel on the left, a font was carved in 1520 by Jean de Rouen in the Manueline and Renaissance styles. In the chapterhouse on the south side lies the tomb of Dom Sisnando, first Christian governor of Coimbra, who died in 1091.

Machado de Castro Museum★★ (Z M¹). – *Guided tour (time: 1 hour) 10am to 12.30pm and 2 to 5pm; closed Mondays and holidays; 50esc.*

It is in the old episcopal palace, modified in the 16C. The Renaissance porch opens on to a patio-courtyard the façades of which are decorated with bands of *azulejos*, and on the west side there is a loggia built by Filippo Terzi *(p 24)* which has a charming view of the top of the old cathedral and the lower town, as far as Mondego.

Sculptures. – They fill the ground floor which also has *(on the right of the entry)* important architectural remains of the original church and cloister. The galleries in the right wing have 14C works in limestone: a remarkable little **equestrian statue★** of a medieval knight, a beautiful Christ in the tomb, a pregnant Virgin by Master Pero *(p 21)*; other sculptures of the 15 and 16C show the transition to the Renaissance, works of the Coimbra school *(p 63)* which are spread over the galleries of the left wing; works by Chanterene (Virgin reading, Entombment of eight personages), Houdart (a Paschal feast, in polychrome terra-cotta), Jean de Rouen (altarpieces). A number of 17C statues

Machado de Castro Museum
The medieval knight.

(Pietà in polychrome wood by the monk Cipriano de Cruz) and 18C statues, complete the exhibition.

Objets d'art, **paintings.** – On the first floor (handsome ceilings) there are also a few 18C statues and statuettes (Procession of the Three Wise Men), 17 to 19C Portuguese pottery, gold and silver religious objects, and Oriental art (Persian carpets, Chinese porcelain).

Some of the rooms are of particular interest: a 15C "Arab Salon" with a Mudejar ceiling, a "Macão Salon" (note the 17C black onyx crucifix), a "Bishop's Chapel" where the walls are hung with silk and decorated with 18C *azulejos*. Others are reserved for special collections, such as French furniture of Louis XV period or liturgical ornaments. There are also paintings of the 15 and 16C Portuguese school (works of Simão Rodrigues), and mementoes of Queen St Isabel, including a gold necklace and a coral reliquary.

Two rooms are dedicated to religious, Flemish and Portuguese painting of the 15 to 18C; an altarpiece of Santa Clara by Quentin Matsys (15C), a 16C Assumption by the Master of Sardoal, an Ascension and a Nativity by the Master of Celas (16C), a Christ appearing to the Virgin by the Master of Santa Clara (16C), the same subject treated by Garcia Fernandez (in 1531) and three paintings by Josefa de Óbidos *(p 110)*.

Roman Galleries. – *In the basement.* Cutting across at right angles, there are impressive rows of doors opening on to a multitude of cellars, some of which have prehistoric remains of the Luso-Roman period.

Old University★★ (Velha Universidade) (Z). – The 17C main door opens on to the University courtyard which is dominated by an 18C tower. Take the staircase on the right which leads to a central portico with a triangular pediment. On the first floor is the loggia, formerly for women only, and leading off it the Ceremonial Hall (Sala dos Capelos) *(open 9am to 12.30pm and 2 to 6pm)*, with its fine 17C painted ceiling, is adorned with a series of portraits of the kings of Portugal.

From the balcony there is an interesting **view★** of the old town and the more modern area, built near the Mondego.

The Manueline **chapel★** (Z F), with an elegant door, is by Marcos Pires. It is decorated with 17C *azulejos* and a painted ceiling and also possesses a fine 18C **organ loft★★**.

A small **Museum of Sacred Art** *(guided tour 9am to noon and 2 to 5.30pm; 35esc)* adjoins the chapel.

(After Secretaria de Estado da Informação e Turismo photo)

Old University — The Chapel Door.

The **library**★★ (Z K), built in the reign of João V in 1724, consists of three rooms whose furnishings in carved and varnished precious woods are highlighted by sumptuous Baroque decorations of gilded wood. The ceilings painted in false perspective are by Lisbon artists influenced by Italian art.

■ ADDITIONAL SIGHTS

Monastery of the Holy Cross (Mosteiro de Santa Cruz) (Y L). – *Open 9.30am to 12.30pm and 2 to 6pm; 20esc.*

The monastery, which was built in the 16C on the ruins of a 12C edifice, is preceded by a Renaissance porch by Nicolas Chanterene and Diogo de Castilho (1520). This work has unfortunately weathered badly and, in addition, was disfigured in the 18C.

Inside, the ceiling is in the Manueline style and the lower part of the nave is adorned with *azulejos*. There is a graceful Renaissance **pulpit**★ carved by Nicolas Chanterene and, on either side of the high altar, and the tombs of the first two kings of Portugal in two bays surrounded by a Late Gothic-Early Renaissance decoration, rich with flowers, figurines, medallions, etc. In the gallery *(coro alto)* are beautiful 16C wooden stalls carved and gilded by Flemish artists and the Frenchman, François Lorete. Their crowning head-pieces include armillary spheres, Crosses of the Knights of Christ and, in greatest number, castles and galleons recalling the voyages of Vasco da Gama.

Four early 16C Portuguese paintings (a Calvary, an *Ecce Homo*, a Pentecost and a St Antony) hang in the sacristy *(access through a door in the south transept)*.

A door in the sacristy leads to the Silent Cloister. This was designed by Marcos Pires in 1524, and is a model at its most pure and uncluttered of the Manueline style of architecture. Three low reliefs represent scenes of the Passion after Dürer engravings.

St James's (São Tiago) (Y N). – The church has interesting capitals on its Romanesque main and side doors.

Penedo da Saudade (X). – Pleasant promenade with a wide view of the Mondego Valley.

Celas Monastery (Mosteiro de Celas) (X P). – An old 12C Reformed Cistercian convent which was rebuilt in the 16C.

The church has star vaulting. The sacristy to the right of the chancel contains a 16C **altarpiece**★ by Jean de Rouen showing St John the Evangelist and St Martin. The 13C cloister which is Romanesque in style with Gothic elements, has historiated capitals.

Former Convent of St Clare (Santa Clara-a-Velha) (X Q). – The Mondego sands have gradually reduced to ruins the beautiful Gothic church in which the body of Inês de Castro *(p 41)* lay until it was transferred to Alcobaça.

Portugal in Miniature (Portugal dos Pequenitos) (X R). – *Open 9am to 7pm (5.30pm October to March); closed Easter Sunday, 1 November and 25 December; 50esc.*

A children's garden where may be seen models of the principal monuments and many types of houses to be found in Portugal and its territories. One of these contains a **Children's Museum** (Museu da Criança) *(same opening times as Portugal in Miniature)*.

Villa of Tears (Quinta das Lágrimas) (X S). – *Times and charges not available at the time of going to press.*

A romantic small wooded park where Inês de Castro *(p 41)* is said to have been assassinated.

Botanical Gardens (X). – *Open 9am to 7pm.*

Terraced gardens with a large number of tropical plants.

New Convent of St Clare (Santa Clara-a-Nova) (X V). – *Open 9.30am to 12.30pm and 2 to 5.30pm; closed Mondays and holidays; no visits during services.*

The Baroque church of this convent contains, in the chancel, the 17C silver tomb of Queen Saint Isabel whose statue in wood by Teixeira Lopes is also in the church.

At the end of the lower chancel, behind the wrought iron screen is the queen's original **tomb**★ (14C) in painted Ança stone. The reclining figure dressed in the habit of the Poor Clares has her eyes wide open. The frieze encircling the tomb shows on one side the Poor Clares and their bishop, and on the other Christ and the Apostles; at the foot are St Clare and two effigies of crowned saints; at the head is the Crucifixion.

EXCURSIONS

Buçaco Forest★★★; **Mealhada**. – *Round tour of 48km - 30 miles – about 1/2 day. Leave Coimbra by ②, the N 17 and after 27km - 17 miles bear left towards Penacova.* The road affords beautiful views directly down into the Mondego Valley and of Penacova on its perched site. *Cross the Mondego opposite Penacova and take the N 235.*

Luso. – Pop 2 726. *Facilities p 38.* The radio-active properties of the waters of this spa town are used in the treatment of kidney complaints.

Buçaco Forest★★★. – *Description p 56.*

Mealhada. – Pop 3 097. Mealhada, which is off the main road, the N 1, is famous for its roast sucking pig *(leitão assado)*.

Return to Coimbra on the N 1.

Conimbriga★. – *Round tour of 60km - 37 miles (twisting roads) – about 2 1/2 hours. Leave Coimbra by ③, the N 1. After 15km - 9 miles bear left towards Condeixa.*

Conimbriga Ruins★. – *Description p 67.*

Penela. – Pop 3 877. The village is overlooked by an 11 and 12C castle. From the keep, cut out of the living rock, the **panorama**★ includes the castle, the village and the Serra da Lousã to the east. The Church of Santa Eufémia, south of the castle, contains a Renaissance altarpiece of the Assumption surmounted by the Trinity, by the Coimbra school of sculpture.

Return to Coimbra by the N 110. The road winds its way through a green countryside.

Michelin map **37** fold 14 – 15km - 9 miles southwest of Coimbra

The Roman ruins of Conimbriga situated on a triangular spur bordered by two deep and narrow valleys are among the finest to be seen in the Iberian Peninsula.

A Celtic city stood on this spot as long ago as the Iron Age. The present ruins, however, are those of a Roman town situated on an important road which connected Braccaria – now Braga – in the north, and Olissipo – now Lisbon – in the south; it was founded in the first century and remained prosperous over a long period. In the 3C, before the threat of Barbarian invasion, the inhabitants were compelled to construct ramparts which, however, left part of the town outside the wall. In spite of these measures Conimbriga fell, in 468, to the Suebi and the town declined as Coimbra grew.

TOUR *about 1 hour*

Open 9am to 1pm and 2 to 8pm (6pm in winter); 30esc for the ruins only.

Leave the car in front of the museum and take the path towards the ruins, following the route marked on the plan.

The visitor at the entrance to the ruins walks along part of what was formerly the Roman road from Lisbon to Braga.

House of the Fountains★★. – The bases of the columns, the pavement and the layout of the rooms can be seen. The house which dates from the first half of the 3C was destroyed when the town wall was constructed. Inside are the atrium (**a**) or entrance vestibule, the peristyle (**b**) and the triclinium (**c**) which served as both sitting and dining room. The triclinium was bordered by a pool (**d**).

Around these rooms were the private living quarters and other communal rooms. The mosaics★★ covering the floors show extraordinary variety.

In a room to the left of the triclinium, a fine polychrome composition (**e**) shows hunting scenes, the Seasons and a chariot drawn by 4 horses harnessed abreast.

Another room (**f**) giving on to the impluvium, the tank which received the rain (**g**) presents some most elegant figures at a deer hunt.

A bedroom (**h** – cubiculum) has ornamental tiling with motifs based on geometrical designs and natural vegetation surrounding Silenus astride an ass being pulled forward by its halter. Next door, a sitting room (**k**), opening on to the peristyle, is decorated with a remarkable mosaic: in the centre of an ornament representing wading birds, dolphins and sting rays, a marine centaur surrounded by dolphins brandishes a standard and a fish. Finally in the southwest corner of the peristyle (**m**) Perseus stands, holding in his right hand Medusa's head which he appears to be offering to a monster from the deep.

Aqueduct. – The aqueduct, which was some 3km - 2 miles long, ended at the arch (reconstructed) abutting on the wall.

House of Cantaber★. – This important house is said to have belonged to Cantaber whose wife and children were captured by the Suebi during one of their attacks on the town in 465. A colonnade (**n**) preceded the atrium (**o**); passing from the atrium to the peristyle (**p**), note a special stone (**q**) in the paving, cut away to a rose tracery through which the drain can be seen. The impluvium (**r**) is to the left of the peristyle.

From the triclinium (**s**) you pass through several rooms with pools. The most interesting of these pools (**t**) is encircled by columns of which one has retained its original stucco painted in red. A suite of three rooms (**u**) adjoining the wall has a lovely pool and beds of flowers in the forms of a cross.

The tour of this large house ends at the private baths: the frigidarium (**v**) with its coldbaths; the tepidarium (warm baths) and the caldarium (hot baths – **w**) over the hypocaust (heated space connected with the furnace). The hypocaust's layout gives a clear idea of the plan of the house and the underground system of warm air circulation; a few lead pipes remain.

Other remains. – Lying northwest of the House of Cantaber, excavations have uncovered the monumental centre of the ancient town, in particular the forum, a hostelry and baths. To the southwest the craftsmen's quarter of the town and the monumental baths have also been discovered.

On the other side of the wall, another bath house (**x**) and an interesting hypocaust (**y**) can also be seen.

Return to the Roman way through two other houses where there are some fine mosaics.

Museum (Museu Monográfico). – *Open 9am to noon and 2 to 6pm; closed Mondays and holidays; 30esc for the museum only.*

Ceramics, sculptures, epigraphs, mosaics and various small objects recount the life of a Roman town from the beginning of the Roman Empire to the end of the 6C.

COSTA DA CAPARICA

Michelin map **37** fold 17 – *Facilities p 36*

On a coastal strip of farming land which is backed by an unbroken rampart of wooded cliffs, the Costa da Caparica beach resort is being developed all the time, growing parallel to the ocean from which it is protected by a ridge of sand dunes.

In season, a small train runs along the coast for 3km - 2 miles, giving access to this immensely long beach, where the fishing boats lie dormant, their prows adorned with a painted star or eye.

Capuchos Belvedere. – *3km - 2 miles to the east by motorway, then bear right on a road turning off from the N 377 (follow the road signs). In front of the convent "dos Capuchos" (Capuchins), turn right on to the paved lane leading to the belvedere on the cliff.*

Interesting view of the resort, the cliffs on the left of the belvedere, the Tagus estuary and the north coast as far as Cascais.

DOURO Valley ★

Michelin map **37** folds 2, 12 and 14 (inset) or **441** folds 22, 23 and 24

Only the lower course of the Douro, which is one of the largest rivers of the Iberian Peninsula, flows through Portugal. Tradition links the river's name with that of port wine, the grapes being harvested on the valley slopes near the Spanish border *(p 17)*.

GEOGRAPHICAL NOTES

Physical Characteristics. – The source of the Douro lies in Spain at an altitude of 2 060m - 6 759ft in the Sierra de Urbión, one of the *cordilleras* or transverse mountain ranges of the Iberian Peninsula. For nearly 525km - 325 miles the river winds its way through the Meseta before becoming, for 112km - 70 miles, the frontier between Spain and Portugal in a hilly region where its course drops rapidly as it cuts between high granite walls.

Once past Barca de Alva, as it enters the last 215km - 134 miles of its course, the Douro becomes entirely Portuguese. The valley grows less wild, although always remaining confined by granite and shale rocks, until it opens out into the estuary commanded by Oporto. The river's annual flow is subject, in the lower course, to heavy rain in autumn and winter and is very irregular: almost drought like conditions above Peso da Régua contrast sharply with violent autumn and winter floodwaters in the Oporto area.

The River's Resources. – The Douro has played an important part in the region's economic development since the 18C. It carried the *barcos rabelos,* typical flat bottomed craft with a tall square rig capable of shooting the rapids and used to transport fruit and, more importantly, port wine. This trade virtually ended, however, (except occasionally in periods of winter flooding), when roads and a railway were constructed along the valley from the Spanish border to Cinfães.

Nowadays, the aim is to harness the energy represented by the Douro Basin for the country as a whole. The project is favoured by the impermeability of the rocks, the river's own course and the narrowness of the valleys through which it flows. The exploitation of the river in its international section is shared: the upper waters allotted to Portugal are already controlled by three dams, the Miranda do Douro *(p 105)*, the Picote *(p 105)* and the Bemposta producing in 1983 2 milliard 597 million 10 000 kWh. The downstream waters allotted to Spain are controlled by the Aldeadávilla and Saucelle Dams. Below Barca de Alva 4 dams cut the river's course: Carrapatelo *(p 69)*, Pesó da Régua *(p 70)* Valeria and Pocinho; a fifth dam, Crestuma, is under construction.

Similar undertakings are projected for the Douro's tributaries: seventeen constructions are planned for the Tâmega, the Tua and the Sabor to the north and the Côa, the Távora and the Paiva to the south. The first to be finished is the Vilar Dam on the Távora.

The reservoir lakes formed by the dams will increase production from 6,3 milliard to nearly 8 milliard kWh, which is almost the country's total present hydro-electric production *(p 14)*.

DOURO VALLEY

0 5 10 15 20 25km

■ THE VINHO VERDE REGION★

The lower valley of the river, near Oporto, is not the domain of the great wine of that name but that of the well known *vinho verde* or **green wine** *(p 16)*, the local climate is such that the grapes cannot fully ripen here. The real Porto is made much further east, from Régua to the Spanish frontier.

The Douro, widened by successive dams, runs hemmed in by steep hills and winds round in great twists and turns. The shale and granite slopes, more wooded on the right bank and more cultivated on the left bank, where little white villages seem to hang between the vines, olive groves or fields of corn on terraces, with the river below, make a very sparkling landscape, despite the reminders of industrial civilization evidenced by the railway line, the Carrapatelo Dam, a few factories, and the installations for transporting coal from the Pejão mines (left bank).

Two winding roads, often picturesque, sometimes built into the cliff, sometimes level with the water, hug the banks of the Douro between Porto and Peso da Régua: the N 108 to the north, the N 222 to the south.

TOWNS AND SIGHTS *local map p 68*

Barrô. – Pop 1 475. There is a good view from the village of the valley's wooded slopes; the 12C Romanesque church – *take the path on the left on leaving the village from the east* – has a richly carved tympanum and a beautiful rose window.

Boa Vista Belvedere★ (Miradouro). – *On the N 226 between Samodães and Lamego.* There is a magnificient **view★** from this belvedere, of the Douro Valley. The northern bank especially is striped with vines on stakes and terraced olive groves; there are scattered villages and the occasional *quinta* (estate) then crowded with the houses of Peso da Régua down by the river. High up, cut out against the sky are the dry whitish summits of the Serra do Marão.

Carrapatelo Dam. – This undertaking is a dead-weight Dam, 170m - 558ft long with, on the left bank, a hydro-electric station and a fish ladder. In addition, on the right bank, it has a navigation lock nearly 90m - 295ft long which drops 43m - 141ft making it the lock with the greatest displacement in Europe.

Cinfães. – Pop 3 261. Cinfães is the commercial centre for *vinho verde*.

Resende. – Pop 3 108. Important wine production centre.

Santa Maria de Cárquere Priory. – *9km - 5 1/2 miles from Anreade (N 222), by the road from São Cipriano, to the south. At 5.5km - 3 1/2 miles, bear left.* Only the church and the funeral chapel of the lords of Resende remain, linked by a monumental arch. The church restored in the 13, 14, 16 and 17C (square crenellated tower and a Gothic chancel, the façade and nave are Manueline) still has a Romanesque doorway decorated with small columns and capitals with interlacing; the chancel under diagonal ribbed vaulting, has a door on the left with a high pediment and a double stringcourse of billets. The chapel, which has a remarkable Romanesque window with capitals of sculpted pelicans, contains four stone sarcophagi carved with animals and inscriptions.

THE PORT REGION★★
Round tour from Vila Real

106km - 66 miles – about 3 hours – local map p 68

The richness of the land, the smiling freshness of the countryside, the picturesque grape harvest *(mid September – end of October)* make this part of the Douro Valley a renowned tourist attraction. In summer the temperature can easily rise to 40ºC - 106ºF and help to ripen the grapes which will give **port** *(p 17)*.

Leave Vila Real (p 139) by the N 322 to the east in the direction of Sabrosa.

Mateus★. – *Description p 139.*

Sabrosa. – Pop 1 228. Magellan's birthplace *(p 20)*.

After Sabrosa, the N 323 descends towards the Douro and overlooks the deep valley of the Pinhão. The hillsides are striped with vines (sometimes fig trees) planted on terraces and dotted with white *quinta* houses.

7km - 4 miles before Pinhão there is a fine **view**★ of the Douro bend and the confluence of the Pinhão with the main stream.

Pinhão. – Pop 831. This village is an important port wine production centre. The railway station is decorated with *azulejos* illustrating the sites and the traditional costumes of the valley. Nearby on the river banks, the white vats *(cubas)* are lined up.

São João da Pesqueira. – Pop 1 984. *21km - 13 miles from Pinhão by the N 222 on the east.* The road winds in hairpin bends as far as Ervedosa through the well tended vineyards which cover the slopes going down to the Rio Torto. São João is a village of the plateau: its houses

(After secretaria de Estado da Informação e Turismo photo)

Harvesting the grapes in the Douro Valley.

with their mellowed roofs surround the **main square**★ which is given an unusual charm by the chapel, the arcades, the pretty turrets and the white balconied houses which stand upon it.

After Pinhão, the road (N 222) follows the valley between shale slopes which have been terraced and contained by small dry stone walls. The landscape alters completely, vines becoming the rule apart from the odd orange or almond tree. Then the road passes near the Peso da Régua Dam.

São Pedro de Balsemão Chapel; Lamego. – *23km - 14 miles to the south from the bridge over the Douro, the N 2.* The road rises through a smiling countryside, a bend affords a lovely **glimpse**★ of Peso da Régua and its setting. *After 7km - 4 miles, turn left into a paved road which descends to a bridge. Then an unsurfaced road leads to Balsemão.* The **chapel** *(times and charges not available at the time of going to press)* stands behind the village. Its 17C façade hides the sanctuary which is said to be the oldest in Portugal (7C: Visigothic period). The interior is divided into three naves by two rows of arcades resting on low columns which are crowned by Corinthian capitals.

Note also the sarcophagus of Alfonso Pires, the bishop of Oporto (d 1362), sculptured with low reliefs representing the Last Supper, the Crucifixion and a royal couple. The painted ceiling and the altarpieces date from the 17C.

Return to the N2 and turn left to **Lamego** *(p 87).*

Cross the river and turn right after the bridge to reach Peso da Régua.

Peso da Régua. – Pop 5 685. This small town, at the confluence of the Corgo and the Douro, is responsible for the administration of the port wine trade. It also organizes the transport by rail of the wines of the Upper Douro to Oporto and Vila Nova de Gaia.

Return to Vila Real by the N 2 which overlooks the Corgo Valley.

If you want to find a place name or other item by name refer to the index at the end of the guide.

ELVAS ★ ★

Michelin map **37** fold 7 – Pop 13 507 – *Facilities p 38*

Elvas, a few miles only from the Spanish citadel of Badajoz, is an impressive fortification still surrounded by ramparts. The town was not freed by the Christians from the Moorish occupation until 1226, while Lisbon had been liberated almost a hundred years before. Elvas subsequently resisted many assaults by the Spanish until 1580 when it was invested by Philip II's troops.

Today Elvas is a great agricultural marketing centre whose sugar plums are a gourmet's delight.

The War of the Oranges. – In 1801 Spain, under pressure from Napoleon, sent an ultimatum to Portugal, demanding that Portugal end the alliance with Britain and close her ports to British ships. Portugal refused and Spain declared war, sending her troops under Godoy into the Alentejo. Olivença offered no resistance and capitulated. On hearing the news Godoy, who had just begun the siege of Elvas, sent as a trophy to Queen Maria-Luisa of Spain two orange branches cut down by his soldiers from trees at the foot of the town ramparts. The trophy amused the citizens of Madrid who then gave the war its name.

In spite of the resistance of Elvas and Campo Major the Spanish won the war. In September peace was signed at Badajoz, Portugal lost Olivença and its lands and was obliged to close her ports to the English.

■ SIGHTS *time: 1 1/2 hours*

Ramparts★★. – The Elvas fortifications are the most accomplished example of 17C military architecture in Portugal. The sombre, well armoured merlons contrast with the white façades of the houses within. Fortified gates, moats, curtain walls, bastions and glacis form a remarkable defensive group completed to the south and north by the 17C Santa Luzia and the 18C Graça forts, each perched on a hill.

To appreciate fully the strength of the fortifications make a tour of the city *(5km - 3 miles)*.

Amoreira Aqueduct★. – The aqueduct was constructed between 1498 and 1622 to the plans of Francisco de Arruda *(p 22)*. It begins 7.5km - 5 miles southwest of the town to which it still brings water.
Enter the ramparts on the south side and go as far as the Rua da Cidadela; turn left beneath the 16C Arco do Relógio which opens on to the Praça da República.

Praça da República. – The square, bordered to the south by the former town hall and to the north by the old cathedral, has a mosaic paving of basalt, marble, and sandstone laid in geometrical patterns.

Old Cathedral (Sé). – The cathedral which was originally Gothic was rebuilt in the 16C by Francisco de Arruda in the Manueline style, which is particularly marked in the design of the belfry and the two lateral doorways.

The interior, where the pillars were decorated in the Manueline period, contains an 18C chancel entirely faced with marble.
Take the street on the right of the cathedral which leads to the Largo Santa Clara.

Largo Santa Clara★. – The *largo* is a small "square", triangular in shape, lined by houses with wrought iron grilles and façades bearing coats of arms; beneath a loggia an Arabic door flanked by two towers remains from the original 10C town wall.

The centre of the square is occupied by an interesting 16C marble **pillory**★ which still has four iron hooks attached to the capital.

Church of Our Lady of Consolation★ (Igreja Nossa Senhora da Consolação). – This church on the south side of the Largo Santa Clara was built in the 16C in the Renaissance style. It is an octagonal building whose interior, covered by a cupola resting on eight painted columns, is faced entirely in fine 17C multicoloured **azulejos**★.

The pulpit supported by a marble column, has a 16C wrought iron balustrade.

Elvas — Largo Santa Clara.

Pass beneath the Arabic arch and go up the street to the Largo da Alcáçova, bear left and then right into a picturesque alley which ends at the castle.

Castle. – Open 1 May to 30 September 9am to 12.30pm and 2 to 7pm; the rest of the year 9.30am to 12.30pm and 2 to 5.30pm; closed Thursdays.

The castle was constructed originally by the Moors and reinforced in the 14 and 16C. The 15C keep stands at the northwest corner. From the top of the ramparts there is a panorama of the town and its fortifications and the surrounding countryside scattered with olive trees and isolated farmsteads.

ERICEIRA

Michelin map **37** folds 11 (inset) and southwest of 16 – Pop 4 460 – *Facilities p 36*

A picturesque fishing port and very busy seaside resort where the colourful houses are grouped together on a cliff facing the Atlantic.

It is from here that on 5 October 1910, King Manuel II sailed into exile, while the Republic was proclaimed in Lisbon.

Harbour. – At the foot of the cliff strengthened with stonework shoring where the top forms a parapet for the corniche roads, there is a sheltered fishing beach, also protected on the north by a jetty.

From the square overlooking it *(Largo das Ribas)* there is a continual flow of spectators watching the fishing boats (small boats and trawlers being hauled up on to the sandy shore by tractors, even as far as the top of the steep road which links the beach to the corniche) and the unloading of the catch of fish and octopus.

Church precinct. – Old cobbled alleys with lovely low white houses, their corner-stones painted blue, surround the parish church *(igreja paroquial)*.

The interior of the church has a beautiful coffered ceiling and *azulejos* with polychrome edging.

The association between Portugal and Great Britain goes back 600 years.
For details on "Our Oldest Ally" see p 20.

ESPICHEL, Cape ★

Michelin map **37** fold 18

Cape Espichel, at the southern tip of the Arrábida Mountain Chain *(p 45)*, is a true World's End beaten continuously by violent winds.

It was off this cape that **Dom Fuas Roupinho**, who had already distinguished himself before King Afonso I in the wars against the Moors, vanquished the enemy again in 1180 in a brilliant victory at sea, when Portuguese sailors, although inexperienced in this type of warfare, succeeded in capturing several enemy ships.

In this desolate **setting** ★ in the vast square where the street ends, may be seen the ruins of Our Lady of the Cape. This spot has been a popular pilgrimage centre since the 13C. The arcaded outbuildings were erected during the 18C by pilgrims.

Sanctuary of Our Lady of the Cape (Santuário Nossa Senhora do Cabo). – The church built in the Classical style at the end of the 17C has a Baroque interior decorated lavishly with gilded wood.

Go round the sanctuary by the left and walk to the cliff edge. The church overlooks the sheer drop of 100 m - 350 ft to the sea. To the west and below a second chapel decorated with *azulejos*, lies a small creek.

ESTORIL ★

Michelin map **37** folds 12 (inset) and 17 – Pop 25 230 – *Facilities p 36*
See town plan in the current Michelin Red Guide España Portugal

Estoril has developed as a sea and winter resort, favoured by a mild climate and a temperature which averages 12°C - 54°F in winter. It lies on the *corniche* road linking Lisbon and Cascais, a point on the Costa de Estoril which is famous for its luminous skies.

Formerly a small village known to a few for the healing properties of its waters, Estoril now attracts an elegant international circle who come for the resort's entertainments (golf, casino and sea fishing), its sporting events (motor and horse racing, regattas), its pleasing situation facing Cascais Bay, its park of tropical and exotic plants and trees, palm lined avenues, beaches of fine sand and its highly successful festivals (the Festival of the Sea in July, etc.).

ESTRELA, Serra da ★

Michelin map **37** folds 3 and 4 or **441** fold 34

The Serra da Estrela, a great mountain barrier 60km - 40 miles long by 30km - 20 miles wide is the highest massif in Portugal. Above the cultivated and wooded slopes appear the arid and boulder strewn summits, the tallest of which is the Torre with an altitude of 1 991m - 6 532ft.

Tourism is developing in this formerly isolated area: Penhas da Saúde has become a winter sports resort; Covilhã, Seia, Gouveia and Manteigas, small towns within reach of the plain, have become starting points for mountain excursions.

Geographical Notes. – The Serra da Estrela is a granite block extending further to the southwest, the central mountain range of Spain. It is limited to north and south by two rock fault escarpments which for several hundred yards overlook the Valleys of the Mondego and the Zêzere. The range ends abruptly in the west dominating the shale ridges of the Serra da Lousã. With the exception of the deep cleft formed by the Ice Age in the Upper Valley of the Zêzere, the relief is fairly uniform, the majority of the peaks having an altitude of some 1 500m - 4 800ft.

Tree vegetation – pines and oaks – ceases at about 1 300m - 4 250ft giving place to a close carpet of grass, a few flowers and rocks. Only the valley floors are cultivated with maize and rye; the summits receive 2m - 7ft of rain and snow each year, remaining frozen for nine months out of twelve. Summer, when it comes, is usually hot and very dry.

Formerly only a few shepherds haunted the region, seeking new pastures for their beasts; nowadays great flocks of sheep and herds of goats come from the Mondego Valley to the mountains every summer, providing material for the developing wool industry at Covilhã and Fundão and the manufacture in winter of a delicious cheese, the *Queijo da Serra* (mountain cheese) made from a mixture of ewes' and goats' milk.

① THE MOUNT TORRE ROAD ★★
From Covilhã to Seia – *49km - 30 miles – about 2 hours – local map p 73*

This itinerary includes the highest road in Portugal *(often closed to traffic until the end of April because of snow).*

On leaving Covilhã *(p 74)*, the road rises rapidly through pine and oakwoods which soon thin out, revealing wide views.

Penhas da Saúde. – *Facilities p 38.* Winter sports and summer holiday resort.

The landscape becomes hillier with here and there a reservoir or glacier lake.

Leave the Manteigas road (in poor condition) on the right (described on p 73).

After a bend bringing the road parallel with the Upper Valley of the Zêzere, the **landscape** ★ takes on a desolate appearance from the large quantity of worn granite boulders which lie strewn upon it. A niche hollowed out of the rock on the right hand side of the road *(car park)* shelters a statue of Our Lady of the Holy Star (Nossa Senhora da Boa Estrela) and provides the setting for a religious festival held each year on the second Sunday in August.

There is an interesting **view** ★ from a belvedere arranged in a bend on the left, a short distance from the summit, of the glacial Upper Valley of the Zêzere. The river's actual source is hidden by a 300m - 900ft high granite cone, known locally as the "slender pitcher" *(Cântaro Magro)*, which has been cut into even blocks by freezing ice.

Bear left to the Torre peak.

Torre★★★. – From the summit the **panorama**★★★ includes the Mondego Valley, the Serra da Lousã and the Zêzere Valley.

The road continues over the crest , winding its way between rocks and moss covered boulders and around lakes.

The "long lake", Lagoa Comprida, its deep blue waters controlled by a dam parallel with the road, is the largest single expanse of water in the *serra*. The descent into the Mondego Valley, where both crops and villages are to be found, is swift and the **views**★★ are magnificent. After **Sabugueiro,** a village of granite walled houses the road drops steeply and trees reappear.

Seia. – A small town pleasantly situated at the foot of the *serra*.

② **UPPER VALLEY OF THE ZÊZERE**★★

From Gouveia to Covilhã – *via Manteigas 77km - 48 miles – about 2 1/2 hours – local map below*

The route crosses the massif by way of the Upper Valley of the Zêzere.

Gouveia. – Pop 3 580. Small attractive town built halfway up one of the slopes of the Mondego Valley.

The upper plateaux scattered with rocks are soon reached; some of the granite boulders have been worn by erosion into astonishing forms, as for instance the Old Man's Head (Cabeça do Velho) which rises from a mass of rocks on the left of the road. The source of the Mondego *(Nascente do Mondego-signposted)*, the longest river entirely in Portugal, rises at an altitude of 1 360m - 4 462ft just before Penhas Douradas.

The descent becomes brutal as hairpin bends twist down to the Zêzere Valley; a man-made belvedere affords a **view**★ of the valley upstream which is commanded by Manteigas.

Manteigas. – Pop 3 026. 17C houses with wooden balconies.

At Manteigas leave the N 232 and turn right.

Alternative route★ **by Belmonte.** – *Leaving from Manteigas. Additional distance: 19km - 12 miles.* The road (N 232) follows the Zêzere Valley, here quite different in its cheerful aspect and cultivated land from its glacial part higher up *(see below).*

Belmonte. – *Description p 51.*

Return to the N 18 which, taken on the left, leads to Covilhã.

A little after the small spa of Caldas de Manteigas, note on the side of the road the fish farm *(posto aquicola)* at Fonte Santa *(open 9am to 7pm).* Further on there are still a few sheepfolds, then the mountain solitude takes over. However, cultivated terraces can be seen on the lower slopes.

After the bridge over the Zêzere, the road *(in poor condition)* continues upstream until it reaches the rock face of the glacial valley *(see below)* which it then climbs to the top.

Hell's Well★ **(Poço do Inferno).** – *6km - 4 miles by a narrow unsurfaced road.* The road affords good occasional views of Manteigas in its setting. Hell's Well is a wild but wooded defile given considerable beauty by a **cascade**★.

The road runs level with the edge of the ancient glacial valley where the Zêzere flows.

Zêzere Glacial Valley★ (Vale Glaciário do Zêzere). – This valley is a perfect example of glacial relief: U-shaped contour with consequent steep slopes, hanging tributary valleys and connecting gorges, cirque at the highest point; cascades, enormous erratic boulders strewn on the bottom, and on the slopes, scraggy vegetation.

Half-way along this rectilinear section, jagged outlines appear which, in front and on the right, encircle the glacial cirque, the peak of the Cântaro Magro and the Torre pyramid. The road bears westwards and passes near the source of the Zêzere – signposted "Cântaros" (not visible from the road but it can be reached on foot through huge boulders). A little further on, at a fountain, there is a lovely extensive **view**★ across the glacial valley which one has just skirted.

At the final pass, take the N 339 to the left towards Covilhã.

Covilhã. – Pop 21 689. Covilhã, spread over the first wooded foothills of the southern flank of the Serra da Estrela, close to the rich Zêzere Valley, which at this point is known as the Cova da Beira, is both a climatic resort and an excursion centre and is also the dormitory town for the Penhas da Saúde winter sports resort.

The town is equally well known for its *Queijo da Serra*, a strong cheese made from ewes' milk. Sheep also supply the wool which is woven in this small industrial town into yarn sufficient for two-thirds of the country's woollen industry.

③ THE WESTERN SIDE OF THE SERRA ★
From Covilhã to Seia by Unhais da Serra – *84km - 52 miles – about 2 hours – local map p 73*

This route goes round the *serra* by the west along a road which runs almost constantly at an altitude of between 600 and 700m - 2 000 and 2 300 ft. Throughout there are interesting views to the left, first over the Zêzere Valley and the Serra da Gardunhã, later over the shale hillocks of the Serra da Lousã and finally towards the Mondego Valley.

Leave Covilhã (above) by the N 230 going south.

The Serra da Estrela's high peaks come into sight beyond Tortosendo.

Unhais da Serra. – A small spa and climatic resort in a lovely **setting** ★ at the mouth of a torrent filled valley.

Villages, such as **Alvoco da Serra**, cling halfway up the hillsides or, as does **Loriga**, stand perched upon a spur in the valley. The terraced valley floors are put to full use growing crops (maize) in even sweeps.

Senhora do Desterro. – *3km - 2 miles from São Romão.* The road climbs the Alva Valley to Senhora do Desterro where you leave the car. Take the path on the left cut out of the rock which will bring you *(1/4 hour on foot Rtn)* to the Old Woman's Head (Cabeça da Velha), a granite rock worn by erosion.

Continue to Seia, see the route described p 73.

To find a town, a sight or setting,
a historical or geographical reference
described in this guide,
consult the index pp 160-162

ESTREMOZ

Michelin map **37** fold 7 – Pop 7 869

Estremoz, standing at the centre of a region of marble quarries, is a pleasant city, still possessing its 17C ramparts and dominated by its medieval castle. It is, and has been since the 16C, a well known centre for Alentejo pottery which can be seen most fully and picturesquely displayed on the main square *(Rossio)* on market days *(Saturdays)*.

The Estremoz Potteries. – In addition to wide mouthed jars *(bilhas)* and narrow mouthed jars *(barris)*, the potteries of Estremoz manufacture decorative ware in which to keep water cool and serve it at table. The goglets *(moringues)* with one handle and two spouts and the kings' jugs *(púcaros dos reis)*, their names testifying to former royal favour, although unglazed are decorated with geometrical or stylized foliage motifs which are sometimes engraved and inlaid with white marble chips. A more recent and less elegant ornament consists of sticking on oak twigs. *Fidalgo* is the name by which the large, big bellied, glazed pots ornamented with small bunches of flowers are known.

Estremoz is equally famous for its pottery figurines which are naïve in style and vividly coloured: religious (characters from the Christmas crib and saints) and secular figures (peasants at their everyday tasks, caricatures) and animals are reproduced from old designs whose realism and picturesque qualities have lost none of their savour.

The general view ★. – If you arrive from the south you will get an attractive general view of the old town perched on the hillside round its ancient keep, and below, the modern white town.

(After a P.U.F. photo)

Estremoz — A moringue.

■ THE LOWER TOWN

Enter the 17C ramparts through a gate which opens on to the modern town. Here the houses have wrought iron balconies and are decorated with coloured tiles.

Rural Museum. – *At no 62b of the main square. Guided tour (time: 1 hour) 10am to 1pm and 3 to 6pm (5pm in winter); closed Mondays; 20esc.*

This small but interesting museum uses models of local crafts and costumes to portray the life of the people of Alentejo.

Church of Our Lady of the Martyrs (Nossa Senhora dos Mártires). – *2km - 1 mile south (road to Bencatel).*

The church dates from 1 844 and has a monumental Gothic chevet. In the nave, (the entrance being indicated by a triumphal Manueline arch), and in the chancel there are beautiful *azulejos*.

■ THE UPPER TOWN *time: 1 hour*

Walk to the Manueline pillory at the north end of the Rossio and take a small uphill alley on the right. A 14C doorway marks the entrance to the old town where the houses are either Gothic or Manueline.

Keep. – *Apply to the pousada.*

The keep, which was built in the 13C, is crowned with small pyramid shaped merlons and flanked in its upper part by galleries supported on consoles. On your way to the topmost platform, look at the lovely octagonal room with trefoil windows on the second floor. From the platform there is a circular view of the town and the Alentejo where the Serra de Ossa heights can be seen against the sky to the south.

Chapel of the Queen Saint. – *Guided tour; apply, except on Mondays, to Largo D. Dinis B. Go round the keep and King Dinis's palace and through the grille to enter the chapel.*

The chapel has walls which are covered with beautiful *azulejos* depicting scenes in the life of the **Queen Saint Isabel of Aragon**, wife of King Dinis. The Miracle of the Roses scene is the most delightful: in it the queen, surprised by the king, as she is carrying gold to distribute to the poor, opens the pleats of her skirt to banish her husband's suspicions, revealing only roses within the folds.

Church of St Mary. – 16C. This square church contains paintings by the Portuguese primitives. The majority are in the sacristy which is further embellished with a marble lavabo.

King Dinis's Audience Chamber. – A beautiful Gothic colonnade is the outstanding feature of this chamber whose star vaulting dates from the Manueline period. The Queen Saint Isabel and King Pedro I both died in this room in 1336 and 1367 respectively.

EXCURSION

Crucifix Museum (Museu de Cristo). – *10km - 6 miles to the east by the N 4. In the village of Villa-Lôbos, which is on the right of the road. 3.5km - 2 miles after the turn off to Arcos. Guided tours (time: 1 hour) 9am to 9pm.*

Interesting collections of 3 000 crucifixes, dating from the 8C to the present and 600 mortar bowls (11-19C).

A visit to ecclesiastical and civil buildings will be all the more interesting if you first read pp 21-25.

ÉVORA ★★★

Michelin map **37** fold 7 – Pop 35 117 – *Facilities p 38*

Évora, a walled town since Roman times, is now most attractively Moorish in character with alleys cut by arches, brilliantly white houses, hanging gardens, terraces, *moucharabiehs* or pierced balconies and tiled patios.

From its rich past Évora retains several medieval and Renaissance palaces and mansions which in themselves provide a panoply of Portuguese architecture. The buildings are floodlit during the season from 9pm to midnight, making an evening stroll through the old twisting alleyways a delight.

The Alentejo capital is today the great agricultural market for the province and the base for several dependent industries (cork, leather, woollen carpets, painted furniture).

HISTORICAL NOTES

Évora flowered when the Romans inhabited the town, declined under the Visigoths and in 715 was occupied by the Mohammedans. Their long rule benefited the town which became an important agricultural and trading centre grouped round the Moorish castle and mosque.

Gerald the Fearless (Geraldo Sempavor). – In the 12C internal quarrels among the Mohammedans encouraged the Christians under Alfonso I *(p 19)* to rebel. One, Gerald the Fearless, gained the confidence of the Mohammedan king of Évora and brought off a bold plot: one September night in 1165 he managed alone to take the watchtower northwest of the town; from there he alerted the Mohammedan town guard who promptly hurried to the tower, leaving Gerald's companions-in-arms to advance from the far side and take Évora without difficulty.

A Centre of Humanism. – From the end of the 12C, Évora was the preferred capital of the kings of Portugal and in the 15 and 16C enjoyed brilliant renown. Artists and learned men surrounded the court: humanists such as Garcia and André de Resende, the chronicler Duarte Galvão, the creator of Portuguese drama, Gil Vicente *(p 84)*, the sculptor Nicolas Chanterene *(p 23)* and the painters Cristóvão de Figueiredo and Gregório Lopes. Mansions, monasteries and convents were built everywhere in the Manueline or Renaissance styles; the Mohammedan style of decoration was brought back into favour by some architects and formed part of a new hybrid style, the Luso-Moorish *(p 22)*. Finally a Jesuit University was founded in 1559 at the instigation of the Cardinal patron, Dom Henrique.

But in 1580, following the disaster of El-Ksar El-Kebir, Portugal was annexed by Spain and Evora declined rapidly. Although Portugal recovered its independence in the revolt of 1637 and the Portuguese Crown was restored, the town never recovered its former sparkle and in 1759 *(p 121)* the suppression of the University extinguished its last brilliance.

ÉVORA★★★

■ **MAIN SIGHTS** *time: 3 hours*

Leave the car on the Praça do Giraldo, the bustling centre of the town and follow on foot the itinerary indicated on the town plan.

Rua 5 de Outubro (BZ). – This street is attractively lined with houses with wrought iron balconies and arts and crafts shops; no 30 has a niche decorated with *azulejos*.

Cathedral★★ (**Sé**) (BZ). – The cathedral, built in the 12 and 13C in the Transitional Gothic style, has a plain granite façade flanked by two massive towers crowned by conical spires added in the 16C. The tower on the right consists of several turrets similar to those on the lantern tower over the transept. The nave and aisle walls are cut by crenellations.

The main doorway, preceded by a Gothic porch, is framed with 14C statues of the Apostles.

Interior★. – The nave, with broken barrel vaulting, has an elegant triforium; to the left, a Baroque chapel contains a 15C statue of the Virgin Great With Child in multicoloured stone; opposite is a 16C statue in gilded wood of the Angel Gabriel attributed to Olivier of Ghent.

A very fine octagonal **dome★** on squinches stands above the transept crossing whose arms are lit by two Gothic rose windows.

In the north transept the Renaissance archway to a chapel is decorated with a carved marble head by Nicolas Chanterene. The second chapel in the south transept contains the tomb of the 16C humanist André de Resende. The chancel was remodelled in the 18C by Friederich Ludwig, architect of the monastery at Mafra.

Apply to the sacristan to visit the treasury, the cloisters and the choir stalls 9am to noon (11am Sundays) and 2 to 5pm; closed holidays and Thursday, Friday and Saturday before Easter Sunday and during services; 50esc.

Treasury★. – The treasury consists of sacerdotal ornaments, a large collection of ecclesiastical plate, including a fine 13C French **Virgin★★** in ivory and a 17C reliquary cross in silver gilt and multicoloured enamel decorated with 1 426 precious stones.

Cloisters★. – These 14C Gothic cloisters have a massive appearance, accentuated further by their being built of granite, in spite of the elegance of rounded bays with radiating tracery. Statues of the Evangelists stand in each of the four corners, from which, in the southwest, there is a good view of the Romanesque belfry.

An adjoining chapel contains the 14C tomb of the founder bishop and 14C statues of the Angel Gabriel and a polychrome Virgin whose modelling shows French influence.

Choir stalls★. – The stalls, which are in the gallery *(coro alto)*, are Renaissance in style with a decoration of sacred and secular motifs. A staircase leads to the cathedral roofs from which one can look down on the town.

Roman Temple★ (BY A). – This Corinthian style temple erected in the 2C was probably dedicated to Diana. The capitals and bases of the columns are of Estremoz marble, the column shafts of granite. The temple owes its relative conservation to its having been transformed into a fortress in the Middle Ages and excavated only a century ago.

Palace of the Dukes of Cadaval (**Paço dos Duques de Cadaval**) (BY B). – This palace, protected by two crenellated towers, and with a façade remodelled in the 17C, was given in 1390 by King João I to his councillor, Martim Afonso de Melo, *alcalde* of Évora. The kings João III and João V also lived at different periods within its walls. The north tower formed part of the medieval city walls.

In the **Gallery of the Dukes of Cadaval** *(same opening times as the Dos Lóios Church (see below)* are a collection of the Cadaval family historic documents and two fine Flemish commemorative plaques in bronze, dating from the end of the 15C.

Dos Lóios Monastery★ (**Convento dos Lóios**) (BCY). – The Dos Lóios or St Eligius Monastery, consecrated to St John the Evangelist, was founded in the 15C.

Church★. – *Guided tour (time: 1/2 hour) 10am to 12.30pm and 2 to 5pm; closed Mondays and holidays; 70esc.*

The façade was remodelled following the earthquake of 1755 with the exception of the porch which protects a Flamboyant Gothic doorway. The coat of arms beneath a canopy belongs to the Melos, Counts of Olivença, for whom the church served as a mausoleum. The nave, with lierne and tierceron vaulting, is lined with beautiful *azulejos* (1711) by António de Oliveira Bernardes depicting the life of St Laurence Justinian. Two grilles in the pavement enable one to see, on the left, the medieval castle's cistern and, on the right, an ossuary. There is a 17C Crucifix in the sacristy.

Conventual buildings. – *The conventual buildings have been transformed into a* pousada.

The Late Gothic style cloisters were given extra height in the 16C by the addition of a Renaissance gallery.

The chapterhouse **door**★ has outstanding elegance architecturally and is a good example of the composite Luso-Moorish style *(details p 22)*; the crowning piece over the doorway and the piers topped by pinnacles which serve as a framework to the door, are Gothic inspired; the columns are twisted and Manueline in style and the twin bays with horseshoe arches are, like the capitals, reminiscent of Moorish design.

Note, in some areas, remains of the former Roman wall protecting the city.

Museum of Ancient Art★ (Museu de Évora) (BZ M). – *Open 10am to 12.30pm and 2 to 5pm; closed Mondays and holidays; 50esc.*

The museum is in the former 16 and 17C episcopal palace. The ground floor is devoted to Roman, medieval, Manueline and Luso-Moorish sculpture: outstanding are a fragment of a marble **low relief**★ of a vestal virgin, a 14C **Annunciation**★ also in marble, and a 16C Holy Trinity in Ançã stone. Among the Primitive paintings on the first floor may be seen an early 16C polyptych of the Flemish school representing the Life of the Virgin; the six panels of an altarpiece's predella by the Flemish school showing Christ's Passion and several 16C paintings by the Portuguese artists Frei Carlos and Gregório Lopes.

Mansion of the Counts of Portalegre (BZ C). – A Gothic and 16C Manueline style mansion embellished by a patio surrounded by a hanging garden and a *moucharabieh* balcony.

Garcia de Resende's Mansion (BZ E). – A 16C house in which the humanist Garcia de Resende is said to have lived. Manueline decoration adorns the three sets of paired windows on the first floor.

ÉVORA★★★

Moura Gates Square★ (Largo das Portas de Moura) (CZ). – Two towers, which formed part of the medieval town fortifications command the northern entrance to this picturesque square whose centre is taken up by a beautiful Renaissance **fountain★**. The fountain consists of a column surmounted by a white marble sphere. Several lovely houses border the square: the 16C **Cordovil mansion (F)** on the south side presents an elegant loggia with twin arcades, festooned horseshoe arches and Moorish capitals. A crenellated roof surmounted by a conical spire crowns all.

Soure Mansion (CZ K). – This 15C house was formerly a part of the Palace of the Infante Dom Luis. The Manueline façade includes a gallery of five rounded arches crowned by a conical spire.

Make for the Largo da Graça by way of the Travessa da Caraça.

Church of Our Lady of Grace (Igreja Nossa Senhora da Graça) (BZ L). – This church, built in the 16C in the Italian Renaissance style, has a façade of granite, a portico with Tuscan columns, Classical pilasters and a decoration of bosses and atlantes.

Church of St Francis (Igreja de São Francisco) (BZ N). – This early 16C church, which is preceded by a portico pierced by rounded, tiers-point and horseshoe arches, is crowned with battlements and conical pinnacles, some twisted. The Manueline doorway is surmounted by a pelican and an armillary sphere, the emblems respectively of João II and King Manuel.

The interior, covered by ogive vaulting, surprises by its size – the chancel contains two galleries, that on the right being Renaissance, that on the left Baroque.

The former chapterhouse *(access through the south transept)* is furnished with a balustrade of fluted marble and turned ebony columns and, as a covering to the walls, *azulejos* depicting scenes from the Passion.

(After Secretaria de Estado da Informação e Turismo photo)

Travessa da Caraça.

Take the door to the left of the balustrade in the former chapterhouse.

Ossuary Chapel★ (Casa dos Ossos). – *Guided tour (1/4 hour) 8am to 1pm and 2.30 to 6pm; 20esc.*

This macabre chapel was erected in the 16C by a Franciscan to induce meditation in his fellow men. The bones and skulls of 5 000 people have been used to face the walls and pillars with designs in false relief. At the entrance the braids of young women who are to be married are hung as ex-votos.

Return to the Praça do Giraldo by way of the picturesque Travessa and Rua dos Mercadores.

■ ADDITIONAL SIGHTS

Fortifications★. – A considerable amount remains of the three series of walls which were required to protect the town at different periods. Traces of the 1C Roman wall, reinforced by the Visigoths in the 7C, can be seen between the Palace of the Dukes of Cadaval and that of the Counts of Basto (Largo dos Colegiais). The 14C medieval wall marks the town limits to the north and west and can be seen from the *Estrada da Circunvalação* between ④ and ① on the plan. The 17C fortifications now form the boundary of the public gardens in the south.

Former Jesuit University (Universidade de Évora) (CY U). – The university now occupies the former building of the Jesuit university which was suppressed in 1759. At least visit the inner courtyard *(ask permission of the administration: 9am to 12.30pm and 3 to 5pm; closed Saturday afternoons and Sundays).*

Buildings in the 16C Italian Renaissance style surround what is known as the main Students' Cloister, with its arched gallery – the whole forming a graceful inner court. Facing the entrance, the pediment over the portico to the Hall of Acts is decorated with statues personalizing the royal and the ecclesiastical universities.

The classrooms opening on the gallery are adorned with 18C *azulejos* representing the subjects taught in the different rooms – physics, history, philosophy, mathematics.

Public Gardens (Jardim público) (BZ). – Part of the 16C palace of King Manuel (P) and the ruins of another 16C palace (R) still stand in the gardens. Note the paired windows with horseshoe arches in the Luso-Moorish style.

St Blaise's Chapel (Ermida de São Brás) (BZ S). – This fortified 15C church has rounded buttresses covered with pepper pot roofs, the polygonal chancel is covered by a dome.

Church-Museum "das Mercês" (AZ M²). – *Closed Mondays and holidays; 20esc. If closed apply to the Museum of Ancient Art (p 77).*

The interior of the church (1670) lined with polychrome *azulejos*, has been turned into a museum of 17-18C sacred art. Note particularly a *Pietà*, as well as other statues, one of which is a small Virgin and Child *(chapel on the left)*, two gilded altarpieces, an Indo-Portuguese oratory, and sacerdotal ornaments.

Monastery (Convento) of São Bento de Castris. – *3km - 2 miles to the northwest by* ⑤, *the N 114-4. After passing the aqueduct built in the 16C, turn left to the former Monastery of São Bento de Castris. Ask permission to visit.*

The 16C church in the Manueline style has network vaulting, walls covered with 18C *azulejos* illustrating the life of St Bernard, and a chapterhouse in the Gothic style with traces of Renaissance influence in its decoration.

The **cloister**★ *(first vaulted passage beyond the church)* in the Luso-Moorish style is as cool and elegant as when it was first built in the 16C. Above a gallery of arcades paired beneath horseshoe arches is an upper gallery with depressed arches.

EVORAMONTE ★

Michelin map 🔢 fold 7 – Pop 935

The spruce, little fortified town of Evoramonte has a remarkable **setting**★, having been built at the top of a high hill in the Alentejo.

It was at Evoramonte on 26 May 1834 that the Convention was signed which ended the civil war and under which the liberal son of João VI, Pedro IV, Emperor of Brazil, compelled his brother Miguel 1, an extremist whom he had vanquished at the Battle of Asseiceira, to abdicate in favour of his niece Maria and to go into exile.

Access. – *1.5km - 1 mile from the modern village which is on the N 18, by a very steep road signposted "Castelo d'Evoramonte".*

After skirting the base of the 14-17C ramparts, go through the gate, parking the car in the main street facing the keep. It is peaceful and attractive with the well kept, low built houses, brilliantly white and splashed with colour from the many balconies of flowers.

The Convention House. – One of the houses on the left where the convention was signed bears a commemorative plaque.

Castle★. – *Apply to the caretaker who lives in the Convention House.*

The castle which was first Roman, then Moorish, then radically remodelled in the 14C, emerges as a Gothic style military monument in spite of further reconstruction in the 16C. Three storeys are superimposed, each consisting of a hall with nine Gothic arches resting on robust central pillars, those on the ground floor being massive and twisted.

From the top, there is a **panorama**★ of the surrounding countryside speckled with olive trees and small white village, and to the northeast, Estremoz in its setting.

Parish Church. – The church, with its original transverse bell-gable, has a distinctive outline as it stands at the end of the main street.

FARO ★

Michelin map 🔢 fold 10 – Pop 28 622 – *Facilities p 36*

The capital of Algarve is sited on Portugal's most southerly headland. Faro lives on salt collected from its *ria,* fishing (tunny and sardine), its cork factories and marble works, food processing (beans) and canning, its plastics and building industries. The building of the airport nearby has made Faro the Algarve terminal from which visitors diverge all the year round to the seaside resorts along the coast. The vast sand beach of Faro, situated on an island, attracts a great many tourists.

Historical Notes. – Faro was already an important city when, in 1249, Alfonso III recaptured it from the Moors and so marked the end of Arab power in Portugal. The king presented the city with a municipal charter and its development was such that by the 15C a printing works belonging to the Jewish community was publishing Hebraic incunabula, the first books to be printed in Portugal.

Unfortunately in July 1596, when the country was under the domination of Spain, Charles Howard and Robert, 2nd Duke of Essex, who had been sent by Elizabeth in an expedition against Cadiz, sacked and then burnt the town to the ground. As Faro sought to rise from the ruins two earthquakes in 1722 and 1755, particularly the latter, reduced all to rubble once more. It needed the vigour of Bishop Dom Francisco Gomes, the town's most famous citizen, to undertake its reconstruction. The prelate passed his entire episcopacy encouraging, advising, building and planting throughout his diocese so that the people would learn the best agricultural methods and the best trees and plants to grow for the re-establishment of the town and its environs.

The Algarve Almond Trees. – The Algarve is famous for its beaches, but its hinterland is equally beautiful with groves of fig, orange and almond trees. Legend has it that a Moorish emir married to a Scandinavian princess who languished for her Nordic snows, ordered a vast sweep of almond trees to be planted in his domain. One January morning, the princess was amazed to see the countryside covered in myriad almond flowers whose dazzling whiteness, being no less than that of the snow, greatly delighted her.

■ **SIGHTS** *time: 1 1/2 hours*

Sea front. – The life of this resort revolves round the harbour *(doca),* which has character and a certain elegance due to the 15m - 45ft obelisk (A A) standing in the centre of the Dom Francisco Gomes Square, the wide avenues, as well as the palms bordering the Avenida da Republica, particularly those standing in the Manuel Bivar Gardens.

Maritime Museum (Museu Maritimo) (A M¹). – *Open 9.30am to 12.30pm and 2 to 5.30pm; Saturdays 9.30am to 1pm; closed Sundays and holidays.*

The museum is in the harbour master's office. The outstanding exhibits are the numerous model ships and minatures of different types of fishing vessels.

Old Town. – The old town lies south of the Manuel Bivar Gardens, a peaceful quarter resting in the shadow of the circle of houses which stand like ramparts around it.

Arco da Vila (A). – The Arco da Vila pierces the old Afonso wall. It has Italian style pilasters and, in a niche, a white marble statue of St Thomas Aquinas.

Cathedral (Sé) (A B). – The cathedral, rebuilt in the 18C, stands behind a heavy porch, supporting an exterior belfry at one side. It is decorated throughout, most noticeably in the Rosary Chapel, with 17C *azulejos*.

Municipal Museum (A M²). – *Renovation underway. Open 9am to noon and 2 to 6pm; closed Saturdays, Sundays and holidays; 40esc.*

It is installed in the former 16C Convent of Our Lady of the Assumption *(restored)*.

Archaeological collection (Museu Arqueológico Lapidar do Infante Dom Henrique). – It is housed in the cloister galleries and contains various remains found at Milreu *(below)* – capitals, mosaics, a Roman sepulture of the 1C AD, a 15C sarcophagus, a 16C bishop's throne, and ancient weapons and coins. Moorish earthenware jars and Mudejar *azulejos* evoke the Moslem and post-Moslem periods of local art.

Ferreira do Almeida collection. – It is in the former chapel and includes sculptures (14C statues in jaspar; a lovely 18C Christ in wood, small scale reproductions in bronze or jade of universally known masterpieces), 18C paintings, Spanish furniture, etc.

Carmelite Church (Igreja do Carmo) (A E). – *Open 10am to 1pm and 3 to 7pm, closed Saturday afternoons and all day Sunday.* This Baroque church hides, abutting on its north transept near the tombs of a former graveyard, an **Ossuary Chapel** which is entirely faced with bones and skulls.

Ethnographic Museum (Museu de Etnografia Régional) (B M³). – *Guided tour (time: 1/2 hour) 9.30am to 12.30pm and 2 to 5pm; closed weekends and holidays; 20esc.*

This museum evokes traditional life in the Algarve, with photographs, paintings, everyday objects, models (one of which is a madrague: the huge net formerly used to catch tunny fish), reconstructions (a grocer's shop, interior of a peasant's house with the kitchen, stables, bread oven), and models displaying costumes, etc.

Santo António Belvedere (Miradouro) (B F). – *Open sunrise to sunset. Ring at the doorway of the building to the left of the chapel.*

In the courtyard a small museum devoted to St Antony. From the belfry belvedere at the top of some steep stairs, the **panorama** ★ spreads out over the town and the lagoon (the best time is after midday when the afternoon sun accentuates the relief of the coastal hills).

EXCURSIONS

Faro beach (Praia). – *9km - 6 miles by ①, the N 125 and a signposted road on the left, or by boat – from the Arco da Porta Nova landing stage. Facilities p 36.* This belt of sand connected with the mainland by a bridge has been turned into a beach resort. From the eastern end there is a good **view**★ of Faro and its white houses reflected in the lagoon.

Milreu; Estói. – *10km - 6 miles to the northeast. Leave Faro by ②, the N 2. After 9km - 5 1/2 miles turn right on the Estói road (towards Tavira).*

Roman remains at Milreu. – A square apse and two sections of marble columns, are all that remain of a temple of Roman Ossonoba, a town of the 1C AD. Round the temple, brick foundations of houses and baths surround the dwelling area, as well as pools, some of which have kept their polychrome mosaic facing: in particular note the mosaic with large fish on the wall of one of the swimming baths.

Gardens of the Estói Palace. – *In Estói, 1km - 1/2 mile beyond Milreu.* An alley of palm trees leads to the gardens bordered with orange trees which are built up in terraces as far as the Baroque façade of a small 18C palace *(not open to the public).* The balustered terraces, decorated with pools, statues, busts and marble, bronze or earthenware vases, blue or polychrome *azulejos* with mythological or fantastic subjects, even some Roman mosaics taken from Milreu, make a very picturesque sight.

From the upper terrace, there is a pleasant view of Estói, and Faro in the distance.

The sanctuary at Fátima, one of the most famous in the world, stands at a place called **Cova da Iria** (alt 346m - 1 135ft) in a landscape of green hills still dotted with windmills. Great pilgrimages numbering thousands of believers visit the shrine on the 13th of every month, especially on 13 May and 13 October, the dates of the first and final apparitions. However the 13 May is by far the most frequented. Many travel to the shrine on foot and along every road across the plateau pilgrims may be seen in impressive numbers.

The apparitions. – On 13 May 1917, three young shepherds, **Francisco, Jacinta** and **Lúcia**, were minding their sheep on a hillside at Cova da Iria when suddenly the sky lit up: the Virgin appeared before them standing in an oak tree, and spoke. Her message, which was repeated insistently and gravely at each apparition on the 13th of every month subsequently, was a call to peace. It was particularly apt since Europe had then been at war for three years, Portugal fighting with the Allies. On 13 October 1917, 70 000 people waiting for what turned out to be the last apparition saw the rain suddenly stop and the sun shine and begin to revolve in the sky like a ball of fire. It was only in 1930 that the Bishop of Leiria authorized the celebration of belief in Our Lady of Fátima.

■ THE PILGRIMAGE

Basilica. – Closing the end of the huge esplanade (540m x 160m – 1 772 x 525ft) is the neo-Classical basilica (capacity: more than 300 000 pilgrims) which is extended on either side by a semicircular peristyle and dominated by a 65m - 200ft tower. Inside are the tombs of Francisco and Jacinta who died in 1919 and 1920. The oldest of the three, Lúcia, is now a nun in a convent near Coimbra.

Chapel of the Apparitions. – An evergreen oak, encircled by an iron railing, grows on the esplanade, replacing the one in which the Virgin appeared. Nearby, on the spot where the Virgin appeared, a chapel contains a statue to Our Lady of Fátima.

The Great Pilgrimages. – The great pilgrimages include processions with burning torches, nocturnal vigils, the celebration of solemn Masses on the esplanade, the benediction of the sick and finally "farewell" processions.

The fervour of the thousands of pilgrims at prayer, many of whom cover the approaches to the basilica on their knees, is deeply moving.

■ THE SERRA DO AIRE AND ITS CAVES

To the south and west of Fátima, the chalky heights of the Serra do Aire make an arid landscape which has a certain charm; the roads wind round it, bordered with a few eucalyptus, keeping to the side of white ridges dotted with olive trees and streaked with low drystone walls. The most important towns are **Porto de Mós,** whose restored castle can be seen from afar perched on a hillock with its strange green roof; and Mira de Aire (Pop 3 882) known for its handicraft work *(see under Leiria p 88).*

Mira de Aire Caves★ . – *In the village, to the right of the N 243 going towards Porto de Mós. Guided tour (time: 3/4 hour) 9am to 9pm (6pm November to April); 100esc.*

These caves, the biggest in Portugal, called the **Old Windmill Caves (Grutas dos Moinhos Velhos),** discovered in 1947 and then linked together by artificial tunnels, total a length of more than 4km - 2 1/2 miles *(of which one can visit 600m - 1/3 of a mile)* and reach a depth of 110m - 360 ft. The path spiralling down has 683 steps.

From chamber to gallery the sight is impressive, especially in the two biggest caves, the "Grand Salon" and the "Red Chamber". The reddish tinted walls, due to iron oxide, the opalescence of the rock deposits with evocative shapes ("jewels" from the Pearl Chapel; the Medusa, the Martian, the Organ, etc.), the sound of subterranean water, all exert their fascination. In the vast end gallery you can marvel at the "Great Lake" which collects all the water from the streams and the "Black River" which rises several days a year and floods the lower part of the caves.

São Mamede Caves. – *From Cova da Iria (Fátima), 7.5km - 4 1/2 miles by the N 356 towards Batalha, then the road to Mira de Aire on the left, and the access lane to the caves on the left taken on leaving the village of São Mamede. Times and charges not available at the time of going to press.*

These are the most recently prospected caves (1971). A legend whereby bandits were said to have hurled down the body of a traveller, and his purse too in their excessive haste, has led them to be called the **Money Caves (Grutas da Moeda).** One can count up to nine "chambers", and the variety of colours and folds therein, a waterfall, strange multicoloured calcarious deposits in the Shepherd's Chamber, are worth seeing.

Alvados Caves. – *Access by the N 361 between Alto de Alvados and Serra de San António. Guided tour (time: 1/2 hour) 9am to 9pm (6pm October to March); 110esc; combined ticket with Santo António Caves: 160esc.*

Discovered in 1964 on the northwest flank of the Pedra de Altar Hill. They extend for 450m - 1/3 mile across about ten chambers – linked artificially by long tunnels – each has its small limpid lake and colourful rock deposits. They have an additional attraction due to the golden colour of the walls, the number of stalactites and stalagmites joined together and making pillars, and the zigzag cracks in the ground. In the biggest chamber, 42m - 138ft high, where stray animals used to fall in, remains can still be seen.

Santo António Caves. – *Access by the N 361 to the north of Serra de Santo António. Same opening times and admission as Alvados Caves (see above).*

These caves were discovered in 1955, near the top of the Pedra do Altar Hill. An access tunnel had to be constructed for visitors. The three chambers (the main one with an area of 4 000m² - 4 784sq yards is 43m - 141 ft high) and a short gallery all have delicate rose coloured concretions. In one of the secondary chambers there is a small lake.

The main interest of the Santo António Caves lies in the veritable forest of stalagmites found there, some of which appear as statuesque figures enacting a frozen melodrama.

FIGUEIRA DA FOZ *

Michelin map **37** fold 14 or **441** fold 31 – Pop 13 397 – *Facilities p 36*
See town plan in the current Michelin Red Guide España Portugal

Figueira da Foz, which commands the mouth of the Mondego River, is overlooked from behind by the Serra da Boa Viagem. The most unusual view of the town is from the Galã road to the south as it runs through the local saltmarshes.

Figueira, which was built in the last century, lives primarily from its fishing industry (sardines and cod) and its shipyards. Tourists congregate in the new quarter on the west side of the town, attracted by the vast beach of fine sand which lines the wide curve of Figueira Bay. This bay, then known as Mondego Bay and overlooked by a fort of golden stone captured from the French by students of Coimbra University but a short time before, was where Wellington landed the first British troops in August 1808. From Figueira began the advance south which was to bring the first battles of the Peninsular Campaign not far from Obidos at Roliça and Vimeiro.

A century and a half later Figueiro presents itself as a pleasant resort where the amusements are social, sporting, and traditional – casino, concerts, theatre, swimming, tennis, regattas, and the midsummer festivals of St John on 23 and 24 June and the Pardon of Our Lady of the Incarnation from 7 to 9 September.

Municipal Museum (Museu Municipal Dr Santos Rocha). – *Rua Calouste Gulbenkian. Open 9am to 12.30pm and 2 to 6pm; closed Mondays and holidays.*

The museum, installed along with the public library in a modern building, has an interesting archaeological section (note the stele bearing an Iberian inscription), as well as painting, sculpture and decorative art (earthenware and furniture) sections.

EXCURSION

Serra da Boa Viagem. – *Round tour of 20km - 12 miles – about 3/4 hour. Leave Figueira da Foz by the northwest along the N 109.*

The small fishing village of **Buarcos** can be seen from the road. After going past a large cement works on the left, the road runs beside the sea to reach, again on the left, the Cape Mondego lighthouse, which commands a view out over the Atlantic and along the rocky coastline. The road continues through the forest of pines, acacias and eucalyptus which cloak the *serra.* Turn right towards the village of Boa Viagem. A little before Boa Viagem, the view widens out to beautiful vistas on the right of the Bay of Figueira da Foz and the mouth of the Mondego River.

FLOR DA ROSA *

Michelin map **37** fold 6 – 23km - 14 miles west of Portalegre – Pop 394

The village of Flor da Rosa has for long been a manufacturing centre for pottery, its speciality being the *caçoila,* a round cooking bowl.

Former Monastery*. – *Go into the farmyard beyond the monastery and apply to the caretaker on the right.*

This former monastery of the Order of the Knights Templar of Malta was built in 1356 by Álvaro Gonçalves Pereira, father of Nuno Álvares Pereira who beat the Castilians at the Battle of Aljubarrota *(p 49).* It forms a compact group of fortified buildings within a crenellated perimeter wall.

The **church***, on the right, is a building outstanding for the simplicity of its lines and the impressive height of its nave. The small flower decked cloister, in the centre, is robust in design but is given an overall elegance by its graceful Late Gothic network vaulting.

FREIXO DE ESPADA -À -CINTA

Michelin map **37** southwest of fold 14 (inset) or **441** northeast of fold 35 – *Local map p 69* – Pop 2 338

The shale and granite town of Freixo lies in a fertile basin before range upon range of mountains. It was the birthplace of the satirical poet **Guerra Junqueiro** (1850-1923).

Parish Church*. – This hall church built at the end of the Gothic period has a lovely Gothic doorway adorned by a few Renaissance motifs. The interior, in which stands a fine wrought iron pulpit, is covered by a network vault; the **chancel***, where the vaulting is adorned with emblazoned hanging keystones, contains a gilded wood altar with turned columns and a canopy; the walls are lined with 16C painted panelling.

Pillory. – The Manueline style pillory is crowned with a carved human head.

GUARDA *

Michelin map **37** fold 3 or **441** folds 34 and 35 – Pop 14 803

Guarda was, at one time, the main stronghold of the province of Beira Alta. The best preserved remains of the ancient fortifications are the Blacksmiths' Tower (Torre dos Ferreiros), the 12 and 13C keep (Torre de Menagem) and the King's and Star Gates (Porta d'El-Rei, Porta da Estrela).

Guarda, the highest town in Portugal (alt 1 000m - 3 281ft), is now a pleasant climatic resort.

A strategic site. – Taken over since prehistoric times, the site of Guarda served as a military base for Julius Caesar (so it is believed) before giving support to the Roman town of Lancia Oppidana, and then a Visigothic fortress which was soon overwhelmed by the Arab conquest. The town, recaptured from the Moors by Afonso Henriques *(p 84)* was enlarged and fortified at the end of the 12C, under D. Sancho I. King Dinis I stayed there.

After having driven back the Spanish, Guarda, nevertheless, failed to retain its role of "protector" of the Beira Alta at the time of the French invasion in 1808.

■ SIGHTS *time: 1 hour*

Cathedral★. – The cathedral was begun in 1390 in the Gothic style, but as it was completed only in 1540, Renaissance and Manueline elements are clearly visible in its decoration. The granite edifice is crowned with pinnacles and trefoils which give it a certain resemblance to the monastery at Batalha *(p 49)*.

Exterior. – The northern façade is embellished with an ornate Gothic doorway surmounted by a Manueline window. In the main façade, a Manueline doorway is framed by two octagonal towers emblazoned at their bases with the coat of arms of Bishop Dom Pedro Vaz Gavião, who played an important part in getting the cathedral completed in the 16C.

Interior. – The lierne and tierceron vaulting over the transept crossing has a keystone in the form of a cross of the Order of Christ. In the chancel is a Renaissance altarpiece made of Ançã stone in the 16C, gilded in the 18C. Attributed to Jean de Rouen *(p 23)*, the high relief which includes more than one hundred figures depicts, on four levels from the base to the top, scenes in the Lives of the Virgin and Jesus Christ. A 16C altarpiece in the south apsidal chapel, also attributed to Jean de Rouen, represents the Last Supper.

The Pinas Chapel which opens through a beautiful Renaissance doorway off the north aisle contains a fine Gothic tomb complete with a reclining figure.

A staircase erected at the corner of the south transept round a twisted column leads to the cathedral roofs from which one can look out over the town and the Serra da Estrela.

Old Houses. – Many 16 and 18C houses bearing coats of arms are to be seen surrounding the cathedral square (Praça Luis de Camões) and lining Rua Dom Luis I.

■ THE EASTERN FORTIFIED TOWNS

Distances indicated are from Guarda – local map below.

Medieval strongholds or fortified towns built in the 17-18C to protect the frontier, and numerous fortified small towns or villages, still seem to mount guard at the top of a hillock or a steep headland, in the heart of the Beira Alta.

Almeida★. – Pop 1 497. *59km - 37 miles to the northeast.* Less than 10km - 6 miles from the frontier, the peaceful little town of Almeida crowns a hill 729m - 2 491ft high with its ramparts. Taken by the Spanish in 1762, then by the French under Massena in 1810, it, nevertheless, has kept intact its double **fortifications★**, in the form of a six pointed star in pure Vauban style, completed in the 18C.

Three arched gateways *(sound horn when driving in)* with monumental porches preceded by bridges, give access to the interior, where one can see the old barrack buildings (near the north gate) which were used as a prison from 1828 to 1833, and a few lovely mansions, some covered with *azulejos*.

Castelo Bom. – Pop 205. *47km - 30 1/2 miles to the east.* Medieval fortress dating from King Dinis I, this village clustered round a hill has only one ruined tower left, next to a Gothic gate, and a lovely 16C house.

Castelo Melhor★. – Pop 507. *72km - 45 miles to the northeast.* Visible from the N 222, the village clings to the flanks of a rocky peak dotted with olive trees. A medieval **wall★** reinforced with round towers encircles the grassy and bare summit.

Castelo Mendo. – Pop 230. *39km - 32 miles to the east.* Cobbled alleys crisscross on a rocky hillock amongst the remains of a Gothic wall, where the main gate is wedged between two towers. The village still has the marks of a flourishing past; a few Renaissance buildings and others dating from the Spanish domination, a 17C church with, in front, the highest pillory in the province (7m - 23ft) dating from the 16C. It has an octagonal shaft topped by a cage with small columns. The peasant houses of granite have a flight of steps each side forming a veranda. From the summit, which has the remains of a defence keep and a chapel with a belfry tower, there is a dominating view to the south over the deep valley of the Rio Coa, which is crossed by a railway viaduct.

Celorico da Beira. – Pop 2 096. *28km - 17 1/2 miles to the northwest.* This busy small town is on the extreme north of a wooded ridge at the end of the Serra da Estrela. The large square keep of the ancient castle rises up at the top, surrounded by a small wall. Extensive view.

Linhares. – Pop 463. *46km - 30 miles to the west (the last 6km - 4 miles after Carrapichana are on a winding unsurfaced road).* The very beautiful outer wall of a castle at the time of Dinis I, with its two square crenellated towers runs round the granite top of a headland dominating the Upper Valley of the Mondego. It protects the old village where there are some 16C structures, amongst them, a pillory with an armillary sphere.

Marialva. – Pop 426. *66km - 40 miles to the north.* The remains of a castle built in 1200 cover a rocky ridge which has extensive views over the Bevesa Plain. Between the ruins of the outer wall, a crenellated keep and another tower still set in its wall, there are scattered ruins of the old village, a 15C pillory, and the church with a Manueline doorway.

Sortelha★. – Pop 827. *43km - 27 miles to the south.* This 12C **stronghold★**, hemming in the old village with its picturesque granite houses, rises up at the extreme end of a headland dominating the Upper Zêzere Valley. You enter it by one of the majestic Gothic gates of the fortified wall, where the two existing square towers have their own surrounding wall, with machicolated gateways.

From the watchpath *(mind the wind)*, there are impressive **views★** over the valley.

Other fortresses in the Guarda Region are described in this guide: **Belmonte** *(27km - 17 miles to the south – p 51)*, **Castelo Rodrigo** *(57km - 35 1/2 miles to the northeast – p 120)*, **Penedono** *(70km - 44 miles to the north – p 119)*, **Sabugal** *(33km - 21 miles to the southeast – p 124)*, **Trancoso** *(47km - 30 miles to the north – p 134)*.

GUIMARÃES ★

Michelin map **37** folds 1, 2 and 12 or **441** fold 23 – *Local map p 68* – Pop 22 092 – *Facilities p 38*

In the 10C, soon after it was founded by the Countess Mumadona, Guimarães consisted of a monastery with a defensive tower and a few neighbouring houses. In the Middle Ages and later, new quarters were added to the south until it grew to its present size.

Nowadays Guimarães is a prosperous commercial city with cotton and linen spinning and weaving mills, cutlery, tanning and kitchenware industries and equally successful craft industries such as gold and silversmithing, pottery, embroidery, the weaving of linen damask and the carving of wooden yokes.

The Cradle of Portugal. – In 1095 Alfonso VI, King of León and Castile, bestowed the County of Portucale *(details p 19)* on his son-in-law, Henri of Burgundy. Henri had the tower at Guimarães converted into a castle and installed his wife the Princess Teresa (Tareja) there. In about 1110 Teresa bore Henri a son, Alfonso Henriques, who succeeded his father in 1112. The young prince revolted against the notorious misconduct of his mother, who had acted as regent, and on 24 June 1128 seized power following the Battle of São Mamede. Next he campaigned against the Moors and succeeded in vanquishing them at Ourique on 25 July 1139. In the course of the campaign Alfonso was proclaimed king of Portugal by his troops, a choice confirmed by the Cortes at Lamego *(details p 87)* and his cousin Alfonso VII, king of Léon in the Treaty of Zamora of 1143.

Gil Vicente. – The poet and goldsmith, Gil Vicente, born in Guimarães in 1470, lived at the courts of King Manuel I and King João II. He wrote plays – farces and tragi-comedies – to divert the king and the court, and mysteries *(autos)* to be performed in the churches. His forty-four plays provide a precise if satirical panorama of Portuguese society at the beginning of the 16C, while the variety of his inspiration allied to the lightness of his touch and finesse of his style make him the virtual creator of the Portuguese theatre.

■ MAIN SIGHTS *time: 2 hours*

Palace of the Dukes of Bragança★ (Paço dos Duques). – *Guided tours 10am to 5pm; closed Tuesdays; 100esc.*

Afonso Henriques.

Built in 1401 by Alfonso I, Count of Barcelos and first Duke of Bragança, the palace was abandoned when the dukes moved to Vila Viçosa *(p 140)*. Carefully restored, it has become a national palace and museum. In front of the palace there is a bronze statue of Alfonso Henriques by Soares dos Reis (late 19C).

The palace consists of four buildings with massive corner towers, surrounding a cloister, and crowned with machicolated battlements. The roofs are particularly striking because of the unusual aspect of their 39 brick chimneys.

Interior. – On the first floor the eye is caught by the **ceilings★** of oak and chestnut in the two largest rooms (Dining Hall and Banquet Hall) and the 16-18C **tapestries★** (Aubusson, Flanders and Gobelins). There are also Persian carpets (15 and 17C), Portuguese furniture (17C), Chinese porcelain, weapons and armour, Dutch and Italian paintings, three canvases attribued to Josefa de Obidos *(p 110)* and a 15C sculpture (Virgin and Child sitting on a crescent moon).

St Michael of the Castle (Igreja São Miguel do Castelo) **(A)**. – *Apply at the Palace.*

This small 12C Romanesque church contains a font in which it is said Alfonso Henriques was baptized; also numerous funerary tombstones.

Castle★ (Castelo). – Seven square towers surround the keep. From the ramparts there is a wide view over Guimarães dominated to the south by Mount Penha.

GUIMARÃES

Paio Galvão (R.) 11
Sto António (R. de) 14
Tourai (L. do) 19

Alberto Sampaio (Av.) 2
Dom A. Henriques (Av.) 4
Duques de Bragança (R.) ... 6
João Franco (L. de) 7
Mumadona (Pr. de) 8

Nuno Álvares (R.) 9
Oliveira (L. da) 10
Rainha (R. da) 13
S. Tiago (L. de) 16
Serpa Pinto (R.) 17

Church of St Francis of Assisi (Igreja São Francisco) (**B**). – The church was built early in the 15C but was remodelled in the 17C so that only the main door and the east end retain their original Gothic character. The capitals in the main doorway represent the legend of St Francis. The interior suffered some unfortunate remodellings in the 17 and 18C. The chancel, which contains a Baroque altar carved in wood and gilded, is decorated with 18C azulejos★ depicting the life of St Antony.

In the sacristy★ *(access through the south transept; open 9am to noon and 2 to 5.30pm or 5pm in winter; closed Mondays and holidays; apply to the sacristan)* may be seen a fine coffered ceiling ornamented with grotesques and an Arrábida marble table standing against an elegant Carrara marble column.

Note, to the right of the church, a beautiful façade adorned with *azulejos*.

Alberto Sampaio Museum★ (**M¹**). – *Guided tour (time: 1/2 hour) 10am to 12.30pm and 2 to 5pm; closed Mondays and holidays; 30 esc., free Sundays.*

The museum has been installed in the conventual buildings of the Collegiate Church of Our Lady of the Olive Tree. The 13C Romanesque cloister has interesting historiated capitals. In the east corner of the cloister is a door from the former 10C Monastery of Mumadona. In a Gothic chapel to the right on entering is the fine recumbent figure in granite of Dona Constança de Noronha, wife of the 1st duke of Bragança. Rooms off the cloister contain paintings, in particular those of António Vaz, who was born at Guimarães, and Baroque altarpieces. The chapterhouse has a fine 16C coffered ceiling, and then there is an interesting collection of ceramics and *azulejos*.

On the 1st floor, note first of all several statues including the 15C alabaster statue of Our Lady of Pity and a gilded wood altarpiece of the 17C. The following galleries contain the **ecclesiastical plate★**. The collegiate church's treasure includes in addition to the tunic worn by João I at the Battle of Aljubarrota, the silver gilt **triptych★** said to have been given to the church by the king after he had taken it from the Castilians at the battle. The triptych shows in the centre, the Nativity, on the left, the Annunciation, the Purification and the Presentation at the Temple and on the right the shepherds and the Magi. Among other pieces of the treasure, note a Gothic chalice of silver with enamel embossing, a Manueline monstrance attributed to Gil Vicente *(see opposite)* and a finely engraved 16C silver Manueline **cross★** depicting scenes from the Passion.

Collegiate Church of Our Lady of the Olive Tree (Igreja Nossa Senhora da Oliveira) (**C**). – The original edifice has disappeared completely. Several buildings have since been erected in succession on this same site: the cloister and chapterhouse *(now parts of the Alberto Sampaio Museum)* are Romanesque; the main doorway surmounted by a Gothic pediment is 14C.

A Gothic porch in front of the collegiate church is said to have been built to commemorate the victory over the Moors at the Battle of the Salado in 1340. Legend has it that during the completion of the porch in 1342 the trunk of the olive tree which stood in front of the church suddenly sprouted leaves: it was thus that the church got its name.

Former Town Hall (Paços do Concelho) (**E**). – The arcaded and crenellated building dates from the 16C.

Rua de Santa Maria. – This street, which goes up to the old quarter of Guimarães, is typical of those in the old town where 14 and 15C houses with wrought iron grilles and carved granite cornices line the majority of the streets.

■ **ADDITIONAL SIGHTS**

Largo do Toural. – This picturesque square with a wave-like mosaic pavement is a good example of Classical urban architecture. Old houses with mansard roofs surround it, their vast windows are adorned with fine wrought iron grilles.

Martins Sarmento Museum (**M²**). – *Guided tour (time: 1 hour) 9.30am to noon and 2 to 5pm; closed Mondays and holidays; 30esc.*

The museum, which is installed partly in the Gothic cloister of the Church of St Dominic (São Domingos), includes numerous archaeological exhibits from the pre-Roman cities of Sabroso and Briteiros (p 55).

EXCURSIONS

Penha. – *Round tour of 17km - 11 miles. Leave Guimarães by the N 101 going towards Fafe. After Mesão Frio, turn right towards Penha; the road immediately begins to rise as it winds between pines and eucalyptus trees.*

Penha *(facilities p 38)* stands on the highest part of the Serra de Santa Catarina. *Cross the esplanade before the Basilica of Our Lady of Penha and continue along the road to the statue of St Catherine where you park your car.* There is a vast **panorama**★ of the Serra do Marão to the south and Guimarães and the Serra do Gerês to the north.

To return to Guimarães, bear left at the end of the esplanade into a narrow road, the N 101-2, which winds downwards, working its way between rocks and trees.

Trofa★. – *7.5km - 4 1/2 miles. Leave Guimarães by the N 101 towards Amarante.*

Trofa is a small village where the women make net and lace; they may be seen working and displaying their crafts (cloths and napkins) at the roadside.

Roriz. – *Pop 3 735. 8.5km - 5 miles. Leave Guimarães by the N 105 to the south. Bear left into a signposted road 3km - 2 miles before Lordelo, the N 209-2.* An interesting Romanesque church stands beside an ancient monastery. *Open 9am to noon and 3 to 7pm (5pm in winter). If closed apply at the presbytery or to the caretaker of the monastery.*

The exterior of this granite 11C **church** recalls that of Paço de Sousa *(p 117)*. The plain but harmonious façade is pierced by a doorway adorned with capitals of carved foliage and animals, and columns embellished with shells in relief. As at Paço de Sousa, hemispheres adorn the doorway arches and the border moulding of the graceful rose window above.

LAGOS ★

Michelin map **87** fold 20 – Pop 10 504 – *Facilities p 36*
See town plan in the current Michelin Red Guide España Portugal

Lagos occupies the west end of a bay closed on its northern horizon by the Serra de Monchique. Now one of the Algarve seaside resorts, Lagos is also a fishing port well sheltered by the Ponta da Piedade promontory and an important yachting centre organizing international races.

The most attractive approaches to Lagos are from Aljezur in the north along the N 120 or from Vila do Bispo in the west along the N 125. There are **views**★ from these two roads of the resort and its setting and the development which now lines the bay. It was out to sea from this bay that, in 1693, the French Admiral Tourville succeeded in sinking the eighty ships of an Anglo-Dutch convoy commanded by Admiral Rooke who had beaten him the year before off the Normandy coast in the Battle of La Hougue.

The African Expeditions. – Lagos harbour served as Prince Henry the Navigator's principal maritime base. It was from Lagos that Gil Eanes left in 1434 to round for the first time in history Cape Bojador, a point on the west coast of the Sahara which until then had been the last outpost of the habitable world. On Prince Henry's orders, one expedition followed another down the coast of Africa, always adding to the knowledge of ocean currents and improving techniques of navigation *(p 124)*. A statue of Prince Henry the Navigator stands in a vast square situated between the harbour and the old town.

■ SIGHTS *time: 1 hour*

Regional Museum. – *Up an alleyway, which starts from the Praça da República. Guided tour (time: 1/2 hour) 9.30am to 12.30pm and 2 to 5pm; closed Mondays and holidays; 20esc.*

The archaeological collection and the ethnographical section devoted to the Algarve are especially interesting. Included also is a visit to the adjoining **St Antony's Church.** The plain façade gives no inkling of the exuberance and virtuosity of the Baroque **decoration**★ which reigns inside. Outstanding are the ceiling painted in false relief, the Eucharistic symbols and statues of gilded wood in the chancel, the walls and the gallery ceiling.

Former Slave Market (Mercado de Escravos). – *In the Praça da República, opposite the Santa Maria Church.* Europe's first slave markets (15C) were held in this house with arcades, following the Africa Expeditions. *Temporary exhibits are organized annually.*

EXCURSIONS

Ponta da Piedade★★; Praia de Dona Ana★. – *3km - 2 miles. From the harbour take the road leading to Sagres and at the place called Trinidad take the first road on the left as far as the lighthouse (car park).* The **setting**★★ of this seaside resort is what makes it especially attractive: reddish rocks worn by the ocean into swirling shaped boulders and marines caves *(in summer: visit by boat - apply to the owner)* contrast vividly with the clear green of the sea.

From behind the lighthouse, the **view**★ stretches from Cape St. Vincent on the west to Cape Carvoeiro on the east. By a small road on the left of the lighthouse, a belvedere affords a bird's eye view of the rocks and of the tiny seaside resort of **Praia de Dona Ana**★ *(facilities p 36)*.

Bravura Dam★. – *15km - 9 miles. Leave Lagos by the N 125 going northeast towards Portimão.* The road leading from Odeáxere to the dam winds along an irrigated valley where melons, tomatoes, maize and figs all grow, before climbing the foothills of the Serra de Monchique with extensive **views**★ over the coastal ranges.

The Odeáxere Dam closes the valley of the same name. To its west, a powered conduit directs water to the power station downstream from where it goes on to irrigate the 1 800ha - 4 500 acres of agricultural land which lies between Lagos and Portimão.

Michelin map ⊞ fold 2 or ⊞ folds 23 and 24 – *Local map p 68* – Pop 9 942 – *Facilities p 38*

Lamego is an attractive small episcopal and commercial town known for its sparkling wine and its smoked ham. It lies near the Douro Valley *(p 68)* in a landscape of green hills covered with vines and maize.

The town which is rich in 16 and 18C bourgeois houses is overlooked by two hills on which stand respectively the ruins of a 12C fortified castle and the Baroque Sanctuary of Our Lady of the Remedies, famous for the annual pilgrimages held in late August-early September.

The Lamego Cortes. – The first national assembly of representatives of the nobles, the clergy, and towns, was held in Lamego in 1143; it recognized Alfonso Henriques as first King of Portugal and proclaimed the law of succession by which no foreigner should have power to accede to the throne.

■ **SIGHTS** *time: 1 1/2 hours*

Regional Museum★. – *Guided tour (time: 3/4 hour) 10am to 12.30pm and 2 to 5pm; closed Mondays and holidays; 30esc, free Sundays.*

Housed in the former episcopal palace (18C), it includes 34 rooms. The ground floor contains mainly religious sculpture from the middle Ages to the Baroque period and a Baroque chapel.

The first floor has two more Baroque chapels of carved and gilded wood, one of which has niches and statues; a chinese salon (porcelains, paintings on silk); an interesting collection of *azulejos*, some polychromed, from 16 to 18C; gold and silver religious works (an early 17C chalice with small bells); furniture, pottery and various paintings and sculptures (15C flowered cross).

Two series of works are particularly noteworthy: the five **paintings on wood★** (early 16C) of which one is a lovely Visitation by Vasco Fernandez *(p 23)*, from the altarpiece of Lamego's cathedral; six 16C Brussels **tapestries★**, with mythological subjects (note the rich composition of the Temple of Latone).

Cathedral (Sé). – Of the original 12C Romanesque church there remains only the square belfry whose crown is 16C. The interior was redone in the 18C.

Chapel of the Exile (Igreja do Desterro). – *Apply at no 126 Rua da Calçada or 9 Rua Cardoso Avelino.*

This chapel built in 1640, is decorated inside with 18C carved and gilded woodwork and 17C *azulejos;* the coffered **ceiling★** is outstanding with painted scenes from the Life of Our Lord.

Sanctuary of Our Lady of the Remedies (Santuário Nossa Senhora dos Remédios). – A good overall view of this Baroque building is gained from the bottom of the steps which lead up to it. The 18C façade on which white stucco serves to highlight the elegant granite curves, overlooks the crossed ramps of the staircase ornamented with *azulejos* and bristling with a multitude of pinnacles.

The view from the church parvis *(access by car possible: 4km - 2 1/2 miles)* extends over Lamego to the heights on the horizon which border the Douro.

EXCURSION

São João de Tarouca. – *16km - 10 miles – about 3/4 hour. Leave Lamego south along the N 226 towards Trancoso.*

The road passes near **Ferreirim** *(2km - 1 1/2 miles on the left)* where, from 1532 to 1536, Cristóvão de Figueiredo worked with the help of Gregório Lopes and Garcia Fernandes *(p 23)* on the altarpiece which was to adorn the monastery church.

Bear right 2km - 1 mile beyond the Tarouca road which branches off to the right.

São João de Tarouca. – *Description p 127.*

Michelin map ⊞ fold 12 or ⊞ fold 22 – 8km - 5 miles north of Oporto – *Local map p 68* – Pop 13 659

It is said that after the First Crusade, the domain of Leça do Bailio was given to brothers of the Order of the Hospital of St John of Jerusalem who had come from Palestine probably in the company of Count Henri of Burgundy, father of the first King of Portugal *(p 19)*.

Leça was the mother house of this Order (now the Order of Malta) till 1312 when this was transferred to Flor da Rosa.

Monastery Church★. – *Time: 1/2 hour.* This fortress church built, in granite in the Gothic period, is characterized outside by pyramid shaped merlons emphasizing the entablature by the tall battlemented tower surrounded with balconies and machicolated watchtowers, and by the very plain main façade adorned only with a door with carved capitals below and a rose window above.

The bare interior is well proportioned. The historiated capitals portray scenes from Genesis and the Gospels – of particular note are Adam and Eve with the serpent and the angel.

Several of the Hospitallers are buried here. The chancel, which has star vaulting, contains the 16C tomb of the Bailiff Frei Cristóvão de Cernache, which is surmounted by a painted statue (16C) and in the north apsidal chapel is the prior, Frei João Coelho's tomb, with a reclining figure by Diogo Pires the Younger (1515).

The Manueline style **font★**, carved in Ança stone by the same artist, is octagonal and rests on a pedestal adorned with acanthus leaves and fantastic animals.

Michelin map **37** fold 15 – Pop 12 428 – *Facilities p 38*

Leiria is pleasantly situated at the confluence of two rivers, the Liz and the Lena, and at the foot of a hill crowned by a medieval castle.

Its role as a crossroads near well known beaches – notably that of Nazaré *(p 108)* – the sanctuary of Fátima and the magnificent architecture of Batalha and Alcobaça, makes it a favoured stop off place for the holiday-maker, the pilgrim and the art-loving tourist.

Craftsmanship and folklore. – The Leiria Region has kept alive its old tradition of popular art and folklore. The glazed and multicoloured pottery of Cruz da Légua *(p 51)* and Milagres, the decorated glassware of Marinha Grande, the willow baskets and ornaments and the woven coverlets of Mira de Aire are among the best known crafts of the district.

The traditional festivals and customs have lost none of their spontaneity. The folklore of the Leiria Region is closely associated with that of its neighbour, the Ribatejo. The women's costume, which is not in the least showy, consists of a small black felt hat with feathers, a coloured blouse edged with lace, a short skirt and shoes with wide low heels. It differs from that of the Ribatejo only by the addition of a gold necklace and earrings. Folk dancing displays are held every year at the time of the Leiria exhibition-fair (first to last Sunday in May) and in particular on the 22 May, the town's local holiday.

■ **THE CASTLE★** *time: 1/2 hour*

Open 9am to 7pm (6pm in winter); 20esc.

On a remarkable **site★**, inhabited even before the arrival of the Romans, Alfonso I, first King of Portugal, had a fortified castle erected in 1135. This castle formed part of the defence of the southern frontier of the then Kingdom of Portugal, Santarém and Lisbon still being under Moorish domination.

After the capture of these two cities in 1147, the castle lost its significance and fell into ruin. In the 14C, King Dinis, who undertook first the preservation and then the extension of the pine forest near the coast at Leiria, rebuilt the castle in order that he might live in it with his wife, Queen Saint Isabel. The present buildings, modified in the 16C, were restored.

Enter the castle walls through a door flanked by two square crenellated towers and take a shaded stairway, on the left, to the centre of the castle. The royal palace is then on the left, the keep straight ahead, and traces of the Chapel of Our Lady of Pena on the right.

A staircase leads to the upper storeys of the **royal palace** and in particular to a vast rectangular hall with a gallery adorned with tiers-point arcades resting on slender double columns. The gallery, once the royal balcony, affords a good view of Leiria lying below.

From the keep *(75 steps; walk up carefully)*, built by King Dinis, there is a wide lookout over the castle, the town and the surrounding countryside, which is green and scattered with gardens.

Of the early 15C **Chapel** of Our Lady of Pena there remain only ruins – a tall and elegant Gothic chancel and the arcade, adorned with Manueline motifs, which supported the gallery.

Michelin map **37** north of fold 1 and 11 (inset) or **41** fold 23 – Pop 837

Built like an amphitheatre against the southern flanks of one of the last mountains in the Serra do Soajo, Lindoso sets out its austere granite houses in tiered rows up to a height of 462m - 1 516ft, perfectly integrated into the rocky landscape – despite the presence of a few recent constructions – and surrounded by cultivated terraces (maize, vines). The castle stands on a hillock where there is also an unusual group of *espigueiros (see below)*.

From Ponte da Barca to Lindoso. – *31km - 20 miles.* The road, bordered with pine trees, tangerine trees, oleanders, winds about on the wooded slope of the Serra do Soajo, with a view of the arid and rocky Serra de Peneda which rises on the other side of the Lima Valley. At the crossroads with the road leading to Entre-Ambos-os-Rios, continue on the N 203 which starts a steep climb into the Peneda-Gerês National Park *(p 118)* and has views overlooking the meandering river, which is enlarged by a dam upstream. It ends up as a corniche road, and stops when it reaches the striking castle of Lindoso.

Castle. – Facing the frontier, it was inevitably attacked several times by the army of Philip IV of Spain during the War of Independence in the 17C.

Restored, it appears again as a crenellated feudal keep in the middle of a small 17C square surrounding wall with bastions and watch turrets. From the watchpath there are views over the Lima Valley and the surrounding Portuguese and Galacian mountains.

Granaries★★ (Espigueiros). – Covering a rocky platform at the foot of the castle, these *espigueiros (p 27)*, at least sixty, are strangely grouped together, resembling a cemetery. They are small granite buildings, perched on piles, and most of them have one or two crosses on the roof. Their very careful construction dates back to the 18 and 19C. They are still used today for drying corn.

Your visit to Portugal will be easier and more interesting if you are aware of:

everyday customs; the appearance of the country;

the major facts about the economy; national and local specialities;

the most important dates in the country's history; its artistic originality;

Portuguese folklore and popular festivities.

This information is to be found on pp 6-31.

At the time of the Great Discoverers, Lisbon, according to the Portuguese poet Camões, was the "princess of the world... before whom even the ocean bows". The town, on seven low hills, is naturally favoured by its position at the southwest corner of Europe and its superb harbour commanding the Tagus estuary, which was given the name of the "Straw Sea" because of the golden reflections of the sun upon the water at this spot. The attraction of the Portuguese capital lies in the magnificent vistas along its wide avenues, the deep shade of its many tree lined roads, and squares, the freshness of its public gardens, its medieval quarter clinging to the hillside and, always, the Tagus.

Lisbon is at its most lighthearted when celebrating the feasts of the "popular saints" *(p 9)* in June. St Antony's is the gayest occasion when groups of young men and women *(marchas populares)* parade down the Avenida da Liberdade in traditional costume.

HISTORICAL NOTES

According to legend, the town was founded by Ulysses. Historians, however, attribute the city's foundation in 1200 BC to the Phoenicians who named it the "serene harbour". The town soon became a port of call for Mediterranean ships sailing to northern Europe; it was conquered first by the Greeks, then the Carthaginians and, in 205 BC became a Roman city. Then the Barbarians invaded it and for four centuries it was under Arab rule. In AD 714 the city took the name Lissabona but it was not until 25 October 1147 when King Alfonso I captured it with the aid of part of the fleet from the Second Crusade that the Arab occupation finally ended. In 1255 Alfonso III chose Lisbon in place of Coimbra as the capital of Portugal.

The Age of the Great Discoverers. – The voyage of Vasco da Gama to the Indies in 1497-99 and the discovery of Brazil by Pedro Alvares Cabral in 1500 *(p 20)* made Portugal the greatest maritime power of the age; new trade routes developed, causing a decline in the prosperity of Venice and Genoa; merchants flocked to Lisbon bringing riches in their train: the lower town (Baixa) was packed with small traders buying and selling gold, spices, silver, ivory, silks, precious stones and rare woods. King Manuel embellished every part of the town with buildings on which the decoration is always inspired by the sea.

The Earthquake. – On 1 November 1755 during High Mass the town was shaken by an exceptionally violent earth tremor: churches, palaces and houses collapsed; fire spread from the wax candles in the churches to furnishings and woodwork; survivors rushed to take refuge in the Tagus, but a huge wave came upstream, breaking over and destroying the lower town. Lisbon's riches were engulfed; Voltaire wrote that 40 000 citizens perished.

King José I escaped as did his minister, the future Marquis of Pombal *(p 121)*. The minister immediately began to re-establish life in the city. In collaboration with the civil engineer Manuel de Maia and the architect Eugenio dos Santos, Pombal undertook the rebuilding of Lisbon to plans and in a style utterly revolutionary for the period. The straight wide avenues, the plain and stylized houses to be seen in the Baixa today are due to him.

The Lines of Tôrres Vedras. – The Lines of Tôrres Vedras was the name given to a system of defence lines conceived by Wellington in 1810 to protect Lisbon from attack by the French under the command of Masséna. It was also estimated that, if necessary, British troops could be either landed or evacuated through the lines.

The lines were an assemblage of defensive positions, fortifications, embrasures and roads, rather than a continuous line. The positions, nevertheless, stretched from Tôrres Vedras, 70km - 43 miles north of Lisbon to Alhandra, near Vila Franca de Xira, at the furthest point inland reached by the Sea of Straw. Masséna, after a minor skirmish, during which he could observe personally the system's strength, decided not to attack in the immediate instance and later (December 1810) began what ended as the final retreat northwards out of Portugal altogether.

The Carnation Revolution. – On 24 April 1974, at the instigation of General de Spinola and numerous officers, a coup d'état ended the regime instituted by Salazar and maintained by his successor Caetano. Without encountering any opposition the army occupied Lisbon where soldiers with a red carnation stuck in the barrel of their rifles were acclaimed by the population.

LIFE IN LISBON

The centre of life in Lisbon is in the lower town known as the **Baixa** *(pronounced: baïcha)*. The main shopping streets and offices lie in this quarter, and public and private transport in the form of cars, buses, the Underground and taxis all converge upon it. The Praça Dom Pedro IV known as the Rossio, and the Rua Garrett, known as the Chiado, are the two poles of attraction. The area comes alive in the afternoon (around 3pm) when the cafés lining the Rossio begin to fill.

Many Portuguese women go window shopping in the Chiado and the Rua Augusta looking at the fashions, or they sit about in the cafés sampling the pastries. The men of Lisbon, including those of very modest means, usually wear dark suits and white shirts. After dinner, they are to be seen strolling in the streets or seated outside the cafés. The chief forms of relaxation are watching football – Benfica's fortunes are followed closely by every Portuguese! – going to the cinema (foreign films with original soundtracks and captions), the theatre or spending an evening in a tavern or local restaurant where towards 10pm he can hear *fado (p 30)*. These restaurants and taverns are to be found mostly in the medieval quarters of the city: the **Alfama** *(p 96)* and the **Bairro Alto**, where the *fado* is said to have originated and which is now a centre of nightlife. *Book in advance, the casa de fado are often small.*

■ **THE PORT, THE TAGUS** *plan p 92*

Port (Porto de Lisboa). – The port is one of the main places of call in Europe with docks, quays, warehouses and quayside stations extending over some 20km - 12 miles along the bank of the Tagus from Algés to Sacavém. Traffic in 1983 amounted to 14 million tons, mostly in imports and capital goods. Agricultural products, essentially wine and cork, are shipped abroad through the port. Industrial complexes have developed towards Vila Franca de Xira, including grain silos, cement works, oil storage tanks, steel mills, cork factories and refrigeration plants for storing cod, etc. As the four dry docks at the Rocha shipyard on the right bank of the Tagus were not large enough to take the latest tankers, a larger yard has been built by the Lisnave organization facing Lisbon in Margueira Bay on the left bank of the Tagus. This new yard, which was opened in 1967, has three dry docks, the longest (520m - 1 706ft) is capable of taking the largest oil tankers. The yard, in a latitude through which 75% of the world's tankers pass, also provides, repair, degassing and cleaning facilities for the latter. The passenger port (60 000 passengers in 1983) is situated at Rocha do Conde de Óbidos.

Boat trips on the Tagus. – *Weekly April to October start from the Terreiro do Paço, near Cais dos Colunas: Apply to the Direcção-Geral do Turismo, Palácio Foz, Praça dos Restauradores.*

The trips give a good view of Lisbon and its surroundings and the harbour where, in addition to the commercial traffic, Phoenician style barges with large triangular sails can be seen coasting alongside the largest passenger liners.

The crossing of the estuary in one of the regular ferries *(see plans on pp 92-93 and 94-95)* makes a pleasant trip as well as affording fine views of the town.

Suspension Bridge★★ **(Ponte 25 de Abril)** (BV). – *Toll: 100 to 140esc.* Until 1966 there was no bridge over the Tagus below Vila Franca de Xira, and Lisbon, therefore, was only connected with the country's southern province and the industrial area on the river's left bank (Barreiro, Almada, Cacilhas) by ferry. In 1962 construction of a suspension bridge began; it was opened in August 1966. The bridge was constructed from steel purchased from the United Kingdom and the U.S.A. This suspension bridge with an overall length of 2 278m - approx. 1 1/2 miles has the longest central span in Europe – 1 013m - 3 323ft. The bridge is 70m - 230ft above the waters of the Tagus and is suspended from two pylons 190m - 623ft high while the world record foundations go 80m - 262ft below the river bed to stand on basalt rock, etc. The bridge has been constructed to carry not only the present road traffic but also a double railway line below.

The view★★ from the bridge is especially interesting looking from south to north: the light façades of the town buildings can be seen rising in tiers – to the east lie the medieval quarters of the Alfama, dominated by the Castle of St George, in the centre is the Baixa with neo-Classical houses standing majestically along the banks of the Tagus and in the west the Belém Tower recalls the sumptuous days of the 16C.

Christ in Majesty (Cristo-Rei). – *3.5km - 2 miles from the south toll gate of the suspension bridge, turn right at the second motorway exit to take the Almada road. Then follow the signs and leave the car in the car park near the monument (15esc.).*

The statue of Christ in Majesty (28m - 92ft high) is a small replica of the one in Rio de Janeiro. From the pedestal *(access by lift; 25esc; plus 84 steps)* which is 85m - 279ft above ground level and 113m - 371ft over the Tagus, there is a **panoramic view**★★ over the Tagus Estuary and the plain as far as Setúbal.

■ **THE CENTRE: POMBALINE LISBON**★
From Rossio to Rua Augusta time: 1/2 day
Follow the itinerary indicated on the plan pp 94-95

Rossio★ (GY). – The Praça Dom Pedro IV, which is the main square *(rossio)* of the Baixa, dates from the 13C and was the setting for many *autodafés*. Its present appearance is due to Pombal: 18 and 19C buildings line it on three sides, the ground floors being given over to souvenir shops and cafés, while its north side is entirely bordered by the **Dona Maria II National Theatre** (T), built about 1840 on the site of the former Palace of the Inquisition. The façade, with peristyle and pediment, is adorned with a statue of Gil Vicente, creator of the Portuguese theatre.

Between two Baroque fountains at either end of the square is a column with a bronze statue (1870) of King Pedro IV, after whom the square is named and who was also crowned Pedro I, King of Brazil. Flower stalls add a colourful surround to the fountains.

Rossio Station (Estação) (FY). – The station has an amusing 19C neo-Manueline façade with horseshoe shaped openings.

Praça dos Restauradores (FY). – The square owes its name to the men who in 1640 led the revolt against the Spanish and proclaimed the independence of Portugal – an event commemorated by the obelisk in the centre. To the west the deep red Foz Palace (Palácio Foz, now the Direcção-Geral do Turismo) is early 19C and was designed by an Italian architect.

Avenida da Liberdade★ (FX). – The Avenida da Liberdade, 1 500m long and 90m wide - 1 mile x 295ft is the most majestic of Lisbon's many avenues. On either side of the main highways are side roads which are used by Lisbon's doubledecker buses. The pavements are attractively decorated with black and white motifs. Late 19C buildings on either side include theatres, cinemas, a few hotels and restaurants and company offices for insurance, travel, oil, air transport, etc.

Praça Marquês de Pombal (EX). – In the centre of this circular "square", ringed by large hotels, stands a monument to the Marquis of Pombal. Inscriptions round the foot of the monument recall the great man's most important ministerial achievements *(p 121)*.

Take the Av. Fontes Pereira de Melo then the Av. António Augusto de Aguiar on the left.

Edward VII Park★ (Parque Eduardo VII) (EX). – This elegant, formally landscaped park, crowning the Avenida da Liberdade, was named after King Edward VII of England on the occasion of his visit to Lisbon in 1902 to reaffirm the Anglo-Portuguese Alliance. There is a magnificent **vista★** from the upper end of the park over the lower town and the Tagus dominated on either side by the castle and Bairro Alto Hills.

Cold Greenhouse★ (Estufa fria). – *Open 9am to 6pm (5pm in winter); 30esc.*
Wooden shutters in this cold greenhouse protect from the extremes of summer heat and winter cold the exotic plants which grow beside fishponds or cooling waterfalls near small grottoes. Concerts are given in the garden during the high season.

Return to the Praça dos Restauradores (take the Underground from Parque station) then follow the route marked on the town plan pp 94-95.
The Calçada da Gloria, which rises steeply and can be climbed by funicular (fare: 12.50esc.), leads to the Rua São Pedro de Alcântara.

São Pedro de Alcântara Belvedere★ (FY A). – The belvedere takes the form of a pleasant garden with an extensive **view★** of the Baixa and the eastern part of the town *(viewing table)*.

St Rock★ (Igreja São Roque) (FY M¹). – The Church of St Rock was built at the end of fhe 16C by the Italian architect, Filippo Terzi. The original façade collapsed in 1755.
The **interior★** decoration is strikingly elegant. The wood ceiling painted with scenes of the Apocalypse above the nave is by artists of the Italian school. The third chapel on the right is interesting for its 16C *azulejos* and a painting on wood by the 16C artist, Gaspar Vaz of the vision of St Rock.
The **Chapel of St John the Baptist★★** *(4th on the left)*, a masterpiece of Italian Baroque art, was originally constructed in Rome in 1742 to plans by Salvi and Vanvitelli when 130 artists contributed to its completion; after being blessed by the pope, it was dismantled, transported to Lisbon in three ships on the orders of King João V and re-erected in about 1750 in the Church of St Rock. All is richness: the columns are of lapis lazuli, the altar front of amethyst, the steps of porphyry, the angels of white Carrara marble and ivory, the pilasters of alabaster; the flooring and the wall pictures are coloured mosaics; the friezes, capitals and ceiling are highlighted with gold, silver and bronze. The first chapel on the left contains two paintings attributed to the school of Zurbarán *(Nativity* and *Adoration of the Magi)*, and the sacristy *(access through the north transept)* has a 17C coffered ceiling and paintings of St Francis by Vieira Lusitano and André Gonçalves.

Museum of Sacred Art★ (Museu de São Roque) (FY M¹). – The museum abuts on the church *(access by the last door on the left as you leave the church). Guided tour (time: 15 minutes) 10am to 5pm; closed Mondays and holidays; 10esc, free Sundays.*
This modern style museum contains 16C Portuguese paintings and part of the treasure from the St John the Baptist Chapel. The furnishings, eccleciastical plate by 17C Italian artists, and **sacredotal ornaments★** in silk or lamé bordered in gold are outstanding for their rich Baroque decoration. In the first gallery, a fine canopied altar in chased silver is framed by two silver candelabra, perfect in every detail.
Another section on the right of the sacristy contains a 16C Oriental chasuble, a 14C **Virgin and Child★** (Nossa Senhora dos Ardentes) and a silver gilt sculpture of the Rhineland school.
The Rua da Misericórdia is the main street of the Bairro Alto, the popular quarter dating back to the 16C.

Chiado (FZ). – The name Chiado applies not only to the Largo do Chiado but also to the Rua Garrett and the Rua do Carmo which link the Praça Luis de Camões to the Rossio. The Garrett and do Carmo are the two busiest streets in Lisbon: they contain bookshops, leathershops, pastry and confectioners' shop and fashionable clothes stores.

Carmelite Church (Igreja do Carmo) (FY M²). – *Open 10am to 1pm and 2 to 5pm; closed Mondays and holidays; 50esc.*
This church, built at the end of the 14C by Constable Nuno Álvares Pereira *(p 49)*, was for a long time one of the largest in the capital. The nave caved in in 1755 and the **ruins★** provide one of the most memorable reminders of that devastating earth tremor. An **Archaeological Museum** has been formed round them with additional collections (Bronze Age pottery, marble low reliefs, Romanesque and Gothic tombs, Spanish Arabic *azulejos*).
Return to the lower town by the Santa Justa lift.

Santa Justa Lift (Elevador) (GY). – *Admission 15esc.*
It was contructed by the French engineer Gustave Eiffel who built the Eiffel Tower in Paris. From the upper platform there is a good **view★** of the Rossio and the Baixa.

Rua do Ouro (GZ). – "Gold Street" was, in the 15 and 16C, the gold trading area of Lisbon; today it is lined by banks and money changers, jewelers and goldsmiths.

Terreiro do Paço★ (GZ). – The finest square in Lisbon is the Praça do Comércio, known to all citizens as the Terreiro do Paço – The Palace Terrace – in memory of the palace destroyed by the earthquake. It gives on to the Tagus, was designed as a whole and is an excellent example of the Pombal style. The buildings lining three sides are Classical and uniform, tall arcades supporting two upper storeys with red façades. Today they house government departments. In the centre of the square, which is 192m long by 177m wide - 630ft x 581ft and on which, on 1 February 1908, King Carlos I and his heir, Prince Luis Filipe, were assassinated, is an equestrian statue of King José I. This statue by the late 18C sculptor Machado de Castro is cast in bronze and is the reason for the square also being known, particularly to the English, as Black Horse Square. On the north side a 19C Baroque triumphal arch leads to the Rua Augusta.

Rua Augusta (GZ). – This is a bustling, commercial street.

LISBOA

■ **THE CENTRE: MEDIEVAL LISBON**★★ *time: 1/2 day*

1️⃣ **From the Rossio to St George's Castle** – *Follow the route marked on the town plan p 95. You can take a tram to the cathedral.*

The **Church of St Antony by the Cathedral** (Santo António da Sé) **(GZ B)** stands on the site of the house in which St Antony of Padua was born (1195-1231).

Cathedral★ (Sé) **(GZ).** – Lisbon's cathedral, like those of Oporto, Coimbra and Evora, was once a fortress as can be seen from the two towers flanking the façade and its battlements. It was built at the end of the 12C, shortly after the town had been captured by the Crusaders, by, it is said, the French architects Robert and Bernard who designed Coimbra Cathedral. Remodelling followed each earthquake, particularly that of 1755, when the chancel collapsed, bringing down also the lantern tower over the transept. Clever restoration has given the building much of its former Romanesque appeal.

A Visigothic low relief can still be seen at the base of one of the pillars on the north wall of the church.

The main nave is in plain Romanesque style; however, one of the chapels off the north aisle containing a lovely Baroque crib by Machado de Castro *(p 24)* is pure Gothic. An elegant triforium runs above the aisles and the transept. The chancel is 18C but the ambulatory, pierced with lancet windows, kept the earlier Gothic style of the 14C when it was remodelled; the third radiating chapel starting from the south side contains the 14C **tombs ★** of Lopo Fernandes Pacheco, companion in arms to King Alfonso IV, and his wife.

The **sacristy** *(access through the south transept, 9.30am to 12.30pm and 2.30 to 6.30pm (5.30pm in winter); 20esc. The ticket is also valid for the cloisters and the Machado de Castro crib)* is a Baroque room which has been transformed into a **museum** (**museum do tesouro da Sé** *being rearranged*); it shows precious objets of religious art, including silver plate, an Oriental casket in mother of pearl containing relics of St Vincent, Baroque statuettes, etc.

The **cloisters** *(access – apply to the sacristan – through the third chapel off the ambulatory)* recall the late 13C style of Cistercian Gothic: the lower gallery is supported alternately by massive buttresses and Gothic arches, above which are star-shaped oculi. A Romanesque wrought iron **grille ★** closes a chapel off the east gallery.

LISBOA

Places to stay

A wide variety of places to stay
— inland or by the seaside —
have been selected to make your holiday more pleasant

A map on pp 34-35 shows the location of the places listed on pp 36-39.

Gastronomy. Here are a few Portuguese specialities:

Caldo verde – a hot soup made with fresh kale and potatoes.
Leitão assado – roast suckling pig.
Porco à alentejana – pork marinated in wine and
garnished with clams.

95

Further on two chapels house the tomb of Lisbon's first bishop and the other a *Pieta* carved by Teixeira Lopes *(p 25)*.

Santa Luzia Belvedere★ (Miradouro de Santa Luzia) (HY C). – A small shaded square, bright with flowers, near the Church of Santa Luzia has been arranged as a belvedere on the remains of the old Arabic fortifications.

The square affords an excellent **view★** of the Alfama from which rise the belfries of São Miguel and Santi Estêvão, and over the harbour and the Tagus. The outer walls of the church are covered with small panels of *azulejos*, one of which shows the Praça do Comércio and another Lisbon's capture by the Crusaders and the death of **Martim Moniz**. Moniz was a Portuguese knight who, at the cost of his own life, prevented the Moors from shutting one of the castle gates while Alfonso I was making his attack.

Azulejos covering a wall marking the south edge of the square show a general view of Lisbon.

Largo das Portas do Sol (JY). – *Plan p 97*. The Sun Gateway was one of the seven gates into the Arab city. *Make the square the starting point for the walk through the Alfama described below.*

Museum of Decorative Arts (Fundação Ricardo do Espirito Santo Silva) (JY M³). – *Plan p 97*. *Guided tour (time: 40 minutes) 10am to 1pm and 2.30 to 5pm; closed Sundays, Mondays and holidays; 60esc.*

The museum, which is in a 17C palace which formerly belonged to the counts of Azurara, brings to life the Lisbon of the 17 and 18C. The Portuguese and Indo-Portuguese furniture is particularly interesting; there are also collections of silver and several tapestries from the 16 to 18C. The banqueting hall is enhanced by a fine 18C Venetian chandelier.

Return by the same route to take on the right the Travessa de Santa Luzia (plan p 97) which leads to the castle.

St George's Castle★★ (Castelo de São Jorge) (GY). – St George's Castle, the heart of the city, occupies a remarkable site. Constructed by the Visigoths in the 5C and the Moors in the 9C and then modified during the reign of Alfonso I, it has since been turned into a flower garden.

After passing through the outer wall which provides a perimeter to the old medieval quarter of Santa Cruz, you reach the former **parade ground** from which there is a magnificent **view★★★** of the "Straw Sea" – the Mar de Palha as the Portuguese call the Tagus at this point, for the sun often gives it a gold reflection – the industrial buildings on the left bank of the river, the suspension bridge, the lower town and the Monsanto Park. The **ramp** has become a pleasant walk. The **castle** boasts ten towers linked by massive battlemented walls. *Cross the barbican at the castle entrance, steps lead to the parapet walk and the tops of the towers which provide viewpoints over the town.* Note in passing the door in the north wall where Martim Moniz distinguished himself.

The **Royal Palace** (GY E) built on the site of a former Arabic palace, was used as the royal residence by the kings of Portugal from the 14 to 16C.

Santa Cruz Quarter (GY). – A quarter of narrow streets full of people and lined with old houses with wrought iron balconies and doors with judas windows.

2 Walk in the Alfama – *Follow the route indicated on the plan p 97*

We suggest you make this walk early in the morning when the fish market is open, or late in the afternoon when everyone is out and about the streets and squares. At night the Alfama is frequented almost exclusively by *fado* enthusiasts *(pp 30 and 89)*.

Alfama★★ (JYZ). – The Alfama, which rises in tiers from the banks of the Tagus to the castle, in the area between the cathedral and the Church of St Vincent de Fora – Beyond the Wall – is the oldest part of Lisbon. It was already in existence when the Visigoths arrived. During the period of Arab rule it abounded in fine noblemen's mansions, while its name from the Arabic *alhama* recalls the hot springs to be found near the Largo das Alcaçarias.

When Lisbon was converted to Christianity churches began to be erected everywhere; the first were built in the Alfama, but did not survive the earthquakes; for the same reason all the noble mansions have vanished.

The Alfama then became a quarter of seamen and fisherfolk, although a few middle class houses were erected there at the end of the 18C.

Today, the Alfama, the best preserved of Lisbon's popular quarters, is a cobbled labyrinth of narrow turning alleys, cut by steps and archways, sometimes blocked at the far end; the houses with whitewashed or painted façades are decorated with wrought iron balconies and panels of *azulejos*, usually representing the Virgin between St Antony and St Martial; windows from which lines of washing hang to dry are gay with flowers.

From the Largo das Portas do Sol (p 96) go down the stairs of the Beco de Santa Helena.

Largo do Salvador (JY). – No 22, the 16C mansion of the counts dos Arcos, with its ornamental Baroque balcony, remains as witness to the quarter's former noble style.

Rua da Regueira (JY). – The Regueira is lined with small shops and local restaurants. Picturesque judas windows are to be seen in the doors to the houses. At the corner of this street and the Beco das Cruzes stands an interesting 18C house (JYA) where the overhanging upper floors are supported on carved corbels.

Beco das Cruzes★ (JY). – On the left above a door (B) a panel of *azulejos* shows the Virgin of Conception; from the same spot there is a pretty view up the alley to where it is crossed by an arch surmounted by a cross (C).

Beco do Mexias (JYZ). – A very narrow alley bordered by dozens of small shops. A doorway on the left opens into an inner court (E) occupied by a large fountain at which the local women do their washing.

Beco do Carneiro★ (JY). – This blind alley, Sheep's Alley, is so narrow that the eaves meet overhead and it is almost impossible to pass on foot without stepping into a doorway. From the top there is an attractive view of stepped façades and rooftops.

Patio das Flores (JY). – This charming little square is edged with houses whose walls are faced in *azulejos*.

Largo de Santo Estêvão (JY). – On the east side of the square there is a corbelled house (**F**) decorated with an *azulejos* panel. From the southwest corner there is a **view★** over the Alfama rooftops to the harbour and the Tagus.

Largo do Chafariz de Dentro (Inner Fountain Square) (JZ). – The square was formerly within the ramparts which in the 14C protected the town on its Tagus front. Today it is the place where local people meet to talk in the evenings.

Rua de São Pedro★★ (JZ). – The São Pedro is the busiest trading street in the Alfama. Lined

on either side by small shops and local "taverns", it is filled all day with colourful and noisy crowds: fisher-women *(varinas)* selling fish, pedlars and many others.

Largo de São Rafael (JZ). – On the west side of this small square surrounded by 17C houses, there still stands the remains of a tower (**K**) which formed part of the Arabic wall and later the defences of Christian Lisbon until the 14C when King Fernando ordered that a new wall be built.

Rua da Judiaria (Jewish Quarter) (JZ). – Go down the street and you will see a 16C house (**L**) with paired windows which abuts on the old Arabic wall.

St Michael's (Igreja São Miguel) (JZ). – The church is rich in Baroque wood-work.

Beco da Cardosa (JYZ). – Blind alleys lined with 16 and 18C houses branch off on either side of this picturesque passage with steps and a supporting arch (**JYN**).

Rua Norberto de Araújo (JYZ). – The steps, supported on one side by the Visigothic town wall, lead one back to the Largo das Portas do Sol.

(After Secretaria de Estado da Informação e Turismo photo)

The Alfama.

97

■ THE WEST: MANUELINE LISBON ★★ (Belém Quarter) time: 1/2 day

Leave the Praça do Comércio by car. See plan pp 92-93.

Hieronymite Monastery ★★ (Mosteiro dos Jerónimos) (AV). – This monastery, founded by King Manuel and designed by the architect Boytac *(p 22)*, is considered to be the jewel of Manueline art. Begun in 1502 not long after the return of Vasco da Gama from the Indies and situated near Restelo harbour in Belém from which the explorer's ships had sailed, it benefited from the riches then pouring into Lisbon. The Gothic style adopted by Boytac until his death in 1517 was modified by his successors: João de Castilho, of Spanish origin, added a Plateresque element to the decoration; Nicolas Chanterene emphasized the Renaissance element; Diogo de Torralva and Jérôme de Rouen, at the end of the 16C brought a Classical note. Only the buildings added in the 19C, west of the belfry, seem quite separate and not part of the overall architectural harmony.

St Mary's ★★ (Santa Maria). – The south doorway, the work of Boytac and João de Castilho, combines a mass of gables, pinnacles and niches filled with statues. Crowning all is a screen surmounted by the Cross of the Order of the Knights of Christ. A statue of Prince Henry the Navigator adorns the pier, and two low reliefs showing scenes from the life of St Jerome, the tympanum. Twin windows on either side of the doorway are heavily decorated.

The interior is outstanding for the beauty of the stonework, carved throughout in great detail but never in such a way as to obscure the architectural lines, as for instance, in the characteristic network **vaulting ★★** of equal height over the nave and aisles. This vaulting resisted the earth tremor of 1755, standing on paired columns uniform in sculptural decoration but ever more slender as their distance from the transept increases. The spiral decoration and the design of niches on the pillars and the magnificent vaulting over the transept crossing are by João de Castilho. The transepts are Baroque, designed by Jérôme de Rouen, the son of Jean de Rouen *(p 23)* and contain the tombs of several royal princes. In the chancel, which was reconstructed in the Classical period, are the tombs of Kings Manuel I and João III and their queens. On either side of the lower chancel *(coro baixo)*, are those of Vasco da Gama and also Camões whose recumbent figure wears a crown of laurel leaves.

Go out by the west door to reach the cloister.

This door by Nicolas Chanterene is ornamented with very fine statuettes, particularly of King Manuel and Queen Maria being presented by their patrons. Represented above the doorway are the Annunciation, the Nativity and the Adoration of the Magi.

Cloister ★★★. – This masterpiece of Manueline art is fantastically rich sculpturally. The stone is at its most beautiful when it takes on the warm golden tint of late afternoon. The cloister, forming a hollow square of which each side measures 55m - 170ft is two storeys high. The ground level galleries with groined vaulting by Boytac have wide arches with tracery resting upon slender columns, and Late Gothic and Renaissance decoration carved into the massive thickness of the walls. The recessed upper storey by João do Castilho is less exuberant but more delicate in style.

The chapterhouse contains the tomb of the writer Alexandre Herculano. The sacristy leading off the east gallery and the monks' refectory off the west gallery both have lierne and tierceron vaulting.

Archaeological Museum (Museu Nacional de Arqueologia e Etnologia) (AV M⁴). – *Open 10am to 12.30pm and 2 to 5pm; closed Mondays and holidays; 20esc, free Sundays.*

The museum, in a 19C wing, contains Iberian antiquities.

The Hieronymite Cloister.

Monument to the Discoveries ★ (Padrão dos Descobrimentos) (AV F). – This monument, erected in 1960 beside the Tagus on the 500th anniversary of the death of Prince Henry the Navigator, represents the prow of a ship with the prince pointing the way to a crowd of personages, among whom can be recognized, on the right side, King Manuel carrying an armillary sphere, Camões holding verses from *The Lusiads* and the painter, Nuno Gonçalves.

In the centre of the black and white "wave" mosaic around the monument is a mosaic compass dial and map of the world.

Museum of Popular Art ★ (AV M⁵). – *Open 10am to 12.30pm and 2 to 5pm; closed Mondays and holidays; 50esc.*

A most attractive presentation of artisan life and crafts and the folklore traditions of the provinces of Portugal.

Belém Tower ★★ (Torre de Belém) (AV). – *Not open to the public.*

This robust fortress, built in the middle of the Tagus, is an elegant Manueline tower *(illustration p 22)*, at the water's edge on the north bank, the river having altered course since medieval times. Jutting out to command the mainstream is an artillery platform, protected by battlements each of which is decorated with a shield of the Order of the Cross of Christ. At the corners are rounded sentry boxes with domed roofs. On the terrace, facing the sea, is a statue of Our Lady of Safe Homecoming.

The tower is five storeys high ending in a terrace. On the 3rd floor, paired windows with elegant balconies, a magnificent Renaissance loggia surmounted by the royal arms of Manuel I and two armillary spheres mellow the granite tower's original architectural severity.

Museum of Ancient Art★★ (Museu Nacional de Arte Antiga) (BV M[6]). – *Open 10am to 5pm; closed Mondays and holidays; 100esc.*

Of the collection of 15 and 16C **Portuguese Primitives**★★ on the 2nd floor, the jewel is the famous **polyptych**★★★ of the Adoration of St Vincent painted between 1460 and 1470 by Nuno Gonçalves. The six panels which stand round a statue of St Vincent, patron saint of Lisbon and Portugal, provide a precious document on contemporary Portuguese society. This, the artist's only extant work, reveals his talent to the full. The composition may well show some debt to the tapestries of the period.

① Saint Vincent
② King Afonso V
③ Prince João, future King João II
④ Prince Henry the Navigator
⑤ Queen Isabel
⑥ Isabella of Aragon, her mother
⑦ Nuno Gonçalves
⑧ Prince Fernando
⑨ Knights
⑩ The Archbishop of Lisbon accompanied by two canons
⑪ The Chronicler, Gomes Eanes de Azurara
⑫ Cistercians from Alcobaça
⑬ Fishermen and pilots
⑭ Fernando, Second Duke of Bragança
⑮ His eldest son, Fernando
⑯ His youngest son, João
⑰ A Moorish knight
⑱ A cleric proffering St. Vincent's skull
⑲ A Jew
⑳ A beggar before the saint's coffin

Museum of Ancient Art — The Adoration of St. Vincent.

Outstanding among the other Portuguese Primitives are a late 15C *Ecce Homo,* an Entombment and works by Frei Carlos *(p 23).*

Also on the 2nd floor is a delicious sketch by Domingos Antônio de Sequeria (1768-1837) of the artist's children and a collection of furniture.

The 1st floor is devoted to foreign schools of painting. The most notable works include *Temptation of St Antony* by Hieronymus Bosch, *Virgin and Child* by Memling, *St Jerome* by Dürer, *Virgin, Child and Saints* by Hans Holbein the Elder and the **Twelve Apostles★** by Zurbarán.

Also on the 1st floor is a large collection of gold and silver plate: 16C silver gilt chalice, 16C Indo-Portuguese caskets, and a highly ornate monstrance by the talented dramatist, poet and goldsmith, Gil Vicente *(p 84).* Dated 1506 the monstrance belonged to the Belém Monastery.

On the ground floor are carpets and ceramics.

The museum includes a chapel from the former Convent of Santo Alberto, which is outstanding for its wooden Baroque sculpture and its 16-18C *azulejos.*

■ THE NORTH AND THE EAST: MODERN LISBON *plan pp 92-93*

Modern Lisbon spreads north and east: large avenues (the Avenida de Roma, Avenida dos Estados Unidos da America, Avenida Almirante Gago Coutinho) have been laid, new quarters created and a modern university founded.

Three motorways and the bridge over the Tagus help to clear traffic from the centre of the city into the suburbs and to the country as a whole, and are also assisting the economic development of the region around Lisbon. The airport has become an important link between Europe, America and Africa.

Calouste-Gulbenkian Museum★★★ (CU M[7]). – *Plan p 93. Open 10am to 5pm (2 to 7.30pm Wednesdays and Saturdays July to October); closed Mondays and holidays; 40esc, free Sundays; time: allow 2 1/2 hours.*

Housed on one floor in a wing of the Gulbenkian Foundation, this very modern museum contains the art collections bequeathed to Portugal by the Armenian patron of the arts (1869-1955).

1st section. – Ancient art: there are works from Egypt (an alabaster bowl about 2 700 years old; a stone statuette of "judge Bes"), the Greco-Roman world (a superb 5BC Attic vase, **jewelery,** coins and medals), and Mesopotamia (A 9BC Assyrian stele, a Parthian urn). Oriental art: this is mostly Christian Armenia (a magnificent Ispahan Gospel, dating from 1686) and especially noteworthy, eastern Islamic: an exceptional **collection of carpets,** mainly Persian (16-17C) wonderful **pottery** (12-18C), glazed glass lamps from the mosques of Alep (14C), Korans and collections of poetry of the 15 and 16C *(on view alternately).*

Art from the Far East: that from China consists mainly of lovely **porcelain** (a 14C Taoist bowl; 17C vase of the hundred birds) and "rough stones" (18C green nephrite bowl); from Japan there are etchings *(on view alternately)* and a selection of lacquer-ware of the 18 and 19C.

2nd section (European art). – This takes up the greater part of the museum, with a preferential place for 18C French art.

Medieval religious art: lovely ivories and manuscripts. 15, 16 and 17C paintings and sculpture: an interesting comparison of schools, there is an admirable *Annunciation* by Dierick Bouts, a masterly *Portrait of Helen Fourment* by **Rubens**; several statues of the 14 to 16C and a 17C bronze bust of Turenne by Coysevox. Of the French 18C: paintings by **Lancret** (a *Fête Galante* in shades of pink, blue and mauve), Hubert Robert *(Gardens of Versailles)*, **Quentin de la Tour** *(Portrait of Mademoiselle Sallé*, in pastel), busts by Lemoyne and Caffieri, statuettes by Clodion, Pigalle and Falconet, and a proud Diana in white marble by **Houdon**.

Then from the Renaissance period there are tapestries (Italy, Brussels), pottery (Spain, Italy) and sculptures (Italy, France) and books of the 16 to 18C.

18C French furnishings: luxurious creations by **Cressent,** Jacob, Oeben, Riesener, Garnier, and Carlin; there is a splendid screen of black and gold lacquer; and Beauvais and Aubusson tapestries.

Gold and silver plate, bronzes and pottery (French, 18 and 19C); particularly note the masterpieces of table silverware created by A. Durand, F.-T. Germain, Lenhendrick, Biennais, etc.

18C painting can again be seen in English works by **Gainsborough** (a lovely Portrait of Mrs. Lowndes-Stone), Romney, Turner, etc. and also a Venetian series by Francesco Guardi. French Impressionism, with canvases by **Corot** *(The Bridge at Mantes)*, **Manet** *(Child with Cherries)*; in addition there are sculptures by **Barye** (animals), **Carpeaux** (a charming wounded Cupid in bronze), Dalou and Rodin.

In the last room there are works of the art nouveau period by the French decorator René Lalique (1860-1945), a personal friend of Calouste Gulbenkian.

Zoological Garden★★ (BU). – *Plan p 92. Open 9am to 8pm (6pm in winter); 150esc; children: 80esc.*

This zoo, with a collection of 3 500 animals, is set in a park of some 26 hectares - 64 acres amid flower gardens.

From the small mill *(miradouro dos moinhos)* at the top of the hill *(viewing table)* you get a view looking south of the Águas Livres Aqueduct and the Christ in Majesty statue, southwest, the Monsanto Park and the Marquis of Fronteira estate where there is a patio ornamented with *azulejos,* and northwest the famous Benfica Luz Stadium.

Our Lady of Fátima (CU K). – *Plan p 93.* This modern church is adorned with beautiful **stained glass windows★** by Almada Negreiros.

Numismatic Museum (Museu numismatico) (CU M⁸). – *Closed for reorganization.*
On the 1st floor of the Casa da Moeda. There are about 45 000 ancient coins exhibited, both Portuguese (dating from the 12C, and with the first gold escudo which was struck in the 15C) and foreign. Approximately 5 000 medals as well as forged coins made in the 15-16C can also be seen.

■ **ADDITIONAL SIGHTS** *unless otherwise indicated see plan pp 94-95*

Botanical Garden★ (EX). – *Open 9am to 7pm (5pm in winter); closed Saturdays, Sundays and holidays 1 October to 31 March.*
A fine avenue of palm trees crosses this lush garden with its many flowering plants.

Museum of Modern Art (Museu de Arte Contemporânea) (FZ M⁹). – *Open 10am to 12.30pm and 2 to 5pm; closed Mondays; 100esc, free Sundays and holidays. Apply in advance in writing to the Curator, Rua Serpa Pinto no 6.*
Of particular interest in the museum are the paintings by Columbano (1857-1929), José Malhoa (1855-1933), João Reis *(Pescadores de Lavos),* and Teixeira Lopes's sculpture, *The Widow* (a Viúva).

Star Basilica (Basílica da Estrela) (BV L). – *Plan p 92.* The imposing Baroque Star Basilica was erected at the end of the 18C. Inside, the transept crossing is covered by a fine **cupola★** surmounted by a lantern tower. Note also a manger with lifesize figures carved by Machado de Castro *(p 24).*

Church of the Mother of God★★ (Igreja da Madre de Deus) (DU N). – *Plan p 93.* Rebuilt at the end of the 18C following the 1755 earthquake, the present edifice has conserved a Manueline doorway, a relic of the original church.

Interior★★. – The tall nave has a coffered vault with panels painted to illustrate scenes from the Life of the Virgin; high on the walls paintings represent on the left and right respectively the lives of St Clare and St Francis; the lower parts of the walls are covered with 18C Dutch tiles. The pulpit and altarpieces are Baroque.

The crypt (originally the primitive church) contains an **altar★** of gilded wood; 16C Seville *azulejos* line the walls.

The **chapterhouse★★** is reached by the church gallery *(coro alto)* it contains the reliquary of St Justus. The painted caissons with golden coffering on the ceiling frame 16 and 17C paintings including portraits of João III and his queen which are attributed to Cristóvão Lopes while those on the walls are of the Life of Our Lord.

The Chapel of St Antony (18C *azulejos)* leads to a room containing several 15 and 16C Portuguese and Flemish **Primitive paintings★**.

The sacristy is decorated with panels of polychrome *azulejos* by André Gonçalves and 16C canvases, and has a white marble credence table and a vestment cupboard of precious wood.

Cloisters adjoin the church; the great cloister is Renaissance; the small cloister, a delightful example of the Manueline style, shows Mudejar influences and contains some beautiful multicoloured geometric 16-17C *azulejos.*

Azulejo Museum★ (Museu do azulejo). – Part of the monastic buildings round the cloisters have been converted into a museum showing, in panels or fragments, the main types of Portuguese or foreign *azulejos* since the 14C.

St Vincent Beyond the Wall (Igreja São Vincente de Fora) (**HY P**). – Filippo Terzi built this church between 1582 and 1627. The interior, which is covered with a fine coffered vault, is outstanding for the simplicity of its lines. On the south side of the church, the cloister *(open 9am to 1pm and 3 to 6pm; closed Mondays; 25esc)*, has walls covered in 18C *azulejos* illustrating the *Fables* of La Fontaine. Galleries lead to the former monks' refectory which since the time of João IV has been transformed into a mausoleum for the House of Bragança. In the convent's caretaker's lodge *(portaria)* the ceiling was painted by Vicente Baccarelli (18C) and the large azulejo panel represents the taking of Lisbon from the Moors.

St Encratis (Igreja da Santa Engrácia) (**HY Q**). – Begun in the 17C this church was never completed. In the form of a Greek cross, it is surmounted by a cupola which completes the Baroque façade. The church is now the national pantheon *(guided tour - time: 1/2 hour - 10am to 5pm; closed Mondays and holidays; 20esc)*.

Flea Market (Feira da Ladra) (**HY**). – *Tuesdays and Saturdays 10am to dusk.*
This picturesque market is held on the Campo de Santa Clara.

Our Lady of the Mountain Belvedere★ (Miradouro da Senhora do Monte) (**GX R**). – There is an extensive view★ over Lisbon and in particular over St George's Castle and the Mouraria Quarter from this belvedere.

Military Museum (**HY M**10). – *Open 10am to 4pm; Sundays 11am to 5pm; closed Mondays and holidays; 30esc.*
The collections of arms and armour are displayed in the former 18C arsenal where the ceilings★ and woodwork provide an interesting background.

Municipal Museum (Museu da Cidade) (**CU M**11). – *Plan p 93. Open 2 to 6pm; closed Mondays and holidays.*
The museum, which is in the former 18C Palácio Pimenta, displays a series of documents showing Lisbon's development and growth. Among the pictures exhibited, note the famous canvas by Malhoa *(p 25)*, The Fado.

The House of Facets (Casa dos Bicos) (**GZ S**). – This house, faced with diamond faceted stones, once formed part of a 16C palace which was damaged in the 1755 earthquake.

Old Church of the Conception (Igreja da Conceição Velha) (**GZ V**). – The south face★ of the transept, the only relic of the original church which collapsed in the earthquake of 1755, is a fine example of the Manueline style; the carving on the tympanum shows Our Lady of Compassion sheltering beneath her robe Pope Léon X, King Manuel, Queen Leonor, bishops and others.

Maritime Museum★★ (Museu de Marinha) (**AV M**4). – *Plan p 92. Open 10am to 5pm; closed Mondays and holidays; 30esc, free Wednesdays; enter through the west wing of the Hieronymite monastery.*
This museum of Portugal's maritime past is situated on both sides of the esplanade of the Calouste Gulbenkian planetarium, in two separate buildings; the west wing of the Hieronymite monastery and the modern Galliot Pavilion.

Main building. – Giant statues in sandstone of historical personnages (one of which is Henry the Navigator), ancient cannons, three anchors from the *Niña* of Christopher Columbus can all be seen in the entrance hall, and make an attractive start to the visit. In the Oriental room on the mezzanine floor, there are models of boats of the former Portuguese trading posts in Asia, some of them in ivory or precious metal.

The 1st floor is devoted to the merchant navy (galleons, steamships, cargo boats, oil tankers), river navigation (models of "frigates" of the Tagus, *rabelos* of the Doura, feluccas and *catraios* used in olden days), and to colonial expeditions of the 19C (Overseas room).

On the ground floor there is an immense room devoted to the Discoveries and the Navy, from the 15 to the 18C, with very accurate and often magnificent models of sailing ships, caravels and frigates, including the 18C vessel, the *Príncipe de Beira*. Warships of the 19 and 20C can also be seen (small scale models of gunboats, frigates and corvettes, modern surface ships and submarines), as well as the fishing fleet (**Henrique Selxas' collection**) with models of various kinds of boats which used to fish in the estuaries or along the Portuguese coast: a *muleta* from Seixal, a *calâo* from the Algarve, a *galeâo* from Nazaré, etc. In an annex there is a reconstitution of the luxurious royal stateroom of the yacht *Amelia* (late 19C).

Galliot Pavilion. – It contains a dozen magnificent ceremonial galliots (or galleys). The most remarkable is that decorated by the French ornamentalist Pillement and built in 1785 for the wedding of the future King João VI. It also has finely dressed models representing the crew.

One can also see a whole arsenal of naval cannons, shells, mines and modern torpedos, as well as three sea-planes, one of which, the *Santa Cruz* made the first crossing of the south Atlantic in June 1922. As to sea charts, there are originals or reproductions of old ones.

Coach Museum★★ (Museu Nacional dos Coches) (**AV M**12). – *Plan p 92. Open 10am to 6.30pm (5pm in winter); closed Mondays and holidays; 50esc, free Saturdays and Sundays.*
Installed in rooms with overhanging galleries in the former riding school of Belêm Palace, it has a splendid collection of 74 carriages (coaches, four-wheelers, etc.) either royal, papal or princely of the 16C (coach belonging to Philip II of Spain), 17C (Isabella of Savoy's coach), 18C (Clement XI's coach), 19C (coronation coach of the Portuguese kings João VI, Louis I, Charles I), some of them elegantly light, others heavily encrusted with mouldings and statues (coach of the Portuguese Embassy in Rome); most of them are handsomely gilded and padded. Sedan chairs, figures wearing coach driver's or footmen's costumes, saddles, silver harness, a coat which belonged to Queen Amelia (founder of the museum in 1905) complete the exhibition.

Monsanto Park★ (AUV). – *Plan p 92* – The park is cut by rides affording panoramic views of Lisbon. The northwest part is occupied by the estate *(quinta)* of the Marquesses of Fronteira *(to visit the park during the week, apply at the door no 1, right of the palace); 20esc.*

Aguas Livres Aqueduct★ (BU). – *Plan p 92*. The aqueduct, which is more than 18km - 11 miles long and took from 1728 to 1748 to construct, still brings fresh water to Lisbon. The tallest arch stands 65m - 213ft above the Alcântara Valley.

The best view of the Avenida de Ceuta is obtained from the bridge on the N 7 to the north.

Palace of Ajuda (Palacio Nacional da Ajuda) (AV). – *Plan p 92. Open 10am to 5pm; closed Mondays; 100esc, free Sundays.*

This former, never completed royal palace (18-19C) has some sumptuous furnishings. Worth noticing are the floors, tapestries as well as sculpture by Machado de Castro and canvases by Domingos António Sequeira and Vieira Portuense.

Vasco de Gama Aquarium. – *At Dâfundo, on the N 6, by ③. Open noon (10am Sundays and holidays) to 6pm; closed 1 May; 30esc, free Wednesdays.*

There are numerous tanks with sea plants, fish and shellfish from both hemispheres; ponds with turtles and seals. Upstairs, there is a room with stuffed sea animals.

LOUSĂ, Serra da ★

Michelin map **37** folds 4, 5, 14 and 15

Wooded hills and crests, where the bare rock takes on a violet hue, make up the mountain landscape of the Serra da Lousã where the highest point at Alto do Trevim reaches an altitude of 1 202m - 3 934ft. The range, consisting of shale ridges and a few harder quartz rock crests, ends in the north in a sheer drop to the Lousã Basin. To the south, the Zêzere Valley divides it from the Serra da Gardunha, which on the east is overlooked by the granite mass of the Serra da Estrela.

The local inhabitants, living in scattered hamlets of low lying houses built of shale, subsist on mediocre crops of rye and maize grown on terraces and the raising of sheep and goats. The hillsides have been planted with sea pines in an effort to combat soil erosion.

From Pombal to Coimbra – *124km - 77 miles – about 3 hours*

From Pombal (p 121) take the N 237 going towards Ansião.

The road from Pombal to Pontão winds over chalky hills dotted with occasional olives, oaks and pines.

The countryside becomes greener and hillier as the chalk gives way to marl, which is used in some of the local brickworks. The **drive**★ has great variety as *corniche* roads follow the mountain contours, and views of cultivated valleys below and bare peaks alternate with wooded stretches of countryside.

Figueiró dos Vinhos. – Pop 4 662. Figueiró dos Vinhos is a small town known for its earthenware pots and bowls. The church, with a chancel decorated in 18C *azulejos* illustrating the life of John the Baptist, has a fine Trinity in the south chapel.

Cabril Dam★. – *22km - 14 miles to the east of Figueiró dos Vinhos*. This dam, constructed on a base of granite and shale in a **defile**★ in the Zêzere Valley, measures 132m - 443ft in height and 290m - 951ft along its crest; a slender screen of concrete holds back 614 million m³ - nearly 150 000 million gallons of water in a reservoir which extends 53km - 33 miles back up the valley. The power station produced in 1983 167.5 million kWh a year.

There is a fine **view**★ from the dam crest, downstream over the enclosed valley hillsides scattered with shrubs, and upstream of pine covered hills running down to the reservoir's edge.

The N 236–1, between Figueiró dos Vinhos and Lousã crosses the Serra da Lousã whose southern slope, at first wooded with pine and eucalyptus, gets barer as it rises.

Castanheira de Pera. – Pop 4 825. On the main street of the town, opposite a school, there is a strange public garden with yew trees, box trees and thujas clipped into amusing shapes.

After Castanheira a belvedere at a right hand turn affords a wide **view**★, beyond onto a curtain of pine, below onto a tributary valley of the Zêzere, higher up on to a crestline, with the Zêzere Valley behind it, then a second crestline and the Tagus Basin.

The **descent**★ into Lousã is swift, the *corniche* road affording attractive glimpses of the Arouce Valley.

Candal. – Pop 297. The old village of Candal stands in an unusual setting along the line of the steepest slope.

Nossa Senhora da Piedade Belvedere (Miradouro). – The **view**★ from the belvedere plunges down into the Arouce Valley where a medieval castle and minute white chapels can be seen on the valley floor. Opposite, surrounded by crop covered terraces, stands the perched village of **Casal Novo.**

A little further on Lousã and the Mondego Valley can be seen.

Lousã. – Pop 7 594. Lousã, like **Foz de Arouce** to the north, possesses a considerable number of patrician 18C houses, ornamented with coats of arms and decorated windows.

The road *(the N 236 and later the N 17 on the left)* after crossing the Lousã Basin and going through Foz de Arouce, follows the course of the Ceira and Mondego Valleys before reaching Coimbra *(p 63)*.

Michelin map **37** fold 11 (inset) and south of fold 16 – Pop 10 153

The town of Mafra has developed to the south of the ancient monastery of the same name, which stands foursquare upon the plateau, a solid and impressive mass in sharp contrast to the many nearby windmills.

The Fulfilment of a Vow. – In 1711 King João V, having no children after three years of marriage, vowed to erect a monastery if God would grant him an heir. A daughter was born. The king bought a vast expanse of land and in 1717 entrusted the work of building the monastery to the German architect Friedrich Ludwig *(p 24)*, who was later succeeded by his son. When the king increased the number of monks from thirteen to thirty, he called in two additional architects, which explains why some of the architectural detail is Germanic, some Italian and some truly Portuguese.

The monastery with 4 500 doors and windows covers 4ha - 10 acres of ground. Within are a basilica, a palace and a monastery building prolonged at the end by a park with a perimeter wall 20km - 12 miles long: 50 000 workmen took part in the construction which went on for thirteen years. The materials came from Portugal, then from the Netherlands and Belgium (the bells), France (liturgical objects), Brazil (precious woods), Italy (walnut wood, statues from Rome and Florence and Carrara marble).

The Mafra School. – João V took advantage of the presence of so many foreign artists at Mafra to found a school of sculpture. The first principal was the Italian, Alexander Giusti and among the teachers were such men as José Almeida, Giovanni António of Padua, who carved the most important statues in the cathedral at Évora and, particularly, **Joaquim Machado de Castro** (1731-1822), the famous sculptor of many Lisbon monuments.

The school's studios, patronized by the Canons Regular of St Augustine who formerly occupied the monastery, produced many marble statues and several jasper and marble altarpieces, often embellished with low reliefs, which may now be seen in the basilica.

Attractive glazed ceramics are made at **Sobreiro** *(5km - 4 miles to the northwest).*

■ **THE MONASTERY** ★ *time: 1 1/2 hours*

The 220m - 722ft long façade is flanked at either end by Germanic-style wings surmounted by bulbous domes. The basilica stands in the centre of the façade.

Basilica ★ . – The basilica, like the flanking wings, is built of marble, its façade breaking the monotony of the main face by its whiteness and its Baroque decoration. The towers are joined by a double row of columns; niches high up contain Carrara marbles statues of St Dominic and St Francis and below of St Clare and St Elizabeth of Hungary.

The peristyle is adorned with six statues of which the most remarkables is that of St Bruno; further statues embellish the side chambers of the main parts of the towers.

The church inside is strikingly elegant in its proportions and in the marble ornamentation. The tunnel vaulting rests upon fluted pilasters which also divide the lateral chapels, each of which contains statues and an altarpiece in white marble with a low relief carved by sculptors from the Mafra school.

The jasper and marble altarpieces in the transept chapels and the chancel pediment are also by the Mafra school. Note especially the fine marble altarpiece of the Virgin and Child in the chapel off the north aisle and the sacristy and lavabo where marble of every description may be seen. Four delicately worked arches at the transept crossing support a magnificent rose and white marble **cupola** ★ .

Also remarkable are the bronze candelabra and six fine organs dating from 1807.

Palace and Monastery. – *3rd door to the left of the basilica. Guided tours (time: 1 1/2 hours) 10am to 5pm; closed Tuesdays and holidays; 50esc.*

The tour proceeds through the pharmacy, the hospital, one of the studios of carving, the kitchens, a museum of sacred art and, on the 2nd floor, the royal apartments, the chapel and the monks' cells. The library is an immense gallery decorated in the Baroque manner containing 36 000 volumes.

It is possible to walk across the main roofs to the basilica dome and the belfries.

Comparative sculpture is displayed in a museum to the left of the palace entrance.

Michelin map **37** fold 3 or **441** fold 34 – Pop 8 055

The medieval town of Mangualde is today a busy agricultural and commercial centre.

Palace of the Counts of Anadia ★ **(Palácio des condes de Anadia).** – *Guided tour 9am to noon and 2 to 5pm; 150 to 200esc.*

This 17C seigneurial estate has a Rococo style façade. The interior is interesting for its furniture and its exceptional collection of 17 and 18C **azulejos** ★ ★ which in particular decorate the hall (battle scenes), the monumental staircase (hunting scenes, legend of Diana and Acteon) and upstairs in the "noble salon" (Forge of the Cyclops, Ulysses, Neptune, etc.). There is also a collection of Sevres china.

Church of the Misericord (Igreja de Misericórdia). – *Enter by the courtyard of the adjoining school.* Dating from the 18C, built at right angles, it is charming with its small Baroque façade adorned with statues, and on the courtyard side its first floor gallery with granite colonnades and balusters. Inside, in the nave, *azulejos* depict the Last Supper, the Miraculous Draught of Fishes, St Martin, etc. In the chancel, which has a gilded coffered ceiling and altars decorated with *azulejos,* note the carved wooden brackets on which to hang lamps.

Old Quarter. – In front of the Anadia palace and a fountain is the old part of Mangualde: winding alleys, small granite houses huddled together round the belfry.

EXCURSION

Penalva do Castelo. – Pop 985. *12km - 7 1/2 miles on the N 329-1, to the northeast.*
On the western side of this small town, the **Casa da Insua**, a manor house dating from 1775, rises majestically with its battlemented façade in a pleasant landscape of woods and orchards. One can visit the chapel dating from 1690, as well as the park which is planted with huge trees (sequoias, eucalyptus) and the very carefully kept garden where camelias, magnolias and exotic plants grow.

■ MARÃO, Serra do ★

Michelin map **37** fold 2 or **441** folds 23 and 24

The Serra do Marão is a block of granite and shale bounded to the east by the Corgo, to the west by the Tâmega and to the south by the Douro. The dislocations caused by the mountain range's upheaval in the Tertiary Era are the reason for its variation of altitude; the wildness and desolation of the landscape are due to intense erosion.

From Vila Real to Amarante – *49km - 30 miles – about 1 1/2 hours – local map p 68*

Leave Vila Real (p 139) by the Oporto road, the N 15 going west. As soon as the road reaches the slopes maize, pine and chestnut trees replace vine-yards, apple orchards and olive groves; starting at Granja the villages, built upon rock shelves, work almost exclusively at blackware pottery which is displayed by the roadside.
Beyond Granja, there are **views** of the *serra's* foothills and of Vila Real in its hollow.
After Arrabães, leave the N 304, the Mondim de Basto road (see below) on your right.
The N 15 continues to climb, soon overlooking a large factory in the valley and to the right the road offers beautiful **views**★ of the summit of the Sejarão which is the highest in the *serra's* peaks.

Sejarão Peak★★. – Alt 1 415m - 4 643ft. *9.5km - 6 miles from the N 15 on the left, by a tarred road.* The road rises up through a mineral landscape of laminated cristalline rocks or shale and ends in a flat headland near the summit where a chapel and a radio-television relay station can be seen.
The summit, topped by an obelisk, commands a magnificent **panorama**★★ of the bare summits of the *serra*, the nearest being that of Mount Alto do Espinho (alt 1 036m - 3 398ft) indicated by a stele.

Shortly after the Alto do Espinho Pass (alt 1 019m - 3 343ft) in a bend, you will come on the São Gonçalo Pousada. The steep and winding descent to Amarante continues along a *corniche* road above the Rio Ovelha, a tributary of the Tâmega, which is well stocked with trout. Shortly before Candemil the road enters an enclosed rocky valley.
The last part of the drive through a green landscape of growing crops, pines and chestnut trees affords attractive views to the right of the tributary valleys of the Tâmega.
The N 15 drops down to the Tâmega Valley before reaching Amarante *(p 44)*.

From Vila Real to Mondim de Basto – *48km - 30 miles – about 1 1/2 hours – local map p 68*

Leave Vila Real (p 139) by the N 15, then right into the N 304. After Aveção do Cabo the road rises towards the pass from which there is a **view**★ to the left of the upper basin of the Rio Olo. The **descent**★ ends at Mondim de Basto in the Tâmega Valley.

Our Lady of Grace★ (Nossa Senhora da Graça). – Alt 966m - 3 169ft. *13km - 8 miles from Mondim de Basto by the N 312 to the north and a forest road on the right.* The forest road climbs between the rocks and pine trees (with their resin cups) until it reaches the lovely conical summit crowned by the chapel.
Leave the car at the bottom of the majestic staircase *(68 steps)*, which leads to the chapel. From the steeple *(reached by 54 steps and rungs)* there is a **panoramic view**★ over the Tâmega Valley, Mondim de Basto and the Serra do Marão to the south.

■ MARVÃO ★★

Michelin map **37** fold 6 – 22km - 14 miles north of Portalegre – *Local map p 127* – Pop 309

Marvão is a proud fortified medieval village, clustered at the foot of a castle on one of the peaks (865m - 2 838ft) of the Serra de São Mamede near the Spanish frontier.
When in 1833 the Alentejo became the scene of the civil war *(p 18)*, the liberals and the extremists fought for possession of the Marvão stronghold because of its impregnability. The liberals captured it by surprise in December 1833, repulsing a counter attack by Dom Miguel I's troops the following month.

The Site★★. – The access road which goes round the rock spike by the north gives one a good idea of the military value of Marvão: the village appears like an eagle's eyrie balanced in a crack in the granite wall.
After circling the ramparts, which are still intact, glance at the Gothic doorway of the Church of Our Lady of the Star, before going through to the village by the double doors flanked by curtain walls, watchtowers and battlements.

The Village★. – *A narrow alley leads to a square with a pillory where you leave the car.*
The stronghold is cut by small streets going uphill and downhill, covered alleys and white houses with balconies bright with flowers, wrought iron grilles and Manueline windows; several chapels have Renaissance doorways. In the Rua do Espírito Santo which goes to the castle, there are two magnificent 17C wrought iron **balustrades**★.

The Castle★. – The castle, constructed at the end of the 13C at the western extremity of the rock spur, was remodelled to a certain extent in the 17C. It consists of a series of perimeter walls dominated by a square keep. Four fortified gates in succession have to be passed through before you reach a flight of steps on the right to the parapet walk which you follow to the keep. Impressive downward **views★★** give a good idea of the various walls and particularly of the crenellated towers and watchtowers built on the rock overhangs. The vast panorama extends to the jagged mountain ranges of Spain in the east, the Castelo Branco Region and Serra da Estrela in the north and the Serra de São Mamede in the southwest.

MÉRTOLA

Michelin map **37** fold 9 – Pop 3 347

The village of Mértola, perched on a spur at the confluence of the Guadiana and Oeiras Rivers and still overlooked by the ruins of its 13C fortified castle, retains from its Arabic past a mosque now transformed into a church.

Church. – *To visit apply to the house nearby.* The square plan and forest of pillars give away the church's origin; look at the ancient *mihrab* behind the altar, the niche from which the Imam conducted prayers, and outside at the doorway leading to the sacristy. The fine vaulting is 13C.

MIRANDA DO DOURO ★

Michelin map **37** fold 14 (inset) or **441** fold 26 – *Local map p 69* – Pop 1 841

Miranda is perched on a spur above a sheer drop to the enclosed Valley of the Douro, where this divides Portugal from Spain. It is an old town with its own special dialect, somewhat similar to Low Latin, and known as *mirandês*.

Guarding the entrance to the village from a hillock, are the ruins of a medieval castle which was destroyed by an explosion in the 19C.

The Pauliteiros Dance. – The local men foregather on holidays and especially on the Feast day of St Barbara on the third Sunday in August, to perform the Pauliteiros Dance. Dressed in white flannel kilts, black shirts with multicoloured embroideries and black hats trimmed with scarlet ribbons and covered in flowers, the men step out a rhythmic stick dance. The striking of the sticks or *paulitos* recalls the sword-fighting of long ago which perhaps formed the original basis of the dance.

Former Cathedral. – *Guided tour (time: 10 minutes) 8.30am to 6pm in summer; 9am to 5pm in winter; closed Mondays and holidays.*

(After Amadeu Ferrari photo)

The Pauliteiros Dance.

The former cathedral, a 16C edifice of granite, contains a series of gilded and carved wood altarpieces★: the one in the chancel by the Spaniard, Juan Muniátegui, depicts the Assumption, round which are scenes from the Life of the Virgin, the Evangelists and several bishops. The whole is crowned with a calvary. On either side of the chancel the 17C gilded wood stalls are further embellished with painted landscapes.

An amusing statuette of the Child Jesus in a top hat stands in a glass display case in the south transept. He is much loved and venerated by the people of Miranda who have presented him with a large wardrobe.

There is a good view down from the cathedral terrace to the Douro flowing below. A little further away may be seen the ruins of the espicopal palace cloister.

EXCURSIONS

Miranda do Douro Dam★. – *3km - 2 miles by a narrow road to the east.* Miranda is the first of the five dams – the others are the Picote, the Bemposta, the Aldeadávila and the Saucelle – constructed on the international section of the Douro *(p 68)* where it forms the frontier between Portugal and Spain. It is a buttressed dam, erected in a rocky defile and measures 80m - 262ft high by 244m - 800ft along its crest; the underground power station *(open to the public; ask the EDP, Largo Dr. Tito Fontes no 15 – Oporto, for permission)* produced 766 million kWh in 1983.

Picote Dam★. – *27km - 17 miles by the Mogadouro road, the N 221, and then the 221–6 on the left after Fonte da Aldeia.* After going through Picote, a village created to house those involved in the construction of the dam, leave on your right a road leading to a viewpoint over the enclosed Douro Valley. The Picote Dam, which is a vaulted dam, uses the granite slopes of the Douro as support; it is nearly as high at its crest as it is long – 100m x 136m - 328ft x 446ft. The greatness in the water's fall enabled the underground power station to produce 902 million kWh in 1983.

Michelin map **37** folds 1 and 2 or **44** fold 25 – *Local map p 69* – Pop 8 192

Mirandela looks down upon the Tua, which is spanned by a long medieval bridge.

Távora Palace. – The beautiful 18C Távora Palace, now occupied by the town hall, stands at the top of a hill, its granite façade ornamented with Baroque shells.

EXCURSION

Romeu. – Pop 478. *12km - 7 miles to the northeast.*

In the heart of the Trás-os-Montes, Romeu, together with **Vila Verdinho** and **Vale de Couço,** forms a group of colourful villages gay with flowers, in a landscape of valleys wooded with cork oaks and chestnuts.

Recent restoration work has given them a new life.

Museum (Loja das Curiosidades). – *Guided tour (time: 1 hour), 9am to 7pm; 25esc. Ring the bell.*

The museum contains the personal collection of Manuel Meneres, the benefactor of all three villages. In one room are early machines such as typewriters, sewing machines, stereoscopes and a phenakistiscope – predecessor of the cinema; in another room are objects of all kinds each containing a music box – a chair, dolls, clocks.

On the ground floor note the old velocipede and among several vintage cars a fine 1909 Ford.

If you would rather plan your own itinerary
look at the map in this guide of the principal sights (pp 4-5)

Michelin map **37** fold 20

The Serra de Monchique is a volcanic block which rises more than 900m - 2 953ft above the surrounding shales ridges, forming a barrier against the sea mists which condense upon it; the resulting water flows down, not being absorbed owing to the impermeable nature of rock.

This humidity and the heat combine to produce a lush and varied vegetation, including orange trees and maize on the cultivated terraces, and arbutus trees, carobs and rhododendrons in the wild.

The volcanic nature of the area has given rise to medicinal springs which at **Caldas de Monchique** are used for the treatment of rheumatism and skin ailments.

From Portimão to Nave Redonda – *61km - 40 miles – about 2 hours*

Leave Portimão (p 122) by the N 124 to the north.

After Porto de Lagos bear left on to the N 266, the road climbs up into the wooded Serra de Monchique. Beyond the junction to Caldas de Monchique, in a wide bend to the left, a belvedere *(viewing table)* affords a bird's eye view of the spa and the terraces of maize surrounding it. Southwards the hills cluster around Portimão.

Leave the N 267, the road to Marmelete on the left.

One arrives at Monchique through the slopes of the Fóia and Picota covered with pines, cork oaks and eucalyptus.

Monchique. – Pop 6 765. *Facilities p 38.* Attractively nestled on the verdant east side of the Fóia, this small town possesses a church known for its Manueline doorway. The twisted columns are in the form of regularly knotted cables which end in unusual pinnacles.

From the belvedere situated on the fair grounds *(access by the street which is an extension of the Fóia road)*, there is an interesting view of the terraced quarters facing Mount Picota (alt 774m - 2 540ft).

In Monchique bear left on to the N 266-3 towards Mount Fóia.

The **road**★ goes up the slopes of the Fóia, the highest point in the range. After a few miles drive beneath the pines and eucalyptus, the **view**★ opens out to the south in a right bend (cross and fountain): from left to right can be seen Portimão Bay, Lagos Bay, Odeáxere Lake and, in the far distance, the Sagres Peninsula.

Mount Fóia. – Alt 902m - 2 959ft. A radio-television relay and a restaurant share this rocky site. From the summit (obelisk) there are extensive views of bare ridges to the north and wooded heights to the west.

(After Secretaria de Estado da Informação e Turismo photo)

The parish church door.

Return to Monchique and the N 266 which you take to the left.

North of Monchique the **drive**★ through varied woodland with many passing views of the massif's inner valleys, includes a beautiful descent down the northern slope. The forest disappears as the small arid hills of Alentejo appear on the horizon.

Nave Redonda. – Located at the beginning of the province of Alentejo, this hamlet lives on the cultivation of cork – piles of their bark can be seen waiting for shipment alongside the road.

Michelin map **37** southeast of fold 4 – 24km – 15 miles southeast of Penamacor – Pop 1 902

Monsanto stands upon the slopes of an arid and fragmented granite hill. It is an old picturesque village dominated by the ruins of a castle, whose indomitable site was already in use before the Romans arrived.

Every year in May *(p 9)*, young girls throw pitchers of flowers from the ramparts to commemorate the defiant throwing out of a calf when the castle was once bitterly besieged and those inside wished to convince the assailants that they would never be starved into capitulation.

Village★. – Steep and rough alleys cut across the village which is made up of old granite houses, often abutting on the rock and seeming a part of it. The façades, some of which are emblazoned, are pierced by paired windows and, in some cases, Manueline style doorways.

Castle (Castelo). – An alley and later a steep path lead through an impressive rock chaos to the castle which, although rebuilt by King Dinis, countless sieges have since reduced to a ruin. From the top of the keep, an immense **panorama★★** spreads northwest over the wooded hills of the Serra da Estrela and southwest over the lake formed by the Carmona Dam, the Ponsul Valley and, in the distance, Castelo Branco.

As you return to the village note the detached belfry of a former Romanesque church and, later, several tombs carved into the living rock.

MONSARAZ ★

Michelin map **37** north of fold 8 – Pop 1 290

The old fortified town of Monsaraz occupied a strategic position on a height near the Guadiana Valley on the border between Portugal and Spain. When it lost its military role it also lost its importance in favour of Reguengos de Monsaraz. Because of this the town has retained much of its historic character.

■ **SIGHTS** *time: 1 1/2 hours*

Leave the car before the main gate.

Rua Direita★. – The street retains all its original charm as it is still lined by 16 and 17C whitewashed houses, many emblazoned with coats of arms and all flanked by outside staircases and balconies with wrought iron grilles.

Former Tribunal. – The building, which is on the left side of the Rua Direita, can be distinguished by the pointed arches above its doors and windows. Inside *(apply to the Tourist Information Centre; Praça de D. Nuno Alvares Pereira)*, an interesting fresco depicts true and false Justice (bearing a crooked stick) with, above, a Christ in Majesty with upraised arms.

Parish Church. – The church contains the 14C marble tomb of Tomás Martins on which are carved figures in a funeral procession (monks and knights led by a priest) and, at the foot, falcons at the hunt.

Pillory. – The pillory dates from the 18C.

Misericord Hospital. – The hospital (16C), which stands opposite the parish church, possesses a beautiful meeting hall on the first floor *(apply to the Tourist Information Centre, Praça de D. Nuno Alvares Pereira)*.

Castle. – The castle was rebuilt by King Dinis in the 13C and given a second perimeter wall with massive bastions in the 17C.

The parapet walk commands a vast panorama.

MONTEMOR-O-NOVO

Michelin map **37** fold 17 – Pop 6 458

Montemor-o-Novo, a small peaceful town and agricultural market in the Alentejo, stretches out at the foot of a hill which is crowned by the ruins of a medieval fortified city. The **ramparts**, whose construction goes back to Roman times, make a good viewpoint over the countryside dotted with olive trees.

Montemor-o-Novo was the birthplace of **St John of God** (1495-1550) a Franciscan of examplary charity who founded the Order of Brothers Hospitallers. The statue in the square before the parish church shows the saint carrying a beggar to hospital, whom he had found on a stormy night. The town's present hospital, called after the saint, was founded in the 17C.

Join us in our never ending task
of keeping up to date.

Send us your comments
and suggestions, please.

Michelin Tyre Public Limited Company
Tourism Department
81 Fulham Road, LONDON SW3 6RD.

MONTEMOR-O-VELHO

Michelin map 🔢 fold 14 or 🔢 fold 32 – 28km - 17 miles west of Coimbra – Pop 2 572

The town of Montemor-o-Velho in the fertile Mondego Valley is dominated by the ruins of a citadel built in the 11C to defend Coimbra against the Moors who were occupying the Province of Estremadura in Spain.

Castle★. – *Open 10am to 12.30pm and 2 to 5pm; closed Mondays and holidays. Coming from Coimbra, on entering the town, take the road to the right; go through the outer walls to the castle courtyard.*

Of the original castle there remains a double perimeter wall, oval in shape, battlemented and flanked by many towers; the north corner is occupied by the church, the graveyard and the keep.

From the top of the ramparts there is a **panorama★** of the Mondego Valley spread with vast ricefields, a few fields of maize and groves of poplar trees. On the southeast horizon lies the Serra da Lousã.

MOURA

Michelin map 🔢 fold 8 – Pop 8 427

Moura stands grouped round the ruins of a 13C castle, a small spa whose bicarbonated calcium waters are used in the treatment of rheumatism.

The Pisões-Moura spring, a few miles from the town, provides a table water (Águas de Castelo) which is widely sold in Portugal.

The Legend of Salúquia. – If the legend is to be believed, the town acquired its name – Vila da Moura: the Town of the Moorish Maiden – and the design on its coat of arms – a young girl dead at the foot of a tower – from the fate of Salúquia, the daughter of a local Moorish lord. Salúquia waited in vain on her wedding morning for her fiancé, a lord from a neighbouring castle. He had been ambushed and slain with all his escort by Christian knights who then stripped the dead of their clothes and dressed in them themselves. Thus by treachery they entered and seized the castle – Salúquia, in despair, hurled herself to death from the top of the tower.

■ **SIGHTS** *time: 3/4 hour*

St John the Baptist's★. – The Gothic Church of St John the Baptist is entered through an interesting Manueline doorway decorated with armillary spheres. Inside an elegant twisted white marble column supports the pulpit; the chancel, with network vaulting, contains a beautiful Baroque Crucifixion group and the south chapel is adorned with 17C *azulejos* representing the Cardinal Virtues.

Mouraria. – This quarter recalls by its name the former Moorish occupation, which only ended in 1233 with the liberation of the town. The low houses lining the narrow streets are sometimes ornamented with panels of *azulejos* or picturesque chimneys.

NAZARÉ ★★

Michelin map 🔢 fold 15 – Pop 10 265 – *Facilities p 36*

The name of Nazaré comes from a statue of the Virgin brought back from Nazareth by a monk in the 4C. The town has three distinct quarters: the **Praia** which runs alongside the beach at the foot of the cliffs; the **Sítio** and **Pederneira** on the hills above.

The large beach of fine sand and the hotel accommodation makes Nazaré a popular seaside resort, but it essentially derives its living from fishing.

The construction of a new harbour has, unfortunately, brought about the end of the fishermen's traditional customs which used to attract crowds of tourists in the summer.

It was not so long ago that – because Nazaré had no natural harbour – the Nazaré fishermen docked their boats on the beach. Therefore, before they cast their nets, they had to roll their boats down the beach over logs and launch them against incoming waves. Once the boats were launched the fishermen would hurl themselves on board and row rapidly to the calmer waters beyond the breakers. At the end of the day, when the boats returned with their catch, they were hauled up the beach by cables and chains drawn by a tractor.

The original costumes of the barefooted Nazareans are worn rarely: the men wear black woollen bonnets reaching down to the shoulders,

Nazaré beach before construction of the harbour.

check shirts and trousers; the women have a headscarf or black hat, and a flared skirt under which you can see the hems of seven petticoats of different colours, worn one over the other.

And yet in spite of this loss of traditional customs the long curving beach, the cliffs, the welcoming simplicity of the houses and the fishermen's quarter, always makes for a pleasant stay in Nazaré.

NAZARÉ

República (Av. da) .... A
Sousa Oliveira (Pr.) .... B 16
Sub-Vila (R.) .... B
Vieira Guimarães (Av.) .. B

Abel da Silva (R.) .... A 2
Açougue (Trav. do) .... B 3

Adrião Batalha (R.) .... B 4
Azevedo e Sousa (R.) .... A 6
Carvalho Laranjo (R.) .... B 7
Dom F. Roupinho (R.) .... A 8
Dr Rui Rosa (R.) .... B 9
Gil Vicente (R.) .... B 10
M. de Arriaga (Pr.) .... B 12
M. de Albuquerque (R.) . B 14
Vasco da Gama (Pr.) ..... A 17
28 de Maio (R.) .... A 19

■ SIGHTS *time: 1/2 day*

The picturesque and stylish houses are the main charm of the Praia quarter, whereas in the Pederneira quarter, and above all that of Sítio, the charm lies in the beautiful views and interesting religious buildings.

The Praia (A). – The name *praia*, or beach, has been given to the lower town, laid out geometrically. It is in this area that the local scenes of Nazaré can be best observed.

Fishermen's Quarter★ (Bairro dos Pescadores) (B). – The fishermen's quarter extends between the Praça Manuel de Arriaga and the Avenida Vieira Guimarães. Small whitewashed cottages line either side of the steep and narrow alleys leading down to the quayside.

The Beach. – The beach at the foot of the Sítio Cliffs is being developed towards São Martinho do Porto. Beach tents provide shade for sun bathers in the area, most crowded with tourists in the high season.

The harbour. – South of the vast beach a harbour now shelters the fishing boats.

Part of the catch is sold in the market (sole, whiting, perch, coalfish, skate, mackerel and especially sardines). Another part goes to the local canneries, while the fish the men's families eat themselves is left to dry on the beach.

Pederneira (A). – Pederneira, on a cliff to the east of the Praia, is the cradle of the modern town.

Church of the Misericord (Igreja da Misericórdia) (A A). – The 16C Church of the Misericord at the end of the main street, the Rua Abel da Silva, has a wooden roof and also an unusual colonnade abutting on its south wall.

There is an interesting view of the town and the Sítio quarter from the church terrace.

The Sítio (A). – The Sítio quarter, perched on a cliff top 110m - 361ft high, north of the town, can be reached by funicular *(fare charged)* or by the Marinha Grande road, the N 242.

Belvedere (A). – The **view★★** from the belvedere, built on the edge of the cliff which itself is the tallest cliff face on the coast of Portugal, includes the lower town and the huge beach occupied in the foreground with bathers' tents and, further away, fishing nets and boats.

Chapel (A B). – This minute chapel near the belvedere commemorates the miracle which saved the life of the local lord, Fuas Roupinho *(p 72)*. One misty morning in 1182 Roupinho on horseback was giving chase to a roe deer which suddenly somersaulted into the air off the top of the cliff. Just as the horse, galloping at top speed, was about to do the same thing, Dom Fuas implored Our Lady of Nazaré for help and the horse stopped, saving the life of his rider.

The façade, the roof and the two floors inside the chapel are covered with *azulejos*: those of the façade on the side facing the sea evoke the knight's jump; those of the crypt, the miracle of the Marian intercession. In the staircase leading to the crypt a recess still has the footprint which the roe deer is said to have left on the rock face.

Church of Our Lady of Nazareth (Igreja Nossa Senhora da Nazaré) (A C). – This imposing church built at the end of the 17C is on the main square where the annual festival dedicated to its patron saint takes place. It has a façade with a forepart forming a gallery, and a Baroque doorway opening at the top of a semicircular flight of steps. The interior is vast and remarkable for the profusion of *azulejos* which decorate it: those of the transept depict Biblical scenes (Jonah, Joseph sold by his brothers, etc.).

Lighthouse. – *800m - 1/2 mile west of the church.* The lighthouse is built on a small fort at the furthermost promontory of a cliff. Behind, and lower down, a path with steps and a parapet wall and then an iron staircase *(at an angle of 34 degrees – watch out for vertigo)* leads to a point *(1/4 hour Rtn)* overlooking a magnificent **seascape★★**; a chaotic mass of jagged rocks through which the sea swirls furiously; on the right one can see the northern beach (Praia do Norte) where the waves surge in great rollers. *Go round the headland a little, towards the left:* you get a beautiful view over the gashed rockface of the Sitio Cliffs and the Bay of Nazaré.

EXCURSION

São Martinho do Porto. – Pop 2 318. – *13km - 8 miles. Leave Nazaré by* ③ *, the N 242.*
The seaside resort of São Martinho do Porto *(facilities p 36)* lies to the north of an unusual saltwater lake connected to the sea by a narrow channel pierced between tall cliffs.

Take a road on the right at the end of the quay. A viewpoint offers an interesting **view**★ of the surf and the cove. From higher up you can see Nazaré's vast beach.

The hamlet of **Alfeizerão** *(4km - 2 miles east)* is well known for its *pão de ló*, a delicious light and soft egg pastry.

ÓBIDOS ★★

Michelin map **37** northwest of fold 16 – Pop 825 – *Facilities p 38*

Óbidos, although 10km - 6 miles inland, stands like a watchtower in its setting. The fortified city, protected by its perimeter wall flanked by small round towers and massive square bastions, once commanded the seashore. The silting up of the bay south of the Foz do Arelho beach created a lagoon (Lagoa de Óbidos) which deprived the town of its coastal position and in consequence reduced its military importance. Despite this the town has kept its proud medieval character and still commands the vast countryside of green valleys and heights topped by the occasional windmill.

The Queen's Perquisite. – Óbidos, freed from Moorish domination in 1148 by Alfonso Henriques, immediately began rebuilding feverishly: the walls were consolidated, towers rebuilt, the delightful white houses refurbished so that the city already had a most attractive appearance when in 1228 it was visited by King Dinis accompanied by his young wife, Queen Isabella. Isabella admired the new town, and the king, thereupon, made her a gift of it. Future monarchs repeated this gesture to their consorts until 1833.

In 1491 the Court was in full mourning, for the *infante* had died in an accident while on horseback at Santarém. His body, lost in the Tagus, had been recovered in a fisherman's net. It was to her town of Óbidos that Queen Leonor, wife of João II, came to hide her sorrow and seek peace. The net upon the pillory in the town is a reminder of this sad event.

Josefa de Óbidos. – Josefa de Ayala, born in Sevilla in 1634 and better known under the name of Josefa de Óbidos, came to live in the town when very young and stayed there until her death in 1684. Her paintings with their indecisive colours and stump drawing or blurred line effects show a marked feminine ingenuousness verging on affectation. Her still lifes in rich colours are more popular.

The First Confrontation: Wellington and Junot. – Wellington, in advance of his troops in the march south at the beginning of the Peninsular Campaign, reached Óbidos and saw ahead the French army drawn up, under Laborde, some eight miles away at the village of Roliça. On 17 August 1808 the two armies met and the British gained their first, but inconclusive action.

Within four days both sides had been reinforced and battle was rejoined: this time thirty miles south of Óbidos at the village of Vimeiro, Wellington took full advantage of the terrain, including the famous ridge and Vimeiro Hill, to win a conclusive victory.

A change of command in the British forces failed to follow up the victory and instead the Sintra Convention was signed.

■ THE CITY ★★ *time: 1 hour*

Main Gate (Porta da Vila). – The inside walls of this double zigzag gateway are covered with 18C *azulejos*.

Take the main street on the left.

Main Street★. – The street which is narrow, is occupied at its centre by a paved gully bordered with white houses bright with geraniums, bougainvilleas and medlars. As you walk along you may see craftsmen at work, most frequently weaving cotton carpets, an Óbidos speciality.

Leave the car on St Mary's Church Square, which is shaded with plane trees.

St Mary's Church. – It was in St Mary's that the young King Alfonso V married his eight year old cousin, Isabella, in 1444.

Inside, the walls, which support a painted ceiling, are entirely covered with 17C blue *azulejos* painted with very large plant motifs. In the chancel, in a bay on the left, a Renaissance **tomb**★ is surmounted by a Virgin of Compassion accompanied by the Holy Women and Nicodemus returning from burying the body of Our Lord. This remarkable work is attribued to the studio of Jean de Rouen *(p 23)*. The altarpiece at the high altar is adorned with paintings by João da Costa.

Municipal Museum. – *In the church square. Open 10am to 1pm and 2 to 5pm; closed Mondays; 20esc, free Wednesdays.*

In the entrance hall of this small museum there is a statue of St Sebastian dating from the 15 or 16C and also a 17C polychrome *Pietà*; in the adjoining "Josefa de Óbidos" room, various works by this artist *(details p 110)* as well as other paintings of religious subjects of the 16 and 17C Portuguese school are exhibited; in the first basement there are mementoes of the war against Napoleon (a relief map of the region, weapons, strange coffers made of translucent hide); the second basement contains medieval and Luso-Roman archaeological remains.

Pillory. – In the church square, stands a fountain surmounted by a 15C pillory bearing the coat of arms of Queen Leonor.

Having arrived at St James's Church (São Tiago) at the end of the main street, take the road on the left and then a path on the right. Steps lead to the ramparts.

The Ramparts★★. – The walls date from the Moorish occupation but were restored in parts in the 12, 13 and 16C.

On the north side, which is higher, is occupied by the keep and the castle's high towers. For an interesting view go through the opening in the ramparts and turn a sharp right.

Castle. – Transformed into a royal palace in the 16C, the buildings overlooking the interior courtyard *(access to the right of St James's Church)* are now a *pousada*.

The *pousada* façade still has paired Manueline windows with twisted columns and a Manueline door surmounted by two armillary spheres.

■ ADDITIONAL SIGHTS

Senhor da Pedra Church. – *Open in summer Saturday and Sunday afternoons.*

The church lies north of the town, beside the N 8. It is a Baroque edifice and was built to a hexagonal plan between 1740-47. In a window above the altar is a very remarkable primitive stone cross dating from the 2 or 3C.

Niches round the nave contain Baroque statues of the Apostles.

On 8 September, the coach, which is kept in the church, is used to transport the Virgin from St Mary's Church in Óbidos to the Church of Our Lady in Nazaré *(p 109)*.

Aqueduct. – The aqueduct at the town's southern exit dates from the 15C.

EXCURSION

Óbidos Lagoon. – *21km - 13 miles. Go towards Peniche and at Amoreira turn right going north.* The road, after crossing Vau, reaches the southern end of the lagoon, which is fringed with reeds. It then turns left and climbs amongst pine trees.

A little before the loop at the end of the road there is a vista over the sea on the left, and the lagoon on the right.

Choose the left side of the loop in the descent towards Aldeia, so as to emerge suddenly facing the village of Praia (on the opposite bank); the **view★** is beautiful over the pass, the stretch of water, the beaches and the summer homes of Aldeia.

OLHÃO

Michelin map **37** south of fold 10 – 8km - 5 miles east of Faro – Pop 13 151 – *Facilities p 36*

Olhão, built on the Algarve coast at a point where long coastal sandbanks lie offshore, is a sardine and tuna fishing port and canning centre. In spite of its Moorish appearance with narrow alleys, cube shaped white or pale blue houses stepped with terraces and corner chimneys, Olhão's history does not go back to the Arabic occupation. It was founded in the 18C by fishermen who came to the spot by sea from the Ria de Aveiro and its architectural style came about through its commercial contacts with North Africa.

(After Yan photo — Casa de Portugal)

Olhão — The terraced roofs.

Viewpoints. – The bridge over the railway at the entrance to the town affords a good view of the white houses piled up so close together.

An unusual **panorama★** of the whole town may be had from the belfry of the parish church standing in the main street *(access through the first door on the right as you enter the church; if closed apply to the sacristan)*. Many of the houses are covered by stepped exterior terraces *(açoteias and mirantes)* connected by small stairways.

Finally you can take a pleasant walk in the **Joaquim Lopes Park** beside the river; from the park you can see the fishing port and the vast flat expanse of the islands and the offshore bars, as far as the lighthouse at Cape Santa Maria. There is a covered market near the park which on Saturdays is crowded with stalls and peasants.

Make up your own itineraries

– The map on pages 4 and 5 gives a general view of tourist regions, the main towns, individual sights and recommended routes in the guide.

– The above are described under their own name in alphabetical order (p 41) or are incorporated in the excursions radiating from a nearby town or tourist centre.

– In addition the Michelin Map no 37 show scenic routes, places of interest, viewpoints, rivers, forests...

Michelin map 🔳 fold 4 or 🔳 fold 33 – Pop 3 074

Hills clad with vines, olives and pines trees, form the setting of Oliveira do Hospital whose name recalls the old 12C appurtenances of the Order of the Hospitallers of St John of Jerusalem, now the Knights Templar of Malta *(p 87)*.

Parish Church★. – *Time: 1/2 hour.* The church, originally Romanesque, was reconstructed in the Baroque period.

The interior, covered by a fine ceiling painted in false relief, includes the 13C funerary chapel of the Ferreiros containing the late 13C tombs of Domingos Joanes and his wife. The reclining figures of Ança stone reflect in the delicacy of their carving the evolution from the Romanesque to the Gothic style.

An equestrian **statue★** of a 14C medieval knight reminiscent of the one at Coimbra *(illustration p 65)* has been fixed to the wall above the tombs. Also noteworthy is a beautiful 14C stone **altarpiece★** of the Virgin Mother between St Joachim and St Anne.

EXCURSION

Lourosa Church. – *10km - 6 miles to the southwest by the N 230, the N 17 and a road on the left. Excavations in process. Apply to the neighbours to visit.*

This pre-Romanesque church which probably dates as far back as 950 was built in the form of a basilica, low and squat, with a porch in front. It was restored in 1921 (façade and chancel).

The interior is typically Mozarabic with its horse-shoe shaped arches dividing it into three naves, and supported by short round pillars (ancient Roman columns), and by the small, elegant windows with two bays at each gable end of the central nave. A primitive Romanesque lintel can be seen in the false transept on the right.

Excavations have revealed the remains of a baptistry, and both underneath the nave and outside the sanctuary, numerous sepultures.

Near the church there is a 15C bell tower and a Manueline pillory.

OPORTO ★ (PORTO)

Michelin map 🔳 fold 12 or 🔳 fold 22 – *Local map p 68* – Pop 335 916

Oporto, Portugal's second largest city, occupies a steep **site★** on the right bank of the Douro. On the opposite bank, the Vila Nova de Gaia wine stores house the famous port wines *(details p 17)*, a trade of prime importance in the life of the town.

The nearby elegant villas built overlooking the sea make up the fashionable suburbs of **Foz do Douro** and **Matosinhos** *(p 116)*.

The major industries in this, the centre of the country's most important economic area, are textiles (cotton), metallurgy (foundries), chemical (tyres), food (canning), leather, and ceramics. Craftsmen also work in considerable numbers, mostly at filigree in Gondomar, 7km - 4 miles away.

The creation of the port of **Leixões** *(to the north)*, to duplicate the function of the harbour on the Douro which has suffered periodic silting up by the river, has provided an excellent outlet for local industrial production. The construction of a tankers' wharf and an oil refinery has provided a new field of industrial expansion. Portugal's second largest port, Leixões is also a large sardine fishing port.

General View★. – The best general view of Oporto is from the parvis of the former Convent of Nossa Senhora da Serra do Pilar *(description p 116)* on the left bank of the Douro. The old town, overlooked by the towers of the cathedral and that of the Clérigos belfry, rises in tiers from the riverbank, an overlapping series of hillside alleys lined with corbelled houses with here and there a façade tiled with *azulejos*. Traces of the 14C town wall can be seen to the right of the Dom Luis I Bridge.

Filigree work.

The Bridges. – The riverbanks are linked by three technically remarkable bridges.

The **Maria Pia railway Bridge★** (CX), which is the furthest upstream, was designed by the French engineer Eiffel and is entirely of metal. It was completed in 1877.

The **Luís I road Bridge** (CX) with a span of 172m - 564ft was built in 1886 by the Belgian firm of Willebroeck on the same lines as Eiffel's railway bridge. The originality of this metal construction bridge lies in two superimposed road tracks, allowing it to serve both upper and lower levels of the town on both banks.

The **Arrábida road Bridge★** (BX), which is the furthest downstream and is used by the motorway which goes through Oporto, is a particularly bold structure. It crosses the Douro in a single reinforced concrete span of nearly 270m - 886ft.

Both the road bridges provide interesting viewpoints over the town.

HISTORICAL NOTES

Portucale. – At the time of the Romans, the Douro was a considerable obstacle to communication between north and south Lusitania. Two cities faced each other across the river, controlling the estuary: Portus (the harbour) on the right bank, Cale on the left.

In the 8C the Mohammedans invaded Lusitania but Christian resistance prevented them from settling permanently in the region between the Minho and the Douro. It was this region, already known as Portucale, that the princess Dona Tareja (Teresa), daughter of the King of Léon, brought as a dowry in the form of a county to her husband Henri of Burgundy in 1095. Later this same county was to be one of the mainsprings for the Reconquest, and so give its name to the whole country *(p 19)*.

Tripe in the Oporto Manner. – Within the county of Portucale, Oporto (O Porto in Portuguese, meaning the port or harbour) developed trading relations with northern Europe and grew in importance; in the 14 and 15C its shipyards helped to create the Portuguese shipping fleet; under the direction of Prince Henry the Navigator, who came from this area, Oporto equipped the fleet which in 1415 took part in capturing Ceuta from the Moors *(p 19)*. To victual the squadron all the cattle in the region were taken, the local people in Oporto being left only with the offal – from which they gained the nickname of *tripeiros* or tripe eaters.

The English and Port Wine. – In 1703 England and Portugal signed the Methuen Treaty which assisted the sale of English manufactured goods – wool especially – to the Portuguese; in exchange the wines from the Upper Douro found a ready market in Britain. English merchants established a trading centre in Oporto in 1717 and little by little English companies took over the production of port wine from the harvesting of the grapes to the final bottling.

To combat the English invasion into the wine trade the Marquis of Pombal founded a Portuguese company in 1757 to which he gave a monopoly control of the wines from the Upper Douro. This strict control annoyed many small Portuguese producers and on shrove Tuesday drunkards set fire to the company's local offices. Pombal reacted harshly: twenty-five men were condemned to death.

The Love of Liberty. – The *revolta dos borrachos* – the drunkards' rebellion – was by no means the only demonstration by the inhabitants of Oporto of their love of liberty. Previously they had succeeded in obtaining a royal edict which barred all noblemen from the city's commercial precincts. Later, on 29 March 1809, fleeing before the advance of the French army under General Soult, they rushed the pontoon bridge across the river in such panic that hundreds were drowned. A plaque near the Luís I Bridge recalls this catastrophe.

The pontoon bridge was blown up by Soult at the approach of the British in May 1809, but Wellington managed to get a force across the river in disused wine barges and so surprised and captured the town. The pursuit which followed once more forced the French out of Portugal.

In 1820 Oporto rebelled against the English occupation and the assembly (Junta do Porto) subsequently convened, succeeded in drafting and having adopted (1822) a liberal constitution for the whole country. But in 1828 Miguel I mounted the throne and ruled as an absolute monarch which brought about a new rebellion in the town; in 1833 a liberal monarchy was restored *(p 18)*.

On 31 January 1891. Oporto once more rebelled, under the influence of the Republicans who had begun agitations throughout the country – but the Republic was not to be declared until 1910 in Lisbon.

(After Secretaria de Estado da Informação e Turismo photo)

Oporto.

■ **MAIN SIGHTS** *time: 4 hours*

Wine Stores (BCX). – There are some eighty wine stores occupying the entire quarter of Vila Nova de Gaia. It is here that the wine harvested on the slopes of the Upper Douro is transformed into port. It is held in immense vats (containing about 100 000 litres - 26 400 imperial gallons) for several years before being decanted into 535 litre - 118 gallon barrels in which the porous quality of the wood assists in the ageing process. *The main stores (free tasting) may be visited at all times except Saturdays (a few houses), Sundays and holidays.*

Cathedral (Sé) (BZ A). – The cathedral began as a fortress church in the 12C and was considerably modified in the 17 and 18C. The main façade, flanked by two square, domed towers, has a 13C Romanesque rose window and a Baroque doorway. A Baroque loggia attributed to the architect Nasoni was added in 1736 to the north face.

The interior was transformed in the Baroque period. The Chapel of the Holy Sacrament which opens off the north transept contains a very fine **altar★** with a chased silver altarpiece worked by Portuguese silversmiths of the 17C. Note also in the nave three lovely 17C marble stoups and in the baptistery (left of the entrance) a bronze relief of the Baptism of Christ by St John, by the sculptor Teixeira Lopes. The sacristy *(access through the south transept)* contains a bronze lectern dating from 1616.

Go through a door at the corner of the south transept to reach the late 14C Gothic **cloister** where the walls were decorated in the 18C with *azulejos* illustrating the Life of the Virgin and Ovid's *Metamorphoses*; an ornate Cross stands at the centre of the close.

PORTO

Cathedral Square (BZ 88). – The Terreiro da Sé, which is bordered by the former episcopal palace, dating from the 18C, and a 14C granite tower *(torre)*, has in the centre a neo-Pombaline pillory.

Old Town. – The old quarter of Oporto, with its picturesque alleyways leading down to the harbour, stretches away to the south and west of the cathedral, and is very animated on market days. The Cais (quay) de Ribeira, along the river's edge, is lined with old corbelled houses whose façades are often decorated with a patchwork of colourful laundry.

St Francis'★ (Igreja São Francisco) (AZ). – *Open 9am to 1pm and 2 to 5pm; closed Mondays and holidays.*

This Gothic church, with its original fine rose window, is entered through a main door dating from the 17C.

The **interior★★** is a triumph of Baroque decorative richness: altars, walls, vaulting and pillars disappear beneath a forest of 17 and 18C carved and gilded wood, representing vines, cherubim and birds. Look especially at the high altar and a Tree of Jesse *(2nd chapel on the left)*. The statue of St Francis in polychrome granite in a chapel on the right is 13C.

Stock Exchange (Palácio da Bolsa) (AZ B). – *Guided tour (time: 20 minutes) 9am to noon and 2 to 5.30pm; closed Saturdays, Sundays and holidays; 50esc.*

The exchange, which dates from the 19C, has a fine granite and marble staircase adorned with sculptures. The **Arabian Hall★**, which is a 19C pastiche of the Alhambra at Granada, is ovoid in shape and decorated with stained glass windows, arabesques and gilded stucco.

Clérigos Church (Igreja dos Clérigos) (BZ C). – This Baroque church, designed by the architect Nasoni, is flanked to the west by a granite tower 76m - 249ft high. The **panorama★** from the top *(open 9.30am to 11.30am and 2 to 5.30pm in summer; 10am to 12.30pm and 2 to 4.30pm in winter; Sundays and holidays 10.30am to noon and 2.30 to 6pm in summer and 10.30am to noon and 2 to 5.30pm in winter; closed Wednesdays; 10esc.)* includes the city, the Douro Valley and the Vila Nova de Gaia wine stores.

Soares dos Reis Museum (AYZ M¹). – *Open 10am to 5pm; closed Mondays and holidays; 50esc, free Sundays.*

The museum, which is in the 18C Carrancas Palace, displays, on the ground floor, local 18 and 19C pottery and an interesting collection of Portuguese **Primitives★** (paintings by Gaspar Vaz, Vasco Fernandes and Cristóvão de Figueiredo). The first floor is devoted to sculpture of which the **works of Soares dos Reis★** (1847-89 – *details p 25)*, in particular that of the Exile and the statue of the Count of Ferreira, are the most remarkable. Also well represented are Teixeira Lopes and among numerous 19 and 20C paintings, Silva Porto, Pousão and Columbano. On the 2nd floor are religious works of art, a collection of early 16C Limoges enamels depicting scenes from the Life of Christ and two canvases by the 16C artist, François Clouet (portraits of Marguerite de Valois and Henri II of France).

■ **ADDITIONAL SIGHTS**

St Clara's (Igreja Santa Clara) (BZ E). – St Clara's is a 15 and 16C church whose interior is entirely lined with magnificent 17C carved and gilded **woodwork★**. The ceiling is Mudejar in style, the holy water stoup Gothic.

Church of the Immaculate Conception (Igreja da Imaculada Conceição) (CV F). – The Stations of the Cross and the frescoes in this interesting modern church (1939-47) are by the Portuguese painter Guilherme Camarinha.

Guerra Junqueiro Museum (BZ M²). – *Open 10am to 12.30pm and 2 to 5.30pm (6pm Fridays and Saturdays); closed Mondays, Sundays and holidays; 20esc.*

An 18C house in which are displayed art objects collected by the poet Guerra Junqueiro *(p 82)*, including Hispano-Arabic pottery of the 15 and 16C, 16C Portuguese furniture and 16C Flemish tapestries.

Ethnographic Museum (AZ M³). – *Largo de S. João Novo. Guided tour (time: 1 hour) 10am to noon and 2 to 5pm; closed Sundays, Mondays and holidays.*

The life and customs of the region are evoked through collections of religious works of art, costumes, ceramics, furniture, toys, cribs, decorated yokes, etc.

St Benedict Station (Estação de São Bento) (BZ). – The walls of the waiting room are covered with *azulejos* painted in 1930 by Jorge Colaço of everyday life in Portugal and such historic events as João I's entry into Oporto *(top right)* and his capture of Ceuta *(bottom right)*.

Rua do Cimo da Vila (BZ). – A highly picturesque narrow street bustling with life.

Former Convent of Nossa Senhora da Serra do Pilar (CX K). – The old convent dominating the town is a curious building erected in the 16 and 17C in the form of a rotunda and said to have been designed by Filippo Terzi. The Renaissance **cloister★** is also circular.

EXCURSION

Matosinhos. – Pop 30 456. *Facilities p 36. 8.5km - 5 miles.* Leave Oporto by the Avenida da Boavista. Drive along the Matosinhos beach and then the inner harbour and docks of the port of **Leixões** *(p 113). Pass beneath a viaduct before coming to a crossroads.*

In a shady garden you vill see the **Church of Bom Jesus of Matosinhos.** The 18C façade bristling with pinnacles and four torches is further enriched with several coats of arms. Inside, the woodwork in the chancel is immediately noticeable, the carvings portray scenes from Christ's Passion. The very old statue of Christ carved in wood, standing at the high altar is the goal each year of a large pilgrimage *(p 9)*. A beautiful coffered ceiling covers the nave and chancel.

OURÉM

Michelin map **37** fold 15 – 14km - 9 miles east of Fátima – Pop 4 498

Ourém, an old fortified city lying south of Vila Nova de Ourém, was built around the top of a hillock, the actual summit of which is occupied by the remains of a castle.

The town knew a sumptuous richness in the 15C when the 4th count of Ourém, Dom Afonso the bastard son of João I and nephew of Constable Nuno Alvares Pereira, converted the castle into a palace and built several other monuments.

■ **SIGHTS** *time: 3/4 hour*

Leave the car at the entrance to the town and take a road on the left which leads up to the castle. The arms adorning the fountain at the entrance to the village are those of Count Dom Afonso.

Castle. – Two advanced towers appear on either side of the road; note the unusual brick machicolations on the walls all round the castle. *Pass beneath the porch of the right tower; a path enables one to see a former tunnel and to examine in detail the machicolations on the north face of the tower.*

Steps go up a square tower commanding the entrance to an older triangular castle. Walk round the parapet path to view the belfry of the basilica at Fátima over to the west, the town of Pinhel to the northwest and Vila Nova de Ourém to the northeast.

A path leads back to the village and the collegiate church.

Collegiate Church. – A door off the south transept opens on to a stairway down to the crypt which is supported on six monolithic columns. The Gothic and highly ornate white limestone tomb of Count Dom Afonso in the crypt has a reclining figure upon it, attributed to the sculptor Diogo Pires the Elder. Two lifting mechanisms, engraved on the tomb, illustrate the count's device: "Patience and strength combined triumph over the heaviest burdens."

The times indicated in this guide

when given with the distance allow one to enjoy the scenery
when given for sightseeing are intended to give an idea of
the possible brevity or length of a visit.

PAÇO DE SOUSA

Michelin map **37** east of fold 12 or **441** fold 23 – *Local map p 68* – Pop 3 536

Paço de Sousa has retained from a former Benedictine monastery, founded early in the 11C, a vast (restored) Romanesque church in which lies the tomb of Egas Moniz, the companion in arms of Prince Alfonso Henriques whose loyalty to his royal leader has remained a legend.

A Model of Honesty. – Alfonso VII, King of Léon, to put an end to the claims of independence of the County of Portugal, set siege to Lanhoso where the Queen Regent Dona Teresa *(p 84)* was established and later, in 1127, to Guimarães, where her son, the Infante Alfonso Henriques, was installed. The prince had only a small handful of men with which to oppose his enemy, and so he dispatched his former tutor **Egas Moniz** to plead before the king. In exchange for the king's abandoning the siege of Guimarães, Moniz swore, in the name of the prince, to recognize the sovereignty of the King of Léon. But in 1130, the danger over, Alfonso Henriques forgot his promise and led another uprising against the king. Egas Moniz, accompanied by his wife and children, departed immediately for Toledo where he appeared before Alfonso VII in the garb of a penitent with bare feet and a cord about his neck, prepared to pay with his life the ransom for his prince's treason. Moniz's honesty won him a pardon.

Monastery Church. – *Time: 1/2 hour.* The church façade has a tiers-point doorway with arching ornamented with motifs which are repeated on the surround of the rose window. The capitals are decorated with foliage. The tympanum is supported on the left by a bull's head and on the right by an unusual man's head. On the tympanum on the left, is a man carrying the moon, on the right a man is carrying the sun. Two friezes of Lombard blind arcades run along the sides of the church.

Inside, the three aisles with pointed arches shelter, on the left, a naïve statue of St Peter and, on the right near the entrance, the 12C tomb of Egas Moniz. Low reliefs carved somewhat crudely on the tomb depict the scene at Toledo and the funeral of this loyal preceptor.

A battlemented tower stands to the left of the church.

PALMELA

Michelin map **37** fold 17 – 8km - 5 miles north of Setúbal – Pop 14 444

This picturesque white town is built up in tiers on the northern slope of the Serra da Arrábida *(p 45)* at the foot of a mound crowned by a large castle which became the seat of the Order of St James in 1423.

Means to an end. – In 1484, one year after the execution of the Duke of Bragança *(p 140)*, King João II learned of a new plot intended to overthrow him in favour of the Duke of Viseu, his brother-in-law. In August, when the king was at Alcácer do Sal and about to return to Setúbal down the Sado River, he avoided an ambush by changing plans and returning by road. However, once arrived at Setúbal he sent to Palmela for the Duke of Viseu, received him in his bedchamber and stabbed him to death. The Bishop of Évora, the instigator of the plot, was imprisoned in Palmela Castle in a dungeon beneath the keep and died a few days later, probably by poisoning.

- **SIGHTS** *time: 3/4 hour*

St Peter's. – The church, which is in the upper part of the town at the foot of the castle walls, dates from the 18C.

The interior is entirely lined with azulejos★ depicting scenes from the life of St Peter; outstanding are those in the south aisle illustrating the miraculous catch of fishes, Christ walking on the waves and the crucifixion of St Peter.

Castle★. – *Open daily. Leave the car in the outer yard.*

The castle, on a sort of promontory, commands the surrounding countryside.

The castle was constructed at three different periods: enter first the perimeter erected at the end of the 17C and based on the system of the French military engineer Vauban: next go up a zigzag path to the second, somewhat clumsy line of fortifications probably constructed by the Moors. Bearing left you pass near the ruins of a one time mosque, transformed into a church (St Mary's) and then destroyed in the earthquake of 1755. Finally you reach the keep and the parade ground which date from the late 14C. Below ground is the dungeon in which the Bishop of Évora was imprisoned.

Panorama★. – From the top of the keep *(64 steps.)* there is a beautiful view westwards of the Serra da Arrábida; southwards of a line of windmills, Setúbal, the Tróia Peninsula and the Atlantic; eastwards of the Alentejo Plain; and northwards of the village of Palmela and, in the far distance on a clear day, Lisbon and the Serra de Sintra.

Former Monastery of St James. – The western extremity of the castle is occupied by the Church and Monastery of St James which were erected in the 15C by the Knights of St James, who had installed themselves in the castle in 1186. The conventual buildings are now a *pousada*.

The church, constructed in transitional Romanesque style, is a well proportioned building of great simplicity. The Romanesque cradle vaulting of the nave extends over the Gothic chancel; the walls are covered with *azulejos*, 16C in the chancel and 18C in the nave. Carved into the flooring is the blazon of the Order of the Knights of St James. The tomb of Jorge de Lencastre, the son of João II and last Master of the Order, may be seen in a Manueline bay off the north aisle.

PENEDA-GERÊS National Park ★★

Michelin map **37** folds 1 and 11 (inset)

This park was established in 1971 and covers 72 000ha - 178 000 acres in the northern districts of Braga, Viana de Castelo and Vila Real. It is in the shape of a horseshoe, the two halves encircling the southwest point of the Spanish province of Orense.

It is a very hilly region which the deep valleys of the Lima, Homem and Cavádo Rivers divide into *serras* (those of da Peneda, do Soajo, da Amarela and do Gerês). It gets a lot of rain (the Peneda Serra has the highest average rainfall in the whole of Portugal) so the country is very wooded. The park is designed to protect not only the picturesque sites and considerable archaeological remains, but also the flora (oaks, cork-oaks, pines and firs; lilies, ferns...) and fauna (stags, wild horses, eagles...) of particular interest. Its layout attracts many tourists, as do the mineral springs of Gerês.

For drivers, we suggest two routes below, which give an idea of the magnificence of the national park's centre. *For information, apply to Sede do Parque Nacional, Rua de São Geraldo, 29, 4700 – Braga.*

CROSSING THE PARK★

From Rio Cávado to Leonte – *27km - 18 miles from the N 103 – about 1 1/2 hours – local map p 62*

The N 308–1 from Gerês cuts across the middle of the national park, from the Upper Cávado Valley (p 62) to the Spanish frontier.

Leaving the N 103 north of Cerdeirinhas, the road (N 304) begins winding downhill between lovely heather covered rocks. After 2km - 1 mile you pass the beautifully situated São Bento *pousada*, overlooking the river on the right; a little further on there is a panoramic view of the Cávado Gorge.

Caniçada Confluence★. – Two bridges cross successively the Cávado and its tributary, the Caldo, turned into lakes by the Caniçada Dam (which is 10km - 6 miles away to the west). The first bridge crosses over a submerged village which appears when the water level drops. Coming from this bridge on to the peninsula between the two lakes, take the N 308-1 on the right at the intersection, and then immediately cross the 2nd bridge which leads to the national park, and from which you have an attractive view★ over the crescent shaped lake formed by the Caldo River, with its steep wooded banks.

After going along the east side of the Caldo Reservoir Lake, you pass by Vilar da Veiga, a village on the left tucked away in vineyards. The road follows a torrent from above, and on the western slope where a pressure pipeline descends vertically, there are numerous houses.

Gerês – *Facilities p 38.* The pleasant little spa *(season: May to October)* and main excursion centre for the park, lies at the bottom of a wooded gorge of the *serra* of the same name. The waters, rich in fluorine, are used in the treatment of liver and digestive troubles.

After Gerês, the road is lined at first with hydrangeas, then winds up through trees (pines and oaks). 8km - 5 miles from Gerês a sign and the statue of a doe indicate the approach to the nature reserve by a footpath. *Starting from this point the itinerary is 1 km - 1/2 mile further on, a small bridge crosses over a little torrent (Leonte River) which the road follows for a while on the right. Bear left onto the lane leading to the Vilarinho Dam (p 119).*

Barely 1km - 1/2 mile further, after having crossed the Leonte River on a small bridge, the road runs along a clearing which is crossed by a section of the Roman way.

Remains of the Geira (Roman Way). – A number of milestones have been assembled here, some upright (about fifteen) and others lying on the ground among the pines and rocks. You can also see, stretching into the distance towards the small Bargiela Valley on the right of the road, a section of the old Roman way which the milestones originally bordered and which used to link Braga to Asterga in Spain.

SERRA DO GERÊS★★
Excursion starting from Gerês. – *31km - 19 miles - about 2 hours - local map p 62.*

Leave Gerês on the N 308-1 south; after 1km - 1/2 mile bear right on the forest track towards Lamas.
Continue another 3km - 2 miles and stop at the Fragra Negra Fountain.

Fragra Negra Belvedere (Miradouro)★. – *1/4 hour on foot Rtn, 43 steps,* From this belvedere built in the rocky scree of the Fragra Negra (Black Rock), there is a beautiful **view★** overlooking the spa of Gerês which is surrounded by green vegetation.

The road offers lovely views on to Caniçada Dam; it then runs between a forest on the right and a gulf on the left which has a great **outcrop of rocks★** extending downhill and some enormous boulders balanced on top of each other.
9km-5 1/2 miles further on bear right on a road for 3km - 2 miles which leads to the Junceda Belvedere, which has a view of the Gerês Valley.
Return to the crossroads and descend towards S. João do Campo. At a crossroads, signposted by a milestone on which a Christ is sculpted, bear right towards the dam and at the next crossroads bear left.

Vilarinho das Furnas Dam. – *Cars not allowed at the top.* In a rocky and wild **setting★** this vaulted dam, put into service in 1972, matches its 94m - 310ft high concrete arch against the pressure of 118 million m³ of water amassed by the Homem River. In 1983 its power station produced 185 million kWh.

Return to the crossroads and bear left on the forest path (1.5km - 2/3 mile) to Barça da Mó which leads to the Roman way and the nature reserve.
Other routes allow you to visit the nature reserve: either starting at Gerês from Ermida to Cobril or from Arcos to Valdevez which follows the Lima Valley.

Green Tourist Guides

Scenery,
Buildings,
Scenic routes,
Geography, Economy,
History, Art,
Touring programmes
Plans of towns and buildings

Guides for your holidays

PENEDONO
Michelin map **37** folds 2 and 3 or **441** fold 34 – *Local map p 69 –* Pop 912

The town of Penedono, perched on a rocky crest 947m - 3 106ft high in the Beira Alta, is overlooked on its northern side by a fortified castle, graceful and triangular.

Castle. – *Apply to the house on the left at the bottom of the steps.*

A 16C **pillory** stands before the steps leading up to the castle. Pass through the ramparts and turn left towards the simple entrance gate which is flanked by two battlemented turrets. The view from the parapet walk extends south over the village to the Serra da Estrela in the distance and northwards to the mountainous plain which precedes Trás-os-Montes.

PENICHE
Michelin map **37** west of fold 16 – Pop 15 267 – *Facilities p 36*

Peniche citadel, built to command access to the mile long promontory, is today Portugal's second most important fishing port (crayfish, sardines, tunny, etc.). Catches are preserved in the town's canneries. Peniche's other source of prosperity is its dockyard.

The remains of ramparts and the powerful looking citadel recall the former military role played by the city. A pleasant public garden planted with palm trees surrounds the Tourist Information Centre *(Rua Alexandre Herculano).*

The survival of handmade lace. – Peniche has been trying since the end of the 19C to revive its former speciality of bobbin lace, there is an apprenticeship school for this installed in the Industrial and Commercial school *(Avenida 25 de Avril):* on the 1st floor there is an exhibition of samples of past and present production. One can also see the lace-makers at work in the Work House of the Daughters of Fishermen *(Rua do Calvario)* and one can buy handmade lace in the town *(Avenida do Mar).*

■ **SIGHTS** *time: 1 hour*

Citadel. – An ancient 16C fortress, converted in the 17C into a Vauban-style citadel. It stands proudly with its invulnerable high walls and sharp edged bastions topped with watchtowers. Until 1974 it was a State prison, then an emergency city for refugees from Angola. It dominates both the harbour to the east and the sea to the south.

The Harbour. – To the southeast of the town, it lies in a cove which is almost shut in by two jetties. The esplanade *(Largo da Ribeira)* which surrounds it, at the foot of the citadel, is always the scene of a highly coloured spectacle with the **return of the fishing fleet** ★ , under the unceasing overhead ballet of the squawking seagulls when the catch of sardines, tunny fish or crawfish is unloaded.

São Pedro. – 17C. The chancel of this Church of St Peter was embellished in the 18C with gilded woodwork into which were incorporated four huge canvases dating from the 16C and attributed to the father of Josefa de Obidos *(p 110)*.

EXCURSIONS

Cape Carvoeiro ★ . – *3km - 2 miles plus 1/2 hour on foot Rtn. On the northern road out of Peniche, take the N 114 on the left; after a school and a water tower, take the road to Papoa on the right.*

  Papoa. – A small peninsula grafted like a spur on that of *Cape Carvoeiro, Papoa* still has, on the widest part along the east shore, a windmill and the ruins of a fort (Forte da Luzo) which was the northern counterpart of the Peniche citadel. *Leave the car at the end of the lane, after 500m - 1/3 mile.* Footbridges take one to a promontory where you overlook the high cliffs and the rocks which rise out of the sea, one of which is called the Crows' Stone (Pedro dos Corvos). Go as far as the raised monument at the highest point to have the full **panorama** ★ which extends to the east and the Balcal headland, its island and the coast further on, scalloped out by the Óbidos Lagoon; to the northwest over Berlenga; to the west over the cliffs as far as Remédios; to the south over Peniche.

Return to the N 114. The road twists and turns following the precipitous coast, where the numerous crevices are much appreciated by anglers. Several belvederes offer bird's eye **views** ★ over the cliffs; the one situated in the axis of the Remédios Chapel has an admirable view over a strange concentrated mass of piles of flat laminated rocks.

  Remédios. – The small village of Remédios stands grouped round a chapel (Nossa Senhora dos Remédios) which is faced inside with beautiful 18C **azulejos** ★ , attributed to António de Oliveira Bernardes. On the right are the Nativity and the Visitation, on the left the Presentation in the Temple. The ceiling is painted with an Assumption.

The vegetation soon dies away to be replaced by a kind of world's end moorland which continues to the foot of the lighthouse. From the lighthouse there is an impressive **view** ★ of the ocean, the horizon broken only by an isolated rock known as the Crows Ship (Nau dos Corvos) and, in the distance, the squat outline of Berlenga Island *(p 52)*.

Berlanga Island ★★ . – *Access by boat. Time: about 3 1/2 hours including crossing and visit. Description p 52.*

PINHEL

Michelin map 🇬🇧 fold 3 or 🇬🇧 fold 35 – Pop 2 354

  Pinhel, an old village and former fortified outpost on a mountainous shelf near to Spain, has many houses decorated with coats of arms and beautiful wrought iron balconies. In the main square, planted with acacia trees, stands a pillory consisting of a monolithic column topped by a pretty lantern turret.
  The road approaching Pinhel from the southwest (N 221) crosses a countryside covered with olive trees and vines; towards the end, near the town, there is a large group of wine vats, their white pointed domes standing straight up.

Municipal Museum. – *Apply at the library. Guided tour (time: 1/2 hour) 9am to noon and 2 to 5pm (4pm in winter); closed Saturdays, Sundays and holidays.*
  This little museum contains prehistoric and Roman remains, religious works of art (stone altarpiece of Ançã attributed to Jean de Rouen), weapons, Portuguese pewterware and earthenware: upstairs, naive folk art and other paintings.

EXCURSIONS

Serra da Marofa; Castelo Rodrigo. – *20km - 12 miles by the N 221 going north.*
The road linking Pinhel and Figueira de Castelo Rodrigo was known locally as the **Accursed Road** because of the danger presented by its countless bends when crossing the Serra da Marofa.
The road, after passing through a rich agricultural region, gradually becomes more and more hemmed in between rock strewn slopes before entering the green Côa Valley. On emerging it traverses the wild and stony **Serra da Marofa,** to reach the Figueira de Castelo Rodrigo Plateau which is planted with fruit trees.
To the left, the *serra's* highest peak, with an altitude of 977m - 3 238ft commands an interesting view of the ruins of the fortified village of Castelo Rodrigo on a height nearby.

  Castelo Rodrigo. – Pop 276. An important city since the Middle Ages, it was superseded in the 19C by Figueira de Castelo Rodrigo. Good views of the region.

  Figueira de Castelo Rodrigo. – Pop 2 096. In the town a 18C Baroque church contains many gilded wood altars.

Former Convent of Santa Maria de Aguiar. – *2km - 1 mile to the southeast of Figueira.* This is now private property. The church, which lacks all furnishings and has a very tall central aisle, is a Gothic edifice built to a Cistercian plan.

Barca de Alva. – *20km - 12 miles to the north of Figueira.* The blossoming of the almond trees between late February and mid-May, provides a delightful spectacle.

Road to Almeida★. – *22km - 14 miles to the southeast.* This route provides a pictur-esque link between Pinhel and Almeida. *Take the N 324 southeast of Pinhel.* The road then comes to a desolate plateau strewn with enormous blocks of granite forming a lunar **landscape★**. Less than 2km - 1 mile after Valeverde you cross a tributary of the Côa River by a narrow old humpback bridge. *2.5km - 1 1/2 miles further on, at a crossroads turn left on to the N 340: the road then crosses a bridge over the Côa River and rejoins the N 332 which one takes to the left to reach Almeida (p 83).*

POMBAL

Michelin map **37** north of fold 15 – Pop 12 469

The town of Pombal at the foot of its medieval castle evokes the memory of the Marquis of Pombal who acquired a property locally where he died in 1782.

The Despotism of the Grand Marquis. – Born in Lisbon in 1699 in a family of the petty nobility, Sebastião de Carvalho e Melo began life in the diplomatic service. Thanks to the support of his uncle, a canon of the Chapel Royal, he was sent first to London, where he interested himself in the flourishing national economy, and then on to Vienna. On the death of João V in 1750, his successor King José I called Carvalho to power. The minister undertook the task of improving the nation's finances and achieved considerable success, promulgating numerous decrees by which, among other things, the Royal Bank was founded and traffic in slavery of the natives of Brazil was abolished. In 1755 the earthquake gave him the opportunity to demonstrate his capacity for organization and planning *(p 89)*.

Simultaneously he sought to consolidate the absolute power of the monarchy by expelling the over powerful Jesuits (1759) and reducing the power of the nobles. On 2 September 1758 the king was wounded in an attack as he was returning from a private meeting with Maria-Teresa of Távora. Only in December did Carvalho decide to act, arresting the Marquis of Távora and his family. They were broken on the wheel and burned while their accomplices were hanged.

In 1759 the minister became Count of Oeiras and ten years later the king bestowed on him the title of Marquis of Pombal. But the death of José I in 1777 showed up the frailty of such created power; Pombal had to face a number of enemies. In 1781 he was banished from the Court and retired to his lands where he died the following year.

Castle. – *Time: 1/2 hour. Take the Ansião road on the right at the corner of the Law Courts and, on reaching a Cross, bear sharp right into a narrow surfaced road which rises steeply. Leave the car at the foot of the castle.*

The castle, which was built originally in 1161 by Gualdim Pais, Grand Master of the Order of Knights Templar, was modified in the 16C and restored in 1940. From the top of the ramparts, overlooked by the battlemented keep, there is a view of Pombal to the west and to the east, the foothills of the Serra da Lousã.

PONTE DE LIMA

Michelin map **37** fold 11 or **441** fold 22 – Pop 2 655

This is an important road junction on the south bank of the Lima, and an animated market town. Ponte de Lima bears witness to its historical past around the main square which has an 18C fountain with an armillary sphere; there is a large bridge with 16 semicircular arches alternating with openwork piers with pointed buttresses; the remains of ramparts surrounding lovely fortified doorways; and the façade of the old palace of the Marquis of Ponte de Lima dating from 1464 *(converted into a school and offices).*

Parish Church (Igreja Matriz). – Altered in the 18C, it has a Romanesque doorway with arching and a double stringcourse of billets.

The interior has numerous statues of various periods, and in the side chapels there are two Baroque altarpieces.

Church-Museum of São Francisco★ (des Terceiros). – *Avenida 5 de Outubro. Guided tour (time: 1 hour) June to September 10am to noon and 3 to 6pm; the rest of the year 2.30 to 5pm; in winter open Sunday afternoons only; 25esc.*

This church is secularized – *as is the one next to it which is reserved for temporary exhibitions.* The sanctuary dating from 1745 has been converted into a museum of sacred art. There are ancient statues, torches for processions, and above all a rare collection of **woodwork★**: in the nave there are two beautiful built-in pulpits facing each other, and two Baroque altarpieces; in the chancel there is a superb altarpiece, Rococo style in gilded wood; in the sacristy, a remarkable vestment cupboard of imposing dimensions.

PORTALEGRE

Michelin map **37** fold 6 – *Local map p 127* – Pop 15 876

A strategic position in olden times near the frontier, the town was endowed with a fortified castle by King Dinis I in 1290, but only a few ruins remain.

Portalegre, opulent and famous in the 16C through its tapestries, found a new prosperity at the end of the 17C when silk mills were established in the town. The bourgeois of the time filled the neighbourhood with Baroque houses and mansions which may be seen to this day on the foothills of the Serra de São Mamede *(p 127).*

■ **SIGHTS** *time: 3 hours*

Follow the route marked on the plan.

José Régio Museum (M¹). – *Guided tour (time: 1 hour) 10am to 12.30pm and 2 to 5pm; closed Mondays and holidays; 10esc.*

The collection of regional religious and folk art assembled by the poet José Régio (1901-69) is the most interesting part of the museum, which is in the house where he lived; there are numerous 16 to 19C crucifixes and naive statuettes of St Antony, as well as antique furniture.

Rua 19 de Junho. – This street is lined with 17 and 18C houses.

Cathedral (Sé). – The 18C façade is characterized by the marble columns of the main doorway, wrought iron balconies and granite pilasters. The 16C interior contains in the second chapel on the right, a fine compartmented altarpiece on the Life of the Virgin and, in the sacristy where the walls are clad with *azulejos*, an 18C cope chest.

Municipal Museum (M²). – *Open 10am to 12.30pm and 2 to 5.30pm; closed Tuesdays and holidays; 10esc.*

Installed in the former diocesan seminary, this museum contains a rich collection of sacred art: a Spanish *Pietà* in gilded wood dating from the end of the 15C, a 16C altarpiece in polychrome terracotta, a magnificent 17C tabernacle in ebony, four ivory high reliefs (18C Italian school), an 18C ivory crucifix, 16C gold and silver plate.

Also on display are 17-18C Arraiolos carpets *(p 46)*, pieces of furniture including a beautiful Dutch wardrobe, earthenware (Hispano-Moorish, 16-17C Portuguese) as well as 17 and 19C porcelain from China.

PORTALEGRE

Luís de Camões (R.)		24
5 de Outubro (R.)		33
Comércio (R. do)		3
Elvas (R. de)		12
Figueira (R. da)		13
G. G. Fernandes (R.)		19
Luís Barahona (R.)		23
M. de Albuquerque (R.)		27
República (Pr. da)		29
S. Vicente (R. de)		31
Sé (L. e R. da)		32

Yellow Palace (A). – The palace has beautiful 17C wrought iron grilles.

Tapestry Workshop (B). – The workshops are in the former Jesuit monastery. *To visit, ring at the door on the left at the top of the stairs on the 1st floor. Open Mondays to Fridays 9.30 to 11am and 2.30 to 5pm.*

The tour takes one successively through the weaving room where all the looms are worked by hand, the design studios where the cartoonists' drawings are adapted, and the exhibition hall.

Portalegre is the starting point for the excursion in the Serra de São Mamede, eastwards (p 127).

PORTIMÃO

Michelin map **37** south of fold 20 – Pop 26 172 – *See town plan in the current Michelin Red Guide España Portugal*

Portimão is a fishing port nestled at the back of a bay. The best view★ is at high tide from the bridge across the Arade at the end of the bay. The town is also an industrial centre specializing in boat building and the canning of tunny and sardines. Brightly coloured carts *(carrinhas)* drawn by mules ensure a picturesque liaison with the seaside resort of Praia da Rocha★★ *(p 123)*.

Largo 1º de Dezembro. – The benches of this small square are covered with 19C *azulejos* portraying various episodes from Portuguese history.

Portimão is the starting point for the excursion in the Serra de Monchique, northwards (p 106).

PÓVOA DE VARZIM

Michelin map **37** fold 12 or **441** fold 22 – Pop 23 846 – *Facilities p 36*

Póvoa de Varzim is partly an old fishing port and partly an elegant and modern seaside resort. It is also the birthplace of the great novelist Eça de Queirós (1845-1900).

The Fishing Port★. – The port lies south of the beach, bordered by the low houses of the fishermen's quarter. In summer it is often both bustling and picturesque: while the women mend nets, the men, in their traditional heavy white wool jerseys embroidered in many colours, see to their boats; nearby freshly caught fish lie on the ground drying in the sun while further away seaweed *(sargaço)* is sorted into great heaps to be used later as fertilizer.

EXCURSIONS

The Romanesque Churches of Rio Mau and Rates. – *15km - 9 miles – about 1 hour. Leave Póvoa de Varzim by the Oporto road, the N 13 going south, and after 2km - 1 mile turn left into the N 206 towards Guimarães.*

Rio Mau. – Pop 1 867. *Turn right opposite the post office into an unsurfaced road.* The small Romanesque Church of St Christopher (São Cristóvão) is built very plainly of granite; the rough decoration of the capitals in the doorway contrast with the much more detailed ornament of the **capitals**★ in the triumphal arch and in the chancel which is later in date.

2km - 1 mile beyond Rio Mau, take an unsurfaced road on the left to Rates (1km - 1/2 mile).

Rates. – Pop 2 219. The granite Church of St. Peter (São Pedro) was built in the 12 and 13C by Benedictine monks from Cluny on the orders of Count Henri of Burgundy. The façade is pierced by a rose window and a door with five arches, of which two are historiated, and capitals decorated with animals and other figures; on the tympanum a low relief presents a Transfiguration. The south door is adorned with a honeycombed archway sheltering a low relief of the Holy Lamb.

The interior is well proportioned and contains beautiful Romanesque capitals.

Vila do Conde. – *3km - 2 miles by the N 13 going south. Description p 138.*

PRAIA DA ROCHA ★★

Michelin map **37** south of fold 20 – *Facilities p 36* – *See town plan in the current Michelin Red Guide España Portugal*

Praia da Rocha which stands in a picturesque **setting**★★ on top of a cliff, has become one of the most popular summer and winter resorts of the Algarve, thanks to the mildness of the climate (an average of 13.5ºC - 57ºF in winter), a magnificent position facing the sun, clear calm water and a vast beach of white sand.

Belvedere★. – From a promontory to the west of the resort near the Dos Castelos Creek, which has been arranged as a belvedere, there is an overall view of the gently sloping beach scattered with rocks and protected by an ochre coloured cliff pierced here and there by picturesque arches and caves. The series of large white buildings, looking down from the cliff top mark the line of the resort's main avenue.

Santa Catarina Fort. – The fort commands, from the west, the mouth of the Arade and, with the fort of **Ferragudo** *(facilities p 36)* on the far bank, guards the entrance to Portimão Bay.

PRAIA DO CARVOEIRO

Michelin map **37** fold 20 – *Facilities p 36*

Built in a narrow indentation in the cliff, this fishing village has become a seaside resort.

Belvedere of Our Lady of the Incarnation (Nossa Senhora da Encarnação). – At the top of a steep slope, to the east of the beach *(in front of a chapel and a police station)* this belvedere offers an extensive view over the cliffs of Cape Carvoeiro.

Algar Seco★★. – *500m - 1/3 mile beyond the belvedere of Our Lady of the Incarnation, plus 1/2 hour on foot Rtn. Leave the car in the car park.*

Below Cape Carvoeiro, the **marine site** of Algar Seco is reached through a maze *(including 134 steps)* of reddish rocks sculpted by the sea in the shape of peaks, arches, rounds of Swiss cheese, etc. The site gives the impression of a giant heart beating as the gaping entrances to several semi-submerged caves throb under the impact of violent whirlpools from confronting currents. On the right *(sign "A Boneca")*, a short tunnel leads under a conical formation ceiling, into a cavern *(converted into a refreshment room in summer)* which has two natural "windows" from which there is a view encompassing the western cliffs. On the left, a path leads to a headland from where one can see the entrance to a deep underwater cave.

The sea caves of Cape Carvoeiro can be visited by boat during the season. Apply to the Algarve agency, Praia do Carvoeiro.

QUELUZ ★

Michelin map **37** folds 12 (inset) and 17 – Pop 47 864

The town of Queluz is known for its royal palace. This graceful edifice, inspired by Versailles, remains intimate in spite of the luxury and fantasy of its decoration.

■ THE ROYAL PALACE★

Guided tour (time: 1/2 hour) 10am to 1pm and 2 to 5pm; closed Tuesdays and holidays; 50esc.

The palace, erected between 1758-94 by the Portuguese, Mateus Vicente *(p 25)* and the Frenchman, J. B. Robillon, was the residence of Queen Maria I (1734-1816) who, during her childhood, had the opportunity to appreciate Versailles while she was officially affianced to Louis XV.

Palace★. – The entrance, with a façade of rose stucco, forms a central building in advance of the wings on either side. The edifice ends in a balustrade.

The tour starts with three rooms of the royal guard to the right of the entrance. In the first, the walls are covered with multicoloured 18C *azulejos* representing landscapes in China and Brazil; in the third room there is a lovely 16C Arraiolos carpet.

The Ambassadors' Hall, decorated with marble and mirrors, has a fine painted ceiling of a concert at the Court of King Dom José, and diverse mythological motifs.

Beyond the queen's boudoir, which is in the French Rococo style, lies the Don Quixote room where eight columns support a circular ceiling, and paintings of Cervantes's hero decorate the walls. In the Tea Room, embellished with gilded woodwork, are several 18C paintings of royal picnics.

To the left of the entrance is the dining hall with gilt frames to the mirrors and a blue toned Arraiolos carpet.

After admiring the fine 18C ceilings in the rooms of the three princesses and the chandeliers in the Music Room one reaches the sumptuous **Throne Room★**. Light is reflected on all sides in this room where mirrors furnish several false doors and magnificent Venetian crystal chandeliers hang from the shallow domed ceiling supported on caryatids.

Gardens★. – The gardens were designed in 1762 by the French architect J. B. Robillon in the style of the 17C French landscape gardener, Le Nôtre. Clipped box trees, cypresses, statues and lakes surrounded by masses of flowers make up the gardens as a whole. Individual attractions include the Amphrytrite Basin from which there is pleasant view of the Neptune garden and the main façade erected in the Gabriel style and, lower down, an Italian style park with pools, cascades and green arbours.

The castle's west wing by Robillon, overlooks the Grand Canal garden. The wing is fronted by a magnificent **Lion Staircase★** which is extended by a beautiful colonnade. Lovely 18C *azulejos* adorn the canal basin.

SABUGAL

Michelin map **37** northeast of fold 4 or **441** fold 35 – Pop 2 164

The small city of Sabugal, grouped on a hillock round its fortified castle, dominates the peaceful Valley of the Côa, a tributary of the Douro.

The town which was founded by Alfonso X of Léon in the beginning of the 13C, became Portuguese in 1282 on the marriage of Isabella of Aragon and King Dinis of Portugal.

Castle. – *Apply at the town hall (Câmara Municipal).*

The castle's present appearances dates from the late 13C; a double crenellated perimeter wall flanked by square towers with pyramid shaped merlons encloses an impressive pentagonal keep with battlemented overhangs.

SAGRES Peninsula ★★

Michelin map **37** southwest of fold 20

The Sagres Peninsula, an arid world's end swept by the ocean winds, was the setting in which Prince Henry the Navigator chose to live and the base from which he was to inspire and instigate the Great Discoveries *(p 19)*.

The Sagres School. – At the beginning of the 15C, after the capture of Ceuta, Prince Henry retired to Sagres where he collected around him the most famous astrologers, cartographers and mariners of the day, so founding a School of Navigation. Theories were tested and put to practical use in expeditions which set out on ever longer voyages *(p 86)*.

Improvements in the astrolabe and the sextant and increased knowledge in their use, enabling calculations to be made far out to sea, led to the prince's introduction of navigation by the stars: mariners who had been used to a chart and compass as guides and had gauged their position from an estimate of the distance travelled, learned to calculate their latitude from the height of the stars above the horizon and chart their positions with greater accuracy.

Cartography also improved. To the Mediterranean portolano, were added maps of the Atlantic which, although ignoring points of latitude, nevertheless demonstrated Portuguese supremacy in the cartographical field.

(After Secretaria de Estado da Informação e Turismo photo)

A Caravel.

Finally the demands of the voyages compelled the Portuguese to design a new type of ship which revolutionized navigation – the **caravel**. This long boat with a shallow draught and a small area of canvas could carry a good-sized crew and had all the advantages of traditional ships without their disadvantages. Its wider hull and high sheathing increased security; the large number of masts enabled it to carry square as well as triangular lateen sails. The latter, pivoting round the mast and taking every advantage of the wind, gave the caravel great speed. Caravels were alone, at that time, in being able to sail close to the wind, a facility much needed when the ships were returning from Africa. Finally the use of a stern rudder made them handle more easily.

The caravel which first appeared in the middle of the 15C was to sail the oceans for nearly a century.

Tour from Vila do Bispo – *26km - 16 miles – about 1 hour*

Vila do Bispo. – Pop 1 097. The Baroque church *(open every morning except Wednesday)* has a chancel in gilded wood and its walls are faced with *azulejos* (1715). A door to the left of the chancel opens into a small museum of art which includes a beautiful old ivory crucifix, another copper Romanesque one, as well as 16C paintings.

On leaving the village take a signposted road going west towards Praia do Castelejo; a short distance along a winding road, bear right; the road ends at the top of the Castelejo Cliff.

Castelejo Cliff. – The **view**★ plunges down over the nearby cliffs and the sea.

Return to Vila do Bispo and take the N 268 to the south.

The road cuts across the windswept plateau where only a few geraniums, agaves and vines exist. *At the crossroads, continue towards Fortaleza; go through the covered way.*

Fortress. – On the ground in the centre of a large square is a mariners' card protected by a chain railing. On the left the old Navigation School and Prince Henry's former residence have been turned into a youth hostel. In an auditorium facing the entrance a film retraces the major events in the period of the Great Discoveries *(English version daily at 3.45pm; 2.50 esc; time: 1/2 hour).*

Sagres Headland★★. – *Bear right, round the headland, following the road which skirts the edge of the cliff.* Views★ open out westwards of St Vincent's Bay and Cape St Vincent and eastwards of the Lagos coast. Two marine caves *(furnas)* in which the deep rumbling of the sea can be heard add to the atmosphere and the wild beauty of the setting.

Sagres. – Pop 2 037. *Facilities p 36.* A small fishing village.

A coast road goes from Sagres to Cape St Vincent.

Cape St Vincent★★. – Cape St Vincent, the most southwesterly point of continental Europe, towers above the ocean at a height of 75m - 246ft. Here, it is said, the vessel landed containing the body of St Vincent after he had suffered martyrdom in Valencia. The legend further recounts how the boat finally reached Lisbon in 1173, following two crows that showed it the way.

The Cape has also served as a backcloth to several British naval victories, notably in 1759 against the French, in 1780 by Admiral Rodney against the Spanish and in 1797 when Nelson's tactical genius was first revealed in a battle with the Spanish.

There is an impressive **view**★ from the lighthouse of the apparently infinite ocean.

SANTARÉM

Michelin map **37** fold 16 – Pop 20 034

Santarém, on a hill on the right bank of the Tagus, overlooks the vast Ribatejo Plain, of which it is the chief town. Its strategic position has made it the scene of several battles since Mohammedan times. It was recaptured from the Moors in 1147 by Alfonso I and later became a royal residence, appreciated by several kings for its setting and its proximity to Lisbon. From this rich past, Santarém retains several monuments, mostly Gothic.

Santarém is well known for Portuguese bullfighting *(details p 31)*. Performances as well as folk dancing and a procession of *campinos (p 30)* take place at the annual Ribatejo Fair.

St Irene. – Irene, a young nun in a convent near Tomar, was assassinated in 653 by a monk called Remigo whose advances she had refused. Her body, thrown in the Tagus, was washed up at the foot of the former Roman city of Scalabis. The king of the Visigoths, who had recently been converted to Christianity, gave the town the new name of Saint Irene or Santarém to commemorate the event.

■ MAIN SIGHTS *time: 2 hours*

Seminary Church (A A). – 17C. The Baroque façade of this former Jesuit college has as its main feature the superimposition of several storeys outlined by cornices and pierced by windows and niches, which gives the church more the appearance of a palace than a place of worship. The niches contain statues of Jesuits whose symbol (Christ's monogram) is above the main doorway. The curvilinear pediment crowning the façade is flanked by heavy scrolls and pyramids.

The interior remains austere in spite of the marble incrustations decorating the altar and the pilasters. The single nave is covered with a ceiling painted to represent the Immaculate Conception and Jesuit evangelical activities overseas.

The frieze of 18C *azulejos*, which lines the corridor walls throughout the building, begins in the vestibule of the former monastery *(entrance to the right of the church)*.

St Clare's (Igreja de Santa Clara) (B B). – This vast Gothic church was once part of a 13C convent. The lack of a doorway on the façade increases the bare appearance of the church's exterior.

Inside, the narrow nave ends with a beautiful rose window above the 17C tomb of Dona Leonor, founder of the convent. Also found in the church is the original 14C tomb of Dona Leonor. On either side of it are Franciscan monks and Poor Clares and at the foot and the head, St Francis receiving the stigmata and the Annunciation.

São Bento Belvedere (Miradouro) (B C). – This belvedere affords a vast **panorama**★ of the Tagus Plain and Santarém where the main buildings can be easily distinguished.

Fonte das Figueiras (B E). – This 13C fountain against a wall is covered by a porch roof crowned with pyramid shaped merlons.

São João de Alporão (B M¹). – This Romanesque-Gothic church, facing the Cale-basses Tower, whose clock formely regulated the life of the city, now contains an **archaeological museum**★ *(open 10am (2pm Mondays) to 5pm; closed holidays)*.

In addition to Arab and Roman pottery, *azulejos*, coins and chinaware, the church's narrow nave has an interesting collection of sculpture, including funerary steles, capitals (two Arabic), coats of arms (in the raised ambulatory), Manueline doors and windows and tombs. The fine tomb, in Flamboyant Gothic style, was erected for Duarte de Meneses, Count of Viana, by his wife to contain a tooth, the only relic of her husband who had been killed by the Moors in Africa.

The beautiful balcony to the left of the entrance was carved by Mateus Fernandes.

Church of Grace (B F). – *Times and charges not available at the time of going to press.*

This Gothic church of 1380 has a fine Flamboyant façade; the doorway is surmounted by a gable reminiscent of the one at Batalha. Above, a lovely rose window has been delicately carved out of a single block of stone.

The beautiful **nave**★ has been restored to its original pure lines. The church contains several tombs including, in the south transept, that of Dom Pedro de Meneses, first Governor of Ceuta *(p 19)*. The 15C tomb, which rests on eight lions and bears the reclining figures of the count and his wife, is carved with leaf motifs and coats of arms. On the pavement of the south apsidal chapel may be seen the funerary stone of the navigator Pedro Alvares Cabral *(p 19)*. In the chapel off the south aisle, a panel of 18C *azulejos* shows St John the Baptist between St Rita and St Francis.

Portas do Sol (B). – From the wall divided by the Sun Gate which has given its name to the garden, one can look straight down on to the Tagus which here makes a wide curve.

■ **ADDITIONAL SIGHTS**

Marvila Church (Igreja da Marvila) (B K). – This 16C church has an elegant Manueline doorway. The interior is lined with *azulejos*, the most interesting being those known as carpet *azulejos* painted in many colours with plant motifs which date from 1620 and 1635.

Chapel of Our Lady of the Mountain (A N). – In the centre of a horseshoe shaped square stands the 16C Chapel of Our Lady. Both sides are bordered by a gallery supported by arcades with capitals decorated with leaf motifs and the heads of cherubim. At the east end is a 16C statue of Our Lady.

Covered Market (A P). – The walls are covered with *azulejos*.

EXCURSION

Alpiarça. – Pop 7 993. *10km - 6 miles. Leave Santarém by* ②, *the N 114. The statesman and art lover, José Relvas, brought together in his beautifully furnished residence at Alpiarça a magnificent art collection. On his death the manor, the Casa dos Patudos, became a* **museum**★. *It stands on the right at the exit to the town on the Lisbon road. Guided tour (time: 1 hour) in summer Thursdays 2 to 7pm, Saturdays, Sundays and holidays 10 to 11am and 1.30 to 6pm; in winter Saturdays 10 to 11am and 1.30 to 5.30pm, Sundays and holidays 3.30 to 5.30pm; closed 1 January, 2 April, 1 May and 25 December; 30esc.*

The vast house contains a remarkable series of **tapestries and carpets**★ dating from the 17 to the 19C. A rich collection of **china and porcelain**★ includes pieces from Portugal, France, Germany and the Far East – some of the ware is displayed in the dining room, which adds a charming touch to the decoration.

A large collection of paintings adorn the museum's walls. In the Primitives' gallery there are some interesting 16C Luso-Flemish pictures, a beautiful Italian *Mother and Child* as well as Portuguese paintings and sculptures.

The walls of one room of the house are faced with 18C *azulejos*.

SANTIAGO DO CACÉM

Michelin map ₃₇ fold 18 – Pop 6 777

Santiago do Cacém clings to the slopes of a hill crowned by a castle built long ago by the Knights Templar.

There is a good **view**★ of the site from the N 120 at the town's south exit.

Castle. – Two restored crenellated perimeter walls encircle the ruins of the castle whose interior is now planted with cypress trees and occupied by a graveyard. Walk round the ramparts to see the panorama which extends as far as Cape Sines.

Roman Ruins of Miróbriga. – *1km - 1/2 mile. Leave the town by the Lisbon road, the N 120 going north; at the top of a hill, bear right (signpost) into a narrow road, then left into a dirt road. Leave the car at the last layby.* A Roman road leads to the relics of the Roman city *(mostly on the hill on the left).*

SÃO JOÃO DE TAROUCA

Michelin map ₃₇ south of fold 2 or ₄₄₁ fold 34 – *Local map p 68* – Pop 1 054

The former Monastery of St John of Tarouca, overlooked by the heights of the Serra de Leomil, lies squat with cypress trees in a hollow in the fertile Barossa Valley. Grouped round the monastery in the valley are a few houses.

Church. – *Apply at the first house on the right in the square, facing the church.*

The church, erected in the 12C by Cistercian monks, was considerably remodelled in the 17C when the interior was given Baroque decoration. The side chapels contain several pictures attributed to the painter, Gaspar Vaz – a picture of **St Peter**★ *(3rd chapel on the right)* is outstanding.

In the north transept the walls are lined with 18C *azulejos* depicting scenes from the life of John the Baptist and the Baptism of Christ. The monumental 14C granite tomb decorated with low reliefs of a boar hunt contains the remains of Dom Pedro, Count of Barcelos, bastard son of King Dinis. Dom Pedro was the author of the *General Chronicle of 1344* and is considered to be the greatest Portuguese writer of the Middle Ages. The *azulejos* in the chancel illustrate the life of St Bernard. The sacristy also contains fine *azulejos.*

*On your way to Portugal visit Spain
with the help of the **Michelin Green Guide Spain.***

SÃO MAMEDE, Serra de ★

Michelin map ₃₇ fold 6 – north of Portalegre

The Serra de São Mamede is a small island of greenery in an arid and stony region; its relatively high altitude (highest point: 1 025m - 3 363ft) and the impermeable nature of the soil combine to provide sufficient humidity for a dense and varied vegetation including among others, chestnut trees, cork oaks, weeping willows, poplars, almonds, pines and eucalyptus.

The triangular shaped massif is composed of hard rock which has resisted erosion; the variations in level on the west face were accentuated by a fault.

Round tour from Portalegre – *69km - 43 miles – about 2 1/2 hours – local map below*

Leave Portalegre (p 121) by the Reguengo road, the N 246–2 going east. The road rises through the woods, affording attractive views of Portalegre and the surrounding countryside.

8km - 5 miles from Portalegre, in a left bend, take a paved path off to the right and after 2km - 1 mile bear left.

From the top there is a vast **panorama**★ south over the Alentejo, west and north over the Serra de São Mamede and east over range after range of the Spanish *sierras.*

Return to the main road. It runs through a landscape of bare moors bristling in places with pines. The descent is swift to the green and wooded plain.

SERRA DE SÃO MAMEDE

Marvão★★. – *Description p 104.*

Castelo de Vide★ ; Nossa Senhora da Penha *(1.5km - 1 mile). – Description p 61.*

Return to Portalegre by the Carreiras *corniche* **road**★.

SERNANCELHE

Michelin map **37** north of fold 3 or **441** fold 34 – *Local map p 68* – Pop 1 060

The old town of Sernancelhe occupies a rocky height in the Beira Alta. It was once a commandery of the Order of Malta which built the castle now standing in ruins.

Church. – The façade of this Romanesque church, flanked by a squat square belfry, is pierced by a beautiful rounded doorway in which one of the arches is adorned with an unusual frieze of archangels. The tympanum is carved with plant motifs. Two niches on either side of the door shelter six granite statues of the Evangelists St Peter and St Paul.

Pillory. – *Opposite the church.* The pillory (16C) is topped by a cage decorated with slender colums.

Carvalhos Manorhouse (Solar). – This elegant Baroque manorhouse (18C) with a façade flanked by pilasters, belongs to the Marquis of Pombal's family.

Christ. – *Take a road which begins to the left of the church and goes towards the castle. It ends in a flight of steps.*

Shortly afterwards, on the right protected by a porch, is a fine stone Calvary (14C). Continuing, one soon gets a view of the church and then of the village.

SESIMBRA

Michelin map **37** folds 17 and 18 – Pop 8 138 – *Facilities p 36*

Sesimbra, at the foot of a southern slope of the Serra da Arrábida *(p 45)*, is a pleasant seaside resort enjoying a magnificently sunny outlook. Underwater swimmers delight in its translucent waters. It is also, for the fisherman, a well know place to catch swordfish.

■ **SIGHTS** *time: 1 1/2 hours*

Castle. – *6km - 4 miles northwest by a steep uphill road.*

The castle, on the crest of a bare rib at an altitude of more than 200m - 700ft occupies a first class defensive position which the first King of Portugal, nevertheless, captured from the Moors in 1165. From its walls there is a good **view**★ of Sesimbra and its harbour.

The Harbour★. – It leans picturesquely against the foot of the cliff, away from the town. The large fleet of trawlers, decorated with an eye or a star on the prow, bring in each morning and evening, sardines, sea-bream, conger eels, swordfish, shellfish, etc. which, unless they have already been sold on the spot, the small boats take on board at once in order to go and sell them by auction in the fishmarket *(at around 9am and 4pm)*.

It is also amusing to watch, next to the harbour, the activity in the small shipyard which is specialized in building and repairing the wooden trawlers.

The Town. – It lies in a pleasant setting, but the traditional features are only to be found now in the charming little steep streets and alleys – sometimes intersected with steps – which go down towards the beach, lined with small shops and houses decorated with flowers where the washing, and quite often a birdcage, hang on the façade, along with fish put out to dry.

Every evening the lines and nets are disentangled in the middle of the street.

Parish Church. – *Halfway up the hill, near the post office.* Inside is a 17C pulpit in the local pink marble and a triumphal arch with Manueline style motifs. A gilded wood altarpiece stands in the 18C chapel.

To find a town, a sight or setting, a historical or geographical reference described in this guide, consult the index pp 160-162.

SETÚBAL ★

Michelin map **37** fold 17 – Pop 97 762

Setúbal, abutting on the last foothills of the Serra da Arrábida *(p 45)* and on the north bank of the wide Sado Estuary, is an industrial town, a port and a tourist centre.

There are several interesting monuments to be seen in Setúbal and, between the Praça Almirante Reis and St Mary's Church, an older quarter with narrow alleys which contrast sharply with the wide avenues of the modern town. The town's muscatel wine and orange marmalade are popular.

Two Portuguese celebrities were born in Setúbal – the singer Luisa Todi and the poet Bocage (1765-1805 – *p 26*).

A Busy Port. – The town's commercial activities are various: cement, standing as the town does close to the slopes of the *serra*, development of the saltmarshes on either bank of the Sado, the assembling of lorries and cars, chemicals, fish canning and the marketing of agricultural produce grown in the region. The shipbuilding industry here is highly developed: at present shipyards are being built at Setenave which when finished will have a greater capacity than those at Lisbon.

Setúbal is Portugal's third port after Lisbon and Oporto (Leixões). It consists of a fishing port (sardines) with a fleet of about 2 000 boats, a pleasure boat harbour and a commercial port. The latter is in contact with the great maritime cities of Germany, the Netherlands, Spain and Great Britain. Trade consists primarily in importing coal and phosphates and exporting cement and paper pulp.

Portuguese Oysters. – The region of Setúbal, like that of Faro, is a production area for molluscs which when eaten are known as Portuguese oysters. The Portuguese prefer the oysters cooked rather than live. In fact, few are eaten in the country so that the oyster farmers direct their activities primarily towards the production of seed oysters, Setúbal virtually holding the monopoly in this Portuguese export trade.

■ SIGHTS *time: 2 1/2 hours*

Church of Jesus★ (A). – This church, constructed of Arrábida marble in 1491, was designed by the architect Boytac and is the first example of a building with Manueline decoration.

It is a Late Gothic building to judge by its Flamboyant doorway – twin doors with bracketed arches framed in ringed columns – and its three lines of vaulting of equal height which make it into a hall church. The Manueline art is seen to particular advantage in the amazingly twisted pillars supporting the vaulting and in the spiral ribs of the vault above the chancel *(illustration p 22)*.

The walls of the nave and chancel are partly covered with 17C *azulejos*.

Museum★ (Convento de Jesus) (M¹). – *Guided tour (time: 3/4 hour) 9am to 12.30pm and 2 to 5pm; closed Mondays and holidays.*

The museum is in the Gothic cloister of the Church of Jesus.

The upper galleries house a large collection of 15 and 16C Portuguese Primitives. All these **paintings★** are said to be by the anonymous artist known as the Master of the Setúbal Altarpiece; some, however, attribute them to two other 16C artists both members of the Lisbon school *(p 23)*, namely Gregório Lopes and Cristóvão de Figueiredo.

In spite of the influence of the Flemish school (stiff attitudes, realistic details) a certain increase in warm tones should be noted, also the imprint on the faces of verisimilitude and mysticism, and especially the expression of the Virgin and the Saints before the Crucifixion and St Francis when receiving the stigmata.

The lower galleries contain 15-18C *azulejos*.

St Philip's Castle (Castelo de São Filipe). – *By Rua São Filipe.* The castle, built in 1590 on the orders of the Spanish in an attempt to control the animosity of the inhabitants of Setúbal and also to prevent the English from establishing themselves at Tróia, is garnished with ramps and stepped bastions. Part of the castle is now a *pousada*.

Cross a covered passage and glance left into a secularized chapel where the 18C *azulejos*, attributed to a master of that art, Policarpo de Oliveira Bernardes, portray the life of St Philip.

There is a wide **panorama★** from the top of the ramparts: to the east lie Setúbal harbour and shipyards, Sado Bay and, on the horizon, the Tróia Peninsula; northwest Palmela Castle and, west and south, the Serra da Arrábida.

St Julian's (Igreja de São Julião) (B). – The trefoil door in the north face of the church is Manueline. Two columns, twisted like cables, frame the door and rise above it in a moulding before ending in pinnacles. Inside, beautiful 18C *azulejos* depict the life of St Julian.

Regional Archaeological and Ethnographic Museum (M²). – *Guided tour (time: 1 hour) 9.30am to 12.30pm and 2 to 5.30pm; closed Mondays and holidays.*

The museum contains prehistoric objects (an idol cut out of bone, Bronze age pottery vase) and Luso-Roman coins, collections of folk art and crafts, costumes, small scale models of boats; the textile industry, agriculture, wood and iron handicraft are depicted by animated models. There are also numerous panels and decorative motifs made of cork.

■ **TROIA PENINSULA** *time: 1 hour*

Access by road. – *98km - 61 miles. Go right round the estuary of the Rio Sado by the N 10, the N 5, and the N 253 until Comporta, then the N 253-1.*

Crossing the estuary. – *By motorboat (1/4 hour); departures from landing stage near the fishing port (Doca dos Pescadores), every 1/2 hour in season, every hour out of season; 30esc. By car ferry (20 minutes): departures near the commercial port (Doca de Comércio), every 1/2 hour in season, every hour out of season; 100esc per car, plus 30esc per passenger.*

An immense strip of fine sand barring the Sado Estuary, lined with dunes and pine trees, the Troia Peninsula is still in the throes of vast development and planning for tourists all along the north and west coasts: hotels, residential villas and high-rise blocks already make it a kind of city, facing the Serra da Arrábida.

Roman ruins at Cetóbriga. – *2.5km - 1 1/2 miles by a sandy path, from the N 253-1 to the east. Apply to the caretaker.* So far only a few remains have been excavated from this important Roman town destroyed by the sea at the beginning of the 5C; vats for salting fish, swimming pools, a sepulchral vault, and the remains of a temple decorated with frescoes.

SILVES

Michelin map ▨ fold 20 – Pop 9 845

Of the ancient Xelb, Moorish capital of the Algarve whose magnificence was said to eclipse even that of Lisbon, only the Alcazaba remains. The red limestone walls dominate the town like an acropolis, but the many mosques have all vanished.

Castle ★ (Castelo). – *Leave the car on the Cathedral Square and go through a gate in the perimeter wall to the castle.*

Two huge cisterns may still be seen below ground in this restored ancient Arab fortress in which the crenellated perimeter walls are reinforced with massive square towers.

As one goes round the circular parapet walk a panorama between the battlements gives interesting views northwest of the irrigated Valley of the Arade and the cork factories and, south, of peach and almond orchards.

Former Cathedral. – The 13C Gothic nave and aisles of the old cathedral have a beautiful and striking simplicity; the transept and chancel are of the later Flamboyant Gothic style. The numerous tombs are said to be of the Crusaders who helped to capture the town in 1242.

The Portuguese Cross. – *At the east exit to the town on the N 124, the São Bartolomeu de Messines road.*

This unusual white Calvary (16C) shows, on one side, Christ crucified and on the other a Virgin of Compassion.

SINTRA ★

Michelin map ▨ folds 12 (inset) and 17 – *Local map p 131* – Pop 20 574 – *Facilities p 38*
See town plan in the current Michelin Red Guide España Portugal

The small town of Sintra, built right up against the north slope of the *serra*, was for six centuries the favourite summer residence of the kings of Portugal, who were attracted by the cool climate and the beauty of the town's setting.

Three different areas make up the town of Sintra: the old town (Vila Velha) which is grouped round the royal palace; the modern town (Estefânia) and the former village of São Pedro. The latter is famous for its market day on the 2nd and 4th Sundays of each month. Horse-drawn carriages drive through the city or as far as Pena Park *(p 131)*.

Sintra has a gastronomic speciality: the delicious small tarts known as *queijadas*.

The Convention of Sintra. – Wellington's victory at Vimeiro in August 1808 *(pp 20 and 110)* was followed by an armistice and subsequently an agreement, known as the Convention of Sintra (30 August 1808). Under this the British made some material gains and the French were granted a passage home on board British ships with their arms and baggage. The terms distressed the Portuguese, who renamed the Dutch Ambassador's residence, where the Convention was signed, the **Seteais** or House of the Seven Sighs.

Royal Palace ★ (Palácio Real). – *Guided tour (time: 3/4 hour) 10am to 5pm; closed Wednesdays and holidays; 50esc.*

The palace's irregular structure is due to the additions made at different times; the central edifice was erected by João I at the end of the 14C and the wings by Manuel I early in the 16C. Apart from the two tall conical chimneys, the paired Moorish style *(ajimeces)* and Manueline windows are the most striking features of the exterior.

The interior is interesting for its remarkable decoration of 16 and 17C azulejos ★★. The finest embellish the dining room or Arabic Hall, the chapel and the Sirens' Hall. The Armoury, which is square, is covered with a **ceiling ★★** in the form of a dome on squinches, the dome itself consisting of caissons painted with the coats of arms of Portuguese nobles of the early 16C – the missing blazon is that of the Coelho family who conspired against João II.

The Reading or Magpie Room has a ceiling painted in the 17C with magpies holding in their beaks a rose inscribed with the words: *por bem* – for good – words pronounced by João I when his queen caught him about to kiss one of her ladies-in-waiting. To put an end to the gossip the king had as many magpies painted on the ceiling as there were ladies at court.

A fine Venetian chandelier adorns the queen's audience chamber.

The Sintra Range is a granite block forming a mountain barrier with the Cruz Alta with an altitude of 529m - 1 736ft as its highest point. Rain from the Atlantic falls upon the impermeable rock giving rise to the dense vegetation which covers the whole massif and largely masks the granite spikes left exposed by the erosion of other rocks. The flora is varied: oaks, cedars, tropical and subtropical trees, bracken, camellias, etc.

The beauty of the landscape has often been sung by poets, including Gil Vicente, Camões *(The Lusiads)*, Southey and Byron *(Childe Harold)*:

> ....Cintra's mountain greets them on their way
> ....
> The horrid crags, by toppling convent crowned,
> The cork trees hoar that clothe the shaggy steep,
> The mountain moss by scorching skies imbrowned,
> The sunken glen, whose sunless shrubs must weep,
> The tender azure of the unruffled deep,
> The orange tints that gild the greenest bough,
> The torrents that from cliff to valley leap,
> The vine on high, the willow branch below,
> Mixed in one mighty scene, with varied beauty glow.

PENA PARK★★

Open in summer 8.30am to 6pm; in winter 9am to 5pm; toll: 50esc per car.

South of Sintra the very beautiful **Pena Park★★** covers 200ha - 500 acres on the granite slopes of the Serra de Sintra; it is planted with rare species of trees, both nordic and tropical, and there are a great number of lakes and fountains. It should be visited on foot to see fully its great charm, but the motorist in a hurry can simply drive along the small roads which cross it, or at least go to the top of the two culminating points; on one the Pena Palace stands, on the other the Cruz Alta (High Cross).

From Sintra to the Cruz Alta by the Moors' Castle

5km - 3 miles – about 2 hours – local map below

Leave Sintra (p 130) by the road to Pena, southwards.

After skirting on the right the Estalagem dos Cavaleiros, where Lord Byron planned *Childe Harold*, the road rises in a series of hairpin bends, between the walls of several fine properties.

At the crossroads with the N 247-3, turn left to Pena.

Moors' Castle★ (Castelo dos Mouros). – *1/2 hour on foot Rtn from the car park.*
The castle, built in the 8 or 9C still has a battlemented perimeter wall guarded by four towers and a ruined Romanesque Chapel.
From the royal tower, which is climbed by a series of staircases, there is a commanding **view★** of Sintra and its palace, the Atlantic coast and Pena Castle perched on its height.

Go through the wrought iron gate at the entrance to Pena Park and leave the car in the car park.

Pena Palace (Palácio da Pena). – *Guided tour (time: 1/2 hour) 10am to 5pm; closed Mondays and holidays; 50esc.*
The palace, which stands on one of the highest peaks of the range, was built in the middle of the 19C by King Fernando II round a former 16C Hieronymite monastery. It is a pastiche in which several styles merge: Moorish, Gothic, Manueline, Renaissance, Baroque. The only remains of the monastery, the Manueline cloister and the chapel – with an alabaster altar by Nicolas Chanterene – are decorated with admirable *azulejos.*

SINTRA, Serra de★★

From the watchpath there is a panoramic **view**★★ of the whole region from the Atlantic coast to the Tagus, straddled by the suspension bridge, and the Costa da Caparica. The Cruz Alta and the statue of the architect of the palace, Count Eschwege, standing as a medieval knight upon a rock, can be distinguished in the nearby *serra.*

Cruz Alta★★. – *It is possible to drive right up to the foot of the cross.*
From this summit, topped by a cross, there is a **panoramic view**★★ over the whole massif (except Sintra and a section to the right of the Pena Summit, hidden by a copse) and the surrounding plain, as far as Lisbon to the south – behind the Pena Palace in the foreground.

A signposted path leads to the Cruz Alta (High Cross) from where there is a wide view over the mountain range, including the southwest area, unfortunately stripped of vegetation by fire, and across the surrounding plain. In the foreground stands Pena Palace.

THE SIDES OF THE SERRA★
Round tour from Sintra – *33km - 21 miles – about 2 hours – local map p 131*

Leave Sintra (p 130) by the road towards Pena then leave it to the left and take the N 247–3 towards Cabo da Roca.

Capuchin Monastery (Convento dos Capuchos). – *Guided tour (time: 20 minutes) 9am to 6pm; closed Tuesdays and 1 January, 1 May, Easter and 25 December.*
The 16C monks' cells have been cut out of the living rock and the walls lined with cork.

A belvedere, constructed on the right side of the road, the N 247–3, affords a glimpse of the coast, Praia das Maçás, with Colares in the foreground.

Peninha. – *2km – 1 1/2 miles from the N 247-3. Road open from 9am to 5pm; closed on Tuesdays; toll: 6esc per car plus 2.50esc per person.* A small chapel with an interior lined with 18C *azulejos,* showing scenes from the life of the Virgin, stands upon this hilltop (486m - 1 594ft). The panoramic **view**★★ from the chapel terrace includes, in the foreground, the vast Guincho Beach *(p 60).*

One can go directly to Cabo da Roca by means of a hilly forest track.

Cabo da Roca. – The Serra de Sintra ends in a sheer cliff nearly 150m - 450ft above the sea, the Cabo da Roca. This Rock Cape, which is topped by a lighthouse is continental Europe's most westerly point. The sea pounds furiously below at the rocks and cliffs, wearing the coastline to the north away into inlets and even small harbours.

Continue along the N 247 towards Colares.

Colares. – Pop 6 921. Colares is a small town known for its red and white wines – wines grown from vines on sandy soil, velvety and light and often with a considerable bouquet.

Azenhas do Mar★. – *6km - 4 miles from Colares* **Praia das Maçás** *(facilities p 36)* is a flourishing seaside resort. Beyond, the road runs along the shore.
A good general view of the **setting**★ of **Azenhas do Mar** can be obtained from the south. It rises in tiers up a jagged cliff at whose foot the Atlantic can be seen ceaselessly breaking. A small creek in a hollow in the cliff face has been made into a seawater swimming pool.

From Colares return to Sintra by the narrow and hilly N 375.

Monserrate Park★. – *Open in summer 8.30am to 6pm; in winter 9am to 5pm.*
The landscape **park**★ surrounding the neo-Oriental palace built in the 18C contains magnificent trees and other flora, including cedars, arbutus, bamboos, bracken, etc.

On the way to Sintra may be seen, on the left, the 16C Quinta da Penha Verde *(not open to the public),* the former palace of a Viceroy of India. An arch of the palace straddles the road.
Further on can be seen the early 19C monumental entrance to the Seteais Palace *(p 130).*

TAVIRA
Michelin map **37** south of fold 10 – Pop 7 282 – *Facilities p 36*

Tavira has a pleasant setting on an estuary of the Rio Séqua at the foot of a hill girdled by ramparts and overlooked by the towers of the Church of Santa Maria do Castelo. There is an attractive view from the left bank of the river, which is straddled by a bridge which goes back to Roman times: white houses stand grouped near the grey stone ramparts and tall palm trees move gently in the air above the public garden.

The recapture of the town dates from 1242 when Dom Paio Peres Correia decided to avenge the death of seven knights of the Order of St James who had been murdered during a truce while they were out hunting near the town.

The town has since suffered many misfortunes. It was not spared by the 1755 earthquake, and the harbour which was once active and a great tunny fishing centre is now silted up.

EXCURSION

Luz de Tavira. – Pop 3 974. *6.5km - 4 miles to the west.*
On leaving the village remark a Renaissance church with a fine Manueline doorway, each corner of the roof is decorated with pots.

Tomar stretches along the banks of the Nabão at the foot of a wooded hill crowned by a fortified castle erected in 1160 by Gualdim Pais, Grand Master of the Order of the Knights Templar.

The Knights of Christ. – In 1314 at the request of Philip the Fair, Pope Clement V ordered the disbanding of the Order of the Knights Templar which had its seat in Tomar since 1160. To replace the disbanded Order, King Dinis created in 1320 in Portugal the Order of the Knights of Christ who, in 1334, took Tomar as their seat.

The golden period of the Knights of Christ was at the beginning of the 15C. The Knights of Christ largely contributed to the first important phase in the period of the Great Discoveries *(p 19);* caravels, bearing the Order's emblem, explored the coast of Africa, rounded the Cape of Good Hope and reached the Indies.

The Tabuleiros Festival. – Every two years *(p 9)* Tomar celebrates the Tabuleiros Festival which keeps alive the ceremonies organized by the Brotherhood of the Holy Spirit – an Order founded in the 14C by the Queen Saint Isabel – to distribute bread, wine and meat to the poor of the town. At the festival, young girls, dressed in white, walk in procession through the streets bearing on their heads a *tabuleiro* or platter. The *tabuleiro* is piled up until it is as tall as the girl bearing it; thirty loaves are threaded on reeds and fixed into a willow basket which is adorned with foliage, paper flowers and blades of wheat *(illustration p 31).*

The festival lasts four days, the procession being followed by secular festivities, folk dancing and fireworks.

■ **THE CONVENT OF CHRIST★★** time: 1 hour

Open 9.30am to 12.30pm and 2 to 6pm (5pm 21 September to 19 March); closed holidays; 75esc.

The 12C walls crowning the summit of the hillock dominating the town enclose the Convent of Christ on which construction began in the 12C and was only completed in the 17C. After passing through the castle walls, park the car near the clipped box tree standing in an attractive formal garden.

Church. – The church doorway, which is reminiscent of the Plateresque style to be seen in Salamanca *(see Michelin Green Guide to Spain)*, is by the Spaniard, João de Castilho, the architect successor of Diogo de Arruda. To the former Oratory of the Templars, which now forms the east end of the church, King Manuel added a nave linking it to the rotunda by means of an arch which he commissioned Diogo de Arruda to design.

The **Templars' Rotunda★★** (Charola) was built in the 12C on the model of the Holy Sepulchre in Jerusalem. Eight pillars support a two storey octagonal construction surmounted by a cupola. An ambulatory with a ring vault divides the central octagon from the exterior polygon which has sixteen sides. The paintings decorating the octagon are by 16C Portuguese artists and the polychrome wood statues date from the same period.

The 16C **nave** is by Diogo de Arruda and is outstanding for the exuberance of its Manueline decoration.

Conventual Buildings★. – The **Main Cloister** (Claustro dos Felipes) was constructed essentially between 1557 and 1566 by the architect Diogo de Torralva, a fervent admirer of Palladio, one of the architects of the Italian Renaissance. The cloister has two storeys, the ground level gallery having Tuscan columns, the upper, Ionic pillars. The bare simplicity of the cloister makes a surprising contrast with the Manueline style decoration of the nave which is unfortunately largely hidden by the cloister.

It is in this cloister that Philip II of Spain is said to have been proclaimed King of Portugal in 1581 following the Portuguese disaster at El-Ksar El-Kebir when Sebastiano I was killed *(p 20)*.

A spiral staircase in the east corner of the cloister leads to terraces from which there is a general view of all the convent buildings.

The terraces of the Renaissance style Santa Barbara cloister can be reached by the same route, and from there can be seen the famous window sculpted by Diogo de Arruda in 1510 on the northwest face of the nave.

TOMAR ★★

This **window** ★★ is the most amazing example of Manueline style ornament to be seen in Portugal. The decoration which rises from the roots ①, of a cork oak supported on the bust of a sea captain ②, climbs two convoluted masts. Among the profusion of natural and marine motifs can be see coral ③, ropes ④, cork for use in the construction of ships ⑤, seaweed ⑥, cables ⑦ and anchor chains ⑧.

The whole is crowned with the royal emblems of Manuel I – a blazon and an armillary sphere – and the cross of the Order of Christ, which recurs as a motif on the balustrades surrounding the nave.

The window is "moored" by cables to two identical turrets encircled one by a chain and the other by a ribbon, which are said to be the respective emblems of the Orders of the Golden Fleece and the Garter.

The **Burial Ground Cloister,** with plant motif capitals, and the **Ablutions Cloister,** which both lie to the east of the rotunda, were erected in the 15C in the Gothic style at the behest of Prince Henry the Navigator.

The Manueline window at Tomar.

■ ADDITIONAL SIGHTS

Chapel of Our Lady of the Immaculate Conception (Capela de Nossa Senhora da Conceição). – *Apply to the tourist information centre.* The chapel stands halfway down the hill on the left as you descend from the monastery into the town. It is a lovely Renaissance building with delicately carved capitals.

St John the Baptist. – *Praça da República.* This late 15C Gothic church flanked by a Manueline belfry has a beautiful Flamboyant **door**★ carved with great skill. The door is said to be the work of a French artist, as is the fine Flamboyant pulpit standing on the north side of the nave. In the north aisle hangs a Last Supper by Gregório Lopes (16C).

EXCURSION

Round tour★ **from Tomar.** – *55km - 34 miles – about 2 hours.*

Leave Tomar south by the N 110, the Lisbon road.

This runs through a fertile area of fruit trees, market gardens, vines and olives.

Atalaia. – Pop 3 424. The Renaissance church presents a façade decorated with a carved doorway framed by pinnacled arcades. Inside the walls are covered with fine multicoloured **azulejos**★ painted with both geometric patterns and figurative designs, those of the central nave represent Biblical *(above)* and evangelical themes *(below).*

Turn left towards Abrantès; shortly after Tancos bear right up a narrow road.

Almourol Castle★★. – *Description p 43.*

On arriving at Constância, cross the Zêzere and bear sharp left into the N 358.2 going towards Castelo do Bode.

The road twists and turns as it follows the left bank of the Zêzere which becomes more and more enclosed; women can be seen at their washing on the occasional sandbanks.

Castelo do Bode Dam★. – *Facilities p 38.* The vaulted dam which is 115m - 377ft high and measures 402m - 1 319ft along its crest produced in 1983 187 million kWh. There is a good **view**★ from the dam crest of the Zêzere Valley downstream as it winds between rocks and hills scattered here and there with olive trees, and upstream the reservoir lake which is used for pleasure boating. A *pousada* has been built on the shore.

Return to Tomar by the N 358 and N 110.

TORRE DE MONCORVO

Michelin map **37** east of fold 2 or **441** fold 25 – *Local map p 69* – Pop 3 154

Arriving from the east along the N 220 you will get a general **view**★ of the town as it lies grouped at the centre of a vast landscape of arid mountain peaks.

The Serra do Reboredo to the southeast contains rich iron ore deposits.

The town itself is known for its *amêndoas cobertas,* a sort of nut sweetmeat.

Parish Church. – This tall 16C church, shelters in its north transept an interesting wooden triptych painted to illustrate the life of St Anne, mother of the Virgin, and her husband, Joachim. On the right, is their first meeting; on the left, their marriage; and in the centre, the presentation of the Infant Jesus to his grandparents.

TRANCOSO

Michelin map **37** fold 3 or **441** fold 34 – Pop 884

The ramparts of the citadel, which are still intact, can be seen from far away on the high plateau which extends the Serra da Estrela to the north. The best overall view is obtained from a rocky hillock (north of the town) near a calvary on the side of the road to Meda.

The city which knew glory in the 13 and 14C reached its peak when the marriage of King Dinis and the Queen Saint Isabel of Aragon on 24 June 1282 took place within its walls.

■ **SIGHTS** *time: 3/4 hour*

Fortifications★. – *To appreciate fully these powerful fortifications go round the city by car.*

The 9C wall, which has been rebuilt several times, is topped by pyramid shaped merlons and flanked by massive square bastions. Two of its gates are decorated.

Castle. – *Apply at the town hall – Câmara Municipal – Largo G. Garces.*

Dominated by a square keep, it occupies the northeast corner of the wall; from the top of the ramparts, the view extends to the hilly landscape of the Beira Alta.

Pillory. – The pillory, an octagonal column supporting a small lantern crowned by an armillary sphere and the cross of the Order of Christ, stands in the centre of the town.

Old Houses. – The façades of some of the houses in the town's narrow alleys are adorned with coats of arms and balconies.

VALENÇA DO MINHO ★

Michelin map **37** fold 11 (inset) or **441** fold 12 – Pop 2 474

Valença, on a hillock overlooking the left bank of the Minho and facing the Galician town of Tuy, has stood guard for centuries over Portugal's northern frontier and the river, which is crossed by the main road from Santiago de Compostela to Oporto. The old town is an unusual double city, consisting of two fortresses in the style of Vauban and a single bridge spanning a wide ditch and continuing through a long vaulted passage.

Fortified Town★. – *Access by car from the south by a shaded road leaving the N 13.*

Each fortress, unchanged since the 17C, is in the shape of an irregular polygon with six bastions with double redans, and watchtowers, in front of which are the defensive outworks and two monumental doorways, north and south, emblazoned with the arms of the kingdom and the governor. Old cannons are still in position on the battlements.

From the north side of the ramparts there is a fine **view★** over the Minho Valley, Tuy and the Galician mountains.

Each enceinte marks out an independent quarter with its own churches and picturesque narrow cobbled streets, fountains, houses sometimes decorated with statues at the corners, souvenir shops, etc.

EXCURSIONS

Monte do Faro★★. – *7km - 4 miles. Leave Valença by the N 101 going towards Monção; bear right towards Cerdal and shortly afterwards left to Monte do Faro.*

The road rises rapidly winding through the pines; views open out ever wider as one climbs. Leave the car at the last roundabout and walk up the path to the summit 565m - 1 854ft which lies to the left of the road. From the summit, the **panorama★★** is very extensive indeed: to the north and west lies the Minho Valley scattered with white houses grouped in villages and dominated in the distance by the Galician mountains: to the east is the Serra do Soajo and southwest the wooded hills of the coastal area and the Atlantic.

Minho Valley. – *50km - 31 miles from Valença to São Gregorio by the N 101, to the east.*

The Portuguese bank of the Rio Minho on the east side of Valença is the most interesting. The river, which at the beginning is majestically spread out, becomes hemmed in until it is practically invisible between the steep green slopes. The road is cobbled and winding, thickly bordered with trees (pines, eucalyptus and even palm trees) and climbing vines which make the well known *vinho verde (p 16)*. It passes through large wine-making villages, one of them, Monção, is also a spa.

Below the road the vines, fields of corn, pumpkins, etc. grow on terraces facing the smiling slopes of the Spanish side, dotted with perched villages. The abundance of cultivation and the isolated houses (roughcast in vivid colours) are particularly striking.

After Melgaço, the N 202 rises offering **bird's eye views** of the Minho, still very hemmed in, until nearing São Gregorio (frontier post).

This route chosen in the opposite direction as a way of entering Portugal, is an attractive way of getting to know the country.

VIANA DO ALENTEJO

Michelin map **37** west of fold 8 – Pop 3 674

This agricultural town in the vast Alentejo Plain, away from the main roads, hides behind its castle walls a church which will please the art lover.

Castle★. – *Open 10am to 12.30pm and 2 to 5pm; closed Mondays, holidays and in August.*

Ramparts. – Fortified walls flanked at each corner by a tower with a pepperpot roof surround the pentagonal shaped edifice. The entrance porch is adorned with worn capitals decorated with animals, including tortoises, lions, etc. The castle courtyard, which is planted with medlars, orange trees and palms, extends along the north side of the church.

Church. – The church façade surmounted by conical bell turrets and merlons, has a fine Manueline **doorway★**: a slender twisted column serves as the supporting pier for twin arches framed by two candlestick shaped pilasters, it also supports the tympanum which is decorated with stylized flowers and the cross of the Order of Christ in a medallion surmounted by the Portuguese coat of arms: a gable formed by a twisted cable ends in a type of pinnacle flanked by two armillary spheres.

The interior, which is Romanesque remodelled in the Manueline style, is outstanding for its size. The walls are decorated at their base with 17C *azulejos*, the chancel has a fine Crucifix.

Michelin map **37** fold 11 or **441** fold 22 – Pop 15 356 – *Facilities p 36*

Viana do Castelo, lying on the right bank of the Lima Estuary at the foot of the sunny hillside slope of Santa Luzia, is a pleasant holiday resort where gardens run down to the river's edge.

A humble fishermen's village in the Middle Ages, it suddenly came to fantastic prosperity in the 16C when, following the Great Discoveries, its fishermen set sail to fish for cod off Newfoundland and trade with the Hanseatic Cities. It was during this period that the Manueline and Renaissance houses were built which today make the old town so attractive. After a period of decline following the independence of Brazil in the beginning of the 19C and the civil war, Viana has once again become an active centre of deep sea fishing; industries (wood, ceramics, pyrotechnics, and boat building) and crafts (costumes and embroidery) also contribute to the town's prosperity.

Romaria of Our Lady in Sorrow (Nossa Senhora da Agonia). – The festival which is held in August *(p 9)*, is one of the most famous in the province of Minho. It includes a procession, bull running in the barricaded streets, fireworks on the Lima, a parade of carnival giants and dwarfs, illuminations, traditional folklore events: a festival of regional dancing and singing and on the last day a procession in regional costumes.

Santa Luzia ★★. – *4km - 2 1/2 miles by the road from Santa Luzia, or 7 minutes by the funicular (departures 9am to 8pm; every hour in the morning, every 1/2 hour from 2pm; 15esc one-way).*

Viana belvedere is on the hill of Santa Luzia, which rises to the north of the town and is topped with a modern basilica, a place of pilgrimage. By car one approaches it by a cobbled road with a series of hairpin bends which climbs pleasantly amongst pines, eucalyptus and mimosas.

Basilica of St Lucy (Basilica de Santa Luzia). – Built in neo-Byzantine style, it has a large parvis in front and a monumental staircase. The interior is lit by three rose windows; the chancel and the apse under the domes are decorated with frescoes. 57m - 187ft above the ground the central dome's lantern turret *(142 steps starting in the sacristy - very nar-*

(After Secretaria de Estado da Informação e Turismo photo)

Viana do Castelo — The Romaria.

row passage-way at the end of the climb, price: 10esc) has a magnificent **panoramic view ★★** over Viana do Castelo and the Lima Estuary, and to the southeast on the horizon, the towering wooded heights of the Barcelos Region, scattered with white villages; beyond the harbour, guarded by the 16C São Tiago de Barra Fortress, the ocean foams along the immense beaches of fine sand.

■ MAIN SIGHTS *time: 2 hours*

Praça da República ★ (B 19). – The 16C buildings surrounding the square make it a picturesque urban feature.

Fountain. – João Lopes the Elder constructed this fountain in 1553, crowning its several basins with sculptured decoration supporting an armillary sphere and a cross of the Order of Christ.

Former Town Hall (Paços do Concelho) (B A). – Only the façade has retained its original 16C appearance. It bristles with merlons above, is pierced with pointed arches at ground level and on the first storey has windows crowned with the coat of arms of João III, the armillary sphere or emblem of Manuel I and the town's coat of arms which includes a caravel, as many sailors from Viana do Castelo took part in the Great Discoveries voyages.

The Misericord Hospice (Misericórdia) (B B). – This 1589 Renaissance edifice, with Flemish influence in its style was designed by João Lopes the Younger. The noble façade, to the left of the highly ornate monumental doorway, rises from a massive colonnade with Ionic capitals as two tiers of flower decked loggias supported on atlantes and caryatids.

The adjoining **Church of the Misericord** was rebuilt in 1714. *Open in August Monday to Sunday mornings; closed holidays.*

Municipal Museum ★ (A M). – *Guided tour (time: 1/2 hour) 9.30am to noon and 2 to 5pm; closed Mondays and holidays; 20esc.*

The former 18C Palace of the Barbosa Macieis houses the museum. The interior walls are covered with lovely **azulejos ★** painted in 1721 by Policarpo de Oliveira Bernardes. They depict hunting and fishing scenes, receptions, distant continents, etc.

The entrance hall and the rooms on the ground floor, with coffered ceilings of varnished wood, contain lovely 17C Indo-Portuguese furniture, carved or inlaid, as well as local pottery work and a small Virgin and Child in ivory of the same period. There are also some prehistoric remains and Roman coins.

The adjoining courtyard has a collection of interesting stone work: statues, votive offerings, tombstones, etc.

On the first floor (beautiful ceilings) where the most interesting *azulejos* are to be found, other carved pieces of furniture can be seen, and above all, a remarkable collection of 18C Portuguese **glazed earthenware** (from Lisbon, Coimbra, etc.).

VIANA DO CASTELO

PONTE DE LIMA 23 km

★★ SANTA LUZIA

52 km VALENÇA N 13 - E 50

PORTO 70 km N 13 - E 50

PRAIA

CASTELO

DOCA

LIMA

Cândido dos Reis (R.)	B	2
Capitão Gaspar de Castro (R.)	B	3
Carmo (R. do)	B	4
Conde da Carreira (Av.)	A	7
Dom Afonso III (Av.)	B	8
Gago Coutinho (R. de)	B	10
Humb. Delgado (Av.)	A	14
J. Tomaz da Costa (L.)	B	15
Luís de Camões (Av.)	B	16
Sacadura Cabral (R.)	B	21
Santa Luzia (Estr.)	A	23
São Pedro (R. de)	B	24

Bandeira (R. da)	B	
C. da Grande Guerra (Av. dos)	B	6
República (Pr. da)	B	19

■ ADDITIONAL SIGHTS

Parish Church (Igreja Matriz) (B C). – The church dates from the 14 and 15C, but the two crenellated towers flanking the façade are Romanesque, their crowning Lombard blind arcades supported by carved modillions. The Gothic doorway has a series of three historiated archivolts which rest on statue columns of St Andrew, St Peter and the Evangelists; the outer archivolt shows Christ surrounded by cherubims holding the emblems of the Passion.

Inside, in the baptistery, a carved, polychrome wooden panel (17C) represents the Baptism of the Infant Jesus. In the third chapel on the left there is a fine 16C painting on wood.

Opposite the church stands a 16C house in the Italian Renaissance style emblazoned with a coat of arms.

The 15C house, north of the church, is said to have belonged to João the Elder.

Church of Our Lady in Sorrow (Igreja Nossa Senhora da Agónia) (A E). – This delightful small Baroque chapel is known for the pilgrimage which takes place on 15 August each year.

Ruas São Pedro and Cândido dos Reis (B 24-2). – The houses fronting these streets have Manueline façades.

VILA DA FEIRA

Michelin map **37** folds 12 and 13 or **441** fold 32 – *Local map p 68* – Pop 4 877

The Castle of Vila da Feira stands on a wooded height facing the town which lies scattered over the opposite hillside.

Castle★ (Castelo). – *Open 9am to 12.30pm and 2 to 6pm; closed Mondays; 20esc.*

The 11C castle was reconstructed in the 15C by the local baron, Fernão Pereira, whose coat of arms can still be seen above the entrance. It is an interesting example of Portuguese Gothic military architecture. A square keep flanked by four tall towers with pepperpot roofs overlooks a fortified perimeter wall whose entrance is defended on its eastern side by a barbican.

A postern gate leads to the parade ground. Follow the wall walk; latrines can still be seen. Stairs lead to the 1st floor of the keep where there is a vast Gothic hall; the upper platform *(60 steps)* affords a panorama of the castle's fortifications, the town, the surrounding wooded hills and the coastline, where one can make out the Ria de Aveiro in the distance.

Church of the Misericord. – The chancel, under a coffered ceiling, has a lovely gilded altarpiece. In a south chapel there are some unusual statues, one of which is a Saint Christopher, 3m - 10ft high.

The companion guides in English in this series on France are
 Brittany, Châteaux of the Loire,
 Dordogne, French Riviera,
 Normandy, Paris, Provence.

Other Michelin Green Guides available in English
 Austria, Canada, Germany, Italy,
 New England, Spain, Switzerland,
 London, New York City.
 England: The West country.

Michelin map 🔲 fold 12 or 🔲 fold 22 – Pop 20 245 – *Facilities p 36*

Vila do Conde at the mouth of the Ave is a quiet seaside resort possessing a few industries conducted on a small scale such as shipbuilding, cotton mills and chocolate making. Pillow-lace making is a traditional craft.

The Feast of St John *(p 9)* is the occasion for picturesque processions by the *Mordomas* adorned with magnificent gold jewelry and by the town's lacemakers who cross the floodlit town on the night of the 23-24 June, and the following evening go down to the beach escorted by Vila's entire population.

1km - 1/2 mile to the south, **Azurara** (Pop 1 517) is a small fishing port with a 16C fortified church built in the Manueline style. Facing the church is a beautiful cross, also Manueline.

Convent of St Clare★ (Mosteiro de Santa Clara). – *The convent has been transformed into a rehabilitation centre.*

Only the church *(to visit apply at the convent, guided tour)* has retained the original Gothic style. It was founded in 1318 and was designed as a fortress, apart from its west face which has a beautiful rose window.

The interior, in the form of a single aisle, is covered with a wooden ceiling with 18C carved caissons. The Chapel of the Conception *(first on the left),* erected in the 16C, contains the Renaissance **tombs**★ of the founders and their children. Wonderfully detailed reliefs have been carved into the Ança stone.

Dom Alfonso Sanches' Tomb. – The low reliefs on the tomb's sides represent scenes from the Life of Christ; that at the head shows St Clare preventing the Saracens from entering the Convent of St Clare at Assisi.

Dona Teresa Martins' Tomb. – The reclining figure of Dona Teresa, dressed in the habit of a religious of the Franciscan Tertiaries, rests upon a tomb on which are depicted scenes from the Passion, on the sides, and St Francis receiving the stigmata, at the head.

The children's tombs have the Doctors of the Church *(left tomb)* and the Evangelists *(right tomb)* carved upon them.

A fine grille divides the nave from the nuns' chancel.

The arches of the 18C cloister can still be seen to the south of the church; the 18C fountain in the centre of the close is the terminal for the aqueduct, of the same date, from Póvoa de Varzim.

From the church parvis there is a good view of the small town bounded on its southern side by the Ave and on its west by the sea.

Parish Church (Igreja Matriz). – This fortified church was erected in the 16C in the Manueline style by Biscayan artists, which explains the existence of the fine Plateresque doorway. The tympanum is decorated with a small statue of St John the Baptist protected by a canopy and surrounded by the symbols of the Evangelists.

The tower to the left of the façade dates from the end of the 17C. Inside are altars and a gilded wood pulpit dating from the 17 and 18C.

Pillory. – *Opposite the parish church.* The pillory, originally Renaissance but restyled in the 18C, supports the arm of justice brandishing a sword.

Michelin map 🔲 south of fold 16 – Pop 19 823

On the right bank of the Tagus, Vila Franca de Xira, this industrial town of the Ribatejo Plain is known for its festivals and bullfights.

The city comes alive, particularly in July *(p 9),* at the time of the Festival of the **Colete Encarnado**, the *campinos'* "red waistcoat" festival. The visitor can see picturesque processions of *campinos (p 30)* and, more memorably, bulls running loose through the streets. Folk dancing, bullfights, open air feasts (grilled sardines) and sometimes boating regattas on the Tagus complete the festivities.

The arenas are on the southern side of the town, on the road to Lisbon (N 10), opposite an unusual raised cemetery with flowered pergolas.

Ethnographic Museum of the Arenas. – *Open 10am to 12.30pm and 2 to 6pm; closed Mondays and holidays.*

This small museum has a few paintings and sculptures relating to the region or the art of bullfighting, and above all 19C traditional costumes (fishermen's, peasants', cattle breeders') and 16 and 18C *campinos.*

Monte Gordo Belvedere (Miradouro). – *3km - 2 miles to the north by the Rua Antonio Lucio Baptista, passing under the motorway, then by a surfaced road which climbs steeply.*

From the belvedere, between two windmills at the top of the hill, there is a **panoramic view** to the west and north over the other hills covered with woods and vineyards (amongst which you can see the farmhouses – *quintas);* to the east over the Ribatejo Plain which stretches to the Vila Franca Bridge crossing the Tagus; to the south over the first two islands of the river estuary.

*When visiting London use the **Green Guide 'London'***

  – *Detailed descriptions of places of interest*

  – *Useful local information*

  – *A section of the historic square mile of the City of London with a detailed fold out plan*

  – *The lesser known London boroughs – their people, places and sights*

  – *Plans of selected areas and important buildings.*

VILAMOURA

Michelin map **37** southeast of fold 20 – *Facilities p 36*

The modern tourist complex of Vilamoura lies in front of a pine forest and at the far end of the well sheltered Bay of Quarteira. There is a marina which can accommodate several hundred yachts. However, the remains of a luxurious Roman city have been preserved.

Roman ruins of Cerro da Vial. – *On the northeast corner of the marina. Times and charges not available at the time of going to press.*

The excavations undertaken here since 1964 have revealed a Roman city underneath Moorish and Visigoth remains; there is a patrician house, a more modest one, thermal baths, a crematorium, wells, silos, stables, a wine press, etc. Beautiful panels and fragments of mosaics, polychrome or black and white, still decorate the floors and pools (the latter subsequently converted into salting vats and fish-tanks).

The small museum, installed in the warden' house, contains all the treasures found on the site, of Arab and Latin origin: terracotta lamps, jewelry, etc.

VILA NOVA DE FOZ CÔA

Michelin map **37** fold 2 or **441** fold 35 – *Local map p 69* – Pop 3 869

In a landscape of bare hills, this small isolated but cheerful village, made lively by students, stretches across a long ridge with vine-covered slopes.

Parish Church. – It has remarkable Manueline granite façade★, a belfry porch, and a doorway surrounded with clustered pilasters and topped by an archivolt decorated with floral and shell motifs under a lintel where the armillary spheres frame a 16C *Pietà* in limestone.

The interior has three naves where the painted wooden ceiling is supported by leaning columns, whose capitals have carved human heads. Baroque altarpieces of gilded wood decorate the apse and a south chapel.

Pillory. – A beautiful Manueline pillory in granite, the stock encircled with cable moulding and the top sculpted with small columns and statues under an armillary sphere and a lily.

VILA REAL

Michelin map **37** fold 2 or **441** fold 24 – *Local map p 69* – Pop 13 876 – *Facilities p 38*

Vila Real, a lively small town, enhanced by numerous patrician houses dating from the 16 and 18C, stands grouped on a plateau at the foot of the Serra do Marão *(p 104)*. A well known car racing circuit takes place here.

Fine black pottery is made in the surrounding countryside and can be bought in the town, particularly on 29 June when quantities are brought in for the St Peter's Fair.

■ **SIGHTS** *time: 1 hour*

The main sights are to be found in the vicinity of the Avenida Carvalho Araújo. *From the central crossroads by the cathedral go down the avenue on the right.*

Cathedral (Sé). – This former conventual church built at the end of the Gothic period, has, nevertheless, preserved certain Romanesque details. These are particularly noticeable in the treatment of the capitals in the nave.

House (Casa) of Diogo Cão. – *At no 19 (door-plate).* So-called because, according to tradition, the well known navigator was born there *(p 19)*. The façade was remodelled in the 16C in Italian Renaissance style.

Town Hall (Câmara Municipal). – Built at the beginning of the 19C, it has a lantern pillory in front, and a remarkable monumental stone staircase with balusters in the Italian Renaissance style.

Continue along towards the cemetery which you skirt round on the right.

Cemetery esplanade. – This shaded walk, on the site of the old castle, overlooks the junction of the Corgo and Cabril Rivers. In direct line with the cemetery and behind it there is a view looking steeply down into the Gorges of the Corgo and its tributary. Further to the left, there is an extensive view over the Corgo Ravine and the houses which overhang it.

Return to Avenida Carvalho Araújo and go up it on the right.

Tourist Information Centre (Turismo). – *At no 94.* It occupies a 16C house which has a lovely Manueline façade.

From there take the first road on the right (by the law courts) to St Peter's Church.

St Peter's (Igreja São Pedro). – St Peter's Church is decorated in the chancel with 17C multicoloured *azulejos* and a fine coffered ceiling★ of carved and gilded wood.

EXCURSION

Mateus★. – Pop 1 865. *3.5km - 2 miles to the east by the N 322 towards Sabrosa.*

Chestnut trees, vines and orchards herald the approach to the village of Mateus, famous for the manor belonging to the Counts of Vila Real and the rosé wine made on the estate.

Mateus Manor★ (Solar). – *Guided tour (time: 1 1/2 hours) 9am to 1pm and 2 to 4pm; 150esc, 50esc garden only.*

Dating from the first half of the 18C, this creation by Nicolau Nasoni *(p 24)* is a perfect example of Portuguese Baroque architecture.

Behind lawns planted with cedars, followed by a garden laid out with clumps of box-wood and a tree-covered walk, the **façade**★★ of the manor appears, preceded by a mirror of water. The central section of the manor is set back, and has a beautiful balustrated stairway and a high emblazoned pediment, surrounded by allegorical statues. The main courtyard is protected by an ornamental stone balustrade. The windows upstairs are topped with moulded gables. Beautiful pinnacles top the roof cornices.

To the left of the façade there is a tall elegant Baroque chapel built in 1750, also by Nasoni.

Inside the palace there are magnificent carved wood ceilings in the main hall and the main salon, a rich library (numerous old French editions), some furniture (Portuguese, Spanish, Chinese and 18C French of painted wood), and in two rooms which have been made into a museum: **copperplate engravings** by Fragonard and Baron Gerard, precious fans, liturgical objects and vestments, a 17C altar and religious sculptures, one of which is a 16C ivory crucifix.

VILA REAL DE SANTO ANTÓNIO

Michelin map 37 fold 10 – Pop 13 379 – *Facilities p 36*

In 1774 the Marquis of Pombal founded a town on the flat and arid land on the right bank of the Guadiana to oppose the Andalusian city of Ayamonte. This new town, which was erected in five months, he called Vila Real de Santo António. Classical style houses, like those of the Baixa in Lisbon, extend outwards in a perfect rectangular plan from the main square, which is surrounded by orange trees and paved with a black and white mosaic radiating from a central obelisk.

Vila Real has become one of the largest fishing and commercial ports on the Algarve and is also a considerable fish canning centre. Yachts for export are also built here.

The white houses of the town of Ayamonte on the Spanish side of the river *(ferry crossing)* can be clearly seen from the beautiful gardens which run down to the Portuguese bank of the Guadiana.

Vila Real benefits also from the existence 3km - 2 miles away on the far side of the pinewoods, of the seaside resort of **Monte Gordo** *(facilities p 36)*. This one time village with miles of sandy beach lined by modern facilities is proving to be highly popular with holidaymakers.

VILA VIÇOSA

Michelin map 37 fold 7 – Pop 4 282

Vila Viçosa, grouped on a hillside slope where oranges and lemons grow, is a town of shade *(viçosa)* and bright flowers. It was at one time the seat of the dukes of Bragança and also the residence of several kings of Portugal.

Since the fall of the monarchy in 1910 Vila Viçosa has become a museum town enlivened only by craft workers in pottery and wrought iron, and the marble quarries in the environs.

North of the town is a huge park of 2 000ha - 4 950 acres which was formerly the Bragança hunt. Only a few miles away was fought, on 17 June 1665, the Battle of Montes Claros which confirmed Portugal's independence from Spain.

The Ducal Court. – It was as early as the 15C that the 2nd Duke of Bragança, Dom Fernando, chose Vila Viçosa as the residence of his Court. The execution of the 3rd duke, Dom Fernando *(see below)*, however, annihilated the ducal power and it was only in the following century that Court life became really sumptuous. In the palace, built by Duke Jaime, great seignorial festivals and princely marriages followed one after the other as did gargantuan banquets, theatrical performances and bullfights.

This golden age ended in 1640 when the 8th Duke of Bragança acceded to the throne of Portugal as João IV.

The Execution of the Duke of Bragança. – On his succession to the throne in 1481, King João II instituted stern measures to abolish the privileges granted by his father, King Alfonso V, to the nobles who had taken part in the Reconquest.

The first to be brought low was the Duke of Bragança, brother-in-law to the king, the richest and most powerful nobleman in the land, and already guilty of plotting against the monarchy. After a summary trial, the duke was executed in Évora in 1483.

■ **SIGHTS** *time: 3 hours*

Ducal Palace (Paço Ducal). – *Guided tour (time: 1 hour) 9.30am to 1pm and 2 to 6pm (5pm in winter); closed Sundays, Mondays, holidays and 16 August; 100esc.*

The palace overlooks the Palace Square in the centre of which stands a bronze statue of João IV by Francisco Franco.

Tired of the discomforts of the old castle which dated from the time of King Dinis, the 4th duke, Dom Jaime I, began in 1501 the construction of the present palace. The plan consists of two wings at right angles, the main wing in white marble being 110m - 311ft long.

The interior is now a museum. The well of the staircase to the 1st floor is adorned with wall paintings depicting the 15C Battle of Ceuta and the 16C Siege of Azamor by Duke Dom Jaime I.

Main Wing. – The wing is decorated with 17C *azulejos*, Brussels and Aubusson tapestries and Arraiolos carpets. The rooms are embellished with ceilings finely painted to represent a variety of subjects including David and Goliath, the adventures of Perseus, the Seven Virtues, etc. There are also portraits of the Braganças by the late 19C Portuguese painters Columbano, Malhoa and Sousa Pinto and in the Teutonic Hall, by the 18C French painter Quillard.

The west face looks over a box tree topiary.

Transverse Wing. – The wing comprises the apartments of King Carlos I (1863-1908), who was a talented painter and draughtsman, and Queen Amelia. There is an interesting 16C triptych attributed to Cristovão de Figueiredo illustrating scenes from the Calvary in the chapel.

The 16C Manueline style cloister is beautifully cool.

Also worth looking at are a small museum of 17 to 19C coaches and an armoury.

Augustine Church (Convento dos Agostinhos). – The church, which was rebuilt in the 17C by the future João IV, stands at the east end of the Palace Square and is now the mausoleum of the dukes of Bragança. Bays in the chancel and the transept contain the veined white marble ducal tombs.

Former Convent of the Wounds of Christ (Antigo Convento das Chagas). – Founded by Joana de Mendonça, the second wife of Duke Dom Jaime I, it stands on the south side of the Palace Square. The walls of the church, which serves as the mausoleum for the duchesses of Bragança, are covered in *azulejos* (1626).

Knot Gate (Porta dos Nós). – The so-called Knot Gate, on the north side of the Palace Square beside the Lisbon road, is one of the last remains of the 16C perimeter wall.

Old Town. – The castle and ramparts erected at the end of the 13C by King Dinis were reinforced with bastions in the 17C. The crenellated walls flanked with towers still gird the old town.

The castle *(same opening times as the Ducal Palace; 50esc)* is surrounded by a deep moat. The tour includes the original building's dungeons. An archaeological museum is installed on the 1st floor.

A fine granite pillory dating from the 16C, stands on the west approach.

(After Yan photo — Casa de Portugal)

The Knot Gate.

If you wish to plan your own tour work it out with the help of the map on pp 4-5 of principal sights.

A vocabulary on p 8 of the guide gives the English translation of current tourist phrases.

VISEU ★

Michelin map **37** fold 3 or **441** fold 33 – Pop 21 464 – *Facilities p 38*

The town of Viseu has developed in the region of the famous Dão vineyard *(p 16)* in a wooded and somewhat hilly area on the left bank of the Pavia, a tributary of the Mondego. It is an important centre of agriculture (rye, maize, cattle and fruit) and crafts (lace, carpets, basketmaking and black clay pottery).

Its egg sweetmeats *(bolos de amor, papos de anjo, travesseiros de ovos moles, castanhas de ovos)* are a speciality.

The Viseu School of Painting. – Viseu, like Lisbon, had a flourishing school of painting in the 16C. It was led by two masters, Vasco Fernandes and Gaspar Vaz, in their turn greatly influenced by such Flemish artists as Van Eyck, Quentin Metsys and Francisco Henriques.

Gaspar Vaz, who died about 1568, developed his style at the Lisbon school. He was gifted with a brilliant imagination and knew how to give to forms and draped figures great intensity of expression. The landscapes he painted, nevertheless, keep their regional flavour. His principal works, still showing considerable Gothic influence, hang in the Church of São João de Tarouca *(p 127)*.

The early works of **Vasco Fernandes** (1480-c1543), to whom legend has given the name of Grão Vasco – Great Vasco – reveal Flemish influence (altarpieces at Lamego – in the regional museum – and Freixo de Espada à Cinta). His later work showed more originality, a distinct sense of the dramatic and of composition, a richness of colour and a violent realism inspired by popular and local subjects particularly in his portraits and landscapes. His principal works are in the Viseu Museum.

The two masters probably collaborated in the creation of the polyptych in Viseu Cathedral, which would explain its hybrid character.

■ **OLD TOWN** ★ *time: 2 hours*

Follow the route marked on the plan starting at the Praça da República.

Old Viseu has all the attraction of an ancient town with narrow alleys paved with granite sets and Renaissance and classical corbelled houses emblazoned with coats of arms.

Praça da República (or Rossio) (Z 22). – Facing the town hall, this pleasant tree planted square is the town's lively centre.

Porta do Soar (Y). – Go through this gate in the town wall built by King Alfonso V in the 15C to enter the old town.

Cathedral Square★ (Adro da Sé) (Y 25). – This peaceful square in the heart of the old town is lined with noble granite edifices: the Grão Vasco Museum, the cathedral and the Misericord Church.

Grão Vasco Museum★★ (Y M). – *Guided tour 9.30am (10am Sundays) to 12.30pm and 2 to 5pm; closed Mondays and holidays; 50esc.*

The museum is in the old Três Escalões Palace which was built in the 16C and remodelled in the 18C.

The ground floor is devoted to 13-18C sculpture. Outstanding are a 14C **Throne of Grace★** of which only a representation of God the Father remains, and a 13C *Pietà*; some 16C Spanish-Arabic *azulejos* are also interesting.

On the 1st floor are Spanish 17C paintings *(St Jerome)* and works by modern and contemporary Portuguese painters (Columbano).

On the 2nd floor are the **Primitives★★** of the Viseu school: a *Calvary* and *St Peter on his Throne* by Vasco Fernandes are the masterpieces of the collection. The second painting which shows greater Italian Renaissance influence is an answer to the *St Peter* painted by Gaspar Vaz and now in São João de Tarouca. The fourteen paintings, which comprise the altarpiece which stood formerly in the cathedral, are by a group of artists from the Viseu school: the *Descent from the Cross* and the *Kiss of Judas* are among the best. In the *Adoration of the Magi*, the Negro King has been replaced by an Indian from Brazil, as the country had just been discovered.

Gaspar Vaz is represented by two works: *The Last Supper* and *Christ in the House of Martha*.

Cathedral★ (Sé) (Y A). – This Romanesque church was considerably remodelled between the 16 and 18C.

The façade was rebuilt in the 17C; the central statue among the six which ornament the façade is of St Theotonius, patron saint of Viseu.

Inside, the reconstruction of the vaulting, in the 16C, transformed the edifice into a hall church. The roof, which rests on Gothic pillars, is supported by twisted **liernes★** which form knots at regular intervals; the keystones are decorated with the arms of the founder bishop and the royal mottos of Alfonso V and João II. The chancel is 17C; the barrel vaulting shelters a monumental Baroque **altarpiece★** of gilded wood; above the high altar is a 14C Virgin carved in Ança stone. The north chapel is decorated with *azulejos* dating from the 18C.

Stairs lead from the north transept to the gallery *(coro alto)* where there is a wood lectern brought from Brazil in the 16C and an amusing statue of an angel musician. Go to the 1st floor of the cloister where the chapterhouse contains a **treasury of sacred art** including two 13C Limoges enamel reliquary caskets, a 12C Gospel in a 16C binding and a 12C Byzantine cross.

The **cloister** is Renaissance. The ground level gallery, where the arches rest on Ionic columns, is decorated with 18C *azulejos*. In the Chapel of Our Lady of Mercy there is a fine 16C low relief of the Descent from the Cross which is said to be by the Coimbra school *(p 63)*.

A beautiful doorway in the transitional Gothic style leads from the cloister back into the cathedral.

Misericord Church (Igreja da Misericórdia) (Y B). – This Baroque building has an attractive rhythmic façade in contrast to its white walls and grey granite pilasters.

The central section, focused beneath an elegant pediment, is pierced by a pretty Baroque doorway surmounted by a balcony.

Old Houses. – Notice: in the **Rua Dom Duarte** (Y 7) a keep (Torre de Menagem) (Y C), embellished with a lovely Manueline window; in the picturesque narrow, bustling **Rua Direita** (Y 6), 18C houses with balconies supported on wrought iron brackets; in the **Rua dos Andrades** (Z 3) (south of the Rua Direita), corbelled houses; and in the **Rua da Senhora da Piedade** (Y 26), houses built in the 16C.

The Misericord Church.

Take the Rua Direita before returning to the Praça da Sé via the Rua Escura.

■ ADDITIONAL SIGHTS

St Francis's (Igreja São Francisco) (Z E). – St Francis's is a Baroque church ornamented with *azulejos* and gilded wood.

St Benedict's (Igreja São Bento) (Y F). – The church has beautiful 17C azulejos★.

THE MADEIRA ARCHIPELAGO

The Madeira Archipelago consists of the main island which has the greatest area (740km² - 286sq miles) and the largest population (254 880), the island of Porto Santo (42km² - 16sq miles), lying 40km - 25 miles to the northeast, and two groups of uninhabited islands, the Desertas or Empty Isles, 20km - 12 miles from Funchal and the Selvagens or Wild Isles, situated near the Canaries 240km - 150 miles.

Access by air. – There are direct flights twice weekly from the U.K. and daily flights from Lisbon *(see p 7 for information on connections between London and Lisbon, and the USA and Lisbon)* to Funchal Airport, Madeira and from Funchal to Porto Santo. Full information from TAP Air Portugal, 19 Regent Street, W1, ☏ 734 41 81.

A Holiday on the Island. – *See p 147.*

MADEIRA ***

Madeira stands out in the Atlantic Ocean, a volcanic island mass rising high above the ocean swell. The "pearl of the Atlantic", 900km - 559 miles from Lisbon, offers tourists a climate which is mild at all times of the year, a vegetation which is subtropical and transforms the island into a blossoming garden all year round, and a landscape, beautiful and varied, which opens out into vast panoramas.

HISTORICAL AND GEOGRAPHICAL NOTES

Discovery and Colonization. – The discovery of Madeira marks the beginning of the first period in the era of the Great Portuguese Discoveries. In 1419, **João Gonçalves Zarco** *(p 147)* and Tristão Vaz Teixeira, leaders of an expedition dispatched by Prince Henry the Navigator, landed first on the island of Porto Santo and later on Madeira itself in what was later known as Machico Bay. The island appeared to be uninhabited and entirely covered in woodland and they, therefore, named it the wooded island, *a ilha da madeira*. The navigators reported their discovery to Prince Henry, who commanded them to return the following year, charging them with its colonization and settlement.

The prince divided the territory into three *captaincies*: Zarco received the land centred on Funchal and extending south of an imaginary line drawn from Oliveira Point to Tristão Point; Tristão Vaz received Machico and all the rest of the island and Bartolomeu Perestrelo *(p 159)* the neighbouring island of Porto Santo. Shortly after the lieutenants had become established Prince Henry made their titles hereditary but in 1497, to avoid further abuses which the explorers' heirs were making of their authority, the islands were restored to the Crown.

In the early 19C during the period of the Napoleonic Wars the island of Madeira was twice occupied by British troops, first in 1801 and later from 1807 to 1814. A few years after Portugal became a Republic in 1902 the archipelago achieved internal self government under the Statute of Neighbouring Islands.

Volcanic Character. – Madeira, together with Porto Santo and the Desertas, rose from the bed of the Atlantic during a period of volcanic eruption in the Tertiary Era. It is divided from the Selvagens and Canary Islands and the continent of Africa by an ocean bed some 2 000m - 6 000ft deep and a marine trough which reaches a depth, in places, of 4 512m - 14 804ft. Later underwater upcasts and convulsions accentuated the geological development of the island. The island's volcanic origin is also visibly confirmed in the Curral das Freiras Crater where the principal heights in Madeira's central relief are to be found, the several lakes and volcano craters and the prismatic basalt piles bordering the valleys and coastline also confirm this theory.

Erosion has modified the relief: streams have cut through enclosed valleys, waves have bitten into the cliffs, wearing them away to shingle.

A Turbulent Landscape. – Madeira is an island of escarpments, outcrops and a mountain chain of over 1 200m - 3 950ft culminating in tall peaks such as the Ruivo Peak (Pico Ruivo 1 861m - 6 016ft). The chain crosses the island from the St. Lawrence Point (Punta de S. Lourenço) to the Tristão Point (Punta do Tristão), dropping to 1 007m - 3 304ft at its centre at the Encumeada Pass from which several minor formations radiate. The island is thus divided into two distinct sectors. One presents a wild and turbulent landscape where high peaks abut deep precipices at whose feet torrents *(ribeiras)* follow courses through to the sea. The only flat area is the Paúl da Serra, a desertlike and inhospitable plateau extending for some 20km² - 8 sq miles at a height of 1 400m - 4 593ft in the centre of the island and which is inhabited only by grazing sheep.

The rock and cliff lined shore is broken at frequent intervals by estuaries where small fishing villages have become established. The rare beaches which exist are usually pebble ones. The only sandy beach is at Praínha, to the east of Machico.

A Privileged Climate. – Madeira, which is almost at the same latitude as Casablanca, enjoys, generally, a temperate climate. Mild and with no extremes, the mean temperature varies only from 16° to 21°C - 61° to 70°F from winter to summer. The weather is best on the south coast which is well protected from the northerly and northeasterly winds by the mountains: rain is scarce and when it falls, falls as downpours in April and October; the summer is very dry. The temperature of the water varies between 18° and 20 °C - 64° and 68°F and so makes bathing pleasant at almost any season of the year. Apart from occasional sea mists the light is excellent.

Inland, where the land rises, has lower and less stable temperatures. Clouds, formed by seawater evaporation, collect round the peaks, keeping the air cool and producing considerable humidity in the mountain regions which are transformed by the abundant spring and autumn rains into the island's watershed.

A Luscious Vegetation. – The climate and relief of Madeira combine to produce three distinct vegetation areas. The subtropical area which extends from sea level to about 300m - 1 000ft includes the north and south coasts where sugar cane, bananas and some vegetables are grown – Barbary figs have invaded all the non irrigated areas along the south coast. The area from 300 to 750m - 1 000 to 2 500ft is the warm, temperate or Mediterranean zone where vines flourish and also such cereals as maize, wheat and oats.

European and tropical fruits grow well: oranges, pears, apples and plums besides avocado pears, mangoes, custard apples, guavas and passion fruit.

Orchid.

Above 750m - 2 500ft lies the cold temperate zone, a region of pine covered hill slopes, heather, tree laurels and mimosa acacias, and higher still, among the crests, pastures and bracken.

Anthuriums.

The whole island of Madeira is a mass of flowers; every hillside, every garden and road-side verge is covered with hydrangeas, geraniums, hibiscus, agapanthus, bougainvilleas, fuchsias and euphorbias. Certain species like orchids, anthuriums and strelitzias (or Birds of Paradise) are grown in large quantities for export. There also are several species of flowering trees – mimosas, magnolias, sumaumás with red or pink flowers and jacarandas with purple blooms.

Terraces and Levadas. – On this island where more than half the population is engaged in agriculture only one third of the land is fit for cultivation. To clear the soil the early colonists set fire to the forests; this fire, it is said, burned for seven years, sparing a few areas, however, so that trees of 1 000 years or more can be seen in some places – the til (*Oreodaphne jetens*), sesame, vinhático, heaths, tree laurels and cedars.

Strelitzias.

Once cleared, the land had to be brought under cultivation. The peasants hauled earth in hods on their backs (for no draught animals have ever been able to be acclimatised to the island) to build the thousands of **terraces** *(poios)* into the hillsides which now give the island its characteristic appearance. The minute parcels of earth are not ploughed but hoed.

Madeira's agricultural prosperity, however, is due to irrigation: the island lives by the miracles performed by the **levadas.** Their construction, when one considers the relative lack of technical knowledge and equipment, represents a prodigious undertaking, for these stone or cement aqueducts tunnelling through rock faces, bridging abysses, circling hills, bring lifegiving water to the thousands of fields in the less favoured areas near the coast. The *levadas* are owned by the state or hereditary groups. Strict laws govern their working and the complicated system of water allocation is tightly controlled.

In spite of the island's fertility and the intensive cultivation practised, Madeira does not have sufficient land to provide for all her inhabitants. The density of population compels many of the younger members to leave and make their homes abroad (Brazil and Venezuela).

Madeira Wine. – The vine, the banana tree and sugar cane are Madeira's major agricultural crops, and of these the most rewarding is the vine with its harvest of wine.

Vine culture was introduced to Madeira at the beginning of the 15C. The stock, which was imported from Crete and planted in the rich and sunny volcanic soil along the south coast, produced a good quality wine, later famous in England as Malmsey. In the 16C vines became more important than sugar canes which suffered from the Brazilian competition, Madeira wine acquired a certain prestige in Europe: the Duke of Clarence drowned in a butt of Malmsey, François I (King of France, 1515-47) offered it to his guests and later Admiral Lord Nelson was known to be partial to it.

MADEIRA ★★★

The commercial treaty of 1660 between England and Portugal (p 113) encouraged the export of the wine and increased production. Overseas buyers, for the most part English, were drawn to Madeira by the prosperous trade which reached its height in the 18 and 19C, the period when consumption was at its greatest by the two major consumers, England and America.

In 1852 the vines were decimated by phylloxera (a small beetle). A few Englishmen, among whom was Charles Blandy, determined to re-establish the vineyards. In 1872 Thomas Leacock succeeded in overcoming this blight which had attacked the renewed vineyards.

The three principal wines are Sercial, Boal and Malmsey. **Sercial,** made from grapes from vines originally from the Rhine Valley, is a virile, dry wine, amber in colour which is served chilled and drunk as an apéritif. **Boal** originates from Burgundy; the rich, full bodied savour of this red brown wine makes it primarily a dessert wine. **Malmsey,** the most famous, is rare today; again a dessert wine, honeyed in flavour and a deep red, almost purple colour.

A medium sweet all purpose wine, Verdelho, and a Muscatel are also produced.

The grape harvest begins at the end of August. The bunches of grapes are brought to the press and from there the juice is transported to Funchal in skin bottles, each with a capacity of at least 40 litres - 9 gallons, by *borracheiros.* As the wine ferments in the cask various processes are performed: it is fortified with small quantities of alcohol, clarified with the aid of egg whites or isinglass and submitted to the heat of the sun or fire in hothouses.

Madeira improves with age. There is a story which tells how Napoleon put in to Madeira on his way to St Helena and was given a cask of wine by the British Consul. On the emperor's death, the consul reclaimed the cask, which had not been broached, and

Borracheiros carrying skin bottles.

bottled the contents. More than a century later, in 1936, an Englishman was able to boast that he had enjoyed the emperor's wine, by then some hundred and twenty years old.

Madeira Embroidery. – Embroidery is one of the mainstays of the island's economy.

Madeira embroidery owes its origin to an Englishwoman. In 1856 **Miss Phelps,** the daughter of a wine importer, started a workroom where she set women to embroider designs after the manner of *broderie anglaise.* The work was sold for charity. Specimens of the embroidery reached London and were received with such enthusiasm that Miss Phelps decided in future to sell the work abroad. In less than a century embroidery became one of Madeira's major resources; today 70 000 women are employed, sewing, usually in the open air – although there are a few workshops in Funchal *(open to the public).*

The embroidery on linen, lawn or organdie is very fine and very varied in design.

ART

Art in Madeira is almost entirely religious. The churches with their treasures constitute the major part of the island's artistic heritage.

With the arrival of the first colonists, the island began to be scattered with churches and chapels built in the Portuguese ecclesiastical style. Prosperity brought artistic riches, commercial exchanges increased and, through contact with Flanders, Flemish art reached Madeira. Thanks to the gifts and bequests of rich merchants, of Knights of the Order of Christ, of King Manuel I, and of the captains and their descendants between whom the island had been divided, the churches became even more important artistically. The interiors, in contrast to the façades which often continued to be built with a certain austerity of style, were adorned with altarpieces and triptychs brought from Antwerp, Lisbon or Venice in exchange for cargoes of sugar. The benefactors are frequently represented within the churches.

Architectural styles reached Madeira only after some delay and their evolution was also slower than on the Portuguese mainland. The earliest churches are Romanesque, Gothic or Manueline. In the 17 and 18C their interiors were over embellished with Baroque ornament while the majority of new churches erected were almost entirely in the Baroque style.

Their white façades, although often influenced by the Italian Renaissance, remain somewhat restrained except where the details are outlined in black basalt scrollwork. Usually a doorway surmounted by a semicircular arch and a window pierces the face, which is always flanked by one or two square belfries topped by a pyramid shaped roof, covered, in the traditional manner, with faience tiles. The main door is lined by an inner door, a *paravent,* made of precious woods and marquetry.

Inside, the single naves are roofed with barrel vaulting, Baroque frescoes being painted directly on the wood. The altarpieces have a striking exuberance; a profusion of pictures, of which many are of interest, still hang upon the walls and lovely filigree silver lamps can usually be seen adorning the chancels; finally the sacristy is often a fine chamber containing a vestment cupboard made of precious wood and a beautiful Baroque fountain carved out of lava rock.

The palace of the counts of Carvalhal, now the Funchal town hall, and the town hall in Santa Cruz are elegant examples of the island's domestic architecture.

A HOLIDAY ON THE ISLAND

When to go? – The archipelago can be visited in all seasons as the climate is very mild *(see the table on p 12)*.

Where to stay? – *To choose a hotel or restaurant in Madeira, consult the current Michelin Red Guide España Portugal.* The hotels are generally heavily booked in the summer and throughout December. It is essential, therefore, to book in advance, especially fot the small country inns where the accommodation is limited. Most of the sports and tourist facilities are concentrated in the towns of Funchal and Machico, which make excellent excursion centres for visiting the rest of the island.

Tour of the island. – The itineraries suggested can be followed by means of the buses which go to most of the towns *(ask for a timetable, at the Tourist Information Centre, Direcção Regional de Turismo da Madeira)*. Taxis are numerous and are useful for short distances. The best way to get around is to hire a self drive car in Funchal. *Apply to the Hertz Company, Rua Ivens, 12, ℡ 26026 and 23332, to the Avis Company, Largo António Nobre, ℡ 25495, or at other garages with car hire facilities: Garage Ivens, Rua Ivens, 13 B, ℡ 23872; Garage Nunes, Rua Ivens, 12, ℡ 20542.*

> *Before leaving and on the road*
>
> *Do not forget to fill your tank before setting out – there are virtually no filling stations outside the towns. Furthermore, the many steep hills use up more petrol than you might first have reckoned.*
> *For the same reason see that your car is in good order. The cobbled roads, the hairpin bends, the gradients will tax the engine and the car generally to the maximum.*
> *Buses are numerous on the roads. Take care when passing one.*
> *Garages are only to be found in the larger towns – nearly every village, however, has a workshop where simple repairs can be undertaken.*
> *Allow plenty of time for each excursion: the roads permit a speed of only 20 to 30 kph - 12 to 20 mph and the beauty of the countryside encourages frequent halts.*

FUNCHAL ★★

Local map p 155 – Pop 48 239

The island's capital lies at the end of a beautiful bay. Terraces of white houses line the wide open slopes of the encircling green hills whose summits, overlooking the town, are often wrapped in mist.

The remarkable setting which can be admired from many viewpoints, the gardens with their luxuriant vegetation which surround the *quintas* and hotels, the geographical position which makes Funchal a port of call on the major Atlantic routes, combine to form a popular city resort attracting visitors from many countries.

Funchal has a considerable selection of nightlife attractions such as a casino, cabarets, cinemas and theatre. Folklore concerts are organized every evening in one of the town's hotels *(apply to the Tourist Information Centre)*. For those who enjoy active recreation there are tennis courts, swimming pools (on the west side of the town), a golf course at Santo da Serra and a coast which invites fishing, water skiing and sailing. The Clube de Turismo (Estrada Monumental 179 – *leave by ③ on the plan*) welcomes all visitors: swimming pool, restaurant and tea room.

The largest town in what are known as the "adjacent isles", (Madeira and the Azores), is also a business and commercial centre, absorbing the island's main products. Tourists are offered the wine, embroidery and basketwork, although much is now exported, as are virtually the entire output of canned tunny, dairy products, cane sugar, etc. Above all the town has an important role as port of call, receiving 66 000 transit passengers in 1983.

There is a brilliant firework display each year at midnight on 31 December which lights up the whole town and the bay.

In Funchal restaurants the visitor will find meat grilled on skewers *(espetadas)*, cinnamon spiced roasts, tunny steaks *(bifes)*, fried corn and, for dessert, honey cakes and delicious fruits.

Zarco. – João Gonçalves Zarco, born at Tomar of humble origin, abducted the daughter of a noble family whom he wished to marry. He sought the protection of the Infante, who took him into his service and invested him as a knight.

Zarco distinguished himself by his courage at the Battle of Tangier and in the conquest of Ceuta when he was struck in the eye by an arrow. He joined Tristão Vaz Teixeira in the discovery of Madeira *(p 144)* and the following year returned to the island to settle with his family in Funchal, remaining there as ruler for more than forty years until his death (1467). On this site at the meeting of three river mouths – *ribeiras* – where fennel *(funcho)* grew, he drew the plan for the town and gave out land to the colonists to farm. In 1508 King Manuel granted a charter to the town which had by then grown prosperous from its sugar trade (the town's crest includes four sugar loaves).

■ **LOWER TOWN** *time: 3 hours*
Follow by car the route marked on the plan p 148.

The original heart of the city, confined to west and east by the Forts of St Lawrence (São Lourenço) and St James (São Tiago) and clustered around the cathedral, with the animation and industry of its skilled workers and the bustle of trade, contrasts with the peace and quiet of the residential areas.

Praça do Município (Y). – The square is bordered to the south by the former archbishop's palace, now the Museum of Religious Art and to the east by the town hall (Câmara Municipal), 18C palace of Count Carvalhal. The palace tower, rising high, still proudly dominates the surrounding houses. To the north stands the Old College *(p 149)*.

St Mary Major (Igreja da Santa Maria Major) (X A). – The church's elegant 18C Baroque façade, with scrollwork of black lava rock standing out against the rough-cast white stucco, is pierced by a plain door. The Apostle St James the Less is honoured before this doorway each year on May Day in remembrance of the miracles of 1523 and 1538, when epidemics of the plague, which were ravaging Funchal at the time, were dissipated.

Inside, look upwards at the painted cradle vaulting. The sacristy, to the right of the chancel, is ornamented with a pretty Baroque fountain. A glass showcase contains sacred objects, including the Apostle's silver shrine.

Socorro (X). – The flowered Socorro belvedere opposite the church overlooks Funchal harbour; in the foreground stands the Fort of St James which has retained its 17C lookout turrets while below lies the small Barreirinha beach of shingle with its seawater swimming pool.

Avenida das Comunidades Madeirenses (Z). – This promenade, wide, shaded and bordered with flowers, runs the length of the shingle beach.

On the right stands the old 16C customs house (Antiga Alfândega) and beyond the 17C Fort of St Lawrence, the first fort to be built on the island and now the military headquarters, and the governor of Funchal district's residence.

Go through the Pontinha control post and on to the breakwater.

Pontinha (X). – The breakwater which was built at the end of the 18C to link the first islet to the main island has since been lengthened twice so that it now provides a well sheltered harbour and also serves as a mooring quay for ocean liners. The road passes beneath the fortress, Nossa Senhora da Conceição, which was built on a rocky islet at the end of the 19C. On reaching the end of the breakwater *(ask for permission)* climb up the steps of the retaining wall to see the **panorama**★★ which extends over the whole area of the town protected by the Pico das Frias Fort. To the east can be seen the long island mass of the Desertas.

Casino Gardens (Jardins do Casino) (X). – The new Funchal casino, built in 1979 by the Brazilian architect Oscar Niemeyer, is set in a park of beautiful exotic trees. The top of a steep cliff near the Bianchi and Pavão Quintas provides a viewpoint down to Funchal harbour far below.

In the Avenida do Infante, on the left, may be seen the tropical garden of the Dona Amelia Hospital. Its entrance is framed by two fine dracoena, or dragon trees.

St Catherine's Park (Parque de Santa Catarina) (Z). – This public garden forms the setting for the Chapel of St Catherine which was built by Zarco in 1425 and is, therefore, one of the oldest buildings on the island. The garden, which contains a statue to Christopher Columbus erected in 1968, overlooks the promenade and the harbour.

Avenida Arriaga (Z). – The avenue, which is the main street of Funchal, has been planted with jacaranda trees which are covered in purple flowers throughout the spring. The municipal park (Jardim do São Francisco), on the left, is also a **botanical garden**.

Cathedral★ (Sé) (Z B). – This cathedral which was built by Knights of the Order of Christ at the end of the 15C was the first Portuguese cathedral to be constructed overseas. The style is Manueline; the façade is plain, the white rough stucco being relieved by black basalt and red tufa rock. The apse, decorated with openwork balustrades and twisted pinnacles, is flanked by a crenellated square belfry whose roof, pyramid in shape, is tiled with *azulejos*.

In the nave slender columns support arcades of painted lava rock while above, and also over the transept, extends a remarkable *artesonado* **ceiling★** in which ivory inlays in the cedar wood have been used to emphasize the stylistic motifs.

The stalls which adorn the chancel date from the 17C but are nevertheless Manueline in style. They are surmounted by painted and gilded oak niches which contain statues of Apostles, Doctors of the Church and saints. The cheekpieces are ornamented with interesting caricatures carved in sesame wood: grotesque animals and people add a humorous touch to Biblical, satiric or fabulous scenes *(apply to the sacristan to have the chancel lit)*.

Flemish paintings form a beautiful 16C altarpiece above the high altar. Higher still the vaulting is delicately divided.

The Chapel of the Holy Sacrament, to the right of the chancel, is richly Baroque in its gilded wood and marble decoration. The pulpit and the font are of Arrábida marble.

■ ADDITIONAL SIGHTS

Museum of Sacred Art★ (Museu de Arte Sacra) (Y M¹). – *Rua do Bispo, 21. Open 10am to 12.30pm and 2.30 to 5.30pm; closed Sunday afternoons, Mondays and holidays; 50esc, free Sundays.*

The museum, which is in the former episcopal palace, contains paintings and sacred objects from several churches on the island. A gallery on the 1st floor contains a display of 17-18C church ornaments, low reliefs in gilded wood, 17-18C gold and silver plate. Note a moving Entombment in wood, dating from the 16C.

There is an interesting **collection of paintings★** of the 15 and 16C Portuguese and Flemish schools on the 2nd floor. The paintings are on wood – either oak or indigenous woods according to whether they were executed in Europe or Madeira.

In the 1st gallery are a triptych, from the Bruges school, depicting St James and St Philip between the donors of the painting (an Annunciation can be seen on the back); a *Descent from the Cross* attributed to Gérard David, in which the personages involved have great nobility of bearing, and a curious 14C painting in which St George is represented as a child overcoming the dragon.

The next room contains paintings of the Flemish school, including a full length portrait of St James Minor, the town's Patron Saint, in a red toga, attributed to Memling. *The Adoration of the Shepherds,* brought from the church of Ribeira Brava, is a would be subtle painting marred by a slightly stiff design; a Mary Magdalene, sumptuously robed and surprisingly realistic, stands vitally erect before a magnificent landscape. There is also an interesting portrait of Bishop St Nicholas.

The major painting in the 3rd gallery is a fine composition by the Antwerp school of the Adoration of the Magi. It comes from the church at Machico.

Among the paintings in the 4th gallery are the *Meeting between St Anne and St Joachim,* and a *Crucifixion* by the Flemish school, which is full of movement. Among the Portuguese paintings, there is a traditionally hieratic bust of Christ.

In the 5th gallery is a group of two delightful naïvely painted 16C Portuguese pictures: one shows the embalming of Christ with, on the back, Christ appearing to Mary Magdalene, a graceful and unselfconscious painting; the other a Descent from the Cross and on the back, Christ before the Virgin Mary.

The last two galleries exhibit gold and silver plate: there is a fine 16C Gothic Manueline silver cross given by King Manuel I and a beautiful 18C ivory sculpture.

Former College (Colégio) (Y C). – The Church of St John the Evangelist, which abuts on a monastery now converted into barracks, was built early in the 17C in the Jesuit style.

The austere white façade, which is pierced by numerous windows with black surrounds, has also been hollowed out to form four statuary niches. These contain figures on the upper level of St Ignatius and St Francis Xavier, and on the lower of St Francis Borgia and St Stanislas.

The nave, paved with *azulejos,* is superabundantly decorated with exuberant Baroque altars whose ornament derives from the island's own vegetation, particularly bunches of grapes. Go into the sacristy to the left of the chancel. This elegant room has a fine ceiling with painted squinches, a frieze of *azulejos* adorning the walls and a magnificent vestment cupboard with gilt locks.

Municipal Museum (Y M²). – The former mansion of Count Carvalhal in the Rua da Mouraria, which is bordered by several houses with beautiful wrought iron balconies, now houses a natural history museum *(open 9am to 8pm; Sundays and holidays noon to 6pm; closed Mondays, 1 January, 25 April, 1 July, 5 October and 25 December; 20esc. including a tour of the aquarium).*

The aquarium on the ground floor is particularly interesting *(same times and charges as the natural history museum except that on Sundays the aquarium closes at 4pm).*

St Clare's Convent (Convento de Santa Clara) (Y E). – The convent was built in the 17C on the site of the church founded in the 15C by Zarco to provide a burial place for his family.

Inside, the church, which was tiled between the 16 and 18C with *azulejos,* contains, at the end, Zarco's Gothic tomb supported by lions and surmounted by a canopy.

The convent *(to visit ring at the door to the right of the church)* is now a kindergarten run by nuns. The tombstones of Zarco's two granddaughters who founded the original convent of the Order of St Clare on the island may be seen in the cloisters. In the former conventual hall a fine 17C Crucifix may be seen above the altar.

The Crosses' Quinta★ (Quinta das Cruzes) (Y M³). – *Open 10am to 12.30pm and 2 to 5.30pm; closed Mondays and holidays; 50esc.* Zarco's former villa has been transformed into a museum of decorative art.

On the ground floor, low ceilinged rooms which served formerly as wine stores now contain 16C Portuguese furniture collected from private houses in Funchal. Note also the 17C Chinese porcelain and the 18C Limoges enamels.

On the 1st floor are English and French furniture of the 17 and 18C, a carved wood manger (late 18C) and a collection of ivories.

The villa stands in a botanical garden in which may be seen a lapidary collection, as well as two beautiful Manueline windows. At the top of the garden is a hot house of orchids.

Customs House Street (Rua da Alfandega) (Z 2). – This, the Customs House Street, is one of the most picturesque and busy in all Funchal. It is very narrow, unevenly paved with black lava rock and lined with old houses and a large number of shops of which the majority are tinware stores.

Market (Mercado dos Lavradores) (Z). – This "workers' market", which is now housed in a modern building, is particularly lively in the morning.

At the entrance, flower sellers in traditional Madeiran costume – striped skirt, red corselet and hood, leather boots and black tailed bonnet known as a *carapuça* – offer bunches of flowers in myriad colours.

Baskets and stalls overflowing with fruit and vegetables ring the central patio.

In the bustling fishmarket, swordfish, tunny, red mullet, conger eels, etc. are all displayed for buyers and tourists to look over.

Church of the Incarnation (Igreja da Encarnação) (V F). – The entrance to this 16 or 17C Manueline church is through a beautiful side doorway.

Inside, the arches supporting the elegant diagonal ribbed vaulting stand on carved consoles. A keystone to one of the arches bears an armillary sphere.

Quinta da Palmeira (V). – *Take the Rua da Carne Azeda going north then the Rua da Levada de Santa Luzia on the left.* The entrance to the *quinta* (private property) is just before a left turn, its name is in white shingle inlaid in the roadway.

Leave the car near the entrance gate. A steep path leads to the quinta.

A grass path crosses the well kept park, whose terraces overlook Funchal, and leads to a Gothic stone window. This window was formerly in the house in which, it is said, Christopher Columbus stayed when he lived in Funchal.

Fireman's Museum (Museu do Bombeiro) (V M⁴). – *Temporarily closed. This museum is to be transferred to new premises. Apply to the town hall.*

A former fireman has gathered together in a small gallery several interesting examples of old fire engines mounted on sledge runners for pulling by hand. The evolution of firefighting techniques since the late 19C and the different catastrophes which befell the firemen of Funchal are depicted in a series of engravings.

Botanical Gardens (Jardim Botânico) (V). – *Open 8am to 6pm; closed Sundays; 60esc. Take the Rua da Levada de Santa Luzia going east and after passing the Ribeira de João Gomes, turn left into the Rua Carlos Azevedo de Menezes.*

The gardens, where remarkable examples of every type of Madeira flora grow, have been laid out in terraces overlooking the *ribeira* valley on the grounds of an old *quinta* (Quinta do Bom Sucesso). From the topmost balcony, there is a **view★** of Funchal harbour and immediately below of the wild Ribeira de João Gomes Valley.

Nazareth Chapel★ (Capela da Nazaré). – *Leave by ④. At the end of the Rua do Doutor Pita bear left into the Caminho das Virtudes, then, left again, into the Caminho da Nazaré (formerly the Caminho de Avista Navios).* The chapel lies on the left, not far from the crossroads.

The chapel's side walls are clad in 17C **azulejos★**. On one of the walls is a maritime scene in Lisbon harbour in which the artist has included a representation of the legend of Dom Fuas Roupinho *(p 72)*.

The road continues steeply downhill to a roundabout where the Levada dos Piornais, which irrigates São Martinho, ends.

Go round the stadium to return to the Rua do Doutor Pita.

EXCURSIONS *plan pp 154-155*

Quinta do Palheiro Ferreiro★. – *4km - 3 miles.*

Leave Funchal by ②. Turn left, after São Gonçalo, into the first road going towards Camacha. Not far after the second crossroads, in a left turn, bear right, into a small cobbled road. Go through the entrance gate to the quinta and follow the avenue of plane trees up to the villa. Private property. Open 9.30am to 12.30pm; closed Saturdays, Sundays and holidays; 150esc.

The villa *(closed to the public)* stands in a landscaped park★ which is well cared for and a pleasure to wander around, with its remarkable specimens of tropical trees, rose gardens and beds of rare flowers.

Barcelos Peak★★; Eira do Serrado★★★; Curral das Freiras★. – *Round tour of 20km - 12 miles. – Leave Funchal by ④.*

    São Martinho. – Pop 17 277. In São Martinho the parish church stands at the top of a "peak" 259m - 850ft high.

As you come to the cemetery bear right.

    Barcelos Peak★★ (Pico dos Barcelos). – This belvedere, surrounded by aloes and masses of flowers, affords a **panorama★★**: of Funchal set at the foot of the mountain ranges whose ragged outlines can be distinguished massed to the north; of Santo António lying snugly in its valley and clustered round its white village church; of São Martinho whose church stands out in silhouette against the sea.

Continue along the road towards Eira do Serrado.

The road crosses a countryside where houses and their surrounding small fields alternate with eucalyptus groves.

The road nears the Ribeira dos Socorridos – River of the Survivors named as such for the "survivors", who took refuge in its course when the island was set on fire. Soon, there is a striking **sight★** of the deep defile caused by a volcanic fracture through which the stream runs, and far away, its opening to the sea and the few houses of Câmara de Lobos.

The hydrangea bordered road travels on through pine and eucalyptus woods soon affording wide views of the valley. There is a magnificent **view★★** from a balcony on the left, of the defile where the face has been cut into terraces for cultivation and where the occasional white house has been built.

A right fork takes you to Eira do Serrado where you leave the car.

    Eira do Serrado★★★. – A path *(signposted)* goes round the Serrado Peak (1 060m - 3 318ft) by the right to a viewpoint. The **panorama★★★** is outstanding: the white houses of the village of Curral das Freiras lie scattered like stars around a hollow circle of ravine scarred mountains.

Take the road which runs down to Curral das Freiras.

This road, which has taken the place of the old path which zigzagged down the steep hillsides, has been cut out of the completely vertical rock face and passes through two tunnels to reach the small and isolated village of Curral das Freiras.

    Curral das Freiras★. – Pop 2 368. Curral das Freiras lies in an enclosed **setting★** at the foot of a grandiose cirque of extinct volcanoes. It belongs to the sisters of the Convent of St Clare who took shelter here when French pirates pillaged Funchal in 1566. The event was commemorated in the name of the village which in Portuguese means the "nuns' shelter". The road ends before the church which stands in a small square near the cemetery.

As you return uphill pause on leaving the village at a paved terrace on your left, to get an interesting **view★** of the circle of mountain peaks.

Leave the Barcelos Peak road on your right as you enter Funchal.

    Santo António. – Pop 19 775. The 18C Baroque church stands on a terrace to the right of the road.

Return to Funchal by the Caminho de Santo António (VX on the town plan p 148) which drops rapidly into the town between the flower covered walls of several quintas.

Câmara de Lobos★; Cape Girão.★ – *20km - 12 miles. Leave Funchal by ③.* Once beyond the banana plantations occasional glimpses of the coast show it to be lined by shingle beaches. After 3km - 2 miles you come within sight of Cape Girão, its reddish cliff plunging nearly 600m - 2 000ft vertically into the sea. Cross the bridge over the Ribeira dos Socorridos. As you come out of a bend in the road, you get a **view★** of the Cape and the far end of the Câmara de Lobos harbour fringed with rocks.

    Câmara de Lobos★. – Pop 15 099. *In the town, take the first road on the left.* A pergola ornamented balcony directly overlooks the shingle beach and, on the right, the Ribeira do Vigário where the local women do their washing. Sea perch frequented the shores in such numbers when Zarco arrived that he called the village Câmara de Lobos or the Sea Perches' House.

    Go down towards the harbour. Câmara de Lobos is a picturesque village built round a harbour well protected by two cliffs of volcanic rock. Walk westwards along the harbour wall to get an overall view of the village **setting★**. The white houses with their red tiled roofs stand scattered on the banana planted terraces. Below, on the shingle beach, brilliantly coloured boats lie drawn up in the shade of palm and plane trees, bizarre black nets suspended on willow frames hang out to dry above them.

    Return to the main road. At the crossroads, overlooking the harbour is the small terrace where Winston Churchill would sit and paint, when he visited the island in 1950. The modest houses in the fishermen's quarter can be seen rising in tiers up a cliff on the west wide of the harbour, and in the distance, Cape Girão.

Banana plantations give way to vineyards for the vine is virtually the only crop in the region of Estreito de Câmara de Lobos. The low vines, beneath which vegetables are frequently planted, spread over the hillslopes. Malmsey and Verdelho are made from the white grapes; Tinto from the black. Above 500m - 1 500ft in the Jardim da Serra region vines are grown on espaliers, their grapes producing the well known Sercial.

Estreito de Câmara de Lobos. – Pop 11 661. The bustling village is off the main road, its houses grouped round a vast terrace from which rises the white parish church *(open Saturdays and Sundays)*. Inside is a large collection of chandeliers and a cradle vault on which has been painted a highly coloured Baroque scene. The overall impression is richly sumptuous.

The approaches to Cape Girão are clad with pinewoods and eucalyptus groves.

Bear left towards Cape Girão (signposted).

Cape Girão★ (Cabo Girão). – From the belvedere built at the tip of the vertical cliff there is a wide **view★** of the coastal plains as far as Funchal Bay. The sea crashes 580m - 1 900ft below. Even the slenderest ledges on the cliff face are striped by the regular curves of vines planted in line on terraces under cultivation.

Monte★ ; Terreiro da Luta★. – *Round tour of 25km - 16 miles. Leave Funchal by ①.*

One can return to Funchal from Monte, and also Terreiro da Luta, in the traditional sledges (carros de cesto). *Two men in white control these toboggans which hurtle down the Caminho do Comboio.*

Quinta do Til (V *on town plan p 148*). – The beautiful grille in the gateway is well worth looking at as you pass the entrance to the *quinta.*

The road rises between small fields of sugar cane to pass the Marmeleiros belvedere, on the right, which affords a bird's eye view of Funchal whose houses lies scattered over the hillsides right down to the sea. Pinewoods precede the **setting★** in which Monte stands.

Monte★. – Pop 7 803. Monte, at an altitude of nearly 600m - 1 800ft is a country resort much appreciated for its cool climate and rich vegetation. Enhancing the surroundings further are several *quintas,* in their lovely gardens. The Quinta do Monte, which lies below the former Belmonte Hotel, became the house of the last Emperor of Austria and his family when they went into exile and came to live on the island in 1921. Karl I died in the house the following year.

Our Lady of the Mountain (Nossa Senhora do Monte) rises from a hillock in the centre of a magnificent park. The church dates from the end of the 18C when it was built on the site of a chapel erected in 1470 by Adam Gonçalves Ferreira, who with his twin sister, Eva, were the first children to be born on the island of Madeira. The façade with a Baroque pediment, great windows and arcaded porch is highly decorative.

The church contains, in a chapel to the left of the nave, the iron tomb of the Emperor Karl I of Austria. A tabernacle worked in silver above the high altar shelters a small cloaked statue of Our Lady of the Mountain *(to illuminate, apply to the sacristan)*. The figure which was discovered in the 15C at Terreiro da Luta at the spot where the Virgin appeared to a young shepherdess, is the goal of a popular pilgrimage held on 14 and 15 August each year. Our Lady of the Mountain is the Patron Saint of Madeira.

The sacristy, on the right of the chancel, contains religious objects presented by the Empress Zita, wife of Karl I, and also a few mementoes of the latter.

At the foot of the church stairway *(the departure point for the sledges)*, the Largo das Babosas leads to a square shaded by plane trees and overlooked by the **Chapel of Our Lady of the Holy Conception** (Nossa Senhora da Conceição). From the chapel which was built in 1906 in the Baroque style, there is a view across the wooded valley of the Ribeira de João Gomes to the place known as Curral dos Romeiros.

Return to the main road.

The road to Terreiro da Luta passes through pine, acacia and eucalyptus woods.

Terreiro da Luta★. – When the bombardment of Funchal by German submarines in 1917 had stopped, the Bishop of Funchal made a vow to erect a monument to the Virgin, provided peace followed within a short space of time. The monument to Our Lady of Peace stands where Our Lady of the Mountain is said to have appeared. Encircling the monument are anchor chains from the torpedoed ships.

From the café terrace near the monument there is a **view★** of Funchal and the three hills which mark the limits of the town on the right.

Take the road running downhill towards Camacha.

The Levada dos Tornos which runs on the far side of the Ribeira de João Gomes soon comes into view, and shortly afterwards (belvedere) Funchal and the Santo António Valley.

Leave the road to Camacha (p 155) on the left.

Boa Nova Church. – The new church constructed to the right of the road on a terrace overlooking Funchal incorporates the Baroque remains of a 17C Funchal convent chapel. The façade is bare except for a Classical doorway of black lava rock, the pediment serving as a perch for an eagle. The plain interior is adorned with a ceiling painted in the Baroque style and an interesting gilded wood altarpiece whose dimensions seem perfect in this new setting. A lovely balustrade surrounds the chancel.

Shortly after Boa Nova take a downhill road on the left to return to Funchal by ②.

BOAT TRIPS

From Funchal it is possible to make most attractive boat trips along the coast as far as Ponta do Sol via Câmara de Lobos in the west or Caniçal via Machico in the east. It is also possible to sail to the Desertas *(allow one day)* or to Porto Santo *(p 159)*.

Apply to the Tourist Centre (Direcção Regional de Turismo de Madeira), Avenida Arriaga, 18, or to travel agents.

Itinerary ① on the map on p 155 – 67km - 42 miles starting from Funchal – about 3 hours.

Leave Funchal by ②.

Pináculo Belvedere ★ ★ (Miradouro do Pináculo). – 2km - 1 mile beyond São Gonçalo, a belvedere at the summit *(pináculo)* of a rocky promontory affords, through the flowers on its pergola, a wonderful view of Funchal, lying spread out at the end of its beautiful bay. Cape Girão stands out on the horizon.

The *corniche* road passes through uninhabited areas where man has not yet succeeded in cultivating hillsides dried out by the sun and where there are, as yet, no irrigation channels. The Desertas can be seen far out to sea.

Caniço. – Pop 7 249. Caniço is a small town whose inhabitants live by fishing and the cultivation of bananas and sugar cane.

4km - 2 miles further on, the most easterly part of Madeira comes into sight, the St Lawrence Headland. The desolate countryside bears traces of terraces once cultivated and now falling into ruin as Barbary figs invade the area.

Santa Cruz. – Pop 6 166. Santa Cruz, a fishing village edged with a shingle foreshore on which brightly coloured boats lie idle in the daytime beneath the palms, possesses several Manueline monuments, mementos of the early period of colonization.

The **Church ★** of São Salvador borders the main square, whose centre is a public garden. It was erected in 1533 and is said to be the oldest now standing on the island. The exterior is white, flanked by a belfry with a pyramidal roof. At the end of the apse is girdled by a balustrade of crosses. The interior, divided into three aisles, is covered with a painted ceiling. The chancel, where the vaulting is supported on twisted columns, contains a metal memorial plaque to João de Freitas. The tomb of the Spinolas is in the north aisle off which lies a beautiful Manueline chapel. There are two good paintings above the door to the sacristy. The former **domus municipalis**, with twin Manueline windows, stands in the church square. The small street on the east side of the square leads to the present **town hall,** a fine 16C building.

The road skirts the **airport,** constructed in 1966 in the midst of the banana plantations.

Francisco Álvares Nóbrega Belvedere ★ (Miradouro Francisco Álvares Nóbrega). – A road to the left leads to this belvedere named after a Portuguese poet, known also as the Lesser Camões (1772-1806), who sang Madeira's praises. From the belvedere there is a **view** of Machico and, not far away, a vast grey shingle beach. In the east lies the elongated reddish mass of the St Lawrence Headland.

Machico. – Pop 12 129. The town of Machico, situated at the mouth of a fertile valley, is divided by a river: the fishermen's quarter, the Banda d'Além, lies on the east side, the old town on the west. It was at Machico that Zarco and his companions landed *(p 144).* The following year, Tristão Vaz Teixeira was invested by Prince Henry as Governor of the Captaincy of Machico.

There is a legend that in 1346 an English ship sank in a tempest at the mouth of the river. Robert Machim and Ana d'Arfet, who had fled from Bristol to get married in spite of their parents' opposition, survived the shipwreck but died a few days later. Their companions took to sea again on a raft, were captured by Arab pirates and taken to Morocco. The story of their adventure was told by a Castilian to the King of Portugal who thereon decided to equip an expedition to rediscover the island. When Zarco landed at Machico he found the lovers' tomb at the base of a cedar tree and named the village after the young Englishman, Machim. The Manueline **parish church** built at the end of the 15C stands in a square shaded by plane trees. The façade is pierced by a lovely rose window and a doorway adorned with capitals carved with the heads of animals. The side doorway, which was given by King Manuel I, consists of paired arches supported on white marble columns.

A Manueline arch in the north wall leads to the St John Chapel which serves as pantheon to those who donated the church.

As ruler, Tristão Vaz Teixeira had a chapel constructed in 1420 on the east bank of the river on the site of the English lovers' tomb. This chapel, the **Chapel of Miracles** (Capela dos Milagres), was destroyed by river floods in 1803. The original Manueline doorway was reinstalled when it was rebuilt. In 1829 Robert Page, an English merchant, maintained that he had found the cedar cross which had originally stood upon the grave of Robert Machim and Ana d'Arfet *(Ask to see the framed cross* (quadro) *discovered by Robert Page).*

The **St Rock Chapel** (Capela São Roque), which stands at the end of the avenue bordering the west side of the harbour, was founded in the 15C also by Tristão Vaz Teixeira, this time in fulfilment of a vow. It was rebuilt in the 17C. The interior is ornamented with an interesting frieze of *azulejos* dating from the 17C, based on the life of St Rock. The birth of the saint, on the right, can be easily distinguished *(to visit apply to the house on the right in the last path on the right before the church).*

Praínha. – *13km - 8 miles from Machico by the Caniçal road.* There are views, as the road rises, of the Upper Valley of Machico dominated by mountain summits. The road leaves the valley through a tunnel bored through the base of Mount Facho.

Caniçal (Pop 3 210) is a small fishing village where life remains traditional.

The road, which is not surfaced, next crosses a desolate landscape of rust coloured earth and rock. Near the coast, in the foreground on the right, a small factory extracts oil from cetacea brought in from the sea by the Caniçal fishermen.

A stairway leads down to a **small beach** (Praínha) which lies in a little creek, well protected by basalt cliffs. It is the only sand beach on the island. Above, on a hillock, standing guard, is the hermitage of Nossa Senhora da Piedade.

At Machico take the road to Portela. As you climb, the banana and cane sugar plantations of the valley floor give way to pine and eucalyptus trees.

MACHICO TOUR ★

Portela Pass. – At the Portela Pass crossroads, go up to look at the view from the belvedere overlooking the green Machico Valley.

A road in deep shadow leads to Santo António da Serra.

Santo António da Serra. – Pop 1 295. Santo da Serra which was built on a forest covered plateau (pines and eucalyptus) at an altitude of 800m - 2 500ft has become popular with the residents of Funchal as a country resort with a cool climate in a restful setting. The golf course is famous. Go from the main square where the church stands, into the Quinta da Junta Park, formerly the property of the Blandy family *(p 146)*. At the end of the main drive, a chalet converted into a belvedere provides a bird's eye view of the Machico Valley; in the distance can be seen the St Lawrence Headland and, in clear weather, a white speck which is the Island of Porto Santo.

The Camacha road goes through a wooded area where occasional fields of early vegetables draw one's attention to the odd hamlet.

A signpost on the left marks a **viewpoint** over the Levada dos Tornos which flows across the valley on the far hillside.

Camacha. – Pop 6 193. Camacha is a village set in the woods at an altitude of 700m - 2 300ft. It is famous for its basketwork and equally for its group of folk dancers and musicians. The lively but graceful dances are accompanied by chords from a *braguinha*, a four string guitar, while the rhythm is accentuated by an amusing looking stick caparisoned with a pyramid of dolls and castanets and known as a *brinquinho*.

Boa Nova Church. – *Description p 152.*

Soon after take the road leading downwards on the left and return to Funchal by ②.

The maps and plans are orientated with north at the top.

SANTANA TOUR ★★

Itinerary ② *on the map below.* – *155km - 96 miles starting from Funchal – allow two days.*

Leave Funchal by ①. The route as far as Terreiro de Luta is described on p 152.

Beyond Terreiro da Luta the road, which is lined with flowering hedges, rises in hairpin bends through pine and acacia woods. With the increase in altitude the landscape becomes more barren and the only trees are a few scattered junipers and evergreen oaks.

Poiso Pass. – A few isolated houses have been built on the south side of the 1 400m - 4 600ft Poiso Pass, which is only 13km - 8 miles from Funchal.

Take the road on the left to the Arieiro Peak. The road follows the crest line of the mountains in the centre of the island and there are, therefore, good views from it of both the south coast and Funchal, and the north coast. Flocks of sheep graze on desolate moorlands. At Chão do Arieiro the road passes below a weather station at an altitude of 1 700m - 5 578ft.

Juncal Belvedere ★ (Miradouro do Juncal). – A well designed path goes round the summit of the Juncal Peak (Pico do Juncal: 1 800m - 5 906ft) to *(1/4 hour Rtn on foot)* the belvedere, from which there is an attractive view along the full length of the Ribeira da Metade Valley which runs into the sea below Faial near a curious rock spike, the Penha d'Águia. The St Lawrence Headland (Ponta de São Lourenço) can also be seen.

Arieiro Peak Belvedere ★★ (Miradouro do Pico Arieiro). – There is a magnificent panorama of the mountain ranges in the central part of the island from the Arieiro belvedere built on the very summit of the mountain at an altitude of 1 810m - 5 939ft. The landmarks include the Curral das Freiras crater, the distinctive outline of the crest of the Torrinhas (turrets) and, standing one before the other, the Torres and Ruivo Peaks. To the northeast are the Ribeira da Metade, the Penha D'Águia rock spike and the St Lawrence Headland.

A path has been constructed from the Arieiro to the Ruivo Peak (p 158).

Return to Poiso and take the road on the left going to Faial. The road descends in a series of hairpin bends through pine and arborescent laurels whose dense growth gives an indication of the humidity to be found on the north coast.

Botanical Gardens ★ (Flora da Madeira). – This small well kept garden in the centre of a forest park provides great enjoyment to those who choose to walk in the shade along its flower bordered paths.

Ribeiro Frio. – Near a little bridge over the Ribeiro Frio (meaning cold stream) stands a small hotel, settled in a pleasant site amidst the greenery at an altitude of 860m - 2 822ft. The Levada do Furado which brings water to Porto da Cruz and Machico can be seen flowing near by.

Balcões ★★. – *1/2 hour on foot.* A path *(signposted)* leads off left from the road, after the bend of Ribeiro Frio, and, going alongside the Levada do Furado, brings you to the Balcões belvedere. This stands in the Metade Valley on a hillside surrounded by the last of the high mountains. The **view** extends from the upper valley, which begins among jagged peaks, to the more open valley running down to the coast.

Continuing along the course of the valley you will come to **São Roque do Faial** (Pop 941), a village perched on a long crest between two valleys. The red roofed houses, covered in vines, are surrounded by small market gardens, willow plantations and orchards scattered with straw thatched byres *(palheiros, illustration p 158).*

Turn right towards Portela. From the bridge over the Ribeira de São Roque there is an attractive view of Faial Valley and the village perched on the clifftop. Bananas, sugar cane and vines are grown on the sunniest slopes.

A belvedere constructed on the left side of the road affords an interesting **view**★ of **Porto da Cruz** (Pop 3 680), a village nestled at the foot of a steep cliff bordered by a shingle beach.

At Porto da Cruz turn round and make for Faial by way of a series of hairpin bends.

4km - 3 miles from Faial, two belvederes on the right provide an overall **view**★ of Faial, the Penha d'Águia, the village of São Roque at the confluence of the Metade and São Roque Valleys and, on the horizon, the St Lawrence Headland.

Santana★★. – Pop 4 045. Santana, at an altitude of 436m - 2 433ft, a coastal plateau, is the prettiest village on the island. The villagers still live in attractive cottages made of wood with pointed thatched roofs. Gardens enclosed by box hedges and bright with flowers add to the gaiety and local atmosphere which can be only truly appreciated if you turn off the main road and into the Queimadas Park road.

Parque das Queimadas. – *5km - 3 miles starting from Santana. Bear left after the town hall in Caminho do Barreiro and make for Caminho das Queimadas.* This narrow and unevenly surfaced **road**★, lined with hydrangeas, winds between thatched cottages and flower gardens to the Junta Geral refuge at 883m - 2 897ft. There, in a peaceful setting at the foot of the Ruivo Peak slopes, is a beautiful park where the trees stand reflected in a small pool.

The road soon ends to become a path leading to the Ruivo Peak (p 158).

As you leave Santana there is a splendid panorama to your left of the chain of mountains. The road, pleasantly lined with hydrangeas, arum and cana lilies, crosses coastal valleys where the sunny hillsides bear a variety of crops.

São Jorge. – Pop 2 655. São Jorge's 17C **church,** which stands off the main road, is astonishingly rich in its Baroque ornament. This totally unexpected abundance in a country parish church recalls the sumptuous period of King João V. The eye is drawn immediately to the chancel which is covered by a ceiling painted in false relief and where the decorations include a Flamboyant gilded wood altarpiece with twisted columns, and, on each side wall, one opposite the other, two paintings framed by heavy twisted columns. The fine silver altar lamp dates from the 18C. The sacristy contains an elegant vestment cupboard and a pretty Baroque fountain. An *azulejos* frieze encircles the church.

Before beginning the descent to Arco de São Jorge, a belvedere to the right of the road affords a wide **vista**★ of the coast as it curves to form the São Vicente Bay. Below lies the small valley, worn into a series of steps by erosion, in which Arco de São Jorge was built.

Many vines grow on trellises on the more sheltered slopes, for this is a region which, like the Estreito, produces Sercial wine.

Boaventura. – Pop 2 298. The small village of Boaventura lies scattered among vineyards in a pretty setting on a hill dividing two valleys *(lombo).*

3km - 2 miles on there is a beautiful **view**★ to the right over the harsh coastline which, beyond the nearby Moinhos River, sweeps away in a series of headlands and inlets. To the left is **Ponta Delgada** (Pop 1 472) with its white church and seawater swimming pool. Beyond Ponta Delgada, the coast becomes even harsher. The road passes beneath an immensely high cliff. The trellised vines are, by now, protected from the wind by broom hedges giving the landscape a chequered appearance.

Bear left after crossing the São Vicente Bridge, where a small rock has been hollowed out to form a Chapel to St Rock.

São Vicente. – Pop 4 374. São Vicente stands at the mouth of the river of the same name, grouped in a cliff hollow a little way from the sea.

The coast near Boaventura.

The road follows the wide course of the valley which is green but not cultivated and is overlooked by high mountains. On the left, on a wooded hillock, stands the chapel built in 1952 to Our Lady of Fátima. The vegetation – arborescent laurels and heathers and broom – gets thicker as the road rises.

Encumeada Pass★ **(Boca da Encumeada).** – A belvedere in the Encumeada Pass at an altitude of 1 007m - 3 304ft, in a sort of depression in the mountain chain, looks down over both sides of the island. There is a general **view**★ of Madeira's two central valleys which occupy a volcanic fault area between the Paúl da Serra Plateau and the mountain ranges near the Ruivo Peak.

The Levada do Norte, which passes beneath the road and descends to Serra de Água before irrigating the region between Ribeira Brava and Câmara do Lobos, is 60km - 38 miles long. It was constructed in 1952 and is one of the newest irrigation channels in Madeira.

From the Pousada dos Vinháticos a power station can be seen, on the left, in the bottom of the valley.

Serra de Água. – Pop 1 564. The village of Serra de Água has been built in a pretty setting★ halfway up a slope in the Ribeira Brava surrounded by abundant crops.

The river runs through a narrow valley of gentle contours. The plant life is rich and varied with mostly willows and black poplars along the water's edge.

Ribeira Brava. – Pop 6 217. Ribeira Brava was built in a plain at the mouth of the swift flowing river of the same name. A shaded avenue, always alive with people, runs the length of the beach, upon which a small 17C fort still stands, recalling battles of old with raiding pirates.

In the centre of the village on a square where the cobbles have been laid to form a mosaic, stands a proud little 16C **church** flanked by a belfry whose roof is decorated with small square blue and white glazed tiles. The church *(open 9am to 6pm)* has been remodelled but still retains the original pulpit and an interesting Manueline font.

There is a good view of Ribeira Brava from the road as it leaves the valley and rises *corniche* style over the hillside. It subsequently goes some distance up several of the coastal valleys.

From Cape Girão to Funchal. – *Drive described in the opposite direction p 152.*

PORTO MONIZ TOUR ★

Itinerary ③ on the map on p 154 – 179km - 111 miles starting from Funchal – allow two days.

From Funchal to Cape Girão. – *Description p 151.*

From Cape Girão to São Vicente. – *Drive described in the opposite direction above.*

São Vicente is linked with Seixal by an impressive **corniche road**★ boldly cut into the side of a cliff which plunges vertically to the sea below. It also is the spot from which the falls which drain the Paúl da Serra can be seen cascading down.

The Ribeira do Inferno (the Infernal River) runs into the sea through a picturesque gully. 1 mile - 2km from Seixal the road passes through a tunnel over which a waterfall pours. A belvedere, at the far end, provides a good **viewpoint**★ of this well known spectacle.

Seixal. – Pop 775. This village occupies a pleasant **setting**★ surrounded by vineyards on a promontory which ends in a series of reefs.

Three small islands *(ilhéus)* rise out of the sea at the mouth of the **Ribeira da Janela**. The largest is pierced by a sort of window *(janela)* which has given its name to the river and the village. At a distance from the bridge the unusual formation of this rock islet can be clearly seen.

Porto Moniz. – Pop 2 406. Porto Moniz provides the only sheltered harbour along the north coast. Protection is afforded by a low lying flat tongue of land which stretches out towards a rounded islet, the Ilhéu Mole, on which stand a few fishermen's cottages. North of the village the coast is strewn with a mass of pointed **reefs**★ among which a seawater swimming pool has been constructed. Before you approach the pool go and take a look down from the balconies which overhang the chasms and natural arches hollowed out by the sea in the black lava rocks.

The road, on leaving Porto Moniz, climbs in hairpin bends up the cliff which dominates the village. Two successive belvederes afford plunging **views**★ of Porto Moniz, its houses and other buildings huddled halfway up the slope round the church and surrounded by fields divided squarely as a draughtboard by broom hedges.

Santa. – At Santa, short for Santa Maria Madalena, a curious belfry resembling a minaret flanks the white church.

The west end has fewer inhabitants and is also more traditional than the other parts of the island. The women still wear long smocked skirts and small black kerchiefs.

The road, on either side a mass of flowers, crosses a green countryside where occasional cultivated terraces may be seen scattered amid the laurel woods, briar trees, eucalyptus and pines. The landscape is pleasing but not open enough to afford the panoramic views found elsewhere on the island.

The road passes near the Pargo Headland, the westernmost tip of Madeira and so named because sailors from Zarco's ship when out exploring caught a huge dolphin *(pargo)* offshore at this spot. The lighthouse is half hidden by a hill.

Calheta. – Pop 3 476. *Take the road on the right which goes down in hairpin bends through banana plantations and vineyards to the village.* The church, which stands on the right at a bend in the road, dates from 1639 and is interesting for its Moorish ceiling over the chancel. Motifs, similar to those on the Funchal Cathedral ceiling, are seen here grouped in squares.

Loreto. – The church, on the right, is ornamented with Manueline pinnacles and a fine side door surmounted by a Cross.

Rich crops reappear in this coastal region which profits from good sunlight, a mild climate and permanent irrigation. The Dr Trigo de Negreiros belvedere gives a wide view over these characteristic slopes of the south Madeira coast.

Paúl da Serra. – *12km - 8 miles off the main itinerary road.* The road, bordered at times by masses of flowers, goes through pine, chestnut and eucalyptus woods before crossing the more arid areas which precede the Campo Grande. This vast plain, which is not in the least typical of Madeira in its unending flatness and aridity, is grazed in summer by flocks of sheep. In winter it becomes a marshland *(paúl)*. The plain is cut by many paths *(signposted)* which penetrate deep into the centre of the island. *(Visitors wishing to make these long excursions are warned that a guide is indispensable – mountain mists fall suddenly, adding to the expected hazards; apply at the Tourist Information Centre; Direcção Regional de Turismo da Madeira.)*

Ponta do Sol. – Pop 4 404. The village's 15C **church** *(open 9am to 6pm)* with a belfry ornamented with faience tiles is embellished inside with a painted cedarwood ceiling in the Moorish style reminiscent of the one at Calheta. A beautiful Baroque silver lamp hangs above the altar.

Lombada da Ponta do Sol. – *2km - 1 mile from Ponta do Sol bear left into a cobbled road which branches off beneath a levada. On arriving in the village first turn right and then left.* Facing an old house which bears the coat of arms of João Esmeraldo and standing in a small square is the **Chapel of the Holy Spirit** ★ (Capela do Santo Espírito). This chapel was originally constructed in the 16C by João Esmeraldo, the friend of Christopher Columbus *(p 159)*, in the centre of what was then his extensive sugar cane plantation. It was rebuilt in 1720. The sober and elegant façade, where Renaissance and Baroque styles mingle, is pierced by a doorway standing in a trefoil arch.

The interior is outstanding for the richness of the gilded wood Baroque altars and the beautiful *azulejos* panels representing the Virtues.

There is a pretty **view** ★ before you begin the descent to Ribeira Brava, of the valley enclosed by basalt piles, and the village *(see above)* and village church.

From Cape Girão to Funchal. – *Drive described going in the opposite direction p 152.*

RUIVO Peak ★★★

Access from the Arieiro Peak. – *6km - 4 miles on foot starting from the Arieiro Peak (p 155), about 3 hours by a mountain path. Itinerary ④ on the map p 155.*
This is a most rewarding hill walk but the absence of a safety rail at the end and the unevenness of the way make the walk hazardous. People subject to vertigo are advised against the excursion.
It is possible to come back through Queimadas and Santana or to spend the night in the refuges (Casas de Abrigo) on the Ruivo Peak – in which case you must apply for permission to the Governo Regional-Secretariado da Presidêncial.

The path begins by following a rock crest line which, on the left, overlooks the Curral das Freiras Valley and, on the right, that of the Ribeira da Metade.
After the tunnel through the Gato Peak, a second tunnel avoids the climb up to the Torres Peak. On leaving the tunnel one sees a vast circle of mountains, the source of the upper tributaries of the Ribeira Seca. The remains of a remarkable volcanic chimney lie not far from the path.

(After Yan photo — Casa de Portugal)

The Ruivo Peak Massif.

Ruivo Peak ★★★. – The slopes of the Ruivo are overgrown by a giant heather. The refuge stands, on a shelf 10 minutes from the summit. An incomparable **panorama** ★★★ unfolds before you from the summit (alt 1 861m - 6 104ft): from left to right, beginning at the refuge hut are:

– towards the east, the wild valleys of the Ribeira Seca, the Ribeira da Metade and the Ribeiro Frio as they disappear behind the mountains on their way to the sea. In the far distance is the St Lawrence Headland;

– near, to the southeast, is the Torres Peak and behind it the Arieiro; to the right of this the Cidrão (1 802m - 5 912ft);

– to the south and west are the Curral das Freiras cirque and the Ribeira dos Socorridos Defile; above stands the Grand Peak (Pico Grande: 1 657m - 5 437ft) overlooking all, including the distinctive Torrinhas (meaning turrets), and the Casado (resembling a blackcurrant); in the distance lies the Paúl da Serra;

– to the northwest, the Caldeiro do Inferno (Hell's Cauldron) crater;

– to the north, the valleys of the north coast separated by long lines of hills;

– and to the northeast, São Jorge and Santana on their coastal plateau.

THE ISLAND OF PORTO SANTO

The island of Porto Santo, though only 40km - 27 miles to the northeast of Madeira, could not be more different. With a total population of 4 371 and an area of 42km² - 16sq miles it is less densely inhabited – 241 inhabitants to the square mile – and geographically consists of a large plain edged to the northeast and southeast by a few so called "peaks", of which the highest, the Facho, has an altitude of only 511m - 1 676ft. Except in winter when the damp turns the fields green, nothing grows on the chalky soil and the landscape has an ochre tinge, resembling a desert.

A vast **beach of golden sand**★ stretching 7km - 4 miles along the southern shore and a climate milder (mean annual temperature: 19°C - 67°F) and drier than that of Madeira, attract tourists to this island.

The inhabitants of Porto Santo live by fishing and cultivating cereals, tomatoes, melons, watermelons and figs. The island's vines produce an excellent very sweet white wine which, however, is less well known than the local mineral water. The therapeutic value of this water has made it popular not only on the island but also in Madeira and in Portugal, to which it is exported. Fish canneries, limekiln and cement works constitute the island's only other industries.

HISTORICAL NOTES

One year after the island had been discovered *(p 144)* the first captain, Bartolomeu Perestrelo, arrived. The year was 1420. Perestrelo had the unfortunate idea of bringing rabbits to Porto Santo and suffered thereafter from the destruction they caused and their proliferation. He, nevertheless, succeeded in bringing a certain prosperity to the devastated island. For a long time the authorities on the mainland of Portugal ignored Porto Santo's existence so that the inhabitants were left to defend themselves against the Algerian and French pirates, who continued at intervals to pillage and murder until the 18C. In addition the island suffered several periods of drought and famine.

Christopher Columbus. – Christopher Columbus first came to the island when he was charged by a Portuguese merchant to buy a cargo of sugar in Madeira. He sailed on to Porto Santo where he married Isabela Moniz, the daughter of the administrator, Bartolomeu Perestrelo. He left for Funchal, where he lived for some time with his friend, João Esmeraldo, studying the theories then current in navigation and which were later to inspire his voyages of exploration.

■ SIGHTS *map p 155*

Vila Baleira or **Porto Santo.** – This town with its dual name is the island's capital. The small white church contains in a chapel, on its north side, a fine 17C Portuguese painting of Mary Magdalene at the feet of Our Saviour.

The house in which Christopher Columbus is said to have stayed is in an alley behind the church. It stands on the right beyond the bend, surrounded by palm trees.

Opposite the church, the attractive small building emblazoned with coats of arms is now the town hall.

Ponta da Calheta. – This point, which lies separated from Baixo Islet by a channel dangerously strewn with reefs on which the sea never stops breaking, has a beach spiked with black basalt rocks. It is an unusual but pleasant spot.

Portela. – The **view**★ from this hillside, on which stands one of the island's few remaining windmills, extends right across the beach to Calheta Point (Ponta da Calheta) in the far distance.

Castelo Peak (Pico do Castelo). – Follow the road, lined on either side by cypress trees, up the side of the wooded peak to a belvedere *(on the left)*. From this there is a general view of the island, chequered with crops in square fields. Madeira can be seen in the distance.

Fountain in the Sands (Fonte da Areia). – This fountain, in which the local women do their washing, flows near cliffs which overlook a wild and rocky coast and which have been strangely worn by erosion.

INDEX

THE MADEIRA ARCHIPELAGO

(corresponding to the district of Funchal)

MANUFACTURE FRANÇAISE DES PNEUMATIQUES MICHELIN

Société en commandite par actions au capital de 700 000 000 de francs

Place des Carmes-Déchaux - 63 Clermont-Ferrand (France)

R.C.S. Clermont-Fd B 855 200 507

© Michelin et Cie, Propriétaires-Éditeurs 1985

Dépôt légal 12-85 – ISBN 2 06 015 572-X – ISSN 0763-1383

Printed in France 9-85-25
Photocomposition KAPPA, Coulommiers
Impression LAZARE-FERRY, Paris 12ᵉ n° 8130